THE BIBLE AS BOOK

THE TRANSMISSION
OF THE GREEK TEXT

THE BIBLE AS BOOK
THE TRANSMISSION
OF THE GREEK TEXT

Edited by
SCOT McKENDRICK AND
ORLAITH A. O'SULLIVAN

THE BRITISH LIBRARY
& OAK KNOLL PRESS
*in association with The Scriptorium:
Center for Christian Antiquities*
2003

First published 2003 by
The British Library
96 Euston Road
St Pancras
London NW1 2DB

Published exclusively in North and South America by
Oak Knoll Press
310 Delaware Street
New Castle
DE 19720

in association with
The Scriptorium: Center for Christian Antiquities
PO Box 770
Grand Haven
Michigan 49417-0770

British Library Cataloguing-in-Publication Data
A CIP record is available from The British Library

Library of Congress Cataloging-in-Publication Data

The Bible as book : the transmission of the Greek text / edited by Scot McKendrick and
Orlaith O'Sullivan
    p.   cm.
Report of a conference held in 1998 at Hampton Court, Herefordshire, England.
Includes bibliographical references (p.) and index.
ISBN 1-58456-082-7
    1. Bible. Greek – Versions – Congresses. 2. Bible – Manuscripts, Greek – Congress.
3. Bible – Criticism, Textual – Congresses. I. McKendrick, Scot. II. O'Sullivan, Orlaith.

BS38.B53 2003
220.4'86 – dc21

2002192992

ISBN 1-58456-082-7 (Oak Knoll)
ISBN 0-7123-4727-5 (British Library)

Designed by John Trevitt
Typeset in England by Norman Tilley Graphics, Northampton
Printed in England by St Edmundsbury Press, Bury St Edmunds

CONTENTS

Contents

CONTRIBUTORS

J. Neville Birdsall, *University of Birmingham*

John J. Brogan, *Northwestern College, Iowa*

Bart D. Ehrman, *University of North Carolina at Chapel Hill*

J. K. Elliott, *University of Leeds*

Michael W. Holmes, *Bethel College and Seminary*

Karen H. Jobes, *Westmont College of Religious Studies, California*

Warren A. Kay, *Merrimack College, Massachusetts*

Robert A. Kraft, *University of Pennsylvania*

Scot McKendrick, *The British Library*

Bruce M. Metzger, *Princeton Theological Seminary*

Orlaith O'Sullivan, *formerly The Scriptorium: Center for Christian Antiquities*

David Parker, *University of Birmingham*

Stanley E. Porter, *McMaster Divinity College*

Emanuel Tov, *Hebrew University, Jerusalem*

Jakob van Bruggen, *Theological University, Kampen*

John William Wevers, *University of Toronto*

LIST OF ILLUSTRATIONS

(reproduced between pages 100 and 101)

PREFACE

PROFESSOR BASTIANN VAN ELDEREN and the editors would like to offer their thanks to all the scholars who participated in the conference held at Hampton Court, Herefordshire, in 1998. We would also like to thank the Van Kampen family for their great generosity and support, and to all those who helped to make the conference a success.

As the curator of the Van Kampen Collection, it was Orlaith O'Sullivan's privilege to take care of the personal library of Eberhard Nestle for a time. Filled with personal notes, newspaper clippings and letters, Nestle's library offers us a glimpse of the character behind the monumental work that is today the Nestle-Aland Greek biblical text. Our conference celebrated the centenary of the publication of the first edition of the Nestle New Testament, and we trust that this volume continues in the tradition of such worthwhile scholarship as that to which Nestle devoted much of his life.

Finally our thanks to David Way, Anthony Warshaw and Kathleen Houghton of the British Library Publishing Office, for their skill, resolve and patience.

SCOT MCKENDRICK and ORLAITH O'SULLIVAN

FOREWORD

The Bible as Book: The Transmission of the Greek Text is the report of the 1998 conference held at Hampton Court, Herefordshire, under the sponsorship of The Scriptorium: Center for Christian Antiquities, in cooperation with The Van Kampen Foundation. The papers presented at the four-day symposium cover a wide range of topics that bear on the science and the art of the textual criticism of the Greek text of the Septuagint and the New Testament.

The results of the practice of textual criticism applied to the Scriptures have differed from one generation to another, partly because the balance in the quantity and quality of available witnesses has gradually altered as new manuscripts are discovered, and partly because theories and procedures for evaluating textual evidence have varied over the years.

Articles in the present volume provide a rich and rewarding variety of studies concerning materials of ancient books (papyrus and parchment), formats (roll and codex), and methodologies (traditional and innovative). There are surveys of what has been already accomplished as well as suggestions concerning future directions in biblical textual criticism.

Among studies concerned with the New Testament, four papers focus on uncial manuscripts. Even though Codex Alexandrinus has been available for scholarly examination for nearly four hundred years and Codex Sinaiticus for nearly a century and a half, there are still many features of these two manuscripts that call for further clarification. Scot McKendrick re-examines the evidence for the Egyptian or Alexandrian origin of Alexandrinus. He tracks its wanderings from Constantinople to Alexandria and back, and tentatively suggests Ephesus as at least an early home of the Codex. John Brogan is intrigued with the presence in Sinaiticus of what is called 'block mixture' in the text of John's Gospel. Instead of Hort's view that the text of Sinaiticus in the Fourth Gospel is primarily Alexandrian with Western corruptions scattered throughout, it now appears that the textual character of the Codex dramatically changes, with John 1.1-8.38 containing a Western form of text whereas in John 9-21 there is an Alexandrian form of text. The presence of block mixture in Sinaiticus raises questions about the source text(s). Did the scribes who produced Sinaiticus use several exemplars that contained different text-types? Or did they use a single exemplar that already contained a mixed text? Brogan concludes that no matter what angle of investigation is taken, the presence of block mixture tells us something about the history of the transmission of the text of the New Testament. Furthermore, Brogan is struck by the 'uniquely high level of textual affinity between Athanasius's text of the Gospels and scribal corrections in Sinaiticus'. Birdsall returns to the third of the principal uncials, Codex Vaticanus. In his outline of the history and use of the Codex he stresses how little is known of its origins and history before the fifteenth century. In his appraisal of the significance of the Codex he reasserts the importance of the New Testament text of the Codex in respect of its preservation of the common language of the early Christian period and its eschewal of extensive revision for reasons of propriety or sound doctrine.

The bilingual manuscript known as Codex Bezae receives renewed attention in David Parker's paper. Noteworthy are the differences here and there between the Greek and the Latin texts on facing pages. This provides evidence, in Parker's opinion, that the Greek text in Acts (which is the object of his present study) is an evolving text rather than the product of a single individual and occasion.

Several papers discuss aspects of the study of the Septuagint. Robert Kraft considers the 'textual mechanics' involved in the transmission of early Jewish Septuagint manuscripts and/or Old Greek manuscripts, mostly from Egypt. The chief goal of his research is to examine the evidence from some thirty early Jewish biblical and related materials in Greek, reflecting scribal habits and techniques in order to address questions concerning Jewish Greek developments on the one hand, and the relationship between Jewish 'scribal culture' and early Christian literary practices on the other.

In another paper, Karen Jobes explores the survival of two different Greek textual traditions for the books of Judges, Esther, Daniel, Susanna, Tobit, and Judith. Is one a recension of the other, is each a translation independently produced from a Hebrew *Vorlage*, or is one or both of the texts neither a translation nor a recension, but instead a midrashic rewriting of the biblical story? If each is an independent translation, then the question arises whether both translate the same Hebrew *Vorlage*, and if not, what may be the relationship between the Hebrew *Vorlagen* represented by each of the two Greek versions.

In a comprehensive survey of the discoveries of Greek biblical texts at several places in the Judean desert, Emanuel Tov concludes that both the Hebrew and Greek texts from Qumran reflect textual variety and a lack of rigidity, while the discoveries at other sites point to Jewish nationalistic circles that adhered only to the proto-rabbinic (proto-Masoretic) text in Hebrew and the Jewish revisions of the Septuagint towards that Hebrew text.

According to Michael Holmes, a pressing task for textual critics to pursue is the further investigation of the New Testament minuscule tradition. In addition to the identification of groups of manuscripts such as Family 13 or Codex 1 and its allies, Holmes focuses on what has been accomplished more recently by those who have utilised the Claremont Profile Method in finding affinities among minuscule manuscripts, and by the current publication of volumes in the *Text und Textwert* series undertaken by the Münster Institut. At the close of his paper, Holmes reminds us:

How incomplete is our knowledge of the early and later centuries with respect to the history of the text [...] We are unable to link the minuscule families and groups with extant manuscripts, but we nonetheless put forth hypotheses that suggest direct connections and thus protect and preserve both the status of these extant manuscripts and the present theory that there are only a few major textual traditions, a theory that is congenial to our printed texts.

Other papers also raise questions concerning the methodology of New Testament textual criticism. Keith Elliott's discussion of 'thorough-going eclecticism', while acknowledging some of his misgivings in its practice, concludes by citing half-a-dozen of its positive benefits.

Foreword

Jakob van Bruggen's paper about the Majority Text asks 'Why Not Reconsider Its Exile?' and points out that 'we always have to make a choice between criteria that lead to contradictory results in the process of evaluation when applied at the same time: a longer reading is sometimes more difficult, and so on'. His plea is that the Byzantine text-type be granted an unprejudiced hearing in the assessment of textual variation.

In his paper on 'The Use of the Church Fathers in New Testament Criticism', Bart Ehrman deals with a variety of questions concerning the transmission of text-types. In particular, instead of continuing with Hort's division of the Alexandrian witnesses into Early Alexandrian and Late Alexandrian, Ehrman prefers to speak of primary and secondary witnesses to the one dominant form of the text current in Alexandria. Different witnesses attest it in varying degrees of purity, and therefore 'we should speak of Primary and Secondary Alexandrian witnesses'.

In a lengthy article Stanley Porter touches upon many aspects of the discipline of papyrology in general in order to explore what he regards as inadequacies in the pursuit of a sub-discipline, the study of New Testament papyri.

In the study of the Greek text of the Bible in the last century, the name of Dr Eberhard Nestle (1851-1913) stands out prominently. The 1998 conference commemorated the one hundredth anniversary of Nestle's first edition of the Greek New Testament. Warren Kay's article on 'The Life and Work of Eberhard Nestle' describes the many-faceted interests in both Septuagint and New Testament of a scholar whose accomplishments were formidable. Nestle was the author of about forty book-length publications, as well as several hundred shorter articles and notes. Kay's article rests upon his research while consulting the papers and books of Nestle's private library, which today is housed in The Scriptorium.

The last two papers in the volume consider the future of textual studies of the New Testament and the Septuagint. Despite the hazards confronting would-be prophets, both John Wevers and the undersigned have managed to contribute something that bears on their assigned topics.

BRUCE M. METZGER
Princeton Theological Seminary

THE CODEX ALEXANDRINUS
OR THE DANGERS OF BEING
A NAMED MANUSCRIPT

Scot McKendrick

THE CODEX ALEXANDRINUS (or Alexandrinus, as I shall refer to it hereafter)[1] is one of the three earliest and most important manuscripts of the whole Christian Bible. (The other two are the Codex Sinaiticus and the Codex Vaticanus.) Comprising 773 parchment leaves and now divided into four volumes, the codex contains the whole of the Greek Old and New Testaments and Apocrypha. It concludes with two letters to the Christian community at Corinth ascribed to Clement of Rome. Generally dated to the fifth century and written in a fine biblical majuscule, Alexandrinus constitutes a landmark in the history of the book.

Since its presentation to King Charles I as a New Year's gift in 1627, Alexandrinus has rightly been treasured in Britain. Although it arrived in England too late to be used for the Authorised Version of the Bible, the codex stimulated further study of the text of the New Testament and thus underpins all subsequent editions and translations.[2] Formerly the jewel of the English royal library, Alexandrinus has survived all threats of alienation and destruction to become one of the greatest treasures of first the British Museum and now the British Library.[3]

My purpose here, however, is not a eulogy. Instead I would like to re-examine one crucial aspect of Alexandrinus, namely its place of origin. To this end my paper is divided into two parts. The first re-appraises the historical links of Alexandrinus with Egypt and Alexandria. The second suggests some ways forward to a fresh view of the earlier history and origin of Alexandrinus. Whereas in the first part I have attempted to deal with my subject as fully as possible, in the second I am offering merely some early thoughts. At the very least I hope that my second part will highlight how much work remains to be done on Alexandrinus.

'BOUND TO THE PATRIARCHAL CELL'

The more that I read about Alexandrinus the more that I became convinced of the necessity to set out clearly the bases on which so many writers have identified Alexandrinus's origin as Egypt, or to be more precise Alexandria. For by little steps of incautious thought or wording some of the most influential writers who have described Alexandrinus over the years since Alexandrinus reached this country have given rise to important, but ill-founded assumptions. These assumptions have coloured subsequent descriptions of Alexandrinus. More seriously they also have the power to distort any general history of the transmission and reception of the text of the Bible or any account of early Christian book production, decoration and collection. Take, for example, Jack Finegan's influential introduction to New Testament textual criticism first published in 1975. According to this it is entirely natural that the character of Alexandrinus's text of Acts, the Epistles and Revelation should be Alexandrian, this despite the fact that Finegan chose Alexandrinus as his principal witness of the Byzantine text of the Gospels.[4] Why, one might ask, is the Alexandrian text 'natural'? Another recent example is to be found in Jellicoe's standard monograph on the Septuagint published in 1968. Seeking to explain the eclecticism of Alexandrinus's text of the Old Testament, Jellicoe describes the compiler as aiming at a text 'that would combine and integrate the fruits of the critical labours of Palestine and Syria as well as those of his native Egypt'.[5] And what is the view from Alexandria itself? According to the former patriarchal librarian T. D. Moschonas Alexandrinus 'remained in the Patriarchal Library for nearly 13 centuries'[6] and is a witness of the wealth of the library of the ancient Catechetical School at Alexandria.[7] I hope that these few citations help to explain why I offer what follows and why I consider what follows important.

Cyril Lucar

First, the most obvious question, why is Alexandrinus called Codex Alexandrinus? In 1881, in his revised preface to the historic facsimile produced for the Trustees of the British Museum, Maunde Thompson was clear on the subject:[8]

The title which has been given to this MS is derived from the fact of its having been dedicated to the Patriarchal Chamber at Alexandria, as recorded in a note written by Athanasius the Patriarch, in Arabic, at the foot of the page of Genesis.

In this the eminent palaeographer, Keeper of Manuscripts and later Director and Principal Librarian of the British Museum, was, I regret to say, wrong. And it is not mere carping to say that he was wrong: for his authoritative statement was significantly wrong in its assumptions and significantly unhelpful in its compounding of an already confused understanding of the historical links of Alexandrinus with Egypt and Alexandria.

As has been noted by others,[9] it was Brian Walton in 1657 in one of the prefaces to the London Polyglott Bible who first designated the manuscript as Codex Alexandrinus.[10] Before that it was referred to as either the Codex Regius or Thecla's Bible[11] (I shall return to Thecla a little later). Walton's basis for the designation 'Alexandrinus' was the common understanding that the donor of the manuscript to Charles I, that is Cyril Lucar, had brought the codex with him from Egypt some time after 4 November 1620.[12] At that date Cyril ceased to be Patriarch of Alexandria and took up permanent residence in Constantinople as the Oecumenical Patriarch.[13] As early as 1632 this was the version of events reported by Patrick Young, the Keeper of the Royal Library, who had first received and soon became engaged in the study of Alexandrinus.[14] Indeed, when Walton coined his designation, there was no other evidence of a link with Alexandria accessible to him. On the Arabic inscription to which Maunde Thompson refers (Fig. 1) all seventeenth- and eighteenth-century critics are silent. The Alexandrian reference in it was certainly unknown to them and remained so until early in the nineteenth century.[15] When first coined, therefore, the designation Alexandrinus merely reflected its recent ownership, not its medieval ownership, and certainly not its origin.

Yet within Walton's designation lurks a deceptive assumption. For the designation Alexandrinus refers not only to Lucar's title as Patriarch of Alexandria, but the city of Alexandria. Walton's erroneous assumption was, like that of many others of his own and later times, that the Patriarch of Alexandria and his books resided at Alexandria. This inbuilt falsity of Walton's designation was to prove very influential, for it was all too easy to assume that such an ancient codex as Alexandrinus must have resided for centuries in Alexandria and been directly linked with the city renowned for its learning and books in both pagan antiquity and the early Christian period. From there it was but a little step to see Alexandria no longer as the home of Alexandrinus, but its very cradle.

Such a process of thought is the equivalent of the assumption that an ancient manuscript possessed by the Archbishop of Canterbury at the beginning of the seventeenth century necessarily had its origins in Kent, or more specifically Canterbury. For by Lucar's time and indeed since the last decade of the tenth century the patriarchal seat had been sited in Cairo, not Alexandria.[16] The antique Caesareum, which had been adopted as the official seat of the bishop of Alexandria in the fourth century,[17] was abandoned. Much else changed at Alexandria between the fifth and the seventeenth centuries. As a result of the Monophysite schism in the middle of the fifth century the Orthodox patriarch of Alexandria ceased to be the Christian spiritual leader in Egypt.[18] In 642 the city fell to the Arab general 'Amr Ibn al 'Asi, and, although Alexandria's prosperity continued, serious decline began in the eighth and ninth centuries.[19] The once famous Greek Catechetical School headed by Clement and Origen disappeared,[20] and with it disappeared its presumed extensive library, the Christian successor to the pagan Great Library of Alexandria.

So much for the origins and dangers of Walton's name for the codex. What of the story that lies behind the name, the one consistently retold by Young, Walton and others of the period, namely that Alexandrinus was removed by Cyril Lucar from the patriarchal library in Egypt? Was this merely what these English scholars supposed, were told or given to believe? Or is there some verifiable fact behind the story? Surprisingly little attention has been paid to independent evidence that supports such a story.[21] Alexandrinus is not the only surviving gift that Lucar bestowed on his Protestant friends. Further Greek and Arabic manuscripts were secured through the patriarch for several important English collectors, including the Earl of Arundel and Archbishop Laud.[22] Most importantly, several were personally bestowed on Sir Thomas Roe,[23] the King's ambassador to the Sublime Porte and the key figure in the acquisition of Alexandrinus for the English Crown.[24]

Among the manuscripts which Roe presented to Oxford University on his return from the East in 1628 and are now in the Bodleian Library, two merit particular attention. The first is an Arabic manuscript of the Acts of the early Church Councils (Roe MS 26).[25] Roe appears to have considered this volume his most important manuscript: on three separate occasions he described it as 'the jewel of the East', 'the jewel of his [the patriarch's] library' and 'worth a librarye'.[26] More importantly for our purposes, when in June 1625, soon after his first report of Alexandrinus and its intended donation by Lucar to James I, Roe writes that the Arabic manuscript is on loan to him, he describes it as 'having antiently belonged to the patriarchs of Alexandria, and from thence [note the similarity of the assumptions of Roe and Walton] brought as a great jewell by Cyrillus'.[27] From the manuscript itself all that can be determined is that it was probably written by one Yusuf (Joseph) of the Church of Our Lady in Cairo between 1390 and 1398, upon which later date it became the property of the same Church.[28] Its subsequent incorporation into the patriarchal collection is, however, easy to credit, especially as by Lucar's time the library was based in Cairo.

The second manuscript is a Greek manuscript of the commentaries of Hesychius and St John Chrysostom on the Psalms (Roe MS 13). This volume was written on Mount Galesios, near Ephesus, in 1284/1285 at the request of the head of the monastery there, Galaction the Blind. Although this manuscript has been described in great detail by two eminent Byzantinists of recent times,[29] two significant links with Alexandrinus have escaped notice. Both recent scholars correctly recognized Roe's manuscript as one of two patriarchal books that in a long inscription dated 25 June 1514 a priest named Manuel confesses to having stolen from Alexandria. Despite this they failed to follow up Manuel's own statement that the manuscript contained a 'desmon hierarachikon' threatening with curses or excommunication anyone who should, like Manuel himself, remove the book from its proper home. They did not therefore uncover the significance of a prominent Arabic inscription inserted at the end of the volume (Fig. 5).[30] With the assistance of Colin Wakefield of the Bodleian Library, to whom I am grateful for help with both this and the previous Roe manuscript, I translate the Arabic as follows: 'I have constituted this book an endowment to the See of St Mark and whoever removes it will be excommunicated. Written by Athanasius the humble.'[31]

The closely similar wording and identity of script allows little doubt that this inscription, like that at the beginning of Alexandrinus to which Maunde Thompson refers (Fig. 1), is by Athanasius II, Patriarch of Alexandria from c. 1275 to c. 1315 (I shall return to Athanasius a little later). The See of St Mark is of course that of Alexandria. Without attempting a translation Turyn and Hutter had assumed a further reference to Ephesus.

There is moreover a second link between Alexandrinus and the Roe manuscript, for the Bodleian volume is undoubtedly the 'part of Chrisostome upon the Psalmes' said by Roe to have been part of a consignment of ten books sent to him in February 1628.[32] This consignment came from none other than the Patriarch Cyril Lucar. It therefore seems likely that Manuel's repentant confession of his theft subsequently led to the manuscript's return to the patriarchal library.

The Egyptian provenance of these two gifts of Cyril Lucar to Sir Thomas Roe provides independent evidence of one of Lucar's sources of manuscripts. It also adds flesh to the story that Alexandrinus was brought by Lucar from Egypt. The most likely time of such a transfer is of course that of his own permanent removal from Egypt to become patriarch of Constantinople. The similar history of at least one of the Roe manuscripts (Roe MS 13) as part of the collections of the patriarchs of Alexandria suggests that Lucar made his choice for what Roe described in 1625 as 'a great [personal] collection'[33] directly from those collections. Yet despite what Roe was given to think of the manuscripts given to him neither is ancient and neither a patriarchal heirloom from beyond the fourteenth century. I shall return to this important observation a little later.

The Codex Alexandrinus

Thecla

Another Egyptian story which accompanied Alexandrinus to England in the seventeenth century and subsequently caused much ink to be spilled is the claim that Alexandrinus was written by a woman named Thecla.[34] This claim is made twice in Alexandrinus, firstly in an Arabic inscription on the verso of the parchment leaf bearing the early table of contents and secondly in a Latin note in Lucar's hand now pasted onto a preceding paper flyleaf.[35] A third instance is to be found in a letter from Sir Thomas Roe to the Earl of Arundel dated January 1625 in which the ambassador first announces Lucar's intended gift to his royal master.[36] Being less literally minded and credulous than their predecessors, most modern critics have given short treatment to the Thecla story.[37] For them the reliability of all three statements of the tradition is seriously undermined by their significantly different identifications of Thecla. The possibility of any truth lying behind such statements is negated by their manifest chronological incompatibility with the generally accepted modern dating of Alexandrinus. Further explanation of such claims as arising from an ill-remembered tradition whereby 'written by' supplanted the authentic 'possessed by the monastery (or church) of'[38] now seem forced and implausible.

Yet there are good reasons for stating exactly why we should give little credence to the whole story about Thecla. Apart from the intrinsic virtue of applying clear thinking to this issue, such an approach has two useful purposes. In the first instance we can discredit one piece of evidence which could support an early Egyptian provenance; secondly, we can gain further insight into the context in which Alexandrinus emerged from obscurity.

On the first subject, it is crucially important to note that the Arabic note in Alexandrinus concerning Thecla the martyr was long ago considered by the distinguished Oxford orientalist Nicoll to be neither of the same date nor in the same hand as the Athanasius inscription.[39] Despite what has been so frequently stated, it was his opinion that all these two inscriptions have in common is their language. Whereas Athanasius's note was written around the turn of the thirteenth and fourteenth centuries, the anonymous attribution of Alexandrinus to Thecla was probably written much later, possibly around the beginning of the seventeenth century. According to Nicoll it was written in Lucar's time 'vel paullo antea ea'.

Removing the Arabic Thecla inscription from the time of Athanasius not only increases the temporal distance between what is remembered and its formal record, it eases the possibility that Alexandrinus emerged in Athanasius's time from somewhere other than Egypt. Moving it closer to Lucar's time also starts to make more sense of what Lucar himself and Roe said about Thecla. Indeed comparison of its wording and that of Lucar's Latin note suggest that Lucar's information was directly derived from the Arabic note. Furthermore, Roe's different version is easily explained as either his own garbled version of what Lucar had derived from the Arabic inscription or an intermediary's elaboration of what Lucar knew.

Given all this, it is possible to start to map out the genesis of this story about Thecla. Like many Eastern prelates of his times and later, Lucar came to appreciate the thirst of Western Europeans for Greek manuscripts.[40] Especially prized were manuscripts of the Bible and the Church Fathers, and among these the ideal was an ancient manuscript.

5

Also like other Eastern prelates, Lucar overestimated the advantage to be gained for himself and his cause in supplying such needs (the usual real benefit turned out to be some recent printed editions of the classics); and in his troubled times he might well have mused on the almost unimaginable favours that he might gain if only he could supply that ideal. But Lucar was living many years before the studies of Wanley and Montfaucon made possible the palaeographical appraisal of a Greek manuscript.[41] How was he either to identify such a manuscript or to convince the recipients of his gift of its great antiquity? In this light Alexandrinus, with a tradition that it was copied by no less a person than Thecla, offered Lucar what he described to Roe on two separate occasions as 'the greatest antiquitye of the Greeke church'.[42] Here indeed was a potent diplomatic instrument. Whether Lucar was tempted to forge such a heady provenance or merely credited it unquestioningly we may never know. What is certain is that the Thecla story was for him a story of great convenience.

Athanasius II, Patriarch of Alexandria

Let us now return to the inscription that Maunde Thompson thought the origin of the designation Alexandrinus. In the translation published in the final volume of the reduced facsimile of Alexandrinus it runs as follows: 'Bound to the Patriarchal Cell in the Fortress of Alexandria. Whoever removes it thence shall be excommunicated and cut off. Written by Athanasius the humble.'[43]

As was established beyond doubt by Skeat in 1955,[44] this note (Fig. 1) was added by the Patriarch Athanasius II. Although subsequent research has altered some of the relevant dates,[45] Skeat's other contribution stands firm, namely his perception that Athanasius probably formed the first link between Alexandrinus and Egypt and that as a largely absentee patriarch he probably acquired Alexandrinus outside Egypt.[46] Ironically the most explicit link between Alexandrinus and not only the patriarchs of Alexandria but Alexandria itself is the piece of historical evidence that most seriously undermines any claim of an early Egyptian provenance or origin for Alexandrinus.

From the very time of his election as Patriarch of Alexandria in 1275 or 1276 until the summer of 1305, Athanasius II resided almost without a break in Constantinople. A refugee from the Mamluks, Athanasius became a highly influential figure in the imperial capital, frequently noted as a key player in its political and intellectual life. All of this was brought to an end when Athanasius I, Patriarch of Constantinople, finally secured from the Emperor Andronicus II banishment from Constantinople of the patriarch's great rival and namesake. Athanasius appears to have continued as patriarch until *c.* 1315, but very little of certainty is known about his life after his departure from Constantinople in 1305.[47]

It was during his time in Constantinople that Athanasius acquired the three manuscripts which Skeat first identified as bearing further signed notes by him.[48] Of the two that remain in the library of the patriarch of Alexandria,[49] one (MS 12) includes a Greek inscription by Athanasius stating that it was 'acquired in the Queen of Cities [i.e. Constantinople] and dedicated to the Holy Patriarchal Church in Alexandria' (Fig. 2); the other (MS 34) is said in a similar Greek inscription to have been 'given to me by Master Demetrios Iatropoulos in Constantinople, and was dedicated by me to the most holy Church of God in Alexandria for a memorial of him' (Fig. 3).[50] Like both

The Codex Alexandrinus

Alexandrinus and the Greek Roe manuscript, each bears a patriarchal curse against alienation. Like the Roe manuscript, both are of commentaries by St John Chrysostom, this time on the Pauline Epistles. The third manuscript, now in the Vatican (Ottoboni gr. 452),[51] was recovered for the patriarchy from the monastery of St Catherine, Mount Sinai, in the sixteenth century and remained in the patriarchal collection until early in the eighteenth century.[52] According to a long Arabic inscription by Athanasius (Fig. 4), this volume was 'sought as a gift' from the Emperor Andronicus II, brought from Constantinople as Athanasius's property and made 'an inalienable gift to the Holy Markan cell'.[53] It must have been acquired between 1282 and 1305 and may reflect a successful attempt by Athanasius to secure some visible token of the Emperor's continued goodwill. Reflecting the same interests as Alexandrinus, the Greek Roe manuscript and the two Alexandrian manuscripts, the Vatican manuscript contains the Minor and Major Prophets, with extensive catenae commenting on the text.

Although historians remain uncertain whether Athanasius ever returned to Egypt, there is no doubt that the three manuscripts which he acquired in Constantinople did make the journey there. It is moreover certain that at least the volume donated to him by Andronicus II departed Constantinople with Athanasius himself. The wording of his three notes also suggests that he was writing after his departure from Constantinople. Since not only the Vatican manuscript, but also one of the manuscripts now at Alexandria (MS 34) were recovered for the patriarchy from the monastery of St Catherine, Mount Sinai, in the sixteenth century,[54] Athanasius may have spent his last years in his old monastery or its metochion on Crete. And here it might have been that he had the leisure to add his notes to and ensure the future of his treasured books. It is therefore possible that at least for a short time, both Codex Alexandrinus and Codex Sinaiticus were under the same roof, before the latter's arrival at the British Museum at the end of 1933.

Whatever the exact circumstances of their inscriptions, it is clear that all three of the manuscripts cited by Skeat were Athanasius's personal additions to the patriarchal collection.[55] Yet was this the case for Alexandrinus? Although the inscriptions in these three manuscripts are explicit on the subject, Alexandrinus's is not.[56] It is therefore particularly helpful to be able to state without doubt that the similar inexplicit inscription in the Greek Roe manuscript also records a personal addition of Athanasius to the patriarchal collections. As noted earlier, this Roe manuscript was copied near Ephesus in 1284/1285, and it is very unlikely that this book came into the patriarchal collections in Egypt independently of the reigning patriarch. Moreover, although the person for whom this manuscript was written was a political opponent and an unlikely giver of gifts to Athanasius,[57] there are at least two occasions when the patriarch could have made such an acquisition. His first opportunity came when he was sent by the Emperor in 1289 to win the support of the otherwise unfavourable John Cheilas, Metropolitan of Ephesus.[58] Although Athanasius's mission floundered on Cheilas's intransigence, he may nevertheless have profited in other ways from his visit to Ephesus. The patriarch's second opportunity may have come just before his departure from Constantinople, when on 24 October 1304 Ephesus fell to the Turks under Sasa Bey.[59] Very soon afterwards refugees from Ephesus, including monks from Mount Galesios, were reported in the Constantinople, bearing whatever of their treasures they had managed to escape with. Among these was the head and a manuscript life of their founder, the stylite St Lazarus.[60] Given that Athanasius did not leave the capital until the summer of 1305, there would just have been time for him to benefit from the refugees from Galesios.

For Skeat there were two clear implications of his finds for the history of Alexandrinus.[61] Firstly, it appeared to him almost certain that Athanasius added his Arabic note to Alexandrinus to mark his addition of it to the patriarchal library. Secondly, it appeared a reasonable hypothesis that Athanasius acquired Alexandrinus in Constantinople. The most important consequence of all this was, in his own words, that 'if any future scholar wishes to claim a Constantinopolitan origin for the Codex Alexandrinus, it is at least open to him to do so'.[62] With the further discovery of the Roe manuscript, Skeat's first conclusion, namely that Alexandrinus was a new addition to the patriarchal library, must now turn a near certainty into a complete certainty. With respect to his second point, although the possibility of acquisition at Constantinople remains, some readjustment may be required. For we now know of one further source of Athanasius's acquisitions. Even if, like the other three manuscripts, Alexandrinus was acquired at Constantinople it is possible that it was, like Roe's manuscript, not of Constantinopolitan origin. More positively do we now have a serious contender as the earlier home and even origin of Alexandrinus? It is to this question that I shall return in the second part of this paper.

Meanwhile, what of the frequent assertion that Alexandrinus was given to the patriarchal library in 1098?[63] As perhaps we should be alert to now, this claim is a will-o'-the-wisp, and can be easily reputed. First of all, this claim is clearly based on a Latin inscription in ink that appears on one of the paper flyleaves at the front of the first volume of the four into which Alexandrinus was divided when it reached the royal library. It reads 'donum dedit cubiculo Patriarchali anno 814 Martyrum'. Below this is helpfully added in pencil '+ AD 284 = 1098'. Yet, as was long ago suspected,[65] but appears to have been subsequently lost sight of, this Latin inscription does not derive from an independent source, but is merely an inaccurate attempt at deciphering the Arabic note by Athanasius. Not only does the wording suggest this. 'Cubiculo', for example, is clearly an echo of the Christian Arabic word 'qilāyah' and 'donum dedit' the opening 'bound to'. And the date may be a misunderstanding of the final hastily written Arabic characters. Yet more than all this it is far from difficult with aid of palaeographical knowledge to determine that this Latin inscription could not have been written before the last quarter of the seventeenth century. Although this observation has frequently been made, the implications of such a dating appear to have been ignored. Most obviously, such a dating means that the Latin inscription must have been added in England. The hand is certainly that of a Westerner, and probably that of a Briton.[66] If it was added in England, is it credible that it was based on independent information? In Egypt, or even Constantinople, perhaps so; but surely not in England.

BEFORE ENTRY INTO THE PATRIARCHAL CELL

All that I have said so far suggests that on the historical evidence Alexandria is no more likely as the origin of Alexandrinus than, for example, Constantinople. Indeed common sense might suggest that we should consider all other serious possibilities before returning to consider Alexandria. Such a tactic would of course be absolutely the opposite of what has occurred in the past. For until very recently most writers have assumed Alexandria guilty and examined Alexandrinus with a view to confirming that guilt. Given their assumptions, many previous critics have seen traces of Egypt in Alexandrinus's orthography,[68] script[69] and decoration.[70] However, they have done so merely on the presumption that Alexandrinus originated in Egypt, and it is insufficient as proof that Alexandrinus originated in Egypt that the orthographical, palaeographical and art historical evidence is consistent with such an origin. For it is, as some critics have seen,[71] also consistent with other centres of production. Moreover an honest appraisal would highlight how lamentably little we can say with assurance in several of these areas.

What then are the fundamental constraints on any credible proposal for the origin of Alexandrinus? In the first place, as a luxury manuscript of the full Bible, Alexandrinus must be the work of a sophisticated centre of book production. Full Bibles were never common at any period,[72] and Alexandrinus can justly be compared with, say, the Codex Amiatinus or the Moutier-Grandval Bible, products of two of the most sophisticated centres of western book production. Perhaps such comparisons would have imposed themselves even more forcibly had only Alexandrinus's canon tables survived. Given the decoration found elsewhere in Alexandrinus it is almost certain that its canon tables would have offered us the earliest surviving decorated example of this significant accompaniment to the Gospels.[73] Secondly, the making of Alexandrinus must have required considerable financial input either through a very wealthy Christian individual or within a wealthy Christian institution. Comparable books of later ages certainly required such support. Thirdly, a date of production in the fifth century[74] must be compatible with the known history of any proposed centre of production. All of these constraints seriously reduce the number of credible contenders.

Now let me test out the new hypothesis which I mentioned earlier, namely that Ephesus was the earlier home and perhaps origin of Alexandrinus. As I have already shown, Athanasius did acquire one manuscript that came from Ephesus – so why not two? Alexandrinus's survival and sudden emergence in Athanasius's time could be better explained in terms of Ephesus than Constantinople. If Alexandrinus was not only acquired by Athanasius in Constantinople, but resident in the capital since its origins, we have to suppose that it survived the widespread destruction and pillage that followed the city's fall to the Fourth Crusade in 1204.[75] And why, if Alexandrinus had been in Constantinople since its production, did it become available for removal from that city in Athanasius's time? In the case of Ephesus, Athanasius's sudden availability to Athanasius would be well explained by that city's fall in 1304 or the threatening times that led up to it. Yet it too saw many significant changes between the fifth and fourteenth centuries.[76] In c. 614 large parts of the ancient city were destroyed; by the ninth century its harbour had silted up; and towards the end of the eleventh century it was briefly occupied by the Turks. Monasteries were established on Mount Galesios no earlier than the eleventh century, rapidly declined and were only revived in the thirteenth century within the Nicaean Empire.[77] No manuscript dating from before the tenth century has been identified as having formed part of the library at Galesios.[78]

Moving further back in time, could Ephesus pass muster as a serious contender as Alexandrinus's place of origin? Although there is, as far as I can determine, nothing to suggest that Ephesus was an important centre of book production in the fifth century, there is very little evidence for contemporary production of Christian books else-where.[79] In this context, it should perhaps be noted that in the only modern palaeo-graphical study of Alexandrinus and other manuscripts written in biblical majuscule Cavallo failed to identify Alexandrinus's origin or to link it with either Constantinople, Egypt, Palestine or Syria.[80] What we do know of Ephesus, on the other hand, is sugges-tive and at least not incompatible with my hypothesis,[81] for during the fifth century Ephesus was a very prosperous and thriving city in which many significant Christian establishments were arising or being embellished. Most notable among these was the large fourth-century Basilica of the Virgin, which served as the setting for the two Church Councils in 431 and 449, and the Basilica of St John, which was erected over the purported tomb of the evangelist St John and achieved enormous proportions under Justinian in the middle of the sixth century. Ephesus's strategic and convenient position on the trade route by sea between Constantinople and Alexandria added to its power of attraction and probably contributed to its choice for the two Church Councils in the fifth century. It would be incredible to suppose that such strength and activity on the part of the Church in Ephesus and contemporary prosperity as capital of the wealthy province of Asia were not accompanied by a significant demand for fine Christian books. Whether that demand gave rise to and was fed by well organized local production is perhaps a question worth asking.

Moreover, the list of credible contenders for the origin of Alexandrinus can be seriously reduced if we are prepared to accept certain points regarding the two other great codices of the Greek Bible. For if we accept, as I am inclined to, that both Sinaiticus and Vaticanus issue from Caesarea and are characteristic of the products of that city,[82] it seems most unlikely that Alexandrinus was produced in Palestine. In textual terms alone, the contrast is very marked. Also, if we accept the argument that both these codices were characteristic of the fifty Bibles commissioned by Constantine the Great for the churches of Constantinople,[83] it seems improbable that only one century later that same city should either require another such Bible or produce such a very different text.

Yet, to make a serious claim for Ephesus or any other centre, a lot more research needs to be undertaken. More attention needs to be given to the choice of non-canonical texts contained by Alexandrinus and their implications for the use or purpose of the manuscript. What, for example, are the implications of its inclusion of the two Clementine Epistles? What are the implications of the liturgical apparatus appended to the Psalms? What of its original inclusion of the Psalms of Solomon, the earliest known instance of this text? More study also needs to be applied to the implications of the profuse corrections of Alexandrinus's text, especially those by the near contem-porary Aa.[84] What exactly do his corrections suggest in their textual basis and balance of interest? In a completely different area of study, comparison needs to be made between the decorative aspects of surviving fifth-century works of art from and the striking and understudied decoration of Alexandrinus.[85] Any such study will need to take the widest possible view and avoid isolated comparisons. As Jules Leroy astutely pointed out in 1974,[86] several motifs within Alexandrinus's decoration which also appear in early Coptic and Syriac manuscripts were in fact part of a Graeco-Roman repertoire in use before Christian production and in many different parts of the Empire. And of course fresh consideration needs to be given to the textual character of

The Codex Alexandrinus

Alexandrinus, individually eclectic in the Old Testament and drawing on two separate textual traditions in the New (in the Gospels Alexandrinus's text is Byzantine, but in the Acts, Epistles and Revelation it is later Alexandrian). But here I must admit the limits of my time and abilities and draw to a close. At the very least, I hope that I have highlighted how careful we need to be in dealing with a named manuscript, especially one named after such a famous city of books.

NOTES

For their kind help I am most grateful to my colleague Dr Claire Breay and Dr Colin Wakefield, of the Bodleian Library. I have also benefited from correspondence with T. C. Skeat, as well as from the many traces of his researches on Alexandrinus that I encountered within the Department of Manuscripts of the British Library.

1. Now London, British Library, Royal MSS 1 D.v-viii, Alexandrinus is described in Sir George F. Warner and Julius P. Gilson, *Catalogue of Western Manuscripts in the Old Royal and King's Collections in the British Museum*, 4 vols (London: British Museum, 1921), I, p. 17; also, with bibliography, in *Summary Catalogue of Greek Manuscripts in the British Library*, I (London: British Library, 1999), pp. 223-4. Alexandrinus is completely reproduced, with descriptive introductions, in *Facsimile of the Codex Alexandrinus*, ed. by Edward Maunde Thompson, 4 vols (London: British Museum, 1879-83) and *The Codex Alexandrinus (Royal MS 1 D.v-viii) in Reduced Photographic Facsimile*, 5 vols (London: British Museum, 1909-57). See also H. J. M. Milne and T. C. Skeat, *The Codex Sinaiticus and the Codex Alexandrinus*, 2nd edn, rev. by T. C. Skeat (London: British Museum, 1955), pp. 30-40, and Bruce M. Metzger, *Manuscripts of the Greek Bible: An Introduction to Greek Palaeography* (New York/Oxford: University Press, 1981), p. 86, pl. 8.

2. Sir Frederic Kenyon, *The Story of the Bible: A Popular Account of how it came to us*, 2nd edn (London: John Murray, 1964), pp. 43-5.

3. Warner and Gilson, *Catalogue*, I, pp. xxi, xxiii, xxvii, xxx.

4. Jack Finegan, *Encountering New Testament Manuscripts: A Working Introduction to Textual Criticism* (London: SPCK, 1975), p. 150.

5. S. Jellicoe, *The Septuagint and Modern Study* (Oxford: Clarendon Press, 1968), p. 188.

6. Theodore D. Moschonas, 'Byzantine Alexandria and its Relations with the Bible', *Analecta, Publications de l'Institut d'études orientales de la Bibliothèque patriarcale d'Alexandrie*, 20 (1971), 119.

7. Theodore D. Moschonas, *Hê Patriarchikê Vivliothêkê dia mesou tôn aiônôn* (Alexandria: Anatole Press, 1943), p. 4.

8. Maunde Thompson, *Alexandrinus in Facsimile*, I, 3.

9. For example, Theodore D. Moschonas, 'Codex Alexandrinus', in *Vyzantinon Diptychon: Alexandrinos Kôdix, Vyzantinê Alexandreia* (Alexandria, 1950), p. 32.

10. *Biblia Sacra Polyglotta: complectentia Textus originales, Hebraicum, cum Pentateucho Samaritano, Chaldaicum, Graecum ... edidit Brianus Waltonus* (London: Thomas Roycroft, 1657), I, Prolegomena IX, para. 34, p. 65.

11. See, for example, *Calendar of State Papers, Domestic: The Commonwealth*, ed. by Mary A. Everett Green, 13 vols (London, 1875-86), IV (1651-2), p. 421 (Greek Bible of Tecla); ibid., VI (1653-4), p. 59 (Tecla's Septuagint); also Johannes Kemke, *Patricius Junius (Patrick Young): Bibliothekar der Könige Jacob I. und Carl I. von England* (Leipzig: M. Spirgalis, 1898), p. 103 (Thecla's Greek Bible). Young himself refers to Alexandrinus as the Codex Regius (see, for example, London, British Library, Harley MS 1328, ff. 67-67v). A rare

exception is James Ussher's designation of Alexandrinus in 1639 as 'the Alexandrian Copy' (Kemke, *Junius*, p. 93).

12 'Alexandrinum dicimus, non tam quod ex recensione Hesychii fuerit, a quo exemplaria per Alexandriam & Aegyptum secundum ipsius codicem castigata emanarunt; quam quod ex Alexandria primo allatus sit per Cyrillum Lucarem, nuper Sedis Alexandrinae Patriarcham, qui cum ad Constantinopolitanem translatus erat, hunc librum tanquam magnum thesaurum secum attulit' (*Biblia Sacra Polyglotta*, I, Prologomena IX, para. 34, p. 65).

13 Gunnar Hering, *Ökumenisches Patriarchat und europäische Politik, 1620-1638* (Wiesbaden: Franz Steiner, 1968), p. 27, n. 8; Sir Steven Runciman, *The Great Church in Captivity* (Cambridge: University Press, 1968), p. 269.

14 *Clementis ad Corinthios epistola prior ex laceris reliquiis vetustissimi exemplaris Bibliothecae Regiae, eruit, lacunas explevit, Latinè vertit, & notis brevioribus illustravit Patricius Junius* ... (Oxford: John Lichfield, 1633), preface dated 1632. The same story is repeated in Young's preface to *Catena graecorum patrum in beatum Iob, collectore Niceta Heraclae Metropolita* (London: Royal Press, 1637) and in Thomas Smith, *Miscellanea* (London: Samuel Smith, 1686), p. 136.

15 The first published transcription and translation, made by the royal interpreter, Abraham Salam, appears in H. H. Baber, *Vetus Testamentum Graecum, e codice MS. Alexandrino asservatur, typis ad similitudinem ipsius codicis scripturae fideliter descriptum*, 3 vols (London: Richard Taylor, 1816-21), III, notes p. 1.

16 Joseph Nasrallah and Rachid Haddad, *Histoire du mouvement littéraire dans l'église Melchite du Ve au XXe siècle: Contribution à l'étude de la littérature arabe chrétienne*, III, 1 (Louvain: Peeters, 1983), p. 107; Maurice Martin, 'Alexandrie chrétienne à la fin du XIIe siècle d'après Abû l-Makârim', in *Alexandrie médiévale I*, ed. by Christian Décobert and Jean-Yves Empereur (Cairo: Institut français d'archéologie orientale, 1998), p. 46. *Pace Messages. Millénaire de la Bibliothèque du patriarcat grec orthodoxe d'Alexandrie (952-1952)* (Alexandria: Patriarchal Press, 1952), p. 77, it is unhelpful to talk of one site for a single patriarchal library at this early date. As I show below, several patriarchal books were at Alexandria through the fourteenth and fifteenth centuries.

17 Annick Martin, 'Alexandrie à l'époque romaine tardive: l'impact du christianisme sur la topographie et les institutions', in *Alexandrie médiévale I*, ed. by Christian Décobert and Jean-Yves Empereur (Cairo: Institut français d'archéologie orientale, 1998), pp. 12-15; Alan K. Bowman, *Egypt after the Pharaohs, 332 BC-AD 642, from Alexander to the Arab Conquest* (London: British Museum Press, 1986), pp. 207-8.

18 Edward R. Hardy, *Christian Egypt: Church and People. Christianity and Nationalism in the Patriarchate of Alexandria* (New York: Oxford University Press, 1952), p. 156; George R. Monks, 'The Church of Alexandria and the City's Economic Life in the Sixth Century', *Speculum*, 28 (1953), 350.

19 Christopher Haas, *Alexandria in Late Antiquity: Topography and Social Conflict* (Baltimore: Johns Hopkins University Press, 1997), p. 344.

20 On the Catechetical School see Bowman, *Egypt*, pp. 229-30 and R. L. Wilken, 'Alexandria: A School for Training in Virtue', in *Schools of Thought in the Christian Tradition*, ed. by P. Henry (Philadelphia: Fortress, 1984), pp. 15-30; on its supposed library see Guglielmo Cavallo, 'Libro e pubblico alla fine del mondo antico', in *Libri, editori e pubblico nel mondo antico: Guida storica e critica*, ed. by Guglielmo Cavallo (Rome/Bari: Editori Laterza, 1975), p. 115, and Harry Y. Gamble, *Books and Readers in the Early Church: A History of Early Christian Texts* (New Haven/London: Yale University Press, 1995), p. 161.

21 An exception is Matthew Spinka, 'Acquisition of the Codex Alexandrinus by England', *Journal of Religion*, 16 (1936), 26.

22 Lucar supplied Laud with an Arabic Pentateuch, now in the Bodleian Library (Moschonas,

'Hê Patriarchikê Vivliothêkê', p. 7; Chrysostomos Papadopoulos, *Historia tês Ekklêsias Alexandreias (62-1934)* [Alexandria: Patriarchal Press, 1935], p. 680; Ian Philip, *The Bodleian Library in the Seventeenth and Eighteenth Centuries* [Oxford: Clarendon Press, 1983], p. 122, n. 72). He supplied Arundel with twenty-two manuscripts in 1626 (*The Negotiations of Sir Thomas Roe in his Embassy to the Ottoman Porte for the Year 1621 to 1628 inclusive*, ed. by Samuel Richardson [London: Society for the Encouragement of Learning, 1740], p. 500; David Howarth, *Lord Arundel and His Circle* [New Haven: Yale University Press, 1985], p. 91). *Pace* Moschonas, 'Codex Alexandrinus', p. 28, there is no independent evidence of Laud's Arabic Pentateuch coming from the Alexandrian Patriarchal Library; Arundel's Greek manuscripts, which are now in the British Library, almost certainly came from the Monastery of the Holy Trinity on the island of Chalce (see *Summary Catalogue of Greek Manuscripts*, I, pp. 5-6, 8, 18, 20, 21, 222). Lucar also sent a Catena on Job to Gustavus Adolphus II of Sweden in 1632 (Johann Arckenholz, *Mémoires concernant Christine, reine de Suède, pour servir d'éclaircissement à l'histoire de son règne et principalement de sa vie privée, et aux évenemens de l'histoire de son tems civile et littéraire*, 4 vols [Amsterdam/Leipzig, 1751-60], II, pièce justificative LXII [p. 115]; Chrysostomos A. Papadopoulos, *Kyrillos Loukaris* [Tergeste, 1907], p. 56). *Pace* Moschonas, 'Codex Alexandrinus', p. 28, there is no evidence that this manuscript came from the Patriarchal Library.

23 *Negotiations of Sir Thomas Roe*, pp. 414, 499, 500, 613, 618; *Summary Catalogue of Manuscripts in the Bodleian Library*, 6 vols (Oxford: Clarendon Press, 1895-1953), II, p. 10.

24 See Spinka, 'Codex Alexandrinus', pp. 10-29; R. J. Roberts, 'The Greek Press at Constantinople in 1627 and its Antecedents', *The Library*, ser. 5, 22 (1967), 13-43; Theodore D. Moschonas and Colin Davey, 'Codex Alexandrinus', *Analecta: Publications de l'Institut d'études orientales de la Bibliothèque patriarcale d'Alexandrie*, 22 (1973), 206-10; Andreas Tillyridès, 'Cyril Lucaris and the Codex Alexandrinus', *Analecta: Publications de l'Institut d'études orientales de la Bibliothèque patriarcale d'Alexandrie*, 24 (1975), 103-33; Colin Davey, 'Fair Exchange? Old Manuscripts for New Printed Books', in *Through the Looking Glass: Byzantium through British Eyes*, ed. by Robin Cormack and Elizabeth Jeffreys (Aldershot: Aldgate, 2000), pp. 127-34.

25 David Rogers, *The Bodleian Library and its Treasures, 1320-1700* (Henley-on-Thames: Aidan Ellis, 1991), p. 86, no. 72.

26 *Negotiations of Sir Thomas Roe*, pp. 499, 500, 618; Philip, *Bodleian Library*, p. 38.

27 *Negotiations of Sir Thomas Roe*, p. 414; cited by Davey, 'Fair Exchange?', p. 129. The same description is repeated by Roe in April 1626 (*Negotiations of Sir Thomas Roe*, p. 499).

28 Colin Wakefield, letter of 2 April, 1998.

29 Alexander Turyn, *Dated Greek Manuscripts of the Thirteenth and Fourteenth Centuries in the Libraries of Great Britain* (Dumbarton Oaks: Centre for Byzantine Studies, 1980), pp. 33-8; Irmgard Hutter, *Corpus der byzantinischen Miniaturenhandschriften, 1-3: Oxford, Bodleian Library* (Stuttgart: Hiersemann, 1977-82), III, p. 117.

30 The Arabic inscription is written on the concluding page (fol. 224), between the scribal colophon and the note by Manuel.

31 'Awqaftu ('awqafat) ḥaqarātī hāḏā al-kitāb 'alā al-kursī al-marqusī wa-man 'akrajahu 'anhu yakūnu muḥraman + katabahu 'Aṯanāsiyūs al-ḥaqīr (Colin Wakefield, letter of 18 May 1998).

32 London, Public Record Office, SP 97/14, no. 53; cited in Davey, 'Fair Exchange?', p. 133. I am grateful to Dr David Crook for checking the original text. Roe MS 13 matches Roe's description of it as 'very wormeaten' and also retains the repairs which he proposed to have made to it.

33 *Negotiations of Sir Thomas Roe*, p. 414; cited by Spinka, 'Codex Alexandrinus', p. 23 and Davey, 'Fair Exchange?', p. 130.

34 See C. G. Woide, *Notitia Codicis Alexandrini cum variis eius lectionibus omnibus*, ed. by Gottlieb L. Spohn (Leipzig: Breitkopf, 1788), pp. 49-61; Baber, *Vetus Testamentum*, I, pp. xxv-xxvi.

35 London, British Library, Royal MS 1 D.v, ff. 2, 4v.

36 *Negotiations of Sir Thomas Roe*, p. 335; Davey, 'Fair Exchange?', p. 129.

37 See, for example, Milne and Skeat, *Sinaiticus and Alexandrinus*, p. 36; Guiglielmo Cavallo, *Ricerche sulla maiuscola biblica* (Florence: Le Monnier, 1967), p. 80; Thomas S. Pattie, 'The Creation of the Great Codices', in *The Bible as Book: The Manuscript Tradition*, ed. by John L. Sharpe III and Kimberly Van Kampen (London: British Library, 1998), p. 69.

38 First proposed by Walton in *Biblia Sacra Polyglotta*, I, Prolegomena IX para. 34, p. 65; see also Humfrey Hody, *De Bibliorum textibus originalibus, versionibus graecis, & latina vulgata: Libri IV* (Oxford: Sheldonian Theatre, 1705), p. 638. The proposal that Alexandrinus was written at the oratory of Dekheila outside Alexandria (Moschonas, 'Codex Alexandrinus', p. 27) is a whimsical conflation of the two ideas, especially given the widespread nature of the cult of Thecla in late antiquity. In general see Stephen J. Davis, *The Cult of Saint Thecla: A Tradition of Women's Piety in Late Antiquity* (Oxford: University Press, 2001). A further liturgical explanation offered by Tregelles is correctly rejected in Maunde Thompson, *Alexandrinus in Facsimile*, I, 4.

39 Baber, *Vetus Testamentum*, I, p. xxvii n. 92 (Nicoll's note is dated 1827). *Pace* Maunde Thompson, *Alexandrinus in Facsimile*, I, 3 ('13th or 14th century'); *Reduced Facsimile, New Testament*, ed. Frederick G. Kenyon, p. 7 (same date as Athanasius inscription); Milne and Skeat, *Sinaiticus and Alexandrinus*, p. 36 (fourteenth century); Pattie, 'Great Codices', p. 69 (fourteenth century).

40 See Spinka, 'Codex Alexandrinus', p. 23; Roberts, 'Greek Press', pp. 26-7; Davey, 'Fair Exchange?', pp. 127-34.

41 On this period see Patricia Easterling, 'Before Palaeography: Notes on Early Descriptions and Datings of Greek Manuscripts', in *Texte und Untersuchungen zur Geschichte der altchristlichen Literatur*, 124 (1977), pp. 179-87; idem, 'From Britain to Byzantium: the Study of Greek Manuscripts', in *Through the Looking Glass: Byzantium through British Eyes*, ed. by Robin Cormack and Elizabeth Jeffreys (Aldershot: Aldgate, 2000), p. 108.

42 *Negotiations of Sir Thomas Roe*, pp. 335, 618; cited by Davey, 'Fair Exchange?', pp. 129, 132.

43 Maunde Thompson, *Alexandrinus in Facsimile*, I, 3.

44 Milne and Skeat, *Sinaiticus and Alexandrinus*, pp. 31-3; T. C. Skeat, 'The Provenance of the Codex Alexandrinus', *JTS*, 6 (1955), 233-4.

45 See especially Albert Failler, 'Le séjour d'Athanase II d'Alexandrie à Constantinople', *Revue des études byzantines*, 35 (1977), 43-71.

46 Milne and Skeat, *Sinaiticus and Alexandrinus*, p. 33; Skeat, 'Provenance of Alexandrinus', p. 235; *Reduced Facsimile, Old Testament Part IV*, ed. by T. C. Skeat, p. 4.

47 On Athanasius see, in addition to Failler's 'Séjour d'Athanase', John Mason Neale, *A History of the Holy Eastern Church. The Patriarchate of Alexandria*, 2 vols (London: Joseph Masters, 1847), II, pp. 312-25; Chrysostomos Papadopoulos, 'Ho Athanasios II (1276-1316)', *Epeteris Hetaireias Vyzantinôn Spoudôn*, 6 (1929), 3-13; Gerasimos G. Mazarakes, *Symbolê eis tên historian tês en Aigyptoi orthodoxou ekklêsias* (Alexandria: Patriarchal Press, 1932), pp. 60-6; Papadopoulos, *Historia*, pp. 564-74. On contemporary Alexandria see Martina Müller-Wiener, *Eine Stadtgeschichte Alexandrias von 564/1169 in die Mitte des 9./15. Jahrhunderts*, Islamkundliche Untersuchungen, 159 (Berlin: Klaus Schwarz, 1992).

48 Skeat, *Reduced Facsimile, OT, Part IV*, pp. 3-4.

49 Described in N. S. Phirippidis and T. D. Moschonas, *Katalogoi tês Patriarchikês Vivliothêkês*, 3 vols (Alexandria: Patriarchal Press, 1945-7), I, pp. 23-4, 49-51.

50 The inscription in MS 34 was first cited in G. Charitakis, 'Katalogos tôn chronologêmenôn kôdikôn tês patriarchês vivliothêkês Kaïrou', *Epeteris Hetaireias Vyzantinôn Spoudôn*, 4 (1927), 113-16. See also Mazarakes, *Symbolê*, p. 66 and Papadopoulos, *Historia*, p. 574. As Iatropoulos was still alive in 1295 (Erich Trapp, *Prosopographisches Lexikon der Palaiologenzeit*, 8 vols [Vienna: Verlag der Österreichischen Akademie der Wissenschaften, 1976-96], no. 7968), Athanasius must have donated the manuscript after this date.

51 Described in E. Feron and F. Battaglini, *Codices manuscripti graeci Ottoboniani Bibliothecae Vaticanae descripti* (Vatican City: Vatican Press, 1893), pp. 251-2.

52 Giovanni Mercati, 'I codici greci di Abramo Massad Maronita', *Studia Anselmiana*, 27-8 (1951), 34-5.

53 First translated in Skeat, *Reduced Facsimile, OT Part IV*, p. 4.

54 Both were recovered by the industrious patriarch Ioachim (r. 1487-1567), on whom see Papadopoulos, *Historia*, pp. 589-612 and Turyn, *Dated Manuscripts*, p. 36.

55 The two manuscripts (Alexandria, Patriarchal Library, MSS 12, 34), which were destined for the patriarchal church, were undoubtedly intended by Athanasius for St Saba's, the only church in Alexandria which remained under Melchite control. The patriarchal cell to which Alexandrinus was committed by Athanasius was undoubtedly the associated monastery of St Saba in Alexandria. Athanasius may well have intended these donations to form part of the restoration and revival of St Saba's. The fact that one other manuscript donated by Athananius to the patriarchate (Roe MS 13) remained in Alexandria early in the sixteenth century may support the assumption that they eventually reached their intended home at St Saba's. On both church and monastery see Jules Faivre, 'L'église Saint-Sabas et le martyrium de Saint-Marc à Alexandrie', *Bulletin de l'Association des amis de l'art copte*, 3 (1937), 60-7 and Theodore D. Moschonas, 'L'église de Saint-Saba à travers les siècles', *Revue des conférences françaises en Orient*, (1947), 3-14.

56 'Bound to' does reflect a specific context. The two manuscripts recovered by the patriarch Ioachim were said by him to have been 'bound to' the patriarchate by the patriarch's threat to excommunicate anyone who alienated them, and another manuscript still at Alexandria (Patriarchal Library, MS 69) was similarly 'bound to' the patriarchate by the patriarch Silvester (see Phirippidis and Moschonas, *Katalogoi*, I, 77). In each case the word used is part of the Greek verb 'prosêlaô'. The Arabic word used in Alexandrinus appears to be the counterpart of this Greek word. However, in the case of Alexandria MS 69 and another manuscript from Alexandria, now in Princeton (on the latter see Metzger, *Manuscripts of the Greek Bible*, pp. 124-5, pl. 38; Kenneth W. Clark, *A Descriptive Catalogue of Greek New Testament Manuscripts in America* [Chicago: University Press, 1937], pp. 175-6) the patriarchal threat against alienation merely confirms the gift of another individual.

57 On Galaction see Raymond Janin, *Les églises et les monastères des grands centres byzantins (Bithynie, Hellespont, Latros, Galèsios, Trébizonde, Thessalonique)* (Paris: Institut français d'études byzantines, 1975), p. 248; Turyn, *Dated Manuscripts*, p. 34.

58 On this embassy see Failler, 'Séjour d'Athanase', p. 49.

59 On the fall of Ephesus see Clive Foss, *Ephesus after Antiquity: A Late Antique, Byzantine and Turkish City* (Cambridge: University Press, 1979), pp. 143-4.

60 Foss, *Ephesus*, p. 130; Janin, *Églises*, p. 249; François Halkin, 'Manuscrits galésiotes', *Scriptorium*, 15 (1961), p. 225, no. 16.

61 Skeat, 'Provenance of Alexandrinus', p. 235.

62 Ibid., p. 235.

63 See most recently Léon Vaganay, *An Introduction to New Testament Textual Criticism*, 2nd edn, rev. by C.-B. Amphoux, trans. by Jenny Heimerdinger (Cambridge: University Press, 1991), p. 15. I owe this reference to T. C. Skeat.

64 British Library, Royal MS 1 D.v, f. 1.

65 By Nicoll in Baber, *Vetus Testamentum*, I, p. xxviii n. 92.

66 One serious contender is Thomas Smith (1638-1710), chaplain to the British ambassador to the Porte (1668-71) and biographer of Cyril Lucar.

67 See, for example, Baber, *Vetus Testamentum*, I, p. xviii; Kenyon, *Reduced Facsimile. New Testament*, p. 7; Moschonas, 'Codex Alexandrinus', pp. 26-7.

68 Woide, *Notitia*, pp. 29-32.

69 Maunde Thompson, *Alexandrinus in Facsimile*, I, 9-10; Frederic G. Kenyon, *The Text of the Greek Bible* (London: Duckworth, 1937), p. 84.

70 *Codex Alexandrinus. Novum Testamentum Graece*, ed. by B. H. Cowper (London: Williams & Norgate, 1860), pp. xxii-xxiii.

71 Cavallo, *Maiuscola biblica*, pp. 56, 80. For similar remarks on Codex Sinaiticus see H. J. M. Milne and T. C. Skeat, *Scribes and Correctors of the Codex Sinaiticus* (London: British Museum, 1938), pp. 66-9.

72 See T. C. Skeat, 'The Codex Sinaiticus, the Codex Vaticanus and Constantine', *JTS*, n.s. 50 (1999), 616.

73 On Alexandrinus's canon tables see Milne and Skeat, *Scribes and Correctors*, p. 9, and Carl Nordenfalk, *Die spätantiken Kanontafeln* (Gotheburg: Oscar Isacson, 1937), p. 274.

74 This dating remains the consensus view. For a dating to the third quarter of the fifth century see Cavallo, *Maiuscola biblica*, p. 79.

75 On the devastating effect of the fall of 1204 see N. G. Wilson, *Scholars of Byzantium* (London: Duckworth, 1983), pp. 218-19. In contrast it is worth citing that as late as 1304 Ephesus was renowned for many relics of great antiquity, including the purported autograph manuscript of Revelation written in gold (Foss, *Ephesus*, pp. 125-8).

76 See Foss, *Ephesus*, pp. 103-37.

77 Janin, *Églises*, pp. 241-50; Foss, *Ephesus*, pp. 128-30. The revival of scholarship at Ephesus as part of the Nicaean Empire (ibid., pp. 130-1) may, however, be important.

78 See Halkin, 'Manuscrits galésiotes', pp. 221-7.

79 On the paucity of evidence see Gamble, *Books and Readers*, pp. 121-2.

80 Cavallo, *Maiuscola biblica*, pp. 79-80.

81 For what follows see Foss, *Ephesus*, pp. 7-9, 33-45, 52-4, 87-92.

82 Argued most recently by Skeat, 'Codex Sinaiticus', pp. 583-604.

83 See ibid., pp. 604-17.

84 *Reduced Facsimile, OT Part I*, ed. F. G. Kenyon, p. 1.

85 Meanwhile see Gwendolen M. Stephen, 'The Coronis', *Scriptorium*, 13 (1959), 9; Carl Nordenfalk, *Die spätantiken Zierbuchstaben* (Stockholm, 1970), pp. 106-13; Guglielmo Cavallo, 'Iniziale, scritture distinctive, fregi: morfologie e funzioni', in *Libri e documenti d'Italia: dai Longobardi alla rinascita della città*, ed. by Cesare Scalon (Udine: Arti grafici friulane, 1996), p. 30.

86 Jules Leroy, *Les manuscrits coptes et coptes-arabes illustrés*, Bibliothèque archéologique et historique de l'Institut français d'archéologie de Beyrouth, vol. 96 (Paris: Paul Geuther, 1974), p. 63.

ANOTHER LOOK AT CODEX SINAITICUS

John J. Brogan

I F   T H E R E   I S   A N Y biblical manuscript that is known outside of the guild of textual critics among the general public, it is Codex Sinaiticus (Fig. 6). Several events have contributed to Sinaiticus' fame and fortune: the romantic tale of Constantine Tischendorf's initial discovery in 1844 of a portion of the codex at St Catherine's monastery (supposedly saving the leaves from a fiery demise);[1] the suspect circumstances surrounding Tischendorf's removal of the rest of the codex from St Catherine's fifteen years later (1859) and its subsequent 'gifting' to the Czar of Russia;[2] the scandal created by the notorious forger, Constantine Simonides, who claimed that he had written the codex himself;[3] the rallying of the English public in 1933-4 to purchase the codex from the Russian Government for £100,000; the endless parade of visitors over the years to the British Museum and British Library who come to gaze upon the famous codex. All of these things combine to make Codex Sinaiticus larger than life.

This article will begin with a few general remarks about some past studies of the illustrious codex. I will then discuss some of my own observations concerning the corrections of Sinaiticus and their importance for studying the history of the transmission of the New Testament text. Throughout the article, I will suggest further investigations of Sinaiticus that might prove valuable in the future.

PAST STUDIES OF CODEX SINAITICUS

The initial discovery of the manuscript generated a flurry of studies. After removing the codex from St Catherine's monastery in 1859, Tischendorf published a quasi-facsimile edition of the entire text of Sinaiticus three years later (1862),[4] and a critical edition of the New Testament portion of the manuscript the following year (1863).[5] E. H. Hansell (1864) published a full collation of Sinaiticus,[6] and in the same year, F. H. Scrivener also published a collation of the text with a scholarly introduction in English.[7] Helen and Kirsopp Lake produced a photographic facsimile along with a critical introduction (1911-22) shortly before Sinaiticus was relocated to the British Museum.[8] Various articles analyzing the manuscript's antiquity or some of its important/peculiar readings appeared sporadically in the late-nineteenth and early-twentieth centuries.[9] The standard text-critical handbooks of the period soon included discussions concerning the text and importance of Sinaiticus.[10]

The British Museum's acquisition of Sinaiticus in 1933 revitalized interest in the codex. Milne and Skeat published their monumental study of the manuscript, entitled *Scribes and Correctors of the Codex Sinaiticus*, in 1938.[11] This remains the standard work covering the contents, scribes, correctors, paleography, date, and provenance of the manuscript. They provide a detailed description of the manuscript's physical attributes. Their keen paleographic insight greatly simplified the overwhelming number of scribes and correctors proposed by both Tischendorf and Lake. In short, their work epitomizes the attention to detail needed in a study of a text such as Sinaiticus. The identity of a particular scribe or corrector might be disputed in a few places, but overall there appears to be little reason to revisit the major topics of their study.[12]

THE TEXTUAL CHARACTER OF SINAITICUS

In contrast to the advancements made in the study of the physical attributes of Codex Sinaiticus, there have been only modest advancements in understanding the textual character of Sinaiticus since it was first published.[13] According to Westcott and Hort, Sinaiticus was a primary witness to their misnomered 'Neutral' text. As such, Sinaiticus (‫א‬) was second in importance only to the much-revered Codex Vaticanus (B). In describing the text of Sinaiticus, Hort observed:

As in its contemporary B, the text [of ‫א‬] seems to be entirely, or all but entirely, Pre-Syrian [i.e. Pre-Byzantine]: and further, a very large part of the text is in like manner free from Western or Alexandrian elements. On the other hand, this fundamental text has undergone extensive mixture either with another text itself already mixed, or more probably, with two separate texts, one Western, one Alexandrian [...] The Western readings are specially numerous in St. John's Gospel and parts of Luke ...[14]

Studies by von Soden and Hoskier also noted the Western elements found in Sinaiticus.[15] A scholarly consensus developed (which continues today) that Sinaiticus contains primarily an Alexandrian text with a mixture of Western readings. This view can be seen in the descriptions of Sinaiticus found in most of the standard handbooks of New Testament textual criticism.[16]

Gordon Fee presented a modification to the prevailing understanding of Sinaiticus' textual character in his study of the Fourth Gospel in Sinaiticus.[17] Intrigued by Boismard's proposal that Sinaiticus had closer affinities to D than B in John 1-8,[18] Fee completed his own statistical analysis of Sinaiticus' text in the Gospel of John and concluded, 'Codex Sinaiticus is a leading Greek representative of the Western textual tradition in John 1.1-8.38'.[19] According to Fee, the text of Sinaiticus in the Fourth Gospel was not primarily Alexandrian with Western corruptions scattered throughout the Gospel as Hort had suggested. Instead the textual character of Sinaiticus actually changed dramatically at John 8. John 1-8 contained a Western form of the text, whereas John 9-21 contained an Alexandrian text – a striking example of what textual critics describe as 'block mixture'.

Other than Boismard's and Fee's examinations, few scholars have attempted to classify Sinaiticus' textual character with greater precision than the general characterization found in the handbooks. Most textual critics simply accept the descriptions of the text of Sinaiticus 'just as they were handed on to us by those who were eye-witnesses' (to borrow a phrase from Luke). Given the tremendous advancements that have been made in analyzing, classifying, and grouping manuscripts in the last fifty years,[20] especially Colwell's and Tune's quantitative analysis[21] and the various profile analyses developed in more recent years, new textual studies of Sinaiticus are now called for. The type of careful analysis performed by Fee on the Fourth Gospel must be extended to the rest of the codex in order to determine whether there are other places of block mixture and also to develop a clearer understanding of Sinaiticus' overall textual character.

THE IMPORTANCE OF 'BLOCK MIXTURE' IN SINAITICUS

The importance of a fresh analysis of the textual character of Sinaiticus should not be underestimated. Important information about the history of the Alexandrian text and the transmission of the New Testament text in general can be found within the pages of the codex itself. Two features of Sinaiticus' text in particular provide valuable information about the history of the New Testament text: (1) the existence of block mixture, and (2) the large quantity and diversity of corrections of the manuscript.

The existence of block mixture in any manuscript should cause the textual critic to pause. Textual criticism has not yet developed a theory of the transmission of the text that can adequately explain such mixture. The existence of a block of 'Western' text in a manuscript that is otherwise primarily 'Alexandrian' in character raises all sorts of questions that require explanations. For example, the question of place of origin is intriguing. Was the manuscript produced in Alexandria? Caesarea? Elsewhere? If Alexandria, what does the presence of a Western text in Alexandria reveal about the history of the Alexandrian text or the relationship between the Alexandrian and Western textual families? If Caesarea (as some scholars such as Skeat have suggested), what does this tell us about the geographic distribution of the various text-types in the Early Church? What does the existence of block mixture indicate about the concern (or lack thereof) for maintaining a 'pure' or 'correct' text within the early stages of transmission? A careful study of the textual character of Sinaiticus could provide some valuable information for answering these types of questions.

The existence of block mixture in Sinaiticus also raises questions about the source text(s) used by the scribes. Did the scribes of Sinaiticus use multiple exemplars that contained different text-types of the New Testament text? Or did the scribes use a single exemplar that already contained a mixed text? If a scribe used separate texts, as Hort suggested,[22] are there theological, polemical, or stylistic reasons which would have motivated him to use one text over the other? In other words, Sinaiticus should be examined to determine whether it displays the theological tendencies of its scribes and correctors.[23] No matter what angle of investigation is taken, the existence of block mixture in Sinaiticus tells us something about the history of the transmission of the New Testament.

THE IMPORTANCE OF THE CORRECTIONS OF SINAITICUS

In addition to the existence of block mixture, the corrections of Codex Sinaiticus also provide valuable information concerning the history of the New Testament. I developed an interest in the corrections of Sinaiticus in my study of Athanasius' text of the four Gospels.[24] In this study, I gathered all of Athanasius' citations, adaptations, and allusions to the four Gospels that are found in his undisputed writings that are available in critical editions. I collated all these references against representative witnesses of the various textual families (i.e. Alexandrian, Byzantine, Western, and Caesarean texts). A quantitative analysis of these collations revealed that Athanasius preserves an Alexandrian form of the text of the Gospels. A comprehensive profile analysis demonstrated that Athanasius' text has closer affinities to Secondary Alexandrian witnesses than Primary Alexandrian witnesses.[25]

I also discovered that on several occasions, Athanasius 'corrupts' his biblical text.[26] There appear to be two causes of his corruptions. On the one hand, many of Athanasius' corruptions are due to careless citation techniques – for examples, changes resulting from faulty memory or the mixture of two or more texts. I would classify such changes as 'unintentional'. On the other hand, some changes appear deliberate on Athanasius' part. These 'intentional' changes fall into two categories: (1) intentional changes which do not alter the meaning of the text (for example, grammatical changes made to fit the citation into the context of Athanasius' writing), and (2) intentional changes made for theological and/or polemical reasons which alter the meaning of the biblical text. Athanasius corrupts his biblical texts through such means as omissions, additions, grammatical changes (e.g. singular to plural), word substitutions, conflations, and even wholesale inventions of texts.[27] Some of these corruptions produce an altered meaning of the text. The net rhetorical effect of these changes is that Athanasius creates new 'biblical' texts which carry the same authority as the 'original' wording of the texts. These new texts conveniently support his theological and political agendas.

ATHANASIUS AND THE CORRECTIONS OF SINAITICUS

If Athanasius' corruption of biblical texts affected only his own writings, then all of this would have nothing to do with Codex Sinaiticus, and I would be guilty of the old academic 'bait-and-switch' routine – promising an article on Codex Sinaiticus, but instead giving a synopsis of my latest (remotely related) research. I will plead only partially guilty to this charge, however. Athanasius does have a connection to Sinaiticus that can be seen in his close textual affinity to the corrections of Sinaiticus.

Codex Sinaiticus was most likely transcribed during Athanasius' lifetime.[28] Over the centuries, several correctors put their pens to codex, creating a text-critical jigsaw of determining the various hands of the correctors. In the words of Milne and Skeat, 'The study and identification of the various correctors constitutes the most difficult task in the investigation of the manuscript'.[29] Milne and Skeat simplified the 'formidable series' of correctors developed by Tischendorf and elaborated by the Lakes into two main groupings. The first group, comprised of the 'earliest correctors', included all of Tischendorf's and the Lakes' 'A' correctors (seven in number) and 'B' correctors (two in number). Milne and Skeat identify these correctors as two of the original scribes (the scribes designated A and D), and thus the corrections were made at the time of the manuscript's production.[30] The second group of correctors, comprised of all five of Tischendorf's 'C' correctors, dates from the fifth to seventh centuries.[31] Athanasius' text shows a remarkable affinity to both the early and later corrections of Sinaiticus in the four Gospels.

When comparing Athanasius' text with the corrections of Sinaiticus (designated ℵ^c),

TABLE I

Witnesses ranked according to their proportional agreement with ℵᶜ against ℵ* in units of significant variation preserved in Athanasius' Text of the Four Gospels

Witness	Agreement	Percentage
1. 1071	3/3	100%
2. Ath	23/25	92%
3. A	17/19	89%
4. Origen	8/9	89%
5. Ψ	16/19	84%
6. f¹³ 1241	21/25	84%
8. 33	19/23	83%
9. Δ Π 700	20/25	80%
12. 565	19/24	79%
13. Ω	18/23	78%
14. E L Θ f¹ TR	19/25	76%
19. 892	13/18	72%
20. UBS⁴	18/25	72%
21. P⁷⁵	5/7	71%
22. 570	12/17	71%
23. a b	15/22	68%
25. Clement	4/6	67%
26. B	16/25	64%
27. C	7/11	64%
28. W	12/20	60%
29. e	11/20	55%
30. P⁶⁶	7/13	54%
31. Didymus	2/4	50%
32. D	6/17	35%
33. k	1/3	33%

two factors must be considered. First, since the text of the Gospels preserved by Athanasius is fragmentary, the number of corrections to Sinaiticus in these portions of text will be small. Sinaiticus has been corrected a total of forty-two times in the text of the Gospels preserved by Athanasius.[32] Second, only those instances where the correction of Sinaiticus involves a 'unit of significant variation' need to be considered.[33] Thus, singular readings of the original hand of Sinaiticus (ℵ*) that have been corrected are not included in the comparisons.[34] In most cases, these unique readings in ℵ* are due to scribal error and unrelated to any textual tradition, and thus the correction tells us little about textual relationships. Overall, twenty-five of the corrections of Sinaiticus represent units of significant variation. Athanasius agrees with ℵᶜ against ℵ* six out of six times in Matthew,[35] two out of three times in Luke,[36] and fifteen out of sixteen times in John.[37] The total agreement of Athanasius with ℵᶜ is twenty-three out of twenty-five times, an amazing 92 per cent.[38]

Table 1 presents the percentages of agreement between the representative textual witnesses with ℵᶜ against ℵ* over these same twenty-five units of variation. Athanasius' percentage of agreement is the highest of any of the witnesses (with the exception of

1071 which preserves only a statistically-insignificant, three shared units of variation with $\aleph^c$), demonstrating his close textual affinity to the corrections of Sinaiticus. In general, Table 1 reveals that several of the witnesses that agree most closely with $\aleph^c$ are Secondary Alexandrian witnesses (Ath Ψ 33 and possibly Origen and 1241).[39] This alignment between $\aleph^c$ and Secondary Alexandrian will be noted further below.

Taking into consideration Milne's and Skeat's dating of the correctors of Sinaiticus, six of the twenty-five corrections (in units of significant variation) are attributed to correctors 'A' or 'B'.[40] These correctors are contemporaneous with the original scribes of Sinaiticus, and contemporaneous with Athanasius as well. Athanasius' readings agree with all six of these corrections. Since in most cases corrections of a manuscript are made by comparisons to either the exemplar itself or to some other manuscript, then it is likely that the readings shared by Athanasius and correctors 'A' or 'B' already exist within the New Testament textual tradition in the fourth century.

The remaining nineteen corrections of Sinaiticus are attributed to the corrector 'C^a'. According to Milne and Skeat, this corrector corrected Sinaiticus sometime during the fifth to seventh centuries. Athanasius agrees with seventeen of these nineteen later corrections. This means that if the readings attested by Athanasius were not already in the stream of transmission during the fourth century, then they entered the stream sometime between Athanasius' lifetime and the time of corrector 'C^a'.

ORIGEN, DIDYMUS, AND THE CORRECTIONS OF SINAITICUS

Athanasius' close affinity to the corrections of Sinaiticus made me question whether this was a common phenomenon among the Alexandrian Fathers or unique to Athanasius. In order to answer this question, I examined the text of the Gospels of two other Alexandrian Fathers – Origen and Didymus the Blind. I selected these two Fathers because critical editions and studies of their texts have recently been completed.[41] In Origen's text of the Fourth Gospel, Sinaiticus has been corrected in 123 units of significant variation. As can be seen in Table 2, Origen agrees with $\aleph^c$ against $\aleph^*$ ninety-one times (74 per cent). Like Athanasius, Origen stands near the top of the list of witnesses. Yet Origen's text is not as closely aligned to $\aleph^c$ as Athanasius' – Origen's percentage of agreement with $\aleph^c$ is 18 per cent less than Athanasius'. Once again the top six witnesses in agreement with $\aleph^c$ are Secondary Alexandrian (33 L 892 Ψ C and possibly 1241).

In the text of the four Gospels preserved by Didymus, Sinaiticus is corrected in thirty-nine units of significant variation. Table 3 provides the percentages of agreement between the representative witnesses and $\aleph^c$ against $\aleph^*$. Didymus agrees with $\aleph^c$ twenty-five times (64 per cent). Didymus' percentage of agreement with $\aleph^c$ is 28 per cent less than Athanasius'. In contrast to Athanasius and Origen, Didymus appears in the middle of the list rather than near the top. Once again, the Secondary Alexandrian witnesses congregate near the top of the list (five of the top eight witnesses – Ψ L 579 33 892). This corroborates the results of the other two tables concerning the textual affinity between the corrections of Sinaiticus and the Secondary Alexandrian witnesses.

Comparing the three tables, Athanasius exhibits a uniquely high level of textual affinity to the corrections of Sinaiticus. Perhaps Athanasius was familiar with a text that

TABLE 2

Witnesses ranked according to their proportional agreement with ℵᶜ against ℵ* in units of significant variation preserved in Origen's Text of the Fourth Gospel

	Witness	Percentage Agreement
1.	33	86%
2.	L 892	83%
4.	Ψ	80%
5.	C 1241	75%
7.	Origen	74%
8.	P⁷⁵ TR	71%
10.	E Π Ω 565 700	70%
15.	D f¹³ 579 UBS⁴	69%
19.	A	68%
20.	Θ	67%
21.	B	66%
22.	f¹	65%
23.	P⁶⁶	57%
24.	W	52%
25.	b	46%
26.	a	41%
27.	D	40%
28.	e	35%

TABLE 3

Witnesses ranked according to their proportional agreement with ℵᶜ against ℵ* in units of significant variation preserved in Didymus' the Blind Text of the Four Gospels

	Witness	Percentage Agreement
1.	Ψ	88%
2.	Δ	77%
3.	L 579	76%
5.	33	73%
6.	Ω	71%
7.	Θ 892	70%
9.	Π	68%
10.	f¹³ TR	66%
12.	C 1241 Didymus	64%
15.	P⁷⁵ A	63%
17.	E	60%
18.	f¹	59%
19.	P⁶⁶	58%
20.	W UBS⁴	57%
22.	e	56%
23.	a	54%
24.	b	53%
25.	B	52%
26.	k	43%
27.	D	30%

was similar to the text(s) used to correct Sinaiticus. Or, perhaps Athanasius and/or his writings had a significant influence on the text behind the corrections or on the correctors themselves (as will be discussed below). In either case, the alignment of Athanasius and ℵ^c as well as the alignment between Secondary Alexandrian witnesses and ℵ^c requires explanation.

SCRIBES, THE TEXT OF THE NEW TESTAMENT, AND THE INFLUENCE OF THE FATHERS

Readings attested by Athanasius, as well as other Church Fathers such as Origen and Didymus, eventually entered the stream of textual transmission, as can be seen among the corrections of Sinaiticus. The question which remains is how and why did textual changes such as those made by Athanasius become part of the actual text? In order to answer this question, we must examine scribal practices and the existence of interpretive communities in the Early Church.[42]

In his 1993 study, *The Orthodox Corruption of Scripture*, Bart Ehrman examines christologically-significant textual variants within the Greek manuscript tradition.[43] Ehrman observes an analogous relationship between the interpretation of texts, in which interpreters 'rewrite' texts in their minds as they read and ascribe meaning to them, and the scribal activity of copying texts, in which scribes actually *do* rewrite the texts.[44] Based on his text-critical analysis of these textual variants, Ehrman concludes that,

Proto-orthodox scribes of the second and third centuries occasionally modified their texts of Scripture in order to make them coincide more closely with the christological views embraced by the party that would seal its victory at Nicea and Chalcedon.[45]

These modifications do more than merely clarify or correct the questionable text. They actually change the meaning of the text. In Ehrman's words, 'Scribes altered their sacred texts to make them "say" what they were already known to "mean"'.[46] The question remains as to how these unknown scribes – these nameless, faceless shapers of the text – developed their theology, which in turn affected their understanding of particular texts, and which ultimately affected their transcription of those texts. Put simply, how did a scribe come to know what a text 'meant'?

'Meaning' – as ascribed to a text – is a social construct. Most scribes belonged to some sort of Christian community. These communities were defined by their location, their worship practices, their relationship to other communities, their leaders, and perhaps most importantly, their theology. People within these religious communities shared a common set of beliefs. Each community allowed for a certain range of view-points concerning particular points of theology. If a person's (or sub-group's) theology strayed beyond the limits accepted by the community, that person or sub-group was expelled from the community. One way in which a community established and maintained its boundaries (by which the community could identify itself and distinguish itself from rival communities) was by developing a canon of sacred literature – a scrip-ture. In addition, each community established ways of properly interpreting and understanding its sacred scripture. Ehrman speaks of these as being 'communities of like-minded readers'.[47] According to Ehrman, the people who belonged to these communities were bound to an intricate network of social, cultural, historical, and intellectual contexts, contexts that affect both who a person is and how he or she will 'see' the world at large, including the texts within it [...] This nexus of factors does more than *influence* the way texts are interpreted; it actually *produces* interpretations.[48]

In this way, Christian communities can be understood as *interpretive* communities.[49] Scribes were influenced by their interpretive communities – the people with whom they worshiped, ate, slept, and most importantly, with whom they worked in the process of transcribing texts.

In most cases, the development of interpretive communities is not an egalitarian process. Each interpretive community has its leaders – people who are respected for their intellectual, spiritual, and/or political prowess. These leaders are extremely influential in establishing and enforcing community boundaries and in developing the interpretive frameworks by which scripture is understood. In effect, the leaders are the intellectual and theological 'movers and shakers' of these communities.

The leaders of the Early Church, those whom we call the Church 'Fathers', were the key players in the theological controversies of the first four centuries. They met in the great ecumenical councils. They fought the theological battles. They wrote the sermons, the letters, the theological treatises, the apologies, and the biblical commentaries that were read and preserved in their communities. Meanwhile, the nameless scribes were busy with the task of copying the scriptures and other important pieces of Christian literature. They were probably not at the centre of the theological battles of the day.[50] Yet they were still interested and affected by those controversies, and they made their own contributions to them. The scribes read the works of the more prominent Fathers. They heard sermons by the leaders of their community in which the leaders espoused the community's theological views. The scribes pondered over these theological and scriptural questions during times of prayer, meditation, and study. Then, quite naturally, when these scribes engaged in the task of copying texts, they read the parent text through the eyes of their interpretive community, occasionally making changes in their texts to fit their interpretive framework, making the text *read* what they already knew it to *mean*.

The scribes themselves were probably not the originators of many of these theological corruptions of Scripture. Prominent leaders in the Church, such as Athanasius, had already corrupted the biblical texts in their citation of these texts in their writings and sermons. In their original contexts, these corruptions served the authors' polemical purposes by providing the correct meaning of the texts, rather than providing the verbatim wording of the texts. During the process of copying these texts in manuscripts, these interpretive corruptions came into the mind of the scribe (either consciously or subconsciously) because they provided the proper meaning of the text. In some cases, either through unintentional gloss or intentional alteration, the scribe introduced these corruptions into the copy of the text itself, making the corruption a part of the ever-changing stream of transmission.

How does this process relate to the corrections of Sinaiticus? In a few cases, Athanasius is the *earliest* witness of a reading that appears in later biblical manuscripts and/or the corrections of Sinaiticus.[51] It is likely that some of the readings attested by Athanasius did not exist in the textual tradition before or during the fourth century. In those cases, Athanasius could have created these variant readings in citing the Gospels for theological and polemical reasons.[52] Since readings created by influential Fathers influenced scribes who were copying texts, then in the case of Athanasius, his corruptions would have influenced either the correctors of Sinaiticus themselves or earlier scribes who transcribed the texts used by the correctors.

SINAITICUS, ITS CORRECTIONS, AND THE ALEXANDRIAN TEXT

My comparison of the text of the Gospels found in the writings of Athanasius, Origen, and Didymus indicated that the corrections of Sinaiticus were most closely aligned to Secondary Alexandrian witnesses. This correlation can be see in the tendency of the Secondary Alexandrian witnesses to congregate near the top in all three tables. From these limited comparisons, it appears that the corrections of Sinaiticus change it from being a Primary Alexandrian witness to a Secondary Alexandrian witness. Obviously, the texts I used to come to this hypothesis are limited in scope and randomly chosen – texts that happened to be preserved in the writings of these particular Church Fathers that also happen to display corrections in Sinaiticus. Yet this randomness further supports my hypothesis. Biblical texts taken from three different Fathers, over a wide range of time and types of texts, compared with the full spectrum of correctors of Sinaiticus demonstrate a remarkable affinity between ℵ[c] and Secondary Alexandrian witnesses. These preliminary findings call for a full-scale quantitative and profile analysis of the various correctors of Sinaiticus in order to determine accurately the textual character(s) of those corrections. Only then can ℵ[c] be classified as being a Secondary Alexandrian witness with any degree of certainty.

My proposal that the corrections of Sinaiticus change its textual character from a Primary to a Secondary Alexandrian witness is contrary to suggestions made by other scholars. One commonly held view is that two of the primary 'C' correctors ('C[a]' and 'C[b]') were located in Caesarea.[53] Based on this view, some scholars suggest that the later corrections, especially those of 'C[a]', support many 'Caesarean' readings.[54] Skeat holds a different view concerning the textual character of the corrections. He states that 'C[a]' (whom Skeat considers to be the most important of the 'C' correctors), 'carefully revised the entire manuscript (excepting the Epistle of Barnabas), bringing it into conformity with the Byzantine texts familiar to him'.[55] These conflicting views about the textual character of the 'C' corrections further demonstrate the need for a thorough statistical analysis of the corrections of Sinaiticus.

The preceding discussion evokes the question as to what is meant when one speaks of a 'Secondary Alexandrian' witness. Stated simply, what makes a witness 'Secondary' as opposed to 'Primary' Alexandrian? My investigation of Athanasius' text of the Gospels and initial observations into the corrections of Sinaiticus lead me to make some preliminary suggestions. First, there are some readings that are supported exclusively or primarily among the Secondary Alexandrian witnesses.[56] My initial observations, however, indicate that there are not enough of these distinctive readings to make the Secondary Alexandrian witnesses a distinct text-type. This is due to the nature of the changes being made to the Alexandrian text. These changes appear sporadic and diverse. They are created in the polemical context of the theological controversies of the

Early Church. These corruptions are created and disseminated by highly respected and influential leaders in their sermons and writings. These new readings are eventually introduced into the actual text of the New Testament by scribes who have been influenced by these leaders. Some changes are widely supported among Secondary Alexandrian witnesses; others are preserved by only a few. Perhaps what we observe in the Secondary Alexandrian witnesses is a movement towards a distinct text-type. Yet this movement is aborted due to the ascendancy of the rival Byzantine text in the late-fourth and fifth centuries.

CONCLUDING REMARKS

Let me draw together the major points of this paper. My primary purpose is to emphasize that even though Codex Sinaiticus has been available to scholars nearly 140 years, there are still many things we do not know about this manuscript. Throughout this paper, I have suggested several possible areas of study. These include:

(1) Further studies into the textual character of Sinaiticus. Descriptions of the text given by such eminent textual scholars as Hort, von Soden, Lake, and Metzger need to be confirmed (or altered) on the basis of thorough statistical textual analysis.

(2) Further investigations into the existence of additional examples of 'block mixture' in Sinaiticus. The existence of a significant block of Western text in John 1-8 makes the textual integrity of the rest of the manuscript suspect. Detailed textual analysis will determine whether other areas of block mixture exist in Sinaiticus. Studies into theological tendencies of the scribes and correctors of Sinaiticus might provide further information as to why different types of the text appear in the manuscript. Finally, studies of the phenomenon of block mixture in manuscripts in general are needed.

(3) Further study into the corrections of Sinaiticus. These corrections, made both at the time of the manuscript's production and centuries later, provide a unique window into the history of the transmission of the New Testament text. The corrections need to be analyzed using more recently developed statistical methods of textual analysis.

One final appeal – the study of Sinaiticus, or of any other biblical manuscript, should not be done in a vacuum of paleography and/or rote collation of manuscripts. Hopefully, my analysis of Athanasius' text of the Gospels, my arguments concerning his corruption of the New Testament text and the influence of the Church Fathers on scribal activity, and my preliminary observations into the relationship of a few of the Fathers' texts with the corrections of Sinaiticus have demonstrated the value of other disciplines (e.g. the social history and the polemical settings of the Early Church) for studying a manuscript and for textual criticism in general. Textual criticism needs to continue to explore new ways of integrating the methods and results of other disciplines into its own methods and results. Only in this way will we be able to construct an adequate and accurate history of the New Testament text.

John J. Brogan

1 Tischendorf's own account of his discovery of and subsequent dealings with Codex Sinaiticus can be found in *Codex Sinaiticus, The Ancient Biblical Manuscript Now in the British Museum: Tischendorf's Story and Argument Related by Himself* (London: Lutterworth Press, 1934). Abbreviated accounts can be found in H. I. Bell, *The Mount Sinai Manuscript of the Bible* (London: Trustees of the British Museum, 1934), pp. 3-11; T. C. Skeat, *The Codex Sinaiticus and the Codex Alexandrinus*, 2nd edn (Oxford: University Press, 1955; repr. 1963), pp. 5-11; A. J. Collins, 'The Codex Sinaiticus', *British Museum Quarterly*, 8 (1933/34), 91-2.

2 In addition to Tischendorf's own account (see note 1 above), a more critical evaluation of Tischendorf's activities and the events surrounding the removal of Codex Sinaiticus from St Catherine's can be found in Ihor Ševčenko, 'New Documents on Constantine Tischendorf and the *Codex Sinaiticus*', *Scriptorium*, 18 (1964), 55-80.

3 A detailed discussion of Tischendorf, Simonides, and Codex Sinaiticus is found in J. K. Elliott, *Codex Sinaiticus and the Simonides Affair*, Analeka Vlatadon, 33 (Thessalonica: Patriarchal Institute for Patristic Studies, 1982).

4 C. Tischendorf, ed., *Codex Sinaiticus Petropolitanus*, 4 vols (Leipzig: F. A. Brockhaus, 1862; repr. Hildesheim: George Olms, 1969).

5 C. Tischendorf, ed., *Novum Testamentum Sinaiticum cum epistola Barnabae et fragmentis Pastoris, etc.* (Leipzig: F. A. Brockhaus, 1863).

6 E. H. Hansell, *Novum Testamentum Graece*, vol. 3, appendix I (Oxford: Clarendon, 1864).

7 F. H. A. Scrivener, *A Full Collation of the Codex Sinaiticus*, 2nd edn (Cambridge: n.p., 1867).

8 Helen and Kirsopp Lake, *Codex Sinaiticus Petropolitanus*, 2 vols (Oxford: Clarendon Press, NT-1911; OT-1922).

9 Ezra Abbot, 'On the Comparative Antiquity of the Sinaitic and Vatican Manuscripts of the Greek Bible', *Journal of the American Oriental Society*, 10 (1872), 189ff; J. W. Burgon, 'On the Relative Antiquity of the Codex Vaticanus (B) and the Codex Sinaiticus (ℵ)', in *The Last Twelve Verses of the Gospel according to Mark* (Oxford: James Parker, 1871), pp. 291-4; H. S. Cronin, 'An Examination of Some Omissions of the Codex Sinaiticus in St. John's Gospel', *JTS*, 18 (1912), 563-71; Charles Hay, 'Peculiarities of the Codex Sinaiticus', *The Lutheran Quarterly*, (1880), 153-75; M.-J. Lagrange, 'Le Manuscrit sinaitique', *RB*, 35 (1926), 89-93.

10 F. G. Kenyon, *Our Bible and the Ancient Manuscripts* (London: n.p., 1895), pp. 121-8; 5th edn, rev. by A. W. Adams (New York: Harper & Row, 1958) pp. 119-20, 191-8; M.-J. Lagrange, *Critique textuelle II: la critique rationelle* (Paris: Gabalda, 1935), pp. 90-107; F. H. A. Scrivener, *A Plain Introduction to the Criticism of the New Testament*, 4th edn, rev. by E. Miller (London: G. Bell, 1894), pp. 90-7; B. F. Westcott and F. J. A. Hort, *The New Testament in the Original Greek: Introduction* (Cambridge/London: Macmillan, 1881; repr. Peabody, MA: Hendrickson, 1988), pp. 151, 210-30, 246-71.

11 H. J. M. Milne and T. C. Skeat, *Scribes and Correctors of the Codex Sinaiticus* (London: The British Museum, 1938).

12 Some additional insights into the physical characteristics of the manuscript, especially concerning the number of letters per column, are provided in Christian A. Tindall, *Contributions to the Statistical Study of the Codex Sinaiticus*, ed. by T. B. Smith (Edinburgh and London: Oliver and Boyd, 1961).

13 Here I limit my discussion to the New Testament portion of the codex. I acknowledge my lack of familiarity with studies on the textual character of the Old Testament portion of Sinaiticus, and its importance for Old Testament and Septuagintal textual studies.

14 Westcott and Hort, p. 151.

15 Hermann von Soden, *Die Schriften des Neuen Testaments in ihrer ältesten erreichbaren Textgestalt hergestellt auf Grund ihrer Textgeschichte*, 4 vols (Gottingen: Vandenhoeck & Ruprecht, 1911-13), and H. C. Hoskier, *Codex B and Its Allies: A Study and an Indictment*, 2 vols (London: Quaritch, 1914).

16 For example, Metzger in *The Text of the New Testament: Its Transmission, Corruption, and Restoration*, 3rd enlarged edn (New York: Oxford University Press, 1992), p. 46 describes Sinaiticus as follows: 'The type of text witnessed by Sinaiticus belongs in general to the Alexandrian group, but it also has a definite strain of the Western type of readings'.

17 Gordon D. Fee, 'Codex Sinaiticus in the Gospel of John: A Contribution to Methodology in Establishing Textual Relationships', *NTS*, 15 (1968-9), 23-44; reprinted in Eldon J. Epp and Gordon D. Fee, *Studies in the Theory and Method of New Testament Textual Criticism*, SD, 45 (Grand Rapids: Eerdmans, 1993), pp. 221-43.

18 M.-E. Boismard, 'Le Papyrus Bodmer II', *RB*, 64 (1957), 363-98.

19 Fee, 'Codex Sinaiticus', p. 243.

20 For an excellent summary of some of the developments in analyzing and classifying texts, see Bart D. Ehrman, 'Methodological Developments in the Analysis and Classification of New Testament Documentary Evidence', *Novum Testamentum*, 29 (1987), 22-45.

21 Ernest C. Colwell and Ernest W. Tune, 'The Quantitative Relationships between MS Text-Types', in *Biblical and Patristic Studies in Memory of Robert Pierce Casey*, ed. by J. N. Birdsall and R. W. Thomson (Freiburg: Herder, 1963), pp. 25-32; reprinted as 'Method in Establishing Quantitative Relationships between Text-Types of New Testament Manuscripts', in E. C. Colwell, *Studies in Methodology in Textual Criticism of the New Testament*, New Testament Textual Studies, 9 (Grand Rapids: Eerdmans, 1969), pp. 56-62. In addition, see the following articles in Colwell's *Study in Methodology*: 'The Significance of Grouping New Testament Manuscripts', pp. 1-25; 'Method in Locating a Newly-Discovered Manuscript', pp. 26-44, and 'Method in Establishing the Nature of Text-Types of New Testament Manuscripts', pp. 45-55.

22 Westcott and Hort, p. 151.

23 Here I am suggesting studies of Sinaiticus such as Eldon J. Epp performed on Codex Bezae in his groundbreaking work, *The Theological Tendency of Codex Bezae Cantabrigiensis in Acts*, Society of New Testament Studies Monograph Series, 3 (Cambridge: University Press, 1966).

24 John J. Brogan, 'The Text of the Gospels in the Writings of Athanasius' (unpublished doctoral dissertation, Duke University, 1997). This dissertation will be published as John J. Brogan, *Athanasius and the Text of the Gospels: Transmitter and Transformer of the Alexandrian Text*, Society of Biblical Literature, The New Testament in the Greek Fathers Series (Atlanta: Society of Biblical Literature, forthcoming).

25 The comprehensive profile analysis was developed by Bart D. Ehrman in *Didymus the Blind and the Text of the Gospels*, SBL NTGF, 1 (Atlanta: Scholars Press, 1986), pp. 223-53. For a description of 'Secondary' and 'Primary' Alexandrian witnesses, see Ehrman, *Didymus*, pp. 263-7.

26 Textual critics use the term 'corruption' in a variety of ways. Some use 'corruption' as a value-neutral term that describes any change in the text, no matter how that change was generated. Others use 'corruption' to describe only those changes in a text that have been deliberately made by someone who desired to alter the meaning of the text for some reason. Oftentimes, changes made in the wording of a text in order to change the text's meaning are theologically motivated. I will use the term 'corruption' to signify any change in the text, whether intentional or not.

27 For a full description of the types of changes Athanasius makes, examples of each type, and a discussion of their significance, see Brogan, 'The Text of the Gospels in the Writings of Athanasius', pp. 261-84.

28 The consensus dating of Sinaiticus is early-to-mid fourth century. See H. and K. Lake, *Codex Sinaiticus Petropolitanus*, vol. 2 (NT), pp. ix-xv; Milne and Skeat, pp. 60-5; Metzger, p. 42; and Kurt and Barbara Aland, *The Text of the New Testament: An Introduction to the Critical Editions and to the Theory and Practice of Modern Textual Criticism*, trans. by Erroll F. Rhodes (Grand Rapids: Eerdmans; Leiden: E. J. Brill, 1987), p. 106.

29 Milne and Skeat, p. 40. For additional discussion of the correctors as well as the identification of the actual correctors, see the 'Prolegomena' to Tischendorf, *Novum Testamentum Sinaiticum*, pp. xxiii-xxxvi, and the introduction to H. and K. Lake, *Codex Sinaiticus Petropolitanus*, pp. xvii-xviii and xxi-xxiv. Tischendorf's classifications are used in the collations of Hansell, *Novum Testamentum Graece*, vol. 3, and Scrivener, *A Full Collation of the Codex Sinaiticus*.

30 Milne and Skeat, pp. 40-6 (especially p. 41). See also T. C. Skeat, *The Codex Sinaiticus and the Codex Alexandrinus*, p. 17. According to Milne and Skeat, the source of some of Tischendorf's 'A' and 'B' corrections in the New Testament was the examplar itself, but they go on to state that 'there are signs of further revision, of actual collation with another textual tradition [...] whether such variants were already recorded in the exemplar or transferred from other manuscripts cannot as a rule be ascertained' (*Scribes and Correctors*, p. 45).

31 Different scholars date the 'C' correctors anywhere from the fifth to seventh centuries. See K. Lake, *The Text of the New Testament* (London: Rivington, 1928), pp. 13-14; B. Metzger, p. 46; F. G. Kenyon, *A Handbook to the Textual Criticism of the New Testament* (London: MacMillan, 1912), p. 65; and E. H. Hansell, *Novum Testamentum Graece*, vol. 3, p. xxii. Concerning the dating of the correctors, Milne and Skeat conclude: 'The A and B corrections we have shown to be contemporary with the manuscript, since they are attributable to the scribes of the text themselves. The C correctors have been assigned by some to the fifth, by others to the seventh century, and lack of comparative material enforces caution upon whosoever would decide between the two dates' (*Scribes and Correctors*, p. 65).

32 For a complete listing and comparison of the texts preserved by Athanasius and corrected in Sinaiticus, see Brogan, 'The Text of the Gospels in the Writings of Athanasius', pp. 192-3, 205, 213-14, 284-92.

33 For a discussion of the classification 'unit of significant variation', see Eldon J. Epp, 'Toward the Clarification of the Term "Textual Variant"', in *Studies in New Testament Language and Text*, ed. by J. K. Elliott (Leiden: E. J. Brill, 1976), pp. 153-73; reprinted in Eldon J. Epp and Gordon Fee, *Studies in the Theory and Method of New Testament Textual Criticism*, Studies and Documents, 45 (Grand Rapids: Eerdmans, 1993), pp. 47-61, (especially 57-61). Briefly stated, a 'significant variant' is a variant where two or more readings exist and each reading is attested by two or more witnesses. Furthermore, the alternate reading(s) must not be a nonsense reading, must not be due to obvious scribal error (e.g. errors due to haplography or dittography), and must not be an inconsequential orthographic difference (e.g. differences in spelling due to itacism).

34 A 'singular reading' is a reading in ℵ* not supported by any other textual witnesses. Corrections of singular readings occur a total of fifteen times (Matthew 1.23; 6.28(2x); 18.20; 24.1; Luke 21.8; John 1.17; 7.6; 8.12; 8.36; 14.16; 16.25; 17.4; 17.17; 18.37). I also did not include corrections of the spelling of proper names (a total of two occurrences: Matthew 24.15; 24.26).

35 Matthew 6.25; 6.26; 6.28; 13.25; 18.20; and 24.17.

36 Luke 1.27; 17.2; and 24.39. Athanasius agrees with ℵ* against ℵᶜ in Luke 17.2.

37 John 1.3; 1.13; 1.18(2x); 6.38; 6.39; 6.46; 8.59; 12.32; 14.28; 16.15; 17.5; 17.22; 18.37; and 19.39(2x). In John 1.18, Athanasius disagrees with both the readings found in ℵ* and ℵᶜ.

38 If corrections of singular readings and proper names are included (see note 34 above) and if John 1.18 is excluded (since Athanasius does not agree with either ℵ* or ℵᶜ against the

other), then Athanasius agrees with ℵ^c against ℵ* a grand total of forty out of forty-one times (97.6 per cent).

39 The textual character of Origen's text and 1241 has not been fully ascertained. Origen's text has not yet been analyzed. The Secondary Alexandrian character of 1241 has been called into question by Ehrman (*Didymus*, pp. 192-3, 205, 212, 219, 250).

40 A correction by corrector 'A' occurs in Matthew 6.28. Corrections by corrector 'B' occur in Matthew 6.25; 6.26; 13.25; 18.20 and possibly John 1.18 (Hansell designates this correction as 'B?').

41 The reconstruction and collation of Origen's text of the Fourth Gospel is found in Bart Ehrman, Gordon Fee, and Michael Holmes, *The Text of the Fourth Gospel in the Writings of Origen*, SBL, The New Testament in the Greek Fathers, 3, vol. 1 (Atlanta: Scholars Press, 1992). A reconstruction, collation, and textual analysis of Didymus' text of the four Gospels is found in Ehrman, *Didymus the Blind*.

42 Much of the following material is taken from Brogan, 'The Text of the Gospels in the Writings of Athanasius', pp. 292-8.

43 Bart D. Ehrman, *The Orthodox Corruption of Scripture: The Effect of Early Christological Controversies on the Text of the New Testament* (New York/Oxford: Oxford University Press, 1993).

44 Ehrman, *Orthodox Corruption*, pp. 29-31.

45 Ehrman, *Orthodox Corruption*, p. 275.

46 Ehrman, *Orthodox Corruption*, pp. 275-6.

47 Ehrman, *Orthodox Corruption*, p. 30.

48 Ehrman, *Orthodox Corruption*, p. 30.

49 The notion of 'interpretive communities' and their role in writing and reading texts is developed by Stanley Fish in his article, 'Interpreting the *Variorum*', in Stanley Fish, *Is There a Text in the Class? The Authority of Interpretive Communities* (Cambridge, MA: Harvard University Press, 1980), pp. 147-73 (especially 167-73). Also in the same volume, see Fish's articles, 'What Makes an Interpretation Acceptable?' pp. 338-55, and 'Demonstration vs. Persuasion: Two Models of Critical Activity', pp. 356-71. Fish's theory and its influence on biblical interpretation is discussed in Stephen D. Moore, *Literary Criticism and the Gospels: the Theoretical Challenge* (New Haven, CN: Yale University Press, 1989), pp. 108-30.

50 Ehrman states: 'The controversies transcended the rarified atmosphere of the Christian *literati*. The heresiologists who produced better known sources – for example, Justin, Irenaeus, Tertullian, Clement of Alexandria, and Origen – clearly enjoyed a rhetorical education. Even though scribes too were by and large among the literary elite [...] there is nothing to suggest that they were all, or even mostly [...] among the intelligentsia of the faith' (*Orthodox Corruption*, p. 278).

51 Athanasius is the earliest witness of particular readings in at least two places in the Gospels (Matthew 24.17 and John 8.59) and possibly in Matthew 6.26. In Matthew 24.17, Athanasius and ℵ^c (corrector 'B') are the *only* two witnesses that support that particular reading. In John 8.59, Athanasius is the oldest witness of a variant reading that is supported *exclusively* by Secondary Alexandrian witnesses.

52 See Brogan, 'Text of the Gospels in the Writings of Athanasius', pp. 261-84.

53 This view is held by Bruce Metzger, p. 46 and A. J. Collins, p. 92.

54 See C. A. Phillips, 'The Codex Sinaiticus and the Codex Alexandrinus', *Expository Times*, 51 (1939-40), 299.

55 T. C. Skeat, *The Codex Sinaiticus and the Codex Alexandrinus*, p. 18.

56 For example, the reading καὶ διελθὼν διὰ μέσου αὐτῶν ἐπορεύετο καὶ παρῆγεν οὕτως in John 8.59 is supported solely by Secondary Alexandrian witnesses and is properly designated

as a 'distinctive' Secondary Alexandrian reading. Furthermore, some of the agreements between Athanasius and the correctors of Sinaiticus represent 'exclusive' Secondary Alexandrian readings. For definitions of 'distinctive' and 'exclusive' readings, see Ehrman, *Didymus the Blind*, pp. 226-8; and Brogan, 'The Text of the Gospels in the Writings of Athanasius', pp. 227-31.

THE CODEX VATICANUS
ITS HISTORY AND SIGNIFICANCE

J. Neville Birdsall

PALAEOGRAPHICALLY, the Codex Vaticanus[1] (Fig. 7) is one of the few extensive examples of the canon of calligraphy to which Guiglielmo Cavallo[2] has given the soubriquet of 'Biblical majuscule'. The style is known from the late second century after Christ to the beginning of the ninth century, with its heyday in the third century.

By consensus, this codex is dated approximately to the early fourth century. This ascription owes more to an argument from internal consideration than to any precisely objective criterion. This argument rests upon the coincidence of the written contents of the manuscript with the list of canonically acceptable books in the thirty-ninth Festal Letter of Athanasius,[3] to be dated to AD 367. In that archiepiscopal instruction, we find for the first time evidence of canonical status given to the sacred literature of the Old and New Testaments, of the same extent as has since been generally accepted in the Church. This we find in Codex Vaticanus. It also contains the same 'deutero-canonical' books of the Old Testament that the Letter commends (since the codex has lost its last folia, we do not know if it ever contained the Didache or the 'Shepherd' which the Letter equally recommends for edification). The date of the Letter thus gives us a marker for the period within which a manuscript with such limits of content might have been produced, yet is only one point in the locus of that period, and thus at best approximate.

Internal considerations are also the basis of the assertion constantly made in catalogues and other repertoria that Vaticanus originated in Egypt. Several textual coincidences in readings otherwise unique to the Coptic versions are adduced, which together with the Egyptian canonical limits are held to point to Egypt as the place where Vaticanus must have been produced. These arguments are basically inconclusive, and have not, I believe, been checked for a long time. The orthography of the manuscript has also been interpreted as showing Coptic interference with the spelling of the Greek, but the arguments are weak for two reasons. Firstly, the incidence of the types of spelling in question is much lower than in many other majuscules. Moreover, as is well known in the debates of this linguistic area, a majority at least of the data in this category are characteristic of Hellenistic and later Greek, and are thus likely to have no relevance to the local linguistic background of the scribe, but rather to be universals of the demotic pronunciation of Greek at that date.[4]

Constantine Tischendorf believed that the codices Sinaiticus (in hand D) and Vaticanus (in hand B) had a scribe in common. This opinion never attracted much support. It was discussed finally by Milne and Skeat in their important monograph

Scribes and Correctors of the Codex Sinaiticus.[5] They concluded that between Vaticanus 'B' and Sinaiticus 'D' there is no affinity. In respect of Vaticanus 'A', however, they outlined a considerable number of points of affinity. Some are palaeographical items such as the form of colophons, the use of the 'diplé', and so forth; others are drawn from aspects of marginal annotation. Nevertheless, they did not allow themselves to argue for the identity of the scribes responsible for these features in the two manuscripts. Such a conclusion, as they say, would be 'hazardous'. The presence of a long-pronged omega in marginal corrections written by Sinaiticus 'D', but never found in the work of Vaticanus 'A', appears to be the major obstacle to identification. (We clearly encounter here the omnipresent problem in questions of scribal identity raised by the uniformity of a dominant style.)

Many difficulties are encountered in attempting to identify this codex with one sent by Athanasius to Constans, or as one which was earlier ordered with others by Constantine from Eusebius (in this case together with the Sinaiticus).[6] Such attempts as these exemplify a tendency often seen in biblical, classical and Near Eastern studies, to identify some striking artefact with one alluded to in literature.

Yet more uncertain are the guesses hazarded in attempting to define the location or locations of the manuscript before it appears in a catalogue of the Vatican library in the late fifteenth century.[7] The suggestion of a domicile in South Italy has been proposed, since many codices of the Vatican Greek collections had come from there. However, the codex had suffered neglect and a partial repair had been carried out; recent discussion has pointed out that the poverty of the South Italian monastic houses at the time of the repair makes it unlikely that such a repair, imperfect though it is, could have been done there at all. Constantinople has also been proposed, but the arguments are inconclusive.

Several of the original leaves are lost, and have been supplemented by a later fifteenth-century hand. At a like period, some decoration has also been added, such as capitals in the margins and so on. Attempts to identify the scribe have been made, but these have not stood the tests of further scrutiny by the Jesuit scholar Janko Šagi.[8] His article of 1972 was summarized and expanded by T. C. Skeat in 1984. In contradistinction to C.-M. Martini in his introductory remarks to the reduced New Testament facsimile of 1965/1986,[9] Skeat believes that the various attempts at embellishment, which now show a high degree of incompetence, are part of one attempted partial restoration. This he hypothetically associates with an otherwise unattested gift to the Pope by Greek delegates to the Council of Florence and conjectures that it was carried out in Constantinople. Earlier attempts to identify the scribe of the added leaves with Joannes Chortasmenos are rejected following Šagi, supported by Canart and the Vatican 'microfilmotek' of fifteenth-century scribal hands. This same resource leads to no further identification, although Skeat evidently felt in 1984 that there were hopes of that shortly in the future, in the wake of ongoing research. It would seem that they are for the present unfulfilled since the three volumes of *Repertorium der griechischen Kopisten 800-1600*[10] available to date contain no reference to our codex at all.

In short, we cannot be certain of the exact date nor the place of origin of Codex Vaticanus, nor, in spite of scholarly efforts, can its history before the fifteenth century be traced. Two catalogues of the Vatican Library,[11] respectively from 1475 and 1481, have survived in which there are unmistakeable references to this manuscript as a complete Bible on parchment bound in red, and, in the later list, 'in three columns'.

The Codex Vaticanus

Apart from a brief mention of the codex by one of the correspondents of Erasmus, little about the details of the manuscript was known for a long time. Some collations were made during the eighteenth century, and the Danish scholar Andreas Birch included the results of his own collations in his editions. J. L. Hug made a study of Vaticanus during the years when it lay in Paris (published 1810), but after that time the manuscript, restored to Rome, became inaccessible, or could be studied only under conditions of difficulty. An edition by Angelo Mai, Prefect of the Vatican Library, posthumously published in 1857, is notorious for its inaccuracy. Then, beginning in 1868, the Vatican authorities produced a series of editions of the text – a facsimile by typographical means in 1868-72, and a photographic reproduction in 1889-90.[12] The use made of the manuscript by late nineteenth-century scholars post-dates the facsimile of 1868. The Alands[13] state that the edition was used intensively by Westcott and Hort. A further facsimile was produced in 1904-7, which is superseded in its New Testament part by the reproduction edited in 1968 by C. M. Martini[14] (now Cardinal Archbishop of Milan).

Although in this sketch I have thus far used palaeographical and codicological material irrespective of the part of the canon of Scripture that is contained on the leaves of the manuscript, in proceeding to the second half of my remit, namely the significance of the Codex Vaticanus, I shall not attempt to deal with the Greek Old Testament. It is only in the land of Kenneth Grahame's *The Wind in the Willows* that 'clever men at Oxford', or anywhere else, 'know all that there is to be knowed'. I once sat for a memorable year at the feet of Peter Katz, and afterwards received many an offprint from him, but I have never attained to know the field of Septuagint and all that is in it 'to be knowed'. The nearest I have come to a contribution is to identify some fragmentary manuscripts and Hexaplaric marginalia preserved in Georgian. I gather from the handbooks[15] on my shelves that while Vaticanus has in some parts been a trustworthy road to knowledge of the Old Greek, in others it presents texts marked in different degrees by Hexaplaric characteristics. Clearly this raises the question whether this has come about simply by the chance availability of exemplars, or whether any critical judgement of the compilers of the pandect is reflected here. I was grateful to learn from a contribution of Professor J. W. Wevers in the discussion of my lecture that this mélange of text-types must be purely fortuitous. This raises a question in the relation of a point to be made later. Its answer will need input from both Septuagint and New Testament scholars. Behind the quality of the New Testament text in this codex, there appears to be critical 'know-how'. If this be true in the case of the New Testament text chosen to be copied for the manuscript's production, why was it lacking in the choice of exemplars which lie behind its Old Testament? Is the excellence of the New Testament part of the codex also fortuitous, rather than the sign of a continuing school?

Isolated and scarcely studied as Codex Vaticanus remained between the fifteenth century and the mid-nineteenth century, it made little impact on the theory and analysis of the data of New Testament manuscripts. Nor was it, I consider, the printing of its text or the facsimile reproduction alone that made it spring into the prominence that it has held ever since. It was the discovery of the Codex Sinaiticus in the same period that enabled scholars to perceive the distinctive form of text that these two majuscules presented distinctively and outstandingly, primarily by reason of their greater age, even amongst the other manuscripts that for Bengel and Griesbach had formed the

'Alexandrian' family. Once this text was more clearly perceived, its foil was to hand in the 'Western' text, already identified as an entity by Griesbach beneath the accidents of its transmission history.[16]

So the stage was set, once Patristic evidence began to be compared with the data of these texts, for the debate in which we are still engaged. The evidence of the Alexandrian text was intrinsically better to the critical eye, but the objective evidence of quotation was that it had appeared upon the scene later. Was it a revision or was it the survival of a good ancient text, which had been overshadowed by a text more suited to popular taste?

The work of Westcott and Hort[17] was careful and painstaking. In the form in which it lies before us, it clearly presents an argument erected after there had emerged within those scholars' discussions a conviction of the excellence of the text of B. That is to say, the argument from intrinsic probability (the concluding stage of the defence of their position) must have been the conviction from which they began the final erection of their argument. Otherwise, the logical stage of removing conflate readings, and the historical stage of dating the respective texts on the evidence of Patristic quotation would have clinched the matter, as it has done for some subsequent generations. If one has lived in a period, as my generation did, when the Hortian construct was presented as a kind of dead and scholastic theorem, one has to rediscover the force of Hort's arguments, as Hort did, by examining the evidence.

I hope that I may be indulged by my readers and allowed to present some further points autobiographically. When I studied at Cambridge, immediately after the Second World War, *The New Testament in the Original Greek* was still the recognized text for biblical examination, even though one had to have recourse to the second edition of Souter for an apparatus criticus! The atmosphere was however inclement to Hortian orthodoxy. A little instruction in text-critical theory was given by J. N. Sanders, a fine scholar who died prematurely, but not a specialist in textual criticism. In his lectures, he aroused my interest in the subject, by his recommendation of the booklet of Kirsopp Lake in its last revision by Silva New.[18] In reading that, my love affair with textual criticism began. Both in Sanders' lectures and in the last form of Lake's introduction, it was suggested that in the second and early third centuries, not only was there no Antiochian or Byzantine text, but no 'Neutral' or Alexandrian text either. The Lakes say nothing of the criteria of that creation, but Sanders, a fine Classicist before he turned to theology, believed that the 'Neutral' text of Hort was characterized by an adaptation of a rough-hewn original to classical norms. He gave no working examples, but in one's simplicity one believed him.[19]

This was underpinned by another great voice of the Cambridge past, that of F. C. Burkitt. His book, *The Gospel History and its Transmission*,[20] was standardly recommended – and I have, incidentally, no complaint or criticism to make of that, as I consider it a book still of value and grossly neglected. If one, however, followed up the textual points on which certain of its arguments rested, or investigated the regular contributions of Burkitt to every number of the *Journal of Theological Studies* from its inception to 1935, the year of his death, one's mind was led in the same direction textually as by Lake and Sanders. The earliest text, still visible on the periphery of Christendom in late minuscule families, or at an earlier date in remote versions, or the quotations of exegetes, was rather a kind of Western text than any text to which

Vaticanus might be deemed related. The Chester Beatty papyrus of the Gospels appeared to support this reconstruction, simply by its third century date, for it was with witnesses of those kinds that its text was often found to agree. It certainly appeared as if the earliest manuscripts that were coming to light were telling the same tale already told by Patristic citations in Hort's day.

It was this situation that lay behind the work of G. D. Kilpatrick.[21] The presupposition from which he starts is that the Western Text, as found in some particular manuscripts or other witnesses, is no more the original text than is that of Vaticanus. Rather, in witnesses previously termed 'Western', original readings might be found. The primary task was the discovery of criteria, amongst which was to figure Atticism as a cause of ancient revision and a reason for present-day rejection. This led Kilpatrick on to thoroughgoing eclecticism, jettisoning the notion of text-types as irrelevant to the recovery of the original text.

One of Kilpatrick's guides on this way – Father Lagrange of Jerusalem – had not arrived at like conclusions. His unfinished work on textual criticism reached only one part, published in 1935, which deals with praxis.[22] It is numbered as the second part on the title page; the first volume was in fact committed to his junior confrère Pierre Benoit from whom I learned this, gaining the impression that work on it had never progressed very far. One presumes that the upheavals of the Second World War and the foundation of the State of Israel contributed to this aborting of the work. Changes of interest after Lagrange's demise may also have played a part, together with the discoveries of the Dead Sea Scrolls, in which the École Biblique et Archéologique played a significant role.

To return to Lagrange and the work he did produce, subtitled 'La critique rationelle'. This rested on the *examinatio* of the variations which identifiable witnesses or families of witnesses presented. (I use the term of older classical textual criticism as, for example, in Maas's handbook.) The criteria were largely stylistic, and preference was given to, for example, rough readings contrasted with smooth, subtle readings contrasted with banal, and so on. The main groups of evidence (a basically Hortian framework was utilized) were assessed for nearness to the original by their presentation of these features. The upshot of the argument, to which this brief summary does scant justice, is that the text of which the Codex Vaticanus is the chief witness is judged to be nearest to the original text. It is an extension of the argument from intrinsic probability in Hort. Although Kilpatrick was evidently unconvinced by this ultimate conclusion of Lagrange, it was a book to which he sent at least one of his pupils. It made a lasting impression.

Before the publication of the Bodmer papyri XIV-XV, and following the analysis of the first Johannine papyrus from that collection (P. Bodmer II), I clearly considered that any further examination of the textual history of the Gospels would reveal a primitive text of which only developments and adaptations remained in the manuscript evidence to hand. I have discovered, in preparing this paper, the beginnings of an article with that gist, of which I had only written the introductory paragraphs. After the publication of the Luke-John papyrus, which I think must have occurred during the composition of this unpublished work, I changed my mind. In reviewing Martini's monograph,[23] I claimed that my own use of the term 'recension' hitherto had intended editorial work which was preservative, not innovative. I do not think that Martini's work in itself had convinced me of that, but the earlier research of which I will shortly remind you. That, however, did not appear in print until the Kilpatrick Festschrift of 1976.[24]

Martini's thesis of the relation of the texts of P[75] and B did something to strengthen my view, but the main impact had already come from the application of rational criticism to the differences between P[75] and P[45] in Luke, where these shared the same extent of text. I had not used, however, stylistic criteria as I had done in studying P[66],[25] but mainly had looked for changes which would evince the Atticizing corruption which Kilpatrick suspected was present in the second century. To my astonishment, I found that it was the P[75] text (that is to say, in essence the B text) which was nearer to the koiné of the day, and P[45] which showed itself inclined to edit with a view to improvement of the language, sometimes in a specifically Atticizing way.

My personal circumstances in the past two years have precluded any possibility to collate the data used from P[75] in that research with that from the parallel passages in Codex Vaticanus. The general consensus based on the analysis of Martini is that the two manuscripts stand in close relationship with one another. In genealogical metaphor, it could be put that the exemplar of Vaticanus was a 'sibling' of P[75]. In light of this, we may for the present consider that my result for P[75] will be found valid for Vaticanus. It preserves a lowly style, and shows thus the tendency to preserve rather than to polish. Martini wrote a short introduction to the reduced New Testament facsimile produced in 1965 for presentation to the Fathers of the second Vatican Council, and later available commercially.[26] In this he describes the characteristics of 'the textual type of which Codex B and the Codex Sinaiticus are the best representatives' as follows: 'brevity and conciseness, the absence of harmonizing amplifications, the preservation of popular forms, and the preoccupation with deleting all suspected interpolation'. It is a careful text: the editing lying behind it has a tradition of careful preservation of what has been received, assessed in the light of knowledge of transcriptional probabilities.

Günther Zuntz, in his monograph of 1953,[27] was able to compare Vaticanus with its papyrus predecessor, P[46]. In that investigation, he was led to posit in the case of the Paulines a careful tradition reaching back even into the first Christian century. In his posthumously published work on the Gospels,[28] he has asserted the function of a like careful philological technique and method in the restoration of a reliable Gospel text. This work would have begun in the mid-second century, and we can trace successive stages in its progress. Codex Vaticanus, 'although two hundred years later', is described as a well-known witness to the text developed by these techniques about AD 200, and Zuntz continues that 'the confidence reposed in it by Westcott and Hort, which their critics found exaggerated, is justified' by the demonstration of such earlier critical activity which discovery now enables us to make.

Hort's immediate successors and later generations may have treated the text he published as if it were in all respects without fault. I have outlined in my article in *Aufstieg und Niedergang der Römischen Welt*[29] how, in spite of that tendency, the more perceptive scholars quickly began to work at the problems which the theory and practice of Hort had left unresolved. Hort was a pioneer, and his work was that of blazing a trail as much as of bringing to a conclusion a process two centuries old. The problem of the 'Western non-interpolations' is still a debating point, and there are many similar but smaller points of almost equal importance. I think that the text of the future will follow the text of Codex Vaticanus in the characteristics named by Martini, but will have been produced by scholars not afraid to restore some of the more startling readings which lurk on the outskirts of the text preserved by the earliest Christian philology.

It has been instructive throughout my scholarly life, but particularly in the relative leisure of recent years, to view the textual criticism of the New Testament against the background of that of Homer.[30] There are of course some very marked differences which must be borne in mind. The unknown critics of the New Testament text in early days were working with material which was only a few centuries old, rather than originating almost one millennium before. The earliest of them indeed might have dealt with material less than one century old. They did not face the amazing linguistic phenomenon of the co-called 'Homeric dialect', whose history extended back into an oral period, perhaps in some matters of formulae and metre into a pre-Greek past. Over the centuries in which the Alexandrian critics were active, their methods became refined, but mistakes and ill judgements still remain and ambiguities on which the experts of today still disagree. We know the names of some of them, and the scholia often enable us to perceive their principles. Modern scholarship, while remaining critical, respects its ancient predecessors. The other factor common to the Alexandrian critics was their concern about the moral influence of the myths and other incidents in the poetry which they sought to restore and preserve. These two components stand out to the newcomer in the field as dominant still in the modern Homerists' methods, namely close attention to language and awareness of the moral judgements on which the ancient critics might draw.

We do not possess for New Testament textual study any equivalent for major components of the equipment of the Homeric textual critic. We do not know the names of the leading practitioners, and records of their judgements are most rare. We are reduced to inference from the choices we see reflected in the main groups of evidence that reveal themselves. If we examine texts such as that of Vaticanus, or its predecessors – the Bodmer papyri of the gospels, or the Chester Beatty papyrus of the Paulines – we see conservation of language often practised, although corrections based on literary standards sometimes intrude. Similarly, we may see that those whose judgements lay behind those texts were convinced that it was a sacred text with which they were dealing. This is why alterations not only specifically doctrinal, but also due to propriety, came from their hands. This they had in common with all whose hands are evident in the variants of the earliest centuries, but the biblical scholarship of Alexandria was restrained in contrast with the other perceptible strands. It seems in its practice to be the inheritor of the methods of the critics of the Museum. For all that, there does not seem to be any evidence that its practitioners were consciously aware of their debt, or it may be the case that they did not choose to make the links obvious to the communities that they were serving. There is scope here for further research and circumspect historical imagination.

I believe that the emphases of the Alexandrians and other ancient critics were sound, and should dominate the New Testament textual field still. Using their two foci, the textual critic of today and tomorrow will find that the text of Vaticanus and its allies frequently preserved the common language of the period when the Gospels were created, and did not press too far demands of propriety or sound doctrine.

J. Neville Birdsall

NOTES

1 Biblioteca Apostolica Vaticana (Città del Vaticano) Ms. graec. 1209. For bibliography, consult J. K. Elliott, *A Bibliography of New Testament Manuscripts*, 2nd edn (Cambridge: University Press, 2000), pp. 47-9 *sub siglo* '03 B', and the three bibliographies to the manuscripts of the Vatican Library published in the series Studi e Testi, 261 (1970), ed. by P. Canart and V. Peri; vols 318, 319 (1986), ed. by M. Buonocuore; and Studi e Testi, 342 (1991), ed. by M. Ceresa (in these, references are *sub siglo* Vat. gr. 1209).

2 G. Cavallo, *Richerce sulla maiuscola biblica*, Studi e testi di papirologia 2 (Florence: Le Monnier, 1967).

3 CPG 202. The Greek text is conveniently given by Theodor Zahn, *Geschichte der Neutestamentlichen Kanons: Zweiter Band* (Erlangen/Leipzig: A. Deichert, 1892), pp. 210-12; an English version is given by B. J. Kidd, *Documents Illustrative of the History of the Church*, Volume 2, *313-461 A.D.* (London/New York: SPCK/Macmillan, 1932), pp. 80-2.

4 Such a recent study of post-classical Greek as Robert Browning, *Medieval and Modern Greek*, 2nd edn (Cambridge: University Press, 1983) will give guidance to the massive bibliography of the essential linguistic background to these aspects of textual study.

5 H. J. M. Milne and T. C. Skeat, *Scribes and Correctors of the Codex Sinaiticus* (London: British Museum, 1938), pp. 89f.; cp. *The Beginnings of Christianity Part 1: The Acts of the Apostles*, ed. by F. J. Foakes Jackson and Kirsopp Lake, vol. 3, *The Text of Acts*, by James Hardy Ropes (London: 1926), pp. xliv, xlv.

6 James Hardy Ropes, *The Text of Acts*, pp. xxxiv, n. 2; xxxvl, n. 4; xxxvii, notes 1-4.

7 For the points discussed in the next two paragraphs, see T. C. Skeat, 'The Codex Vaticanus in the Fifteenth Century', *JTS*, n.s., 35 (1984), 454-65.

8 Janco Šagi, 'Problema Historiae Codicis B', *Divus Thomas: Commentarium de Philosophia et Theologia*, 85 (1972), 3-29.

9 C. M. Martini (ed.), *Novum Testamentum e codice Vaticano graeco 1209 (Codex B) tertia vice phototypice expressum in civitate Vaticana* (Vatican: Bibliotheca Vaticana, 1968). Copies were first printed in 1965 for private circulation.

10 E. Gamillscheg and D. Harlfinger, *Repertorium der griechischen Kopisten 800-1600*, Veroffentlichungen der Kommission für Byzantinistik, Oesterreichische Akademie der Wissenschaften, Band 1: *Handschriften aus Bibliotheken Grossbrittaniens* (Vienna: 1981); Band 2: *Frankreichs* (1989), Band 3: *Roms mit dem Vatikan* (1997).

11 James Hardy Ropes, *The Text of Acts*, pp. xxxi, n. 1.

12 C. R. Gregory, *Textkritik des Neuen Testamentes* (Leipzig: J. C. Hineichs, 1900-09), pp. 35-40.

13 Kurt Aland and Barbara Aland, *The Text of the New Testament* (2nd edn, trans. by Erroll Rhodes; Grand Rapids/Leiden: 1989), p. 109, *sub siglo* B 03.

14 C. M. Martini (ed.), *Novum Testamentum e codice Vaticano graeco 1209 (Codex B)*.

15 For example, Sidney Jellicoe, *The Septuagint and Modern Study* (Oxford: Clarendon Press, 1968), *passim*.

16 For a wider bibliography in this and succeeding paragraphs, may I draw attention to the survey requested from me by the editors of *Aufstieg und Niedergang der römischen Welt (Teil 2, Bd. 26.1)* (Berlin/New York: 1992), pp. 99-198, 'The Recent History of New Testament Textual Criticism (from Westcott and Hort, 1881, to the present)' (on pages 100 and 102, I have inadvertently implied that Hort was a Fellow of Trinity College only, whereas he was later for a longer period Fellow of Emmanuel College).

17 Brook Foss Westcott and Fenton John Anthony Hort (eds), *The New Testament in the Original Greek*, 2 vols (Cambridge/London: Macmillan and Company, 1881).

40

18 Kirsopp Lake, *The Text of the New Testament* (Oxford Church Text Books; London: Rivingtons, 1900), 6th edn revised by Silva New, 1928.

19 It is to be regretted that Sanders left nothing on text, having ceased to give his course on the return of Robert P. Casey to Cambridge. There is in his early work nothing referring to textual matters at all, and in his posthumously published commentary on St John's Gospel no theoretical treatment.

20 Third edn (Edinburgh: 1911). See also his *Evangelian da-Mepharreshe* (Cambridge: 1904).

21 *The Principles and Practice of New Testament Textual Criticism: Collected Essays*, BEThL, 96 (Leuven: 1990), ed. by J. K. Elliott.

22 M.-J. Lagrange, *Introduction à l'étude du Nouveau Testament. Deuxieme partie: Critique textuelle II: La critique rationnelle* (Paris: Gabalda 1935).

23 Carlo M. Martini, 'Il problema della recensionalità del codice B alla luce del papiro Bodmer XIV', *Analecta Biblica*, 26 (1966).

24 J. Neville Birdsall, 'Rational Eclecticism and the Oldest Manuscripts: A Comparative Study of the Bodmer and Chester Beatty Papyri of the Gospel of Luke', in J. K. Elliott (ed.), *Studies in New Testament Language and Text* (Leiden: 1976), pp. 39-51.

25 J. N. Birdsall, 'The Bodmer Papyrus of John', *The Tyndale New Testament Lecture for 1958* (London: Tyndale Press, 1960).

26 See note 9 above.

27 Günther Zuntz, *The Text of the Epistles* (London: British Academy, 1953).

28 Günther Zuntz, *Lukian von Antiochien und der Text der Evangelien* (Heidelberg: C. Winter, 1995), esp. pp. 33-6.

29 See note 16 above.

30 The literature is vast. Amongst others, I have found valuable and stimulating the following: Paul Mazon, *Introduction à l'Iliade* (Paris: Les Belles Lettres, 1943); Alan J. B. Wace and Frank H. Stubbings, *A Companion to Homer* (London: MacMillan, 1962); Ian Morris and Barry Powell, *A New Companion to Homer* (Leiden: Brill, 1997); *The Iliad: A Commentary*, ed. by G. S. Kirk (Cambridge: University Press, 1985-93); *A Commentary on Homer's Odyssey*, 3 vols, ed. by A. Heubeck and others (Oxford: Clarendon Press, 1988-92); P. Chantraine, *Grammaire Homérique*, 2 vols (Paris: Klincksieck, 1958-63).

CODEX BEZAE

THE MANUSCRIPT AS PAST, PRESENT AND FUTURE

David Parker

THE OPEN PAGE OF A manuscript appears essentially two-dimensional. In fact, it contains a third dimension, a perspective through time. The more interesting and complicated a textual history it represents, the more evident this third dimension will be. As Umberto Eco wrote, in a phrase which I have quoted elsewhere, 'It is impossible to write except by making a palimpsest of a rediscovered manuscript'.[1] In our own field, this re-use of the labours of a predecessor is most productively found not in the dramatic palimpsesting of a codex, but in that process of improving and annotating which is so significant a feature of certain manuscripts. By observing the annotations in the manuscript we can see its use and development, and sometimes even its influence, and by reconstructing the alterations that must have been made in earlier copies for the scribe to have written what he did, we can discern the ghostly palimpsests of lost texts. Codex Bezae is not the least suitable manuscript for such treatment, since it has had a sequence of correctors, and a complicated earlier history which, thanks to the stereophony of its twin Greek and Latin columns, we can recover with remarkable frequency. To attempt this journey through time, we will take a fairly full double page of the manuscript, although we may need to turn to others to produce a complete picture. The opening selected is fols 423b-424, containing Acts 2.42-3.4 (Fig. 8). This passage is easily legible and contains some interesting annotations.

We start in the middle of time, as it were, with the manuscript's present rather than its past or future, that is, with the scribe.[2] He wrote in Greek and Latin, a scribe trained in copying Latin, perhaps legal texts. Berytus has been suggested as a likely place in which he worked.[3] The style of writing used is known as b-d uncial for the Latin and Biblical majuscule for the Greek.[4] He used the same letter forms for Greek and Latin characters of similar appearance. Thus, the Greek upsilon is written as Latin Y; a genuine Greek upsilon would be different. As for the text which he used, I will come to that later.

The manuscript contains the four Gospels, Acts, and the end of 3 John.[5] The Greek is written on the left page, the Latin on the right. The layout is significant, for the following reasons. First, it allows us to locate the manuscript in a tradition of Graeco-Latin manuscripts.[6] Second, each column had an influence on the other, at least on the visual level and sometimes as the scribe tried to keep the two texts in tandem. This is not to adopt the outmoded view that the distinctive character of the Greek text is due to extensive 'Latinization'.[7] But it would be surprising in such a manuscript if there was *no* reciprocal influence at work.

43

After that briefest of glances at the scribe, we need to step into the future, first by noting the numbers 338 and 424 in the top right hand corner of the right hand page. This is nineteenth-century foliation inserted in Cambridge University Library. The lower figure numbers the extant pages, the higher one takes account of missing leaves. In the bottom right hand corner of the right hand page is Hh2, another nineteenth-century addition in pencil, this time of quire numeration. These numberings are evidence of the recent conservation of the manuscript. The pale oblong of parchment in the bottom right corner of the left page in the facsimile is probably a nineteenth-century repair. The leaves at that time were disjoint and the manuscript disbound, but in 1965 the pairs of leaves were re-joined, and the manuscript bound. The paler parchment visible between the leaves in modern photographs are what join the leaves together.

Elsewhere (there is no example on this page) one finds an occasional mark or phrase of eighteenth-century date. These are likely to be from the pen of Richard Bentley, who had the manuscript on loan from Cambridge University Library for a number of years. The manuscript had by then already been in Cambridge for 150 years, in fact since 1581. It was a gift from the Genevan Reformer Theodore Beza, who had himself acquired it from a monastery in Lyons, after the town's sacking in 1562.

Moving back another 200 years, we find evidence of sixteenth-century use: on line 19, there is a half bracket in the left margin and *IV Cap¯* in the right margin of the right hand page; there is also *II.III* in the top left corner of the left page and bottom right corner of the right page. This is evidence of reading and consulting the manuscript in the Renaissance and Reformation. We know that the manuscript was owned by Beza between 1562 and 1581, that he used it as an authority in his first edition of the Greek New Testament, and that in 1550 it was one of the witnesses cited in the first ever *apparatus criticus*, that of Robertus Stephanus. Perhaps the chapter numbers were inserted by one of these two scholars.

Stepping up through the centuries even more briskly, we find ourselves in ninth-century Lyons. The manuscript was probably there throughout the Middle Ages. In the ninth century, supplementary leaves (abbreviated as d^suppl) were added in order to replace several lacunae, consisting of Matthew 3.7-16 (Greek), 2.21-3.7 (Latin); John 18.14-20.13 (Greek), 18.2-20.1 (Latin); Mark 16.15-20 (Greek), 16.6-20 (Latin). We know that Lyons was the place where this was done because of the form of the question mark, and because of the use of blue ink in the replacement colophon to Mark.[8] It has for some time now been possible to associate this work with Florus, a Lyonnaise scholar of great distinction. Florus died in 860, and so this restoration may be dated rather precisely to the middle of the ninth century. Amongst other things, Florus was responsible for the preservation of a number of ancient texts and manuscripts, including without a doubt Codex Bezae. Another point of connection with Lyons is that it is possible that the Latin column of these replacement leaves was copied from a manuscript of a similar date also produced in Lyons. This one, unlike Codex Bezae, has remained in Lyons to the present day.[9] The texts are close, there are corrections in Lyons 431 which are followed in d^suppl, and one whole line of Lyons 431 is missing in d^suppl. The Greek text which was copied was of good quality.

The manuscript's future from this point lay in western and northern Europe. But provenance is no indication of origin, and there is no reason to suppose that because the manuscript was found in Lyons it must have been written there. Rather, there are a number of good palaeographical reasons against this.[10] The preceding centuries are at first glance somewhat less certain. However, a study of the successive hands reveals useful information about the kind of contexts in which the manuscript was used, although to associate these contexts with particular places must contain an element of speculation. What we do not know is the stage at which the manuscript came to Lyons. A date in the seventh century, as a result of the Arab conquests in the eastern Mediterranean, seems possible. Certainly, one may say that it was between approximately 650 and around 800. Before that, the evidence of the correctors and my theory of Berytus as its place of origin suggest, the manuscript had been moved in the middle of the sixth century. While I had suggested a local move at that time, perhaps to Sidon,[11] Birdsall has advanced the theory that the manuscript was removed from Berytus to Sicily or southern Italy in the sixth century, and from there to Lyons as a safe place in the eighth.[12] It is to the period just before 650 that we now move. A symbol indicating a beginning of a lection may be observed to the left of line 19 of the Greek page, opposite 3.1. This is written by a hand known as M[4], which added indications of the beginnings and ends of lections in Mark and Acts.[13] It may be dated to the period 550-600. Evidently, the manuscript was at that time being used for the public reading of the Scriptures. The markings are slightly later than the other lectionary annotations just above on the page opposite line 12 (2.46, but referring to 3.1). Later cropping of the margin has reduced what was originally

Αννα]γνοσμα [his usual spelling] [περ]ι του σα[ββατου τ]ω της [διακουνι[σι]μου (*scil.* διακινησιμου ('Reading for the sabbath on the making to walk'.

This hand, datable to the second half of the sixth century, provided the Ammonian Sections in the Gospels, and lectionary annotations throughout the codex. Palaeographically, it is perhaps closest to a group of manuscripts of Syrian and possibly Antiochene origin.[14] There was thus a fairly lengthy period of lectionary use of the manuscript.

From the same period come the *sortes* in Mark's Gospel, a sequence of sentences at the foot of the page, used for telling fortunes or determining one's future.[15]

The remaining annotations are all to the text.[16] There are just over 800 to Acts all told. That is a dozen to a page, a rather large number. The next most recent is in lines 10-11 and it is by Corrector F. Before this correction can be understood, it is necessary to explain one of the most significant things about Codex Bezae: its text of Acts. It is far longer than that found in other witnesses, and in addition contains many re-writings. Here, it reads (2.45-6)

ΚΑΙ ΔΙΕΜΕΡΙΖΟΝ ΑΥΤΑ ΚΑΘ ΗΜΕΡΑΝ ΠΑΣΙ ΤΟΙΣ ΑΝ ΤΙ ΧΡΕΙΑΝ ΕΙΧΕΝ ('And parted them day by day to all those who had need')[17]

Most other manuscripts read

Καὶ διεμέριζον αὐτὰ πᾶσιν καθότι ἄν τις χρείαν εἶχεν· καθ' ἡμέραν ... ('and distributed them to all, as any had need. And day by day... ')

Corrector F changes the text of D to read

και διεμεριζον αυτα καθ ημεραν πασι καθ τοισ αν τι χρειαν ειχεν καθ ημεραν ('And distributed them day by day to all those who had need. And day by day...')[18]

45

In fact it makes a fudge, a compromise between the two readings. This line thus shows a new form of the text in process of coming into being. A copy taken from this emended text would be distinctive in this error. As it happens, no manuscript is known to have this correction, either because Codex Bezae was never copied in Acts, or because no descendant of such a copy has survived, or because a copyist rejected Corrector F's version.

In line 1 there is a quite small correction, the addition of καί ('and'). This is made by the corrector who is probably the most interesting hand to have revised the Greek text, Corrector B (abbreviated as D^B). This work may be dated to before the middle of the fifth century. What is particularly interesting is that the reading which the corrector introduces is often that introduced into Codex Sinaiticus by the so-called C group of correctors (abbreviated as $\aleph^c$). So it is here. In this instance we have a grammatical point – is Luke giving a sequence of four items or two pairs of items? B was the most active corrector, making over 300 changes, half of them to the text of Acts. This is an average of two a page. I have suggested that the relationship between D^B and $\aleph^c$ may be a sign of contact between Codex Bezae and the scholarly traditions of Caesarea.

The next corrector, still working backwards in time, is found three times on the left hand page, in lines 4, 21 and 30. This is C, to be dated shortly before B. The addition of τε follows most manuscripts. The reading of D* may simply be an error. In line 24 D^C changes ενατη τη προσευχης to της προσευχης την ενατην, that is to the text of other manuscripts. Finally, in line 30 it alters ειναι to εισειεναι (sic). These corrections show a careful reader who is tidying up the text.

We move back now to A, the oldest corrector to concentrate on the Greek column. In line 29, ιδων is changed to ειδων. Again, this was a corrector who was keen on tidying up the text here and there.

There are also correctors who are hard to identify. In line 13, αν is erased (unless there is a substitution, an erasure is anonymous, though if there is a washing out of letters, this must have been done by the scribe before the ink had dried). In lines 22 and 27 there is the deletion of ιδου and αυτων. Certain habits in this can sometimes be discerned, but if two or more correctors use the same method of indicating a deletion (for example with a point or a cancelling line), it may be impossible to distinguish between them. In line 26, παρ αυτων is changed to παρα των. Finally, in line 33 ν και has been erased.

All these correctors were concerned almost exclusively with the Greek column. They show that the text of D fascinated as much in the fifth and sixth centuries as it does today. A number do not feature on this page. They are: D, who appears to have been a scholar, and who went to some pains to change the text to agree with that of good manuscripts; E, who made about forty-five changes to Acts; H, the majority of whose fifty-two changes to Acts are orthographic, but some others of which show a somewhat distinctive text; and J^1, who added some missing text on one double opening of John.

We turn now to a quite different hand, the oldest. This corrector works almost exclusively with the Latin column, and almost wholly in Matthew and the early part of Acts. Known as G, he is contemporaneous with the scribe. There are several corrections on this page: line 13, the addition of *in*; line 18, the correction of *cottie* to *cottidie*; line

23, the substitution of *u* for *o* in *baiolabatur*. G may also have been responsible for the deletions in lines 17 and 29: the way that it is done is consistent with his methods elsewhere.

These corrections are rather dull compared to G's activities elsewhere. In Matthew he was active, not just in correcting the Latin but in improving it. Matthew 17.25 is a good example, where he wrote *facit aut prae[stat]* in the margin against *ETIAM*. The fact that this corrector felt so confident led F. C. Burkitt to conclude that he was the bishop of the church for the codex was produced.[19] He makes a good case, though it cannot be proven.

We come at last to the scribe. He makes one of his own corrections at line 18: αυ is washed out under εν.

So far, this survey has dealt with the easy part, the physically visible levels of the text. A copy made from Codex Bezae would have been different between each stage of correction. These processes of correction led to endless complications and confusions in the text of the New Testament, and we may see the process in action on these open pages. However, the text as the scribe produced it was already the product of over three centuries of such processes. How do we move back to discern older levels of the text beneath what is before us? First, by examining the scribe's habits, practices and typical errors. These can be used to eliminate distinctive aspects of the manuscript, including singular or unusual readings, from further investigation. Second, with D, there are in fact *two* texts, the Greek and the Latin, and the opportunities to compare them furnish unique opportunities for recovering and examining the earlier strata of the tradition.

Various theories have been put forward to explain the relationship between the two columns. Eberhard Nestle, for example, believed that the 'Latin text d is not translated directly from its own Greek but from the Greek of the parent manuscript'.[20] He was right in recognizing that the texts represent different generations. My own method has been to look for differences between the two columns, and to find a theory that accounts for them. There are two of them on these two pages. In lines 8-9 (2.45), there are the following readings: in the Greek:

ΚΑΙ ΟΣΟΙ ΚΤΗΜΑΤΑ ΕΙΧΟΝ Η ΫΠΑΡΞΕΙΣ ΕΠΙΠΡΑΣΚΟΝ

In the Latin,

ET QUI POSSESSIONES HABEBANT ET FACULTATES DISTRAHEBANT

The reading of most other Greek manuscripts is

καὶ τὰ κτήματα καὶ τὰς ὑπάρξεις ἐπίπρασκον

The reading of the Latin column of Codex Bezae seems to show a compromise between the two.

In lines 13-14 (2.46), we find in D

ΚΙ ΚΑΤΟΙΚΟΥΣΑΝ ΕΠΙ ΤΟ ΑΥΤΟ ΚΛΩΝΤΕΣ ΤΕ ΑΡΤΟΝ
ΜΕΤΕΛΑΜΒΑΝΟΝ ΤΡΟΦΗΣ

The Latin has

ET PER DOMOS (+ IN D[G]) IDIPSUM CAPIEBANT PANES
ACCIPIENTES CIBUM

The reading of other Greek manuscripts is

κλῶντές τε κατ᾽ οἶκον ἄρτον, μετελάμβανον τροφῆς

Again, D seems to present a half-way house between the Greek texts. One is reminded of the correction by F in the previous verse, and sees that the attempt to improve the text to another standard often led to fresh corruptions and to conflations of different forms. This pattern is common in the D text of Acts. It provides strong evidence that the D text of Acts is evolving rather than the product of a single individual and occasion. The Latin column is derived from a Greek text which contains some of the distinctive features of the Greek column in particular points of variation, but not all of them – that is, it is in some ways older, lacking many of the characteristic additions and paraphrases of D. There is similar evidence elsewhere in the manuscript, particularly in Luke and Mark. I consider this finding to be an important conclusion of my study of the manuscript.

There are a number of other features which enable one to trace the earlier history of the text that are not particularly evident on this page. These include the *nomina sacra*. The examples on this page are not significant, but others make it possible to discern the hands of several scribes in the antegraphs of Codex Bezae.[21] Secondly, there is the orthography.[22] One interesting example on this page is the spelling ÏΩANHN in lines 29 and 33. This form with a single *nu* is found in Luke and Acts, while the double-*nu* form (ïωαννης) is found in Matthew and Mark; the use changes from double- to single-*nu* in John in the course of Chapter 5. In the Latin, we find *Iohannes* in Matthew, Mark and Acts, *Iohanes* in Luke, and a slightly less clear situation in John. Thirdly, there is the evidence of the sense-lines, the division of the text into lines irregular in length containing units of sense.[23] In fact, on this page they accord between the two columns, but elsewhere there are many differences in line-breaks between the two columns. This evidence has led me to the conclusion that the scribe of the manuscript ran together shorter lines from his exemplar of the Gospels, but preserved those of its text of Acts, which was probably a separate manuscript.[24] From the first two classes of evidence, I concluded that the Gospels part of the manuscript was copied from one that contained the Gospels in Greek and Latin in the order Matthew-Mark-John-Luke, and that it was the work of two scribes, who divided their work somewhere around the end of the first third of John.[25] This in turn was derived from another bilingual copy, also of the Gospels, in the order Matthew-Mark-Luke-John.[26] Behind this may lie monolingual copies, but I could not discover any evidence for earlier copyings.

Again, this evidence points to a text that evolved. This is not to deny that through this evolution there emerged a distinctive text, nor that there may have been points in this evolution that were particularly important in the attainment of this distinctive character. Holmes has shown that Codex Bezae in Matthew is definitely a recension,[27] but it is not a recension that was reached in a single stage. Moreover, behind the development may be discerned a yet older textual layer. It has long been agreed that where D agrees with the earliest Old Latin witnesses and with the Old Syriac, we have evidence of a second-century text. This is a matter which deserves continuing examination. The importance of the Latin column in understanding the development of the Old Latin versions can hardly be overstated.[28]

Starting with the composition of Codex Bezae, we have looked from that point both

Codex Bezae: The Manuscript as Past, Present and Future

forwards at the manuscript's use, and backwards through the earlier strata which may be recovered. The findings should encourage us to look forwards to new developments in our discipline, and backwards to the exploration of the most interesting of all the challenges of our discipline, the text of the early second century and before.

NOTES

1 *The Island of the Day before*, quoted by me in *The Living Text of the Gospels* (Cambridge: University Press, 1997), p. 148.

2 I am rather well aware that all the matters with which I deal briefly here are handled, often at considerable length, in my study *Codex Bezae. An Early Christian Manuscript and its Text* (Cambridge: University Press, 1992). I do not reproduce here the evidence for my statements, though I provide a reference where it draws the reader's attention to a case which I have made. Altogether, in my relationship with Codex Bezae I am beginning to feel too like David Copperfield's friend Mr Dick, who was unable to keep King Charles' head out of any conversation. So I have used this paper as the opportunity to imitate the amiable Mr Dick in another of his habits, that of flying kites. This paper is an attempt to present some of the main findings of my study of Codex Bezae from a particular perspective and according to a particular idea. For full bibliographies, the reader is referred to my book and to the Lunel conference papers.

3 *Codex Bezae*, Chapter 15. For a full survey of various theories that itself advocates Jerusalem, see J. N. Birdsall, 'The Geographical and Cultural Origin of the Codex Bezae Cantabrigiensis: a Survey of the *Status Quaestionis*, mainly from the Palaeographical Standpoint', *Studien zum Text und zur Ethik des Neuen Testaments* (F/S H. Greeven), ed. W. Schrage (Berlin, 1986), pp. 102-14. More recently, see J. N. Birdsall, 'After Three Centuries of the Study of Codex Bezae: the *Status Quaestionis*', in Parker and Amphoux, pp. xix-xxx; A. D. Callahan, 'Again: the Origin of the Codex Bezae', in Parker and Amphoux, pp. 56-64.

4 *Codex Bezae*, pp. 27-30.

5 In my opinion it originally contained Revelation and the Johannine epistles between Mark and Acts: *Codex Bezae*, pp. 8-9. A different view has been advanced by C.-B. Amphoux, 'Schéma d'Histoire du Texte grec du Nouveau Testament', *New Testament Textual Research Update*, 3/3 (1995), pp. 41-6. See my reply, 'Professor Amphoux's History of the New Testament Text: A Response', *New Testament Textual Research Update*, 4/3 (1996), pp. 41-5.

6 *Codex Bezae*, Chapter 4.

7 *Codex Bezae*, Chapter 12.

8 *Codex Bezae*, pp. 45-8, building on the work of others, including expecially E. A. Lowe ('The Codex Bezae and Lyons', *JTS* 25 (1924), 270-4, reprinted in *Palaeographical Papers 1907-1966*, ed. L. Bieler (Oxford, 1972), vol. 1, pp. 182-6), and C. Charlier ('Les Manuscrits personnels de Florus de Lyon et son activité littéraire', *Mélanges E. Podechard* (Lyons, 1948), 71-84). There is now scientific evidence to substantiate the blue ink theory: B. Guineau, L. Holtz, J. Vezin, 'Étude comparée des tracés à l'encre bleue du ms. Lyon, B.M. 484 et du fol. 384v du Codex de Bèze', in Parker and Amphoux, pp. 79-94.

9 Lyons, Bibl. Mun. 431. *Codex Bezae*, pp. 172-3.

10 E. A. Lowe, 'A Note on the Codex Bezae', *Bulletin of the Bezan Club* 4 (1927), 9-14, reprinted in *Palaeographical Papers 1907-1966*, ed. L. Bieler (Oxford, 1972), vol. 1, pp. 224-8. Yet see recently L. Holtz, 'L'écriture latine du Codex de Bèze', in Parker and Amphoux, pp. 14-55. See further J. N. Birdsall, 'The Geographical and Cultural Origin'.

11 *Codex Bezae*, p. 282.

12 'After Three Centuries', in Parker and Amphoux, pp. xxii-xxiii.

13 The original listing of correctors, each with a letter of the alphabet, was made by F. H. Scrivener in his transcription of the manuscript. It was subsequently emended by J. R. Harris, in *The Annotators of the Codex Bezae (with Some Notes on Sortes Sanctorum)* (London: C. J. Clay and Sons, 1901). I have further revised their findings.

14 *Codex Bezae*, pp. 42-4, citing G. Cavallo, *Ricerche sulla maiuscola biblica*, Studi e testi di papirologia 2 (Florence: Le Monnier, 1967).

15 There are other manuscripts with these, including a number of papyri and parchment manuscripts of John's Gospel. See especially B. M. Metzger, 'Greek manuscripts of John's Gospel with "Hermeneiai"', in *Text and Testimony. Essays on New Testament and Apocryphal Literature in Honour of A. F. J. Klijn*, ed. T. Baarda, A. Hilhorst, G. P. Luttikhuizen and K. S. van der Woude (Kampen: Kok, 1988), pp. 162-9; B. Outtier, 'Les Prosermeneiai du Codex Bezae', in Parker and Amphoux, pp. 74-8.

16 The full sequence of correctors who supplied lectionary notes of various kinds are:
   550-600   J, M^1/M^2 (probably only one hand), L
   600-650   I, M, M^4, N, O, O^2

17 The translations of D are taken from J. M. Wilson, *The Acts of the Apostles TRANSLATED from the CODEX BEZAE with an INTRODUCTION on its LUCAN ORIGIN and importance* (London, New York and Toronto, 1923). Translations by the text of most manuscripts are from the RSV.

18 *Codex Bezae*, pp. 139-49.

19 F. C. Burkitt, 'The Date of Codex Bezae', *JTS* 3 (1902), 501-13.

20 *Introduction to the Textual Criticism of the Greek New Testament* (London, Edinburgh, Oxford and New York, 1901), p. 65.

21 *Codex Bezae*, Chapter 6.

22 *Codex Bezae*, Chapter 7.

23 *Codex Bezae*, Chapter 5.

24 *Codex Bezae*, pp. 95-6.

25 *Codex Bezae*, Chapter 8.

26 The diagram on page 119 of *Codex Bezae* has the blatant error of 'Mt-Mk-Jn-Lk' for this manuscript. It should of course read 'Mt-Mk-Lk-Jn'.

27 M. W. Holmes, 'Codex Bezae as a Recension of the Gospels', in Parker and Amphoux, pp. 123-60.

28 See J.-M. Auwers, 'Le texte latin des Évangiles dans le Codex de Bèze', in Parker and Amphoux, pp. 183-216.

THE 'TEXTUAL MECHANICS' OF EARLY JEWISH LXX/OG PAPYRI AND FRAGMENTS

Robert A. Kraft

CONTEXT AND OVERVIEW

A major goal of this research is to explore more closely the preserved evidence from early Jewish biblical and related materials in Greek reflecting scribal habits and techniques in order to address questions about Greek Jewish developments, on the one hand, and the relationship between Greek Jewish 'scribal culture' and early Christian literary practices on the other.[1] My intuition is that the continuities between 'Jewish' and 'Christian' will outweigh the discontinuities in such matters, but the thrust of earlier scholarship (with some exceptions) has not tended in that direction. Thus I have attempted to select and examine closely some thirty biblical and related Greek fragmentary manuscripts, all of which are either clearly Jewish in origin or have a reasonable claim to be so, with a view to building up a more carefully controlled set of criteria for addressing ambiguities in other, even more ambiguous (with regard to origin) materials. It will be clear from this evidence that there was a variegated 'scribal culture' in pre-Christian Jewish circles (not unlike the situation in the non-Jewish Greek world!); how much of it may have carried over into 'Christian' practices, and under what conditions, remain less clear, but hopefully will receive further light from this study.

My work on this topic in many ways parallels and supplements the research of my colleague, Emanuel Tov, who focuses even more than I have attempted on the significance of various 'physical' characteristics (spacing, punctuation, etc.) for the ancient preparers and users of the texts. I also view my efforts as continuations of the suggestive but relatively little known study by the late Kurt Treu, in his essay mentioned below (which is readily available in English through the Internet home page mentioned in footnote 1). That I am often critical of the conclusions of the late Colin Roberts on these subjects does not detract from my appreciation of and respect for his pioneering efforts as one of the papyrological giants of the twentieth century, on whose shoulders we all must stand.

SETTING THE SCENE

Among the 120 or so papyri and other early fragments of Greek Jewish scriptures ('LXX/OG') and related materials dated paleographically from the fourth century and earlier, we find more than a dozen that are clearly of Jewish origin, and another dozen or so for which this identification has also been strongly suggested.[2] The vast majority of the remainder has been assumed to have been produced by Christian copyists, although the evidence is seldom unambiguously clear. This study attempts to re-examine the situation with a focus especially on details of format and presentation ('textual mechanics'), without any special attention to text-critical content.[3]

The basis for scholarly discussion of these materials in the past twenty-five years was established primarily by the publications of Treu's article and Roberts' Schweich Lectures (the latter is hereafter referred to as *MSB*). Treu attempted to view the early fragments in the larger framework of how Judaism adapted to, or perhaps reacted to the Graeco-Roman world in which it existed and often flourished. While Treu did not ignore textual matters (see footnote 2), he was much more focused on the sorts of 'physical' and immediately visible criteria that could reasonably be employed in attempting to identify 'Jewish' scriptural materials. The appendix to his 1973 article presents a challenge to previous analyses, and sets the stage for subsequent discussion.

Roberts, in his attempt to extract information from the early papyri for reconstructing the development of Christianity in Egypt, shows sympathy for some of Treu's observations while at the same time defending aspects of the 'older' approach, with its tendency to focus on early Christianity.[4] Perhaps unwittingly, in his quest to identify characteristic 'Christian' traits in the early manuscripts and fragments, Roberts actually opens some new lines of investigation applicable to the Jewish materials as well; especially suggestive are his comments about the 'documentary' tendencies exhibited in some aspects of the presentation of early Christian materials (use of spacing, punctuation, enlarged letters, etc.), and his attempt to distinguish the resultant paleographical 'style(s)' of his 'Christian' witnesses from a more 'elegant' literary approach in (some of) the clearly Jewish fragments.

THE MAIN ISSUES

The older 'criteria' to which Treu, especially, reacts, and the new issues introduced into the discussion by Roberts (with further elaboration recently by Lawrence W. Hurtado),[5] may be summarized as follows – we will want to be especially alert to such matters when we survey the data:

(1) Scroll or codex format: As a rule of thumb, and especially when other evidence is lacking, the equation of scroll with Jewish and codex with Christian has tended to prevail. Admittedly, Christians continued to use the roll format well after codices became popular, and clearly codices came to be used among Jews at some point, but there is little clarity or agreement on the history of such developments. In the survey of thirty Jewish and possibly Jewish texts that follows, all but items 17, 18, 19, 20, 22, 24 (ostrakon) and 25 are scrolls.

(2) Papyrus or parchment material: It is clear now that early Jewish scriptural copies could be inscribed on either material (see the Dead Sea Scrolls, for example), but in 1973 Treu felt the need to argue against the idea that authentic Jewish copies could be written only on animal skins. Of the unambiguously (by date) Jewish manuscripts listed below, all but items 1, 4, 11, 12 and 13 (see also 20, 24 [ostrakon], 26, 30) are on papyri.

(3) Use of *nomina sacra*: Roberts especially (developed further now by Hurtado)

has championed the view that a widely accepted 'system' of abbreviation by contraction of certain key words with 'sacral' connotations (especially 'Jesus', 'Christ', 'Lord', and 'God'; but also several others) developed early in Christian scribal circles, although the modern inventor of the term *nomina sacra* (Ludwig Traube – at a time when virtually no early Jewish evidence was available) thought that the practice must have had Jewish roots.[6] No unambiguously Jewish manuscripts with abbreviated *nomina sacra* in Greek (as opposed to Tetragrammaton representations, on which see below) have yet been agreed upon by the debating scholars, but items 19, 21, 23, 27 (and 29?) below (see also footnote 12 on POxy. 2068) would seem to offer a strong challenge to Roberts' position.

(4) Treatment of the Tetragrammaton: The presence in many of the clearly Jewish fragments of a special way of representing the four lettered divine name יהוה, in contrast to the use of the Greek substitute term 'LORD' (ΚΥΡΙΟΣ) in most LXX/OG manuscripts, has led to discussions of the origins and history of such practices, including the relationship between this phenomenon and the development of 'nomina sacra'.[7] None of the unambiguously (based on date) Jewish manuscripts described below preserves representations of the Tetragrammaton with ΚΥΡΙΟΣ, but the evidence from the first hand as well as the corrector/enhancer of item 19 deserves to be noted, along with the contracted forms found in items 21, 23, 27 and 29 (see above; note also the blank in item 22).

(5) Treatment of numbers: Roberts also argued that Christian copyists tended to use number symbols rather than spelling out the numbers in good Greek literary style. He saw this as another 'documentary' influence. (This feature, if accurate, could strengthen Hurtado's theory that the abbreviated use of IH = 'Jesus' associated with its numerical value as '18' reflects an early Christian development; see note 5 above.) The only manuscript to preserve abbreviated numbers discussed below is item 17, of ambiguous origin.

(6) Use of *scriptio continua* (continuous writing, without word or sense division) or of spacing and other visual aids for the reader: Roberts attempted to claim that influences from 'documentary' scribal practices may have led early Christian scribes and copyists to abandon the strict literary convention of writing an unbroken string of letters and introduce various sorts of sense divisions and similar indicators (using blank spaces, punctuation, enlarged letters, marginal marks, etc.); similar features also seem to be present in many of the early Jewish texts (as Roberts also noted, rather in passing).[8] Of the unambiguously Jewish manuscripts listed below, only items 3 and 5 show completely unbroken strings of writing in their very limited fragmentary remains. Thus it makes no sense to employ this feature as a sign of 'Christian' origin.

(7) Assessment of literary style: Roberts saw in most of the early Jewish materials an 'elegance' of writing style distinct from most of the early Christian examples. He noted especially the use of 'serifs' (decorative strokes) on certain letters. I have also tried to pay attention to 'shading'; that is, the relative thickness of horizontal, vertical, and oblique strokes (shading occurs when one type of stroke tends to be thinner than another). The general comments of Eric Turner on these matters in the Greco-Roman world at large deserve attention, since in what follows attempts will be made briefly to describe the various Jewish hands:

Several 'styles' of writing were simultaneously in use [in the Ptolemaic as in the Roman period]. Contemporary with each other, they cross-fertilize and hybridize easily. Study of these reciprocal influences is rewarding, provided only that the investigator is not trying to prove a derivation of one 'style' from another.

Then Turner lists some of the 'objective considerations' on which his classifications are based, such as degree of formality or informality in writing, speed and skill in execution, size, shape, and tilt of the letters, and consistency of spacing between letters and lines (ed. 1, p. 24 = ed. 2, p. 20 f.).

Turner's resulting general categories of classification for literary hands of the first four centuries are: (1) Informal round hands; (2) Formal round hands (with three subdivisions: Round/Square, Biblical Majuscule, Coptic Uncial); (3) Formal mixed hands. Most of the materials described below will fit into Turner's second category of formal round/square decorated hands. Indeed, it may help to nuance his 'round/square' style by noting the extent of formal decoration present – 'highly decorated' indicates that most non-rounded strokes terminate with full serifs (short perpendicular strokes to both sides) or half serifs (to only one side); 'moderately decorated' would include the use of hooks or blobs as well as some serifs; 'sporadically/minimally decorated' and 'undecorated' complete the scale.[9]

THE MANUSCRIPT FRAGMENTS

The following are brief descriptions of the Jewish and possibly Jewish fragments (including a few unidentified, perhaps 'parabiblical' early pieces) arranged roughly in chronological order (according to paleographical approximations).[10] Attention will be given especially to the aforementioned 'presentational' issues, as described by the respective editors and re-evaluated, when possible, by the present author from available photographs – and with the problematic issues described above also in mind.

1. 4Q122 = LXXDeut, Deuteronomy 11[#819; unknown to vh]; parchment roll, 2nd century BCE; Rockefeller Museum, Jerusalem.

From Qumran, cave 4; ed. E. Ulrich, *DJD* 9 (1992), 195 (plate 43), with paleographical comments by P. Parsons, 11-12.

Very few consecutive letters are preserved on these tiny, misshapen fragments, making precise judgements especially problematic. The manuscript seems to have contained 26-9 letters per line, but the length of each column cannot be determined.

The hand is literary, but not elegant, tending to be a thick informal upright bilinear round style, perhaps with some tendencies to ligatured and to cursive forms, which might suggest 'documentary' influence. It is moderately decorated, with small flourishes on the top and base of most verticals (and the left upper diagonal of Y) in the form of short hooks or blobs (mostly to the left). No shading of ink strokes is evident.

There is some evidence of spacing between at least three of the possible seven word breaks, but no preserved left margins and not enough words to determine the extent and nature of the use of spacing or associated devices.

No nomina sacra or other special markings are preserved.

2. PRyl. 458, Deuteronomy 23-8 [#957 = vho57 = AT28]; papyrus roll, 2nd century BCE; John Rylands University Library, Manchester, England.

Location of the find is unknown (purchased with other papyri in 1917 by Rendel Harris; cartonnage, possibly from the Fayum); ed. by C. H. Roberts, *Two Biblical Papyri* (Manchester: University Press, 1936) (with one photo) and *PRyl.* 3 (1938) (no photos); additional photos are found in E. Würthwein, *The Text of the Old Testament* (Oxford: Basil Blackwell, 1957; 2nd edn Grand Rapids: Eerdmans, 1995).

The papyrus itself is light coloured and of good quality. Originally it was about 28 cm tall with at least 30 lines per column, and columns about 10 cm wide with 27-9 letters per line (average). These fragments are written in a relatively bilinear highly decorated 'elegant' formal book hand, with no clear evidence of shading.

The use of spacing is noteworthy, with both smaller and larger spaces employed between various word groups, but no word division as such. Roberts comments: 'our text [...] shows no sign of documentary influence and we cannot ascribe to this cause the systematic use of [spacing] found here' (26), and wonders about possible influence from Hebrew or Aramaic. See now the investigations by Emanuel Tov mentioned above.

No nomina sacra occur, or other special markings.

3. 7Q1 = LXXEx, Exodus 28 [#805 = vho38 = AT18]; papyrus roll, *c.*100 BCE; Rockefeller Museum, Jerusalem.

From Qumran, cave 7; ed. by M. Baillet (with J. T. Milik and R. de Vaux), *DJD* 3 (1962), 142-3 and plate 30. Brief paleographical comments by P. Parsons in *DJD* 8 (1990), 25.

Probably 19-20 letters per line average; column height cannot be determined on the basis of the two small preserved fragments. The hand is a highly decorated formal upright with strict bilinearity in the few preserved letters – none protrude above or below the projected lines (there are no occurrences of ΦΨ); no shading is obvious.

No unusual formatting appears in the small extant fragments and there are no occurrences of nomina sacra or other special markings.

4. 4Q119 = LXXLev/a, Leviticus 26 [#801= vho49]; parchment roll, *c.*100 BCE; Rockefeller Museum, Jerusalem.

From Qumran, cave 4; ed. by E. Ulrich, *DJD* 9 (1992), 161 and plate 38; paleographical analysis by P. Parsons, 7.

Full scroll height about 20 cm, with at least 1.3 cm top margin and 1.5 cm bottom; about 28 lines per column, with an average of 47-8 letters per line (about 10 cm wide, with at least 0.8 cm between columns). There are faint traces of horizontal guidelines, with the letters dropped from the line. This produces greater linearity at the top of the roughly bilinear upright informal round (tending to oval in places) rather cramped writing. Sporadic ornamentation, with left hooks at the feet of some PΦ letters, and a downward hook sometimes on the left horizontal of T. No shading. See Turner's 'informal round' style?

A textual break marked by an inline blank of about 3-4 letter widths and a horizontal paragraphos mark below that line on the left margin indicates the start of Leviticus

26.21. Otherwise there are a few possibly intentional short spaces between some words or clauses at other points in the fragment, but no observable pattern.

No nomina sacra are preserved in the fragment, or other special markings. Iota adscript is used. An interlinear correction occurs (apparently by the original copyist), and perhaps a couple of 'strike-over' corrections as well.

5. 7Q2 = LXX EpJer, Epistle of Jeremiah (Baruch 6) [#804 = vh312 = AT144]; papyrus roll, c. 100 BCE; Rockefeller Museum, Jerusalem.

From Qumran, cave 7; ed. by M. Baillet (with J. T. Milik and R. de Vaux), *DJD* 3 (1962), 143 and plate 30.

Parts of 5 lines (21 total letters) are preserved, with probably originally 23-4 letters per line; there is no way to know the size of the column(s). The hand appears to be bilinear, formal upright round/square, relatively thick but perhaps shaded on some horizontals and obliques, with subtle ornamentation (small but full serifs, curved flourishes) on most non-rounded letters. There are no preserved examples of the letters ΚΜΡΦΨ, among others, and both a larger and a smaller form of Σ appears.

No spacing appears in the preserved material, although it is tempting to reconstruct it for one of the lacunae. There are no abbreviations, nomina sacra, or other special marks.[11]

6. PFouad 266a, Genesis 3-38 [#942 = vho56 = AT3]; papyrus roll, 1st century BCE; Egyptian Papyrological Society, Cairo.

Unknown provenance (acquired by P. Jouget in 1943); ed. by Zaki Aly and Ludwig Koenen, *Three Rolls of the Early Septuagint: Genesis and Deuteronomy* (Bonn: Habelt, 1980) (includes plates); the descriptions and notes are by Koenen.

The height of the roll is unknown, while the preserved columns are about 15 cm wide (about 38 letters per line on average), and the width of vertical margins is unknown. It is good quality papyrus, written by the same hand or in the same scribal tradition as #848 (item 8 below) in a highly decorated rigorous bilinear formal upright; horizontal strokes tend to be thicker than verticals (obliques are mostly thick).

Spacing of about half the width of a letter is occasionally found, especially before and after some proper names.

No examples of the Tetragrammaton have survived on these eight small fragments, nor any unusual markings, but ΘΕΟΣ is found (Genesis 4.6) uncontracted and unaccompanied by the Tetragrammaton, contrary to the majority of witnesses in this passage (compare #905, item 19 below). Iota adscript is frequent.

7. 4Q120 = LXXLev/b, Leviticus 2-5 [#802 = vho46 = AT22]; papyrus roll, 1st century BCE; Rockefeller Museum, Jerusalem.

From Qumran, cave 4; ed. by E. Ulrich, *DJD* 9 (1992), 168 (plates 39-41), with paleographical analysis by P. Parsons, 10.

A tall scroll, about 31 cm high (about 38 lines per column), with columns of about 10-11 cm in width (23-9 letters).

This fragment is written in a highly decorated bilinear script, with no significant shading (compare #848 and #943b, items 8 and 13 below).

Spacing is used before and after the divine name (represented by IAW) and occasionally between sense-divisions or sentences. Paragraph signs also occur at the left margin. The manuscript also uses iota adscript (usually); and contains some corrections.

8. PFouad 266b, Deuteronomy 17-33 [#848 = vh56 = AT27]; papyrus roll, 1st century
   BCE; Egyptian Papyrological Society, Cairo.
Unknown provenance (acquired by P. Jouget in 1943); ed. by Zaki Aly and Ludwig Koenen, *Three Rolls of the Early Septuagint: Genesis and Deuteronomy* (Bonn: Habelt, 1980) (includes plates); the descriptions and notes are by Koenen.

The height of the roll was about 24 cm, with 21-3 lines per column, while the preserved columns vary from about 15.5 to 16.5 cm wide (about 37 letters per line, average, but line endings are irregular and the final letters sometimes cramped), and the width of vertical margins varies from about 1.5 cm down to 0.2 cm(!), with a tendency for the lower lines gradually to 'move' their beginnings more to the left ('Mass' Law'). Similarly, there is a tendency for the top lines in a column to have more space between them than those at the bottom.

The text is written on good quality papyrus, by the same hand or in the same scribal tradition as #942 (item 6 above) in a highly decorated rigorous bilinear formal round/square upright; horizontal strokes tend to be thicker than verticals (obliques are mostly thick).

Paragraph markers are frequent at the left margin between the lines, and spacing of varying widths is found throughout to indicate various units (or sometimes with no apparent function). Spacing around proper names does not seem to be a feature of #848, unlike its sister MS #942 (item 6 above). At Deuteronomy 21.1, along with a paragraph sign, there is a large diagonal slash in the left margin. Its function (if any) is not clear. There are a few corrections, and a marginal gloss at the bottom of one column. Iota adscript is normal.

The Tetragrammaton appears frequently, in small square Aramaic/Hebrew letters (resembling ΠΙΠΙ) that are oriented to the base line (not hung from the top), preceded but not followed by a high dot with the entire ensemble occupying the space of about 5-6 letter widths of which perhaps half (distributed on each side of the Tetragrammaton) is blank. The first copyist left the dot marker and blank space, which was filled in later, presumably by another hand.

9. PFouad 266c, Deuteronomy 10-33 [#847 = vh56 = Aland 01]; papyrus roll, late 1st
   century BCE; Egyptian Papyrological Society, Cairo.
Unknown provenance (acquired by P. Jouget in 1943); ed. by Zaki Aly and Ludwig Koenen, *Three Rolls of the Early Septuagint: Genesis and Deuteronomy* (Bonn: Habelt, 1980) (includes plates); the descriptions and notes are by Koenen.

The height of the roll may have been about 24 cm (as with #848, item 8 above), with about 21 lines per column, but the width of the columns was much smaller, around 17 cm (about 24 letters per line on average, but with a great deal of variation), and the width of vertical margins may have been around 1 cm.

The text is written on good quality papyrus, and although in some ways the hand is similar to #942 and 848 (items 6 and 8 above), it is less formal in execution, while still generally bilinear and round/square (with some oval tendencies in the rounded letters); highly decorated; no obvious shading.

One paragraph stroke is preserved, and small spacing is used similarly to #848 (item 8 above) but also in connection with the start of proper names (as in #942, item 6 above), but not after such names.

There are no instances of the Tetragrammaton, but ΘΕΟΣ is uncontracted, as expected. Interlinear corrections appear. The dieresis/trema is found once on an initial vowel, but no other diacritics or explicit punctuation marks occur.

10. 4Q127 Exodus Paraphrase (?) [no Göttingen #; unknown to vh]; papyrus roll, late 1st century BCE; Rockefeller Museum, Jerusalem.
From Qumran, cave 4; ed. by E. Ulrich, *DJD* 9 (1992), 223 f. (plate 47), with paleographical analysis by P. Parsons, 12 f.

Dimensions undetermined (no complete line or vertical fragment extending through an entire column's height has been preserved). The writing is similar to #802 (see above, item 7); an informal round/square highly decorated (but no shading) literary script ('ineptly written', so Parsons). Some spacing (e.g. with proper names) and paragraph markings, plus a marginal 'coronis' (as in #848, item 8 above) and a few corrections by the original hand. No occurrences of nomina sacra or Tetragrammaton are preserved.

11. 4Q126 unidentified Greek [no Göttingen #; unknown to vh]; parchment roll, late 1st century BCE; Rockefeller Museum, Jerusalem.
From Qumran, cave 4; ed. by E. Ulrich, *DJD* 9 (1992), 219 (plate 46), with paleographical analysis by P. Parsons, 12.

The dimensions represented in these eight fragments are undetermined. The hand is similar to #802 (item 7 above) and #803 (item 12 below) – a highly decorated bilinear, but with no shading.

Some use of spacing occurs for larger as well as smaller units. Fragment 2 seems to have ΚΥΡΙΟ, preceded by a short space.

12. 4Q121 = LXXNum, Numbers 3-4 [#803 = vh051]; parchment roll, turn of the Common Era; Rockefeller Museum, Jerusalem.
From Qumran, cave 4; ed. by E. Ulrich, *DJD* 9 (1992), 188 (plates 42-3), with paleographical analysis by P. Parsons, 11.

Large format, more than 25 cm tall (34 lines per column), with columns about 10.5-11 cm wide (27-34 letters per line) and perhaps a 1.5 cm margin between. Some use of spacing. Iota adscript. Highly decorated pronouncedly bilinear round/square hand (some oval letters, which tend to lean backwards) with no shading, similar to #802 (item 7 above). No occurrence of the Tetragrammaton. A few corrections.

13. 8HevXIIgr = Naḥal Ḥever Minor Prophets [#943 = vh285]; parchment roll(s), turn of the Common Era; Rockefeller Museum, Jerusalem.
From the Cave of Horror, Naḥal Ḥever (Wadi Habra), Israel; ed. by E. Tov, *DJD* 8 (1990), with paleographical analysis by P. Parsons, 19-26.

Dimensions can vary somewhat from column to column (especially widths), but in general the material was about 35 cm tall (42 lines per column for hand A, 33 for hand

B) with column widths averaging around 9 cm (7.5-11.5 range), and about 1.7 average margins between. It is possible that the original scroll was around 10 metres long, if it was a single scroll containing all the Minor Prophets. It is also possible that two separate scrolls (hand A and hand B, thus #943a-b) are represented by the fragments. The leather inscribed by hand B is also coarser than that by hand A.

Scribe A uses spacing for sections and sub-sections (with some enlarged initial letters), but not for words as such; scribe B spaces between most words as well. Both hands are bilinear round/square in conception (but not necessarily in execution; hand A is especially inconsistent) and heavily ornamented (but not with full serifs). Hand A shows no consistent shading, while hand B does. Parsons concludes that hand B was 'a much more fluent and consistent copyist than hand A' (22). Paragraph marks also occur in hand A, and some marginal marks.

Each of the respective sections (A and B) has a different rendering of the archaic Hebrew Tetragrammaton, and probably hand A actually wrote the material in continuity with the Greek (not after the Greek was completed), from left to right. It is not clear whether hand B followed the same procedure (see Tov, *DJD* 8, p. 14).

It is possible that we have remnants of two scrolls here; in any event, two different hands worked on the materials that have survived, and the second hand presents virtual word division in those sections.

14. POxy. 3522 Job 42 [Göttingen #??; unknown to vh]; papyrus roll, 1st century CE; Ashmolean Museum, Oxford.
From Oxyrhynchos; ed. by P. Parsons, *POxy.* 50 (1983) 1 (with plate).

Dimensions may be as small as 14 cm tall (15 lines per column), or as large as 29 cm (39 lines) or even 32 cm (46 lines), depending on the identification of the poorly represented (three legible letters!) second column, with 19-22 letters per line. Informal (even careless) upright bilinear (some ovals, tending to lean left) with moderate ornamentation (mostly by hooks on some vertical strokes); no shading; some ligatures and cursive tendencies; dieresis/trema on the initial letter of ΙΩΒ.

Use of spacing followed by an exaggerated letter for sense divisions. Tetragrammaton in paleo-Hebrew, written consecutively by the original scribe from left to right.

15. POxy. 4443 Esther E + 8-9 [Göttingen #??; unknown to vh]; papyrus roll, 1st/2nd century CE; Ashmolean Museum, Oxford.
From Oxyrhynchos; ed. by K. Luchner, *POxy.* 65 (1998) 4 ff. (with plate).

About 30 cm tall, with writing block 20 cm (31 lines) by 7 cm (25 letters average) and about 2 cm between columns. Has paragraph markers with enlarged initial letters of next line projecting into the left margin, and initial letters of most other lines also enlarged. Otherwise relatively bilinear with minimal ornamentation (some hooks and flourishes), and various 'documentary' tendencies (ligatures, cursive forms, etc.).

Some spacing for word/phrase separation and at line ends before paragraph markers; dieresis/trema occurs several times, and iota adscript (not always where expected!). Otherwise no punctuation or special markings.

No occurrence of Tetragrammaton; 'nomina sacra' are uncontracted – e.g. ΘΕΟΥ, ΣΩΤΗΡΙΑΝ, ΑΝΘΡΩΠΟΙΣ in E.16 (reconstructed) and 18, 23, 24.

16. PFouad 203 prayer/amulet? [no Göttingen #; vh911]; papyrus roll, *c.* 1 0 0 CE; Egyptian Papyrological Society, Cairo.

Unknown provenance; ed. by P. Benoit, *RB*, 59 (1951), 549-65.

From the top of the middle column (of three), 19 lines (about 17-18 letters per line) are preserved, but it is not possible to determine how much has been lost below. I have not seen a photo of this material but the editor provides an extensive paleographical description and classes the hand as clearly 'literary', carefully written without any cursive forms.

Roberts *MSB* 78: 'There can be little doubt of the Jewish origin [of this manuscript], a prayer against evil spirits, written on a roll of papyrus and attributed to the late first or early second century'.[12]

17. PYale 1, Genesis 14 [#814 = vh012 = AT6]; papyrus codex, 2nd century CE; Beinecke Library, Yale University, New Haven, Connecticut, USA.

Largely bilinear upright round/square lettering with minimal decoration at the top of some diagonals (see ΑΔΚΛΥ). The writing almost fits Turner's 'Formal Round: Biblical Majuscale/Uncial' style (ed. 1, 25 f. = ed. 2, 21 f.) but is less disciplined, with horizontal strokes (especially on tau and epsilon) frequently touching the adjacent letter; no consistent shading.

The text includes mid-points after most proper or gentilic names, some breaks between verse-units, possibly some smaller breaks as well, and mid-points to offset number shorthand TIH (318).

The editor, Bradford Welles, dated PYale 1 to around the year 90 and especially because of the codex form considered it unquestionably Christian. Treu would date it at least a century later, and wonders if it might be of Jewish origin. Turner also dates it to late second or early third century [Codex 'OT 7', pp. 90, 164].

Roberts also dates this text later than 100 [see van Haelst], but considers it definitely of Christian origin not only because of its codex form but because 'the numeral 318 is written not in words but in symbols, contrary to the usual practice of Graeco-Jewish manuscripts' [*MSB* 78].

18. PBodl. 5, Psalms 48-9 [#2082 = vh151 = AT68]; papyrus codex, 2nd century CE; Bodleian Library, Oxford.

Ed. by J. W. B. Barns and G. D. Kilpatrick, *Proc. Br. Acad.*, 43 (1964), 229-32 (plate). Originally 35-40 lines per page.

The photographs are difficult to read, but the hand appears to be a 'delicate' round/square minimally decorated bilinear similar to #905 (item 19 below).

Stichometric format (with some long lines continued at the end of the next line and marked with lines accordingly). Uncontracted forms of ΘΕΟΣ and ΑΝΘΡΩΠΟΣ are restored ('conclusively', so Treu, but not so confidently Roberts *MSB* 78) in the gaps. Roberts thinks it 'definitely' Christian (as did the original editors, because of the codex format), Treu is less sure.

19. POxy. 656, Genesis 14-27 [#905(U4) = vh013 = AT8]; papyrus codex, 2nd/3rd century CE; Bodleian Library, Oxford.

Oxyrhynchos; ed. by Grenfell & Hunt, *POxy.* 4 (1904), 28 f. (plate).

Page dimensions at least 11 by 24 cm, 41-2 lines per page (Turner, *Codex*, OT 9).

Carefully written in a round/square large upright hand with minimal decoration (similar to #2082, item 18 above). Some use of spacing as well as explicit high and middle stops. No abbreviations except the stroke representing N at the end of some lines – ΘΕΟΣ and ΚΥΡΙΟΣ are uncontracted in the first hand. Some corrections have been made by a second hand, which also seems to have added the numeration at the top of each page.

Treatment of Tetragrammaton passages warrants further comment. At Genesis 15.8 (where the absence of ΚΥΡΙΕ is a variant in the manuscripts) there was a blank, four letters in width, filled in with ΚΥΡΙΕ by another hand. Presumably the manuscript being copied represented the Tetragrammaton here in non-Greek letters, and space was left to be filled in by someone expert in the desired script. In Genesis 24.40, no attempt is made to represent the Tetragrammaton, in accord with a minority textual variant.

The remaining two passages are especially interesting since they both occur at the end of lines at Genesis 24.31 (line 122) and 24.42 (line 166; see the photo), and in neither case is the full form of the word ΚΥΡΙΟΣ preserved! In the first of these passages, only the first letter K can be seen before the fragment breaks off (where space for 1-3 letters would have remained, based on the format of the surrounding lines), and in the second passage only ΚΥ appears, although there is some room for additional letters after that on the preserved blank surface (the editors complete the word by supplying ΡΙΕ in the margin of the lacuna preceding the next line, which would be highly unusual!). It seems to me more likely that only the abbreviated ΚΥ (without any mark of abbreviation) was supplied in the second instance, and possibly in the first as well!

20. POxy. 1007 = PLit.Lond. 199, Genesis 2-3 [#907 = vh005]; parchment codex, 3rd century CE; British Library, London.

From Oxyrhynchos; ed. by A. S. Hunt, *POxy.* 7 (1910) 1-3 (plate).

Relatively square page format, about 16 cm high, with two columns of about 33 lines each and 20-5 letters per line.

Basically upright 'formal mixed' bilinear lettering, with oval tendencies and minimal decoration – some loops/hooks on some vertical strokes, but no serifs as such. A blank space of about one letter width appears between chapters 2 and 3; otherwise no clear evidence of punctuation or word division.

The Tetragrammaton is represented by paleo-Hebrew double yod (two yods with a line through them both; a form found already on coins from the second century BCE), and ΘΕΟΣ is contracted, but no other nomina sacra contractions occur (e.g. ΑΝΘΡΩΠΟΣ is fully written several times). Treu, following Kahle (Cairo Geniza), considers the text to be of Jewish origin. Roberts is more cautious:

Either we have an instance of a Jewish scribe being influenced by Christian practice or we must assume that a Christian copying a Jewish manuscript preserved the Hebrew form of the Name, as a few later manuscripts, e.g. the Marchalianus [MS Q], do' (*MSB*).

Apparently Roberts does not consider the possibility that the tradition of abbreviating QEOS may itself be of Jewish origin, along with abbreviating the Tetragrammaton.

21. POxy. 1166 = PLit.Lond. 201, Genesis 16 [#944 = vh014 = AT9]; papyrus roll, 3rd
    century CE; British Library, London.
From Oxyrhynchos; ed. by A. S. Hunt, *POxy.* 9 (1912) (plate).

At least 28 lines per column, about 14-15 letters per line.

The calligraphic style in this scroll fragment differs significantly from all that we
have seen above; this is in an attractive large undecorated bilinear round/square
'biblical uncial/majuscule' with thick strokes except for the horizontals (thus 'shaded').
ΚΥΡΙΟΣ and ΘΕΟΣ (as reconstructed) are contracted, but not ΑΝΘΡΩΠΟΣ. A medial
point occurs two (or three?) times, once clearly followed by a short blank space; no
other spacing appears. A rough breathing mark also occurs.

This is an especially important text for the discussion of Jewish or Christian scribal
practice. Roberts sees the evidence as ambiguous, finally concluding: 'It is perhaps more
likely to be Christian than Jewish' (*MSB* 77; but see his earlier comments in *JTS* 50
[1949], 157). Treu is less sure.[13] If this text is Jewish in origin, it suggests that the
'biblical majuscule' style may have come into Christianity from Judaism, and that the
use of nomina sacra was no less Jewish than Christian in this early period!

22. PBerl. 17213, Genesis 19 [#995 = vh015 = AT10]; papyrus codex, early 3rd
    century; Staatlichen Museen, Berlin.
Unknown provenance ; ed. by K. Treu, *Archiv für Papyrusforschung*, 20 (1970), 46 f.
(plate).

Fragments of 8 and 9 lines from a page that originally contained 27-8 lines of about
26-7 letters each. The script is in a relatively bilinear round/square hand that tilts
slightly to the left at the top, with little obvious decoration (some feathering) or
shading, and regular ligaturing of some letters (e.g. alpha, epsilon, and tau with what
follows them).

There is a mid-stop with a space at the end of 19.17, and a space of about three letter
widths at the end of 19.18, where most texts have a form of ΚΥΡΙΟΣ. Treu comments:
'… as though the scribe omitted the word unintentionally … Or perhaps this resulted
from a vorlage that had the Hebrew divine name here?' Roberts suggests that this is
'a secular sense' of the designation 'lord' (*MSB* 77 n. 2), but it is at best ambiguous,
referring to one or two divine messengers, and the textual variants in the context show
that a Tetragrammaton type of understanding was not impossible.

23. POxy. 1075 = PLit.Lond. 203, Exodus 40 [#909 = vh044 = AT21]; papyrus roll,
    3rd century CE; British Library, London.
From Oxyrhynchos; ed. by A. S. Hunt, *POxy.* 8 (1911) (plate).

The remains of 23 lines plus a simple subscription at the end of the book of 'Exodus',
with about 19-23 letters per line. On the reverse side and in a different and slightly later
hand from the third or fourth century CE are 17 lines from near the beginning of the
Apocalypse (POxy. 1079 = vh559 = NT18).

The Exodus scroll is clearly written in a 'sloping uncial hand of medium size',
bilinear in concept but erratically executed without literary formalism; there is sporadic
ornamentation (no serifs as such) and appears to be some consciousness of word or
phrase division (a few very small spaces, and some slightly enlarged letters) in addition
to the one high-stop and space after 40.28. Dieresis/trema occurs on the first letter of

'Israel'. At the end of the text are found three pointed space fillers (> > >) after the last word (underlined, to separate it from the subscription?) and then centred (or indented) on a separated line the title EXOΔOΣ[...] with short lines above and below to set it off as well.

KYPIOY is contracted as KY with an overstroke (in slightly enlarged letters followed by a small space – it is possible that this was originally a blank space filled in later, probably by the same hand) but not 'sons of Israel'.

The reuse of this roll within a generation or so to inscribe a Christian apocalypse inclines one to believe that the Exodus text was also Christian in origin, but as Treu is quick to point out, 'Jewish manuscripts in the possession of Christians are attested' (as well as the opposite – see the reused Cairo Geniza copies of the Hexapla and of some Church Fathers). Roberts does not discuss this fragment in *MSB*.

24. Cairo Ostrakon 215, Judith 15 [#999 = vho8o]; ostrakon, latter 3rd century CE; Egyptian Papyrological Society(?), Cairo.
From the Fayum; ed. by J. Schwartz, *RB*, 53 (1946), 534-7 (plate).

This unusual fragmentary piece containing at least 19 lines (often with 50 letters or more) from Judith 15.1-7 is written in a sloping but neat semi-cursive hand with minimal ornamentation and no evidence of spacing or added marks of any sort. 'Israel', 'sons of Israel', and 'Jerusalem' are spelled out in full.

The editor discusses some pros and cons of whether to classify the fragment as Jewish or Christian, and leaves the question open. Treu (143 f. and n. 81) and Roberts (*MSB* 78) seem to agree.

25. PLit.Lond. 202 = BL Pap. 2557, Genesis 46-7 [#953 = vho30 = AT14]; papyrus codex, *c.* 300 CE; British Library, London.
Unknown provenance ; ed. by H. J. M. Milne, *Catalogue of Literary Papyri* (1927) 165 f. (no plate).

The page was originally about 14 by 17 cm, with 16-17 lines per page, written in a 'medium-sized upright laterally compressed cursive hand of a type familiar in documents of the period of Diocletian. Punctuation by a middle point and a small space in the line. The I has the diaeresis once [on the first letter of the name Joseph, but not normally]' (Milne). An apostrophe separating double consonants 'gg' and 'ng' also seems to be present (judging from the transcript). 'Father' and 'Israel' occur without contraction.

26. PVindob. 39777 = Stud.Pal. 11.114 = PWien Rainer 18, Ps 68/69, 80/81 (Symmachus) [Göttingen #?? = vh167]; parchment roll, 3rd/4th century CE; Vienna.
From the Fayum or Heracleopolites Nome; ed. by C. Wessely in *Mélanges ... Chatelain* (1910) 224-9 [identified as Aquila], with handwritten replica in *Studien zur Palaeographie und Papyruskunde ... Theologischen Inhalts* 2 (1911) [corrected identification to Symmachus].

Roberts *MSB* 77: 'The Tetragrammaton is in the archaic Hebrew characters; the writing is noticeably elegant'. In the handwritten facsimile, it appears to be moderately decorated with cursive tendencies and frequent ligatures and no pattern of spacing. ΘΕΟΥ is uncontracted.

27. PAlex. 203, Isaiah 48 [Göttingen #?? = vh300]; papyrus roll, 3rd/4th century CE; Alexandria Museum, Egypt.
Unknown provenance; ed. by A. Carlini, *Ann. Sc. Norm. Sup. Pisa*, series 3, vol. 2.2 (1972), 489-94 (plate).

The two best preserved columns (of three) differ significantly in width, with the first averaging about 11 letters, and the second about 15; the columns seem to have contained 24-5 lines (not 27 as the editor estimates).

The writing style fits Turner's 'formal mixed' classification, with a combination of petit rounded letters (except omega), some medium-sized forms (e.g. alpha, iota, rho) and otherwise bold strokes. The result is a relatively attractive upright hand with minimal decoration and a hint of shading (the photo is somewhat blurred, making subtle judgements difficult). One dieresis/trema is visible, on the first letter of the name Jacob. There is a wider space than normal between the last line of 48.11 and the first line of 48.12, and possibly a space was present in the line on which 48.16 begins. Otherwise, no spacing between letters is obvious.

The editor claims that ΚΥΡΙΟΣ is contracted at one point (48.17), although the photo is not clear, and my reconstruction suggests that it was also contracted in the two other occurrences in this material. Possibly the one reconstructed occurrence of ΘΕΟΣ was similarly shortened. Other nomina sacra – Israel and heaven – do not seem to have been contracted (although the evidence for 'Israel' seems ambiguous in both instances).

28. PHarris 31, Psalm 43 [#2108 = vh148 = AT67]; papyrus roll(?), 3rd/4th century CE; Central Library of the Selly Oak Colleges, Birmingham, England.
Unknown provenance; ed. by J. E. Powell, *Rendel Harris Papyri* 1 (1936) (plate); identified by G. D. Kilpatrick, *JTS*, 50 (1949), 176-7.

Beginning of six fragmentary lines, stichometric (longest line has 44 letters, shortest 23 – thus perhaps a page rather than a roll?). 'The writing is of the elegant character referred to above [in connection with Jewish biblical manuscripts]' (Roberts *MSB* 77) – shaded and modestly ornamented (mostly by feathering), with slightly enlarged initial letters. ΘΕΟΣ is uncontracted.

29. POxy. 1225, Leviticus 16.33 f. [#947 = vh048 = AT23]; papyrus roll, early 4th century CE; Princeton Theological Seminary, NJ.
From Oxyrhynchos; ed. by A. S. Hunt, *POxy.* 10 (1914) (plate).

Parts of only 12 lines are preserved, with about 15-20 letters per reconstructed line. The style is a heavy, slightly sloping 'formal mixed' tending towards 'biblical majuscule' (but with relatively smaller O E Σ forms). There is a hint of ornamentation by means of some subtle thickening and/or feathering at the end of some strokes, and also a hint of shading. The ink is brownish in colour rather than the more usual black.

In this short amount of text, three instances of dieresis/trema occur, and three middle stops, without any accompanying spacing (which suggests that they may have been added by a later hand). No nomina sacra are visible, although the editor has supplied

– perhaps unnecessarily – the contracted form of 'Israel' in one reconstruction, preceded by the full form of ΥΙΩ[N] (with dieresis/trema on the iota).

30. PLit.Lond. 211, Daniel 1.17 f. (Theodotion) [#925 = vh319]; vellum roll, early 4th century CE; British Library, London.

Upper Egypt, from the cover of a Sahidic codex; ed. by H. I. Bell in Budge, *Coptic Biblical Texts* (1912), xiv (no plate).

Parts of 8 lines are preserved. Since I have not seen a reproduction of this piece, here are Roberts' comments: 'A fragment of a parchment roll of Daniel in the version of Theodotion, written in the first half of the fourth century; ΘΕΟΣ is uncontracted. This too exemplifies the light and elegant script found in other Jewish texts' (*MSB* 77).

SUMMARY AND CONCLUSIONS

'**Style**': A central point in the overall discussion is the assessment of relevant Greek transcriptional styles. Colin Roberts has moved farther than most in this area, in which he was very experienced – although sometimes his desire to illuminate early Christian 'orthodox' development seems to me to problematize aspects of his presentation.

Roberts sees most of the clearly 'Jewish' LXX/OG texts as more professionally written – more 'literary' and 'elegant' in appearance than most of the earliest 'Christian' texts – although exactly what features indicate the degree of 'literaryness' for him would be useful to know with more precision (e.g. 'bilinearity' or consistent height of letters, use of 'serifs' and other embellishments on non-rounded basic strokes, thickness of strokes, shading, etc.). For him this observation goes hand in hand with his explanation of certain 'documentary' (in contrast to 'literary') tendencies in the early Christian materials (e.g. the use of spacing/punctuation, diacritics, abbreviated numbers and special contractions, less formal script, cursive tendencies, ligatures).[14]

The range of hands and styles even within the Judean Desert fragments, which were produced within a fairly limited period of time, is noteworthy, and is also reflected in the Egyptian materials contemporary with the Judean. A detailed comparative analysis of the relevant features remains to be made, but I doubt that it will result in identifying 'schools' or traditions of scribal culture except in very broad terms. Of course, comparison with what was happening at the same time in the larger Graeco-Roman world will also be very relevant.[15] If, in general, the Roman period (moving into the 'Common Era') witnessed a tendency for literature to be copied less elegantly than it had been before, the presence of such a 'decline' in Jewish texts, and its reflection in Christian materials would seem less significant than otherwise.

Nevertheless, progress has been made in this survey simply by recognizing the extent of the problem and sampling some of the possibilities. A next step in assessing these phenomena more carefully would require availability of excellent reproductions of the extant fragments in a framework that facilitates close comparison and contrast (e.g. by computerized paleographic analysis). Hopefully, the Internet can be used to provide such resources in the near future, if permission from the current 'owners' of the materials can be obtained to display high quality digitized images.

Scroll/Codex: Of course, the main vehicle for Greek literary production at the start of the period we are examining was the roll, and a major point of discussion is the introduction of the codex format and its very rapid acceptance in emerging (Egyptian) Christianity – where the roll also survives, but not in such relative abundance.[16] How soon and under what conditions Jewish authors and copyists accepted the codex format is not clear. But as Treu pointed out forcefully, the mere fact that a fragment of LXX/OG is in codex format does not necessarily mean that it must be of Christian origin. Whether there will ever be sufficient evidence to support my suspicion that the codex form came into early Christianity from Judaism remains to be seen – probably not in my lifetime. But it is almost certain that at least one Jewish codex can be identified in the raw data of this report (as even Roberts gradually came to admit) – POxy. 656, from the late second or early third century CE (item 19; see also 20 and 22).

Spacing: Whether roll or codex, comprehending the texts required some mental gymnastics on the part of the reader, especially when little or no visual assistance was available to identify larger or smaller sense units or ideally, words. In general, traditional literary Greek texts are in *scriptio continua* – an uninterrupted flow of letters – with occasional breaks or indicators for larger units. As Roberts correctly points out, in many – perhaps most – of the early Christian texts with which he deals (not only LXX/OG texts), there are various helps for indicating sense units, whether spaces or lines in the left margin (paragraphoi) or punctuation marks, or exaggerated initial letters or letters that protrude into the left margin. Roberts explains this as part of what he calls the 'documentary' influence on early Christian scribal practice.

What Roberts notes (e.g. in editing item 2) but fails to pursue with the same vigour or consistency is that despite their relatively more 'literary' flavour the clearly Jewish fragments almost all show evidence of the same sort of 'aids to the reader' phenomenon. Indeed, the second hand (or, if I am right, second scroll) of the Nahal Hever Greek Minor Prophets materials [#943b, item 13b above] uniquely engages in actual word division of an obvious sort. To me, this kind of evidence deserves much closer exploration than it has received thus far, and Emanuel Tov is making a major contribution to this discussion by his careful analysis of such phenomena in the Judean Desert materials and in other biblical texts (see footnote 8). Spacing occurs in the Jewish materials whether 'elegant' or not, early or late. It also occurs quite early in materials of clearly Christian origin. To view this as coincidental seems highly unlikely, given the fact that early Christianity developed out of Judaism! This not so unambiguously 'documentary' practice – which has not yet received the attention it deserves in the study of Graeco-Roman literature in general[17] – almost certainly has been inherited by Christian scribes, if not from their Jewish examples (which seems to me most likely), then from the scribal culture of the Graeco-Roman world at large.

Special Words: Some of the spacing issues in these early Jewish and Christian texts are associated with the appearance of personal or ethnic names and certain special words that, for present purposes, fall into three categories: (1) the Tetragrammaton, (2) *nomina sacra*, and (3) number symbolism.

Jewish scribes were self-conscious about the representation of the Tetragrammaton – the special revered four-letter name of the Jewish God – and had available a variety of devices, from paleo-Hebrew, to square Hebrew (thus Greek ΠΙΠΙ), to abbreviated Hebrew (ZZ), to the semi-transliteration (also an abbreviation?) ΙΑΩ and the use of substitutes such as אדוני (ADONAI) and ΚΥΡΙΟΣ ('Lord'), or even to using dots and blank spacing. If convincing evidence has not yet emerged that they also used a Greek abbreviated formation such as ΚΣ (see items 19, 21, 23, 27 above), that surprises me less than the claim that such abbreviation must have been a Christian invention.

Roberts certainly wants to see it otherwise, and traces the practice that became so prevalent, if not pervasive, in Christian manuscripts of abbreviating a select group of *nomina sacra* terms to the initial and original Christian sacralizing of 'the Name' Jesus, which then led to similar treatment for 'Lord', and for 'God', and for the other *nomina sacra*. Hurtado introduces some considerations (see footnote 5) to strengthen this argument. Nevertheless, I remain sceptical. Though it remains ambiguous, some of the evidence presented above suggests that Jewish scribes sometimes may have used contractions of ΘΕΟΣ, and perhaps a few other frequently used words, in the development of their scribal traditions (see items 20, 21[?], 27, and n. 11 above).

One other 'special words' detail that comes up in the discussion is treatment of numbers. Roberts argues that good literary Greek texts invariably (or perhaps, normally) spell out numbers rather than using symbols, while Christian texts – again following 'documentary' influences – usually employ the symbols. In our early texts, examples are few, and I have not systematically explored all of the early fragments of Greek Jewish scriptures for this feature. If PYale 1 (item 17), a codex fragment of Genesis that should probably be dated no earlier than the second century CE, is of Jewish origin, Roberts' hypothesis would be in trouble since number symbols are found in that material. But the combination of codex and symbolized number in PYale 1 unites to make it difficult for Roberts even to consider the possibility that the text is of Jewish origin. Treu is not so troubled, and leaves open the possibility. Obviously I agree that this should be an open question.

CONCLUDING REMARKS

This just scrapes the surface of the variety of information and of issues that can emerge from close study of these early LXX/OG materials. Roberts recreates a developmental historical hypothesis about early Christianity in Egypt from the details as he interprets them, and in general, the hypothesis makes a great deal of sense. But he does not consistently engage the question of what we can learn about Greek speaking/writing/reading Judaism in Palestine and Egypt from the same materials, and in that regard, often fails to be convincing about details.

The evidence is clear that prior to the emergence of Christianity, Greek speaking/writing Jews had access to a range of scriptural (and other) works copied in a highly 'professional' manner. That these manuscripts were produced by specifically Jewish copyists cannot be assumed, although in some instances, the treatment of the Tetragrammaton and the apparently self-conscious attention to indicating significant sense units by means of spacing suggests that the task must have been entrusted to persons who were familiar with those sorts of special literary traditions. The differences in overall 'style' between some of the early Jewish manuscripts suggests that our preserved witnesses represent varieties of technique that had developed in Jewish literary circles. Whether on the basis of this evidence one can mount economic arguments (these Jews were rich enough to afford such quality), or liturgical ones (the spacing techniques were developed to assist in oral reading in the synagogues), or even issues of cultural-educational status (these Jews knew what was appropriate to their social station) I will leave to others. The data suggests variety, and that is what we should have expected. And as new situations developed in the transition to Roman rule and influence, we should expect changes to evidence themselves, not only in our Jewish to Christian trajectories, but in the surrounding world as well.

Early Christianity was formed in large measure in close relationship (positive and negative) to the types of Judaism present in the Graeco-Roman world in the first century of the Common Era. The 'scriptural' preoccupations of many early Christian representatives surely were influenced by the established Jewish frameworks of the time. Thus in the end – if one can responsibly speak of such an end – I would expect to find that the debt of early Christianity to its Jewish heritage is even greater in these areas of 'textual mechanics' and transmitted scribal craft than our scholarly traditions and approaches have permitted us to recognize.

ABBREVIATIONS

The main sources cited below are abbreviated as follows:

Aland = Kurt Aland (ed.), *Repertorium der griechischen christlichen Papyri I: Biblische Papyri ...* (Berlin/New York: De Gruyter, 1976).

Roberts (*MSB*) = Colin H. Roberts, Manuscript, *Society and Belief in Early Christian Egypt*, The Schweich Lectures of the British Academy, 1977 (Oxford: University Press, 1979).

Tov = The article by Emanuel Tov in this volume; otherwise also 'Scribal Practices and Physical Aspects of the Dead Sea Scrolls' in *The Bible as Book: the Manuscript Tradition*, ed. by John Sharpe III and Kimberly Van Kampen (London: British Library, 1998), 9-33; *The Text-Critical Use of the Septuagint in Biblical Research*, 2nd edn (Jerusalem: Simor, 1997); and numerous other pertinent publications on scribal practices.

Treu = Kurt Treu, 'The Significance of Greek for Jews in the Roman Empire', with an excursus on Jewish scriptural manuscripts/fragments, originally published as 'Die Bedeutung des Griechischen für die Juden im römischen Reich', *Kairos* nf 15, Hft. 1/2 (1973), 123-44; trans. by William Adler with Robert Kraft (1991) for Internet access as noted above.

Turner = E. G. Turner, *Greek Manuscripts of the Ancient World* (Princeton, NJ: University Press, 1971); 2nd edn revised and enlarged, ed. by P. J. Parsons, Bulletin Supplement 46 (London: Institute of Classical Studies, 1987).

Turner (*Codex*) = E. G. Turner, *The Typology of the Early Codex* (Philadelphia: University of Pennsylvania Press, 1977).

vh### = Joseph van Haelst, *Catalogue des Papyrus Littéraires Juifs et Chrétiens* (Paris: Sorbonne, 1976).

The standard papyrological designations have been used, as listed also in vh, Aland, and elsewhere.

NOTES

1 This study is very much 'in process', and to view the larger picture (including images of manuscripts), as well as to see periodic supplements and updates, the reader is referred to the author's World Wide Web Internet LXX/OG (CATSS) homepage: http://ccat.sas.upenn.edu/rs/rak/papyri.html

2 I have not included several manuscripts listed by Treu as ambiguous but worth consideration when his reasons appear to be less 'mechanical' than seem appropriate for this study. For example, he points out (142 f.) that since we have evidence for Jewish presence at such sites

as Oxyrhynchos and Antinoopolis, it is not unreasonable to suppose that some of the Jewish Greek scriptural materials from those sites might be of Jewish origin, and he offers some text-critical observations in support (e.g. closer affinities to the surviving Hebrew text, 'eccentric text'). From this textual basis, he expands his horizons further; see his notes on PAntin. 8, 9, 10 [vh254, 252, 316]; PGiss. 13... [vh58]; PSorbonne 2250 [vh308]; PBerl. 17035 [vh022]; Freer Minor Prophets [vh284]; Berlin Genesis [#911 = vh004]; Chester Beatty (etc.) Ezekiel-Daniel-Esther [#967 = vh315]; PRanier 4.5 [#2086 = vh105]. Probably POxy. 2745, a Hebrew onomasticon roll [vh1158] mentioned by Treu (144), should be added to my list; see also n. 12 below on liturgical materials (e.g. POxy. 2068). A fresh look at the evidence from the early papyri (third century CE) of Philo's works will also be in order at some point.

3 The text-critical situation seems analogous to what the New Testament papyri have shown – that the textual relationships prior to the imagined watershed of recensional activity in the third and early fourth centuries CE are in many ways just as confused and confusing as afterwards. Of course, the materials from this early period, on rolls and early mini-codices, must be examined book by book (and sometimes even in smaller units within 'books') rather than in generalized 'text types', but even then clear patterns seldom emerge. Did we really expect clear patterns, given what we have learned from the Judean Desert discoveries as well as from other avenues of information about those textually tumultuous early times? For details, consult Emanuel Tov's *Text-Critical Use of the Septuagint*.

4 This was not a new interest for Roberts, as his pioneering early article on 'The Christian Book and the Greek Papyri' (*JTS*, 50 [1949], 155-68) amply attests. It rewards re-reading even now.

5 'The Origin of the *Nomina Sacra*: A Proposal', *JBL*, 117 (1998), 655-73. Hurtado's primary contribution to the ongoing discussion relates to the graphic marker (overline stroke) used to indicate the significance of IH as both a suspension of the *nomen sacrum* IHΣΟΥΣ (the name Jesus) and as the shorthand way of writing the number 18, which number in Hebrew gematria equivalences also is the word for 'life' (חי). Perhaps not to be lost in this discussion is the fact that the Hebrew letter-number for 18 is חי, which in most early orthographies would resemble closely the anticipated (if the numbering system were consistent) Hebrew number 15 יה, but in the development of Jewish tradition this numerical representation is not used, but we find instead טו (nine plus six = 15; also טז or nine plus seven = 16), presumably as protection against careless representation that might be associated with the Tetragrammaton and/or its abbreviated forms, but perhaps also to avoid ambiguity. It would be useful to know when, and under what conditions, such a supposed modification in the Hebrew numbering conventions arose.

6 L. Traube, *Nomina Sacra: Versuch einer Geschichte der christlichen Kürzung* (Munich: Beck, 1907), 26. See also A. H. R. E. Paap, *Nomina Sacra in the Greek Papyri of the First Five Centuries* (Leiden: Brill, 1959), 119 ff., for a similar view of origins (but different details of development).

7 Hurtado's article provides an excellent discussion of these related issues, as well as an extensive (if not exhaustive) bibliography.

8 Roberts, *MSB*, 18 and n. 3: 'Documentary practice may not have been the only influence on Christian scribes. In the manuscript of the Minor Prophets found in a cave near Engedi in Judaea [subsequently identified as Naḥal Ḥever] and dated between 50 BC and AD 50, an enlarged letter, preceded by a small blank space, marks the beginning of a new phrase, while verses are marked off by larger spaces. This may well have been standard Hebrew usage in texts such as this, clearly intended for liturgical reading.' The footnote refers to articles by E. J. Revell in *BJRL*, 54 (1971), 214 ff. and *StudPap*, 15 (1976), 131 ff., comparing this situation with Hebrew Masoretic tradition. Roberts then concludes, 'this might indicate that the method of paragraphing by the initial letter was of Jewish origin'. Study of such phenomena in early Jewish and Christian biblical texts is now underway by Emanuel Tov and

will make it quite clear that this was no uniquely 'Christian' development (in addition to the publications listed above, I have been privileged to see a draft form of his forthcoming 'Scribal Features of Early Witnesses to Greek Scripture' [tentative title]).

9 With such paleographical backgrounding in view, here is my summary checklist of the phenomena that ideally would deserve attention in a complete examination and description of the materials listed below (but for present purposes, a summary treatment will suffice). Note that Aland also tries to follow such a checklist in his descriptions (p. 6):

manuscript identification
    contents (author, work, etc.) and relevant modern editions
    current location, identification number(s), ownership history, etc.
    place and circumstances of discovery
    place of origin, probable date

overall form and format description
    type of material for writing surface (papyrus, leather, etc.)
    type and colour of ink(s)
    mega-format (roll, codex, amulet, etc.)
    specifics of what is preserved (size, letters, etc.)
    mega-dimensions (writing surface, written blocks)

marginal markings (outside the writing blocks)
    column/page numbers
    corona
    paragraph marks
    indicators of special (e.g. quoted) material
    correction marks and marginal corrections
    other

overall style of writing (within the writing blocks)
    relative bilinearity (consistent letter heights)
    letter widths and proportions (square, rectangular, oval)
    letter slant (e.g. upright, slanting right/left at top)
    letter formation (strokes per letter, speed, ligatures, etc.)
    letter shading (thick/thin strokes)
    decoration
        serifs (i.e. horizontal strokes, esp. along the bilinear planes)
        finials, hooks and/or loops (other, less angular flourishes)

use of internal spacing (absence of ink)
    blank lines or unusual vertical spacing
    indentations
    end of line space
    more than one letter width in line
    one letter width in line (or less)
    other (e.g. writing in shapes, like a triangle)

explicit in-line markings (presence of ink)
    enlarged letters
    reduced size letters
    unusual letters (e.g. Tetragrammaton)
    punctuation
    trema/dieresis [diaeresis] ('organic' and 'inorganic')
    apostrophes (e.g. to separate identical consonants)
    breathings
    accents
    contractions and/or suspensions (e.g. *nomina sacra*)

marking number symbols (e.g. between dots, overlined)
other special symbols (e.g. 'year', monetary denominations)
correction marks and correction locations
other (e.g. marked Tetragrammaton space)

10 Items are presented with the Göttingen Septuagint Institute (or 'Rahlfs') number in brackets, where available, followed by the van Haelst number (vh###) and Aland's [AT##]. Other attempts to identify and discuss aspects of the early Jewish biblical papyri are noted by Hurtado (his n. 6), and by Tov in his forthcoming study (above, n. 8).

11 Qumran cave 7 has produced several other small Greek fragments that have not yet been identified convincingly. In general, many of them seem to be bilinear and decorated with serifs and/or hooks. Spacing may be present on 7Q5 and 7Q15, and 7Q16 may have a paragraph mark (see also 7Q7?). Since they are probably of Jewish provenance, they are also of possible relevance as attesting Jewish literary activity and scribal practices. In his forthcoming article (above, n. 8), Tov notes the following suggested identifications with LXX/OG locations, any of which if verifiable would qualify the respective fragment(s) for inclusion in the present list:

7Q4 Numbers 14.23-4
7Q5 Exodus 36.10-11; Numbers 22.38
7Q6.1 Psalm 34.28; Proverbs 7.12-13
7Q6.2 Isaiah 18.2
7Q8 Zechariah 8.8; Isaiah 1.29-30; Psalm 18.14-15; Daniel 2.43; Qohelet 6.3

12 Roberts continues, *MSB*, 78: 'Both PLond. Christ. 5 (=vh921), a leaf from a liturgical book of the third century [vh reports 4th-5th century CE!], and POxy. 2068 (=vh966), some fragments of a papyrus roll of the fourth century, have been thought to be Jewish [e.g. by G. D. Kilpatrick]; but in the latter the contraction of ΘΕΟΣ, the eccentric *nomen sacrum* ΒΣ = ΒΑΣΙΛΕΥΣ, and the apparent echoes of Revelation 15.3 and 1 Timothy 1.17 in l. 7 render the suggestion doubtful. To these should be added the Vienna text of The Penitence of Jannes and Jambres: it was written on the recto of a roll and *nomina sacra* are left uncontracted [p. 61 f. n. 5 calls this PVindob.Gr. 29456 (=vh1068); p. 63 n. 3 refers to the forthcoming edition of Jannes/Jambres material by A. Pietersma and also to the republication of the Vienna fragment by P. Maraval in *ZPE*, 25 (1977), pp. 199 ff.].'

13 The fragment contains a variant that might also be relevant to this discussion: in Genesis 16.11 which parallels the familiar wording of Matthew 1.21 'she shall bear a son', #944 has παιδιον in agreement with some manuscripts of Philo, while all other known witnesses to the Genesis and the Matthew passages have υιον. Was this an old Jewish reading that survived in our fragment (and in Philo) despite the temptation that Christian scribes might have had to harmonize the text with Matthew? Or is it evidence for Christian revisionary activity to make the Genesis text (on the birth of Ishmael) more different from the Matthew wording (Ishmael is a 'servant/son', while Jesus is simply 'son')?

14 Roberts, *MSB*, 76: 'There seems to have been a distinctive style of writing used for Jewish copies of the scriptures in Greek from the second century B.C. onwards and still used, with modifications of course, down to the third century A.D. The style of these Jewish manuscripts needs closer examination and definition than they have as yet been given, especially in the use of serifs (for these see *GMAW*, p. 25); a parallel would be the development of the so-called Biblical Uncial or Biblical Majuscule [...] But not all Greek manuscripts known to be Jewish are written in this style, witness the roll of the Minor Prophets from Engedi [actually, Nahal Hever], and parallels to it can be found among the secular literary papyri.' See also P. Parsons, *DJD* 8 (1990), 23 f., on the Minor Prophets scroll (item 13 above): 'the use of enlarged initials at line-beginning (hands A and B) and phrase-beginning (hand A) and (set out in the margin) to mark a new section (hand A) gives this manuscript a documentary look [...] The fact is itself remarkable. Early Christian books show the same characteristic; copies of the Greek classics

do not. It has therefore been tempting to argue that the texts of the Early Church stood closer to the world of business than to that of literature, and to draw conclusions about the social milieu in which the texts circulated or the esteem in which they were held. Now we see the same thing in a Jewish manuscript of pre-Christian date. This may suggest that the Christians inherited the practice, rather than inventing it; the problem remains, why Greek-speaking Jews should have adopted it in the first place' (23 f.). Parsons adds, in his comparisons of the various Dead Sea Scroll Greek scripts: 'This makes it clear that serifed hands are common enough (but not universal) in Judaean material assignable to the period i B.C.-i A.D.' (25).

15 Note, for example, Turner's strictures on giving too much weight to the use and forms of 'serifs' in classifying styles of Greek hands (ed. 1, 25 = ed. 2, 21)!

16 The previous state of this question has been defined by the study produced jointly by Roberts and T. C. Skeat, *The Birth of the Codex* (London: British Academy, 1983; also released with a 1987 date).

17 A small (yet large!) step in this direction is taken by William A. Johnson in his Yale dissertation on 'The Literary Papyrus Roll: Formats and Conventions – An Analysis of the Evidence from Oxyrhynchus' (1992); witness his long list of corrections to the editions of these literary papyri (22-70), where he regularly notes the omission in the editions of signs of paragraphing, punctuation, and occasionally spacing. See also his brief note on 'The Function of the Paragraphus in Greek Literary Prose Texts', in *ZPE*, 100 (1994), 65-8.

QUANTITATIVE METHODS FOR EXPLORING THE RELATIONSHIP BETWEEN BOOKS OF THE SEPTUAGINT

Karen H. Jobes

ONE OF THE MYSTERIES of the history of the ancient Greek Bible is the survival of two different textual traditions for several books of the Septuagint corpus. There are at least two different Greek versions of the books of Judges, Esther, Daniel, Susanna, Tobit, and Judith. The immediate question that comes to mind is why are double versions of these books extant, and of only these books? Is it an accident of history that a second Greek version of these particular books happened to survive? Or is it the case that a second Greek version existed only for these several books, and if that is so, then why for these books only?

The most fundamental question concerns the relationship between the double textual traditions. Is one a recension of the other, is each a translation independently produced from a Hebrew *Vorlage*, or is one or both of the texts neither a translation nor a recension, but instead a midrashic rewrite of the biblical story? If each is an independent translation, then the question arises whether both translate the same Hebrew *Vorlage*, and if not, what is the relationship between the Hebrew *Vorlagen* represented by each of the two Greek versions.

Eberhard Nestle, whose work is commemorated in this volume, examined the relationship of the two Greek textual traditions of the book of Tobit. Codex Sinaiticus contains one of the versions, the other is found in Codex Vaticanus.[1] Nestle documented that the Sinaiticus text of Tobit more closely represents its original Semitic *Vorlage*, which he presumed to be the Masoretic Text (MT). Each of the two Greek versions for the several biblical books can be examined to determine which more closely or literally represents the extant MT. However, that determination alone does not answer questions about whether the more literal translation is the original translation or a later recension that corrected the original toward MT, or whether each Greek version is an independently made translation, one of which used a more literal style of translation.

Clearly, the relationship of the double Greek versions to each other and to their respective *Vorlagen* is important to textual criticism of both the Hebrew text and its original Greek translation. Therefore, working from the extant texts to distinguish somehow translation style from subsequent recensional activity is one of the fundamental challenges of Septuagint studies and is directly relevant to the task of textual criticism. Methodologies are needed to compare and describe the differences between two or more Greek texts with each other and with MT.

An attempt to define the theory of textual comparisons was described first by James Barr in 1979 in *The Typology of Literalism in Ancient Biblical Translations.*[2] Barr was not content with characterizing a Greek text by the opposing categories of 'free' and 'literal', categories so often used to describe a Greek translation with respect to its presumed Hebrew *Vorlage*. He describes these classifications as 'very rough and impressionistic'.

It is easier to categorize what one means by a 'literal' Greek translation in comparison to the Hebrew than it is to describe the many ways a translation can be 'free'. Therefore, Barr attempted to bring more precision to the term 'literal' by identifying six categories that are 'distinguishable modes of difference between a more literal and less literal rendering of a Hebrew text'.[3] Moreover, Barr made the excellent point that 'there are different ways of being literal and of being free, so that a translation can be literal and free at the same time but in different modes or on different levels'.[4]

About the same time, Emanuel Tov was also working on the problem of providing a more precise definition of the categories 'literal' and 'free' as applied to Greek translations of Hebrew *Vorlagen*. In his classic work *The Text-Critical Use of the Septuagint in Biblical Research*, Tov identified five criteria that are similar to those proposed by Barr:[5]

(1) lexical consistency, defined as whether a given Hebrew word is consistently translated by the same Greek word,
(2) equivalence between units of Hebrew and units of Greek,
(3) the preservation of Hebrew word order in the Greek,
(4) the extent of correspondence between individual elements of the Hebrew unit with elements of the Greek unit, and
(5) the linguistic adequacy of the corresponding Greek expression.[6]

The nature of four of Tov's five criteria is such that they can be counted, thus the degree to which the Greek text adheres to the Hebrew *Vorlage* can be at least partially quantified.

In the same decade, a computer database for Septuagint studies was being designed and implemented by Tov and Robert Kraft. Called CATSS (Computer Assisted Tools for Septuagint Studies), it contains Rahlfs's text of the Septuagint in parallel units with the Masoretic text.[7] This database made possible initial attempts to quantify the characteristics of literal translation technique and the use of the resulting percentages to compare and rank the books of the Septuagint on a scale of literal to free.

For instance, using the five criteria identified by Tov as a theoretical foundation, in 1985 Tov and Ben Wright searched the CATSS database for five syntactical features of the Greek text in thirty books of the Septuagint.[8] For each of the thirty books, they listed the frequency of occurrence of each of the five syntactical items and the ratio of the number of occurrences to an appropriate total, and expressed that ratio as a percentage. One indication of the degree of literalness of the translation technique is how often the Greek preposition ἐν (en, 'in') is used to translate the Hebrew proposition בְּ (bᵉ, 'in, at, with'). Tov and Wright compared the Greek and Hebrew text of each biblical book, counting how often ἐν translated בְּ. They calculated the ratio of the number of occurrences of the Greek preposition ἐν which translated the Hebrew preposition בְּ to the total number of occurrences of בְּ, and expressed that ratio as a percentage. The thirty books were then ranked in descending order of percentages, with Qohelet ranked first at 92.4 per cent and Job ranked last at 27.7 per cent. This ranking indicates that the translator of Qohelet translated this Hebrew preposition consistently, while the translator of Job apparently did not.

This and other similar attempts to quantify translation technique were criticized by Anneli Aejmelaeus. In the introduction to her book *On the Trail of the Septuagint Translators* she makes a distinction between translation technique as understood as an object of study, as if 'the Septuagint translators had a technique or a method of translation that can be discovered and described', and translation technique 'regarded as a question of method followed in the study of linguistic phenomena in the translation'.[9] She associates the attempt to quantify word order, consistency in lexical choice, and one-for-one syntactic equivalence by percentages of occurrence with the first approach, and asks what could such abstract percentages actually mean, since

it is impossible to calculate an ideal percentage for literalness in a certain linguistic phenomenon, still less so if the evidence of several phenomena is combined. Thus, percentages of literalness are difficult to interpret, and for that matter often incorrect, although they give the impression of being accurate.[10]

Her point is well taken, for unlike a perfect 100 per cent on an objective exam to which an individual student's performance can be measured, there is no linguistic ideal external to the texts themselves which defines a perfectly 'literal' translation. However, this problem can be accounted for in a methodology that allows the Greek texts themselves to define the poles of what is meant by 'free' and 'literal' for each syntactical criterion examined. Moreover, although the ranking of books based on relative percentages does move toward quantifying the categories of 'literal' and 'free', a simple ranking of books based on relative percentages still leaves unanswered questions. Since 100 per cent cannot be the standard measure of literalness, how close to 100 per cent must a given criterion be in order to be considered 'literal'? How close must the ranked percentages of a given criterion in two different books be to consider them as representing the same translation technique? And can such information be used to distinguish a translation from a recension?

Aejmelaeus does allow that if one regards translation technique 'as a question of the method followed in the study of linguistic phenomena in the translation', then percentages are useful to facilitate comparison between 'various books containing a different number of cases of a particular kind'. In fact, she uses percentages extensively in her own work.[11] The practical importance of the distinction she makes in what is meant by 'translation technique' can be debated, but what is clear is that in practice of method scholars count the relative frequencies of the occurrence of certain linguistic features of the Greek texts and use those relative frequencies to compare and rank books of the Septuagint with respect to each other.

Since this is being done, quantitative methodologies are needed that are designed:

(1) to directly compare the occurrence of a given linguistic feature in two or more texts;

(2) to determine the overall central tendency of a text by integrating many linguistic features within one book and in comparison to others;

(3) to reveal linguistic patterns that can be used to construct and test theories about the translation technique and recensional development of the Septuagint texts.

Some scholars have been suspicious of the use of percentages to compare the work of different translators. Since there are no ideal control texts available, it is difficult to interpret differences in the percentages between the various books of the Septuagint. As Aejmelaeus asks, 'How much variation can be expected in the work of one translator, and how great a change unmistakably speaks for a different translator?'[12] In the case of such comparisons made between the double Greek texts, one could rephrase the question: how much linguistic variation can we expect between a recension and the Greek text from which it was produced? Is it possible to identify linguistic criteria that help distinguish between the two?

This paper presents a quantitative approach that can be used to explore whether and to what extent a comparative study of syntax can inform the discussion about the characterization of translation technique and whether the identification of recensional activity within a text can be assisted by such syntactical study. There are at least three advantages to using syntax to characterize a Greek text in relation to others. First, syntax extends throughout the entire text and its analysis yields greater amounts of data in comparison to the amount of data involved in studies of morphology or lexicology, which are constrained by their nature to individual and relatively few occurrences within a given text.

Second, the syntax of a text could not avoid reflecting the nature of the translation technique used by the translator or the nature of subsequent concerted recensional activity, for such endeavours by their nature encompass the entire text. Occasional changes made by scribes to harmonize individual readings in the manuscripts or to update individual words by replacing them with more contemporary synonyms should not be considered recensional activity.

Third, the translator or recensor is less conscious of syntactical choices, which operate at the level of linguistic proficiency and personal style, as opposed to lexical choices that are to a greater extent more deliberate, and to additions and omissions that tend to be motivated by very conscious extra-linguistic concerns such as theology or politics. Therefore, to the extent that syntax bears the fingerprint of the translator or recensor it can be used as an indicator in the attempt to identify translation technique from recensional activity *when it is combined with studies of morphology, of lexicology, and of the theological or political Tendenz.*

The assumption that syntax does bear the fingerprint of its author is certainly one that needs more theoretical grounding, but it is being used in other text-based disciplines to explore issues of authorship and textual relationships. Such methods have already been applied by scholars to texts as diverse as Euripides, books of the New Testament, Shakespeare, and the Federalist Papers of early American history, with a view to enlightening issues such as authorship and date of composition.[13] *The Journal of Literary and Linguistic Computing* (*JLLC*) has been published at Oxford University for at least the last decade, and is dedicated to quantitative methods of textual study.

Moreover, it has been generally assumed in past studies of the Greek biblical texts that the distinguishing marks of the translator or recensor are reflected in identifiable syntactical features of the Greek, which can be counted for each book. Beginning with Soisalon-Soininen's work on the infinitive in the Septuagint,[14] others in the Helsinki school have produced a wealth of numerical information about the occurrences of certain syntactical features. For instance, Raija Sollamo has produced countings of the translation of pronouns in the Pentateuch.[15] Ben Wright responded to Ralph Martin's work on syntax criticism,[16] by publishing enumerations of the frequency of Greek prepositions relative to ἐν for each book of the Septuagint.[17]

Whether and to what extent syntax can be used to identify a particular translation style, recension, period of time, or geographical provenance in which the text was produced is an important theoretical question that is worthy of further concerted discussion. It has long been recognized that the syntax of the Greek translation of the Septuagint texts is distinctive enough to distinguish them from texts composed in Greek. But is there enough syntactical variation among the Greek texts of the Septuagint to be used to separate the texts into distinctive groups, and if so, which elements of syntax would serve that purpose, and how much variation is enough? Based on my work with the double versions of Esther and Daniel I suspect the answer to the first question is yes,[18] but much more work needs to be done to establish this hypothesis. The methodology I propose is intended in part to answer that question, and to provide syntactical profiles against which studies of morphology and lexicology can be interpreted.

From my work on the double versions of Esther and Daniel I have developed two quantitative approaches: (1) syntactic profiling of Greek texts and (2) tools for statistical analysis of texts. These methods are intended to compensate for some of the problems and limitations observed in other approaches and are intended to be used along with, *not in place of*, the more traditional approaches. First, these methods are intended to help evaluate selected, isolated examples that are presented as representative of the character of the text by providing an overall profile against which such selected examples can be considered.

Second, recognizing that all Septuagint texts are a mixture of 'literal' and 'free' features, these methodologies are designed to show more specifically which elements of the syntax of a given Greek text can be said to be 'literal' and which 'free' and, furthermore, which elements may be not at all useful for making such distinctions.

Third, these methodologies are designed to provide a quantified measurement of the central tendency and variation of the syntax of a given text in comparison to a norm that is defined by the rest of the corpus of texts themselves, thus addressing the problem identified by Aejmelaeus that there is no external, ideal text to which the texts can be meaningfully compared. Such normalized quantitative analysis moves the discussion beyond simply ranking the books by relative percentages and provides the advantage that the syntax of two or more Greek texts can be directly and meaningfully compared to the norm of the corpus of which they are a member.

I. SYNTACTIC PROFILES

A syntactic profile is a graphic representation of selected elements of syntax of a given text displayed along an axis showing the relative frequency of an individual element of syntax in relation to the average frequency of occurrence of that element in texts known to have been composed in Greek (−1) and in texts known to have been translated from a Semitic source (+1).

A syntactic profile of a text will show at a glance the central tendency and variation in the syntax of the text. Because the axis is normalized, the syntactic profiles of more than one text can be directly compared without the danger of comparing 'apples and oranges'.

The profiles for the double versions of Esther and Daniel (Graph 1) were compiled using seventeen elements of syntax that were originally identified by Raymond Martin as indicators of a Semitic source behind a Greek text. Martin's seventeen criteria are:[19]

Criteria 1-8. The relative frequency of occurrence of eight prepositions with respect to the preposition ἐν:

1. διά with the genitive
   (dia, 'through')
2. διά in all occurrences
   (dia, 'through, because of')
3. εἰς
   (eis, 'into')
4. κατά with the accusative
   (kata, 'according to')
5. κατά in all occurrences
   (kata, 'down, against, according to')
6. περί in all occurrences
   (peri, 'concerning, around')
7. πρός with the dative
   (pros, 'to, toward')
8. ὑπό with the genitive
   (hypo, 'by')
9. the frequency of occurrence of the coordinating καί (kai, 'and') relative to δέ (de, 'but', 'and')
10. the percentage of articles separated from their substantives
11. the relative frequency of dependent genitives following the word on which they depend
12. the relative frequency of occurrence of dependent genitive personal pronouns
13. the relative frequency of genitive personal pronouns dependent on anarthrous substantives
14. the relative frequency of attributive adjectives preceding the word they qualify
15. the relative frequency of attributive adjectives
16. the relative frequency of adverbial participles
17. the relative frequency of the dative case without the preposition ἐν

The axis of the syntactic profile extends between −1 and +1. Minus 1 represents the average of the frequency of occurrence for each of the seventeen elements of syntax in texts known to have been composed in Greek (normalized to −1). Plus 1 represents the average of the same elements of syntax in texts known to have been translated from a Semitic source (normalized to +1).[20] Normalizing the relative frequencies of the syntax in a given text to the average frequency of occurrence within the larger corpus addresses the problem that, language being what it is, there is no ideal standard to which the syntax of a text can be compared. The texts themselves collectively must define the norm against which any given Greek text is compared. The norm for translated Greek was determined by the average frequency of occurrence of the seventeen criteria as they occur in the books of the Septuagint translated from Hebrew. The norm for composition Greek was determined by the average frequency of occurrence of those same

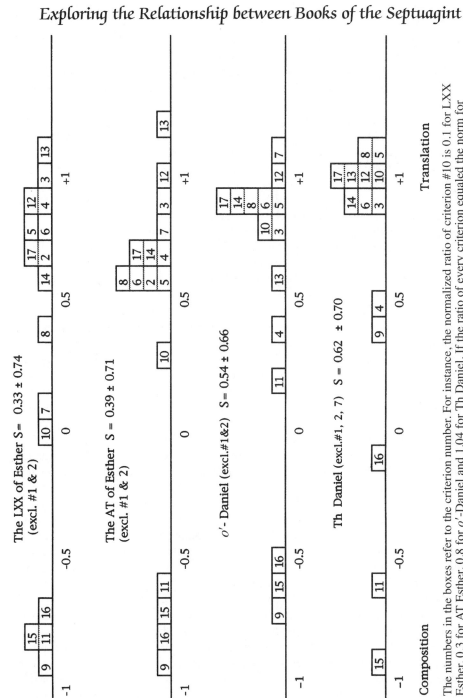

GRAPH 1. The syntax of the Greek versions of Daniel compared to the Greek versions of Esther

The numbers in the boxes refer to the criterion number. For instance, the normalized ratio of criterion #10 is 0.1 for LXX Esther, 0.3 for AT Esther, 0.8 for *o'*-Daniel and 1.04 for Th Daniel. If the ratio of every criterion equaled the norm for translation Greek, all of the boxes would pile up over +1; if the ratio of every criterion equaled the norm for composition Greek, all of the boxes would pile up over –1.

criteria in a total of 1500 lines taken from Plutarch's *Lives*, Polybius, Epictectus, Josephus, and selected papyri.[21] (More texts composed in Greek should be analysed and the norm recalculated, so that the size of the sampling of texts composed in Greek is approximately the same as the size of the texts translated from Greek.)

Martin chose these seventeen criteria because he believed the relative frequency of occurrence of these elements of Greek syntax would reflect the influence of a Semitic *Vorlage*. It is not the mere occurrence of these items in a text that is significant, for all of them could be expected to occur in any Greek text, but it is the *relative* frequency of occurrence that Martin believed identified Greek texts that had been translated from a Semitic source. For example, the rationale behind criterion 9, the relative frequency of καί with respect to δέ is that a Greek translator may choose to render the Hebrew *waw*-consecutive with either the Greek conjunction καί or the postpositive δέ. Martin theorized that a text translated from a Semitic source would contain a higher proportion of occurrences of καί to δέ than would a text originally composed in Greek, because a translator would frequently choose to translate the *waw*-consecutive with καί to retain Hebrew word order. Therefore, the relative frequency of occurrence of καί to δέ could be used as an indicator of a Semitic source lying behind a Greek text. Syntactic profiles can test whether such a criterion actually functions as claimed.

I originally employed Martin's seventeen criteria in my study of whether the alpha-text of Esther (AT) was a translation of a Semitic source or not. However I departed from Martin in the way I analysed and interpreted the resulting ratios.[22] Martin's primary interests were in describing the relationship between the Greek and the Hebrew it translated. My interests began there but moved toward using syntax criticism to explore possible relationships between two or more Greek texts. I developed the methodology of syntactic profiling in order to facilitate the display and interpretation of large quantities of syntactic information and to allow direct comparison of the syntax of the alpha-text with the *o′*-text of Esther, and then with the two Greek versions of Daniel. Using Martin's data for Polybius, Josephus, and some of the documentary papyri, as well as my own analysis of 3 Maccabees, I also profiled these four texts known to have been composed in Greek, as a point of comparison (Graph 2).

Although I used the seventeen criteria identified by Martin, other elements of syntax could be added to the profiles for a fuller characterization of a given Greek text and a broader base of comparison between them. In fact, other syntactic criteria *should* be profiled, because these particular seventeen were chosen by Martin for their presumed value in relationship to a Semitic *Vorlage*, not for providing a broad basis of comparison between two or more Greek texts.

Each numbered box on the syntactic profile represents one of the seventeen elements of syntax, and is numbered accordingly. The position of the box on the axis indicates how close that element of syntax in the given text is to either the norm for texts composed in Greek (−1) or the norm for texts translated from a Semitic source (+1). Note that for texts composed in Greek (Graph 2), the boxes tend to pile up toward −1; for Greek texts translated from a Semitic source, the boxes tend to pile up toward +1. Note also that ±1 are not limits, but merely averages that mark the norm defined by the larger corpus.) The profile also shows at a glance which elements of syntax deviate from the norms, and to what extent.

As an example, consider criterion 9 on Graph 1, the relative frequency of καί

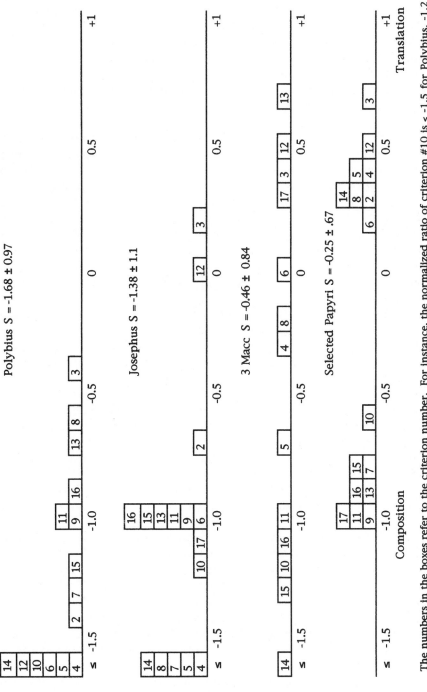

GRAPH 2. A profile of the syntax of texts composed in Greek

The numbers in the boxes refer to the criterion number. For instance, the normalized ratio of criterion #10 is < -1.5 for Polybius, -1.2 for Josephus and -0.6 for the selected papyri. If the ratio of every criterion equaled the norm for composition Greek, all of the boxes for these texts would pile up over -1. (Data from R. Martin, <u>Syntactical Evidence of Semitic Sources in Greek Documents</u> [Missoula: University of Montana, 1974].)

with respect to δέ. The value of this criterion for the alpha-text of Esther was computed by:

(1) Counting the number of occurrences of καί in AT where it is used to coordinate two independent clauses and the total number of occurrences of δέ.[23]
(2) Computing the ratio of number καί/number δέ.
(2) Normalizing that ratio to the norms for translation and composition Greek.
(3) Plotting the normalized ratio on the profile.

Notice that the relative frequency of occurrence of καί with respect to δέ is about the same in the texts known to have been composed in Greek (see Graph 2) as in the two Greek texts of Esther and the Old Greek of Daniel (Graph 1).[24] This data can be argued in at least two different directions. One could use this as one tiny bit of evidence that the two texts of Esther and the o′-text of Daniel are either not translations of a Semitic source, or that they have been so revised as to loose their Semitic flavour. Of course, one would need substantially more evidence to support such a theory. Or, one could conclude – more reasonably, in my opinion – that the relative frequency of καί with respect to δέ is a very weak indicator of the *Vorlage* of these three texts and probably should not be used to retrovert a *waw*-consecutive in the presumed Hebrew *Vorlage* of these particular texts.[25]

Criterion 14 – the relative frequency of attributive adjectives preceding the word they qualify – is also among the eight criteria that occur with approximately the same relative frequency in the papyri as in the Septuagint texts. Since it is certain that the documentary papyri were composed in *koine* Greek and did not undergo any subsequent scribal transmission or recensional activity, the comparison of their profile with the Septuagint books is enlightening. The comparison suggests that the Septuagint translator may simply have been following the standard conventions of *koine* Greek rather than slavishly following the Hebrew *Vorlage*, and that the conventional patterns of usage in *koine* happened for these elements of syntax to be similar to the corresponding pattern in the Hebrew language. Thus syntactic profiles may yield information that guides textual critics in the task of knowing which elements of Greek syntax are useful for detecting Semitic sources, and therefore can be reliably retroverted, and which simply reflect the coincidence of similar syntactic patterns in the *koine* Greek and Hebrew languages.

This example illustrates the value of syntactic profiles for investigating claims that a particular element of Greek syntax reflects its Hebrew *Vorlage*, and is thus useful for reconstruction of the Hebrew, by allowing its relative frequency of occurrence in the given text to be directly compared to the norm for texts composed in Greek. An element of syntax truly distinctive to translation Greek would consistently fall on the +1 end of the axis for Septuagint texts and consistently fall on the −1 end of the axis for texts composed in Greek. This methodology does not *a priori* decide the issue, it simply presents the data in a format that narrows the options and facilitates a more focused discussion.

Even though a given element of syntax may not be a very reliable indicator of a Semitic *Vorlage*, it nevertheless remains a true characteristic of the profile of the given text, and is useful for the purpose of comparing the syntax of two or more Greek texts.

Exploring the Relationship between Books of the Septuagint

For instance, notice in Graph 1 that the relative frequency of the occurrence of καί in Theodotion Daniel is markedly different from the two Greek texts of Esther and the o′-text of Daniel, and in Theodotion Daniel is much closer to the norm for Septuagint texts.

This brings to mind the reigning theory that Theodotion Daniel corrected the o′-text of Daniel toward a Semitic text. Hence, the difference between the o′-text and Theodotion in the number of occurrences of καί with respect to δέ could be interpreted as the introduction of καί wherever there was a *waw*-consecutive in the Hebrew text in circulation at the time and place the Theodotion recension was produced. This brings us to the question of whether, and to what extent, syntax can be used to help identify the characteristics of a recension.

Let us take as a working hypothesis the theory that the o′-text of Daniel was the textual base from which Theodotion Daniel was produced with the intent of 'correcting' the Greek toward a contemporaneous Hebrew/Aramaic text of Daniel. I am not arguing here for or against this hypothesis, but simply wish to show how syntactic profiles can be used to test a hypothesis and how they can suggest specific directions of further study. A comparison of the two profiles of Daniel (Graph 1) shows a distinct shift toward the right for three of the criteria:

Criterion 9, the relative frequency of καί with respect to δέ,
Criterion 13, the relative frequency of genitive personal pronouns dependent on anarthrous substantives, and
Criterion 16, the relative frequency of adverbial participles.

If Theodotion Daniel was produced by one or more revisions of the o′-text, then these profiles suggest that those revisions at least involved (no doubt among many other changes):

(1) replacing post-positive conjunctions, such as δέ, with a coordinating καί;
(2) removing the Greek definite article from nouns qualified by a possessive pronoun;
(3) removing adverbial participles or replacing them with some other construction.

These are the three largest shifts when the syntax of the o′-text of Daniel is compared to Theodotion Daniel that shift the syntax toward what has been described as a more literal rendering. By simply taking the difference between each normalized ratio for each of the two texts and ranking those differences in descending order, the largest shifts in syntax between the double Greek versions can be specifically identified. If one text is a revision of the other, the syntactic profiles identify specifically what effect the revisor's work had on syntax.

On the other hand, notice that two of the criteria – 11 and 19 – shift markedly to the left. If Theodotion is a recension of the o′-text, which is our working hypothesis, then someone must have:

(1) moved dependent genitives to precede rather than follow their substantives, and
(2) added attributive adjectives, but apparently followed Hebrew convention by positioning them most often to follow rather than precede the noun they qualify (because the position of criterion 14, the relative frequency of attributive adjectives *preceding* the word they qualify, remains the same in both profiles).

Seeing shifts in the syntax in both directions raises some questions. Were both shifts in syntax the result of the one and the same revision? If so, the revisor's concern to make the o'-text of Daniel more 'literal' in comparison to his Hebrew text was not consistently executed (not that complete consistency must be expected from one recensor). Or, do these two shifts in opposite directions represent two different strata of recensional activity? For instance, perhaps the shift in syntax toward the norm for composition Greek was contributed to the profile by the various additions to the text of Daniel composed in Greek. These, of course, were untouched by the revisor who 'corrected' the Greek toward the Hebrew, because for those additions there was no corresponding Hebrew. To explore these questions one would return to the Greek texts of Daniel with this very specific information in hand, to compare occurrences of the dependent genitives and attributive adjectives, looking to see if these changes fall with certain portions of the text.[26] The distribution of the changes would then suggest the direction of further investigation of recensional activity.

Note, however, that criterion 14, the relative frequency of attributive adjectives preceding the word they qualify, is among the eight criteria that occur with approximately the same relative frequency in the papyri as in the Septuagint texts. If the recensor of Theodotion Daniel did indeed add attributive adjectives after the qualified substantive, a comparison with the syntactic profile of the papyri suggests that it may have been simply because of the conventions of *koine* and not to conform it toward any Semitic text. This means that the position of the attributive adjective cannot be used to support our working hypothesis that the changes made to produce Theodotion Daniel were in the interests of correcting it toward the contemporaneous Hebrew text. Thus, syntactic profiles are useful for identifying whether given elements of syntax can be used to distinguish recensional activity from general patterns of *koine* usage.

My point here is not to argue for or against the hypothesis about the relationship of the two texts of Daniel, but simply to show that syntactic profiles focus the questions and narrow the field for further research. They do not prove the working hypothesis, but rather present data that must be accounted for by *any* hypothesis claiming to explain the relationship between the two Greek texts. Syntactic profiles organize and graphically display large amounts of syntactic data in a format that facilitates communication and allows hypotheses about translation technique and recensional activity to be raised and tested. I emphasize that this method is not constrained to the seventeen criteria adopted from Martin, but could be used to profile any other syntactic element that can be counted, such as the relative frequency of the articular infinitive, the genitive absolute, and so on.

S-numbers. In order to quantify the overall syntactic profile of a given text and to easily compare it to other texts, the S-number (Syntax-number) of the text can be computed. The S-number is the average value of the normalized frequencies of occurrence for each element of syntax examined (in this case seventeen). An S-number = -1 would indicate that the syntax of the given text perfectly matches, for every element of syntax examined, the norm for texts composed in Greek; an S-number = $+1$ would indicate that the syntax of the given text perfectly matches the norm for texts translated from a Semitic source. Of course, it is very unlikely that such a text exists (Table 1).

Eberhard Nestle, whose work we are commemorating with this volume, discussed

Exploring the Relationship between Books of the Septuagint

TABLE 1. Greek texts sorted by S-number

Where, for all elements of syntax examined, −1 would mean that the syntax of the given text exactly matches the norm for texts composed in Greek, and +1 would mean that the syntax of the given text exactly matches the norm for texts translated into Greek.

Polybius	−1.68 ± 0.97 (using Martin's data)
Josephus	−1.38 ± 1.10 (using Martin's data)
add. E Esther	−0.87 ± 0.88
3 Macc	−0.46 ± 0.84
Selected Papyri	−0.25 ± 0.67 (using Martin's data)
LXX Susanna	0.28 ± 0.73
θ Susanna	0.33 ± 0.67
LXX Esther	0.33 ± 0.74
proto-LXX Esther	0.36 ± 0.62
AT Esther	0.39 ± 0.71
Tobit 𝕰¹ (Alexandrinus & Vaticanus)	0.43 ± 0.70
proto-AT Esther	0.49 ± 0.89
o'- Daniel	0.54 ± 0.66
Th Daniel	0.62 ± 0.70
Tobit 𝕰² (Sinaiticus)	0.63 ± 0.58

the relationship of the double textual traditions of the Greek Tobit, one being found in Codex Sinaiticus, the other in Vaticanus.[27] After examining only a few elements of syntax, he concluded that the Sinaiticus text of Tobit more closely represents its original Semitic *Vorlage*, assuming that the extant MT was in fact its *Vorlage*. A comparison of his conclusion with the S-numbers of the two textual traditions of Tobit shows that Sinaiticus is indeed in overall syntax closer to the norm for Septuagint texts than the text found in Vaticanus. The same general shift in syntax, though of lesser magnitude, is found in the comparison of LXX Susanna and Theodotion Susanna, as well as between LXX Esther and the alpha-text of Esther. How great a shift in syntax could be expected to result from a major revision remains a question for further investigation.

Now one might ask, how are these numbers any better than the simple percentages found in the work of others? The ranking of simple percentages of relative frequency are not indexed to anything, thus making comparisons of those percentages from book to book difficult to interpret. Moreover, comparing simple percentages of occurrence of one element of syntax to another element is like comparing apples and oranges, because there is no inherent relationship between them. For instance, in the study done by Tov and Wright, 'Criteria for Literalness' there is no inherent significance in the fact that in 2 Kings ב is translated by ἐν 83 per cent of the time and that the ratio of occurrence of καί to δέ is 0.39, because there was no point of reference with which to compare the percentage to what might have been expected.[28] There is no common link to relate these two numbers to each other. Such percentages are good as far they go, and they are useful to arrange the books in some *relative* order as Tov and Wright have done.

In contrast to simple percentages, S-numbers are tied to the norm as defined by the other books of the corpus. An S-number greater than zero shows that the syntax of the text in question tends overall toward the norm for Septuagint texts. An S-number less than zero shows that the syntax of the text in question tends overall toward the norm for texts composed in Greek. The difference between the S-number and +1 or −1 shows how far the text varies from the respective norms. Two texts with equal S-numbers would have the same overall syntax, and at glance at their respective profiles would reveal how each element of syntax compares and contributes to the similarity. This is actually true of Theodotion Daniel and the Sinaiticus text of Tobit, whose S-numbers are virtually equal. Such a finding suggests that further investigation of the relationship between these two texts might be especially fruitful (Graph 3).

When the S-numbers are plotted, claims about 'literal' and 'freer' translation technique can be evaluated (Graph 4). It is generally said that AT Esther is the freer of the two Greek versions, because it does not follow the Hebrew Masoretic Text as closely as does the o'-text of Esther. Graph 4 shows that despite the many differences in the minutiae of the two texts, overall there is virtually no difference between the syntax of the o'-text of Esther and AT. Therefore, if we wish to characterise AT as 'freer' than the o'-text of Esther, we must look to other features of the text for that characterization – these seventeen elements of syntax show AT Esther is no more or less 'literal' than that of the o'-text of Esther. And in fact, this was corroborated by my study comparing the agreement of the two texts of Esther to the Masoretic text. The reason that AT Esther gives the impression of being a freer translation than the o'-text of Esther is not found in its syntax, but in the many small pluses and minuses of the two Greek texts that have no correspondence in the Hebrew. Where there is corresponding text that can be compared between all three, the agreement of the AT with the Masoretic text approaches that of the o'-text with MT.[29]

To summarize, the methodology of syntactic profiling:

(1) Provides a profile of the entire text for each examined element of syntax.
(2) Allows the texts themselves to define the norms for texts translated from a Semitic *Vorlage* and for those composed in Greek.
(3) Presents large amounts of syntactic data in a format that facilitates its communication and interpretation.
(4) Allows the syntax of two or more texts to be directly compared.
(5) Provides a method for testing the claim that the frequency of occurrence of a certain syntactic element reflects Semitic influence rather than general *koine* usage.
(6) Allows the testing of hypotheses about the relationship of Greek texts.
(7) Specifies what elements of syntax should be investigated further as potential indicators of recensional relationship.

II. TOOLS FOR THE STATISTICAL ANALYSIS OF GREEK TEXTS

The fact that the study of the Greek biblical texts has not been devoid of quantitative aspects suggests that statistical methods can be appropriately applied to further explore the relationship of the Greek versions and to aid in reconstructing their recensional history. The work of Tov and Wright cited above is but one example of a quantitative study of the Greek texts. Another example is the work of the Helsinki school, which has produced a wealth of quantitative information about the Greek Pentateuch. The work of Soisalon-Soininen on the infinitive,[30] Raija Sollamo's work on the translation

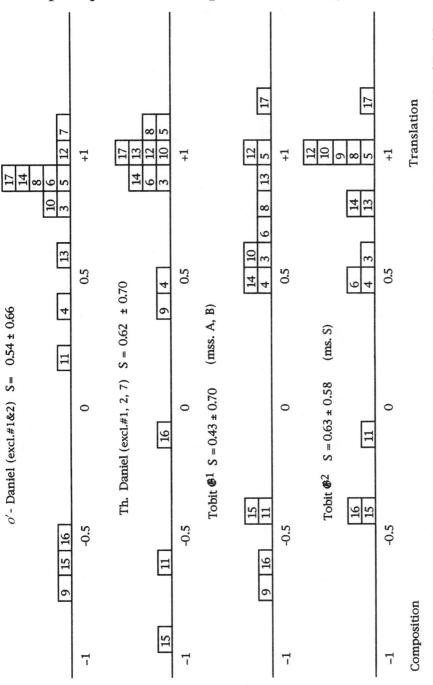

GRAPH 3 . The syntactic profiles of the Greek versions of Daniel and Tobit

Composition

The numbers in the boxes refer to the criterion number. For instance, the normalized ratio of criterion #10 is 0.82 for *o'*-Daniel, 1.04 for Th Daniel, 0.69 for Tobit $\mathfrak{G}^1$ and 1.00 for Tobit $\mathfrak{G}^2$. If the ratio of every criterion equaled the 'norm' for translation Greek, all of the boxes would pile up over +1; if the ratio of every criterion equaled the 'norm' for composition Greek, all of the boxes would pile up over −1.

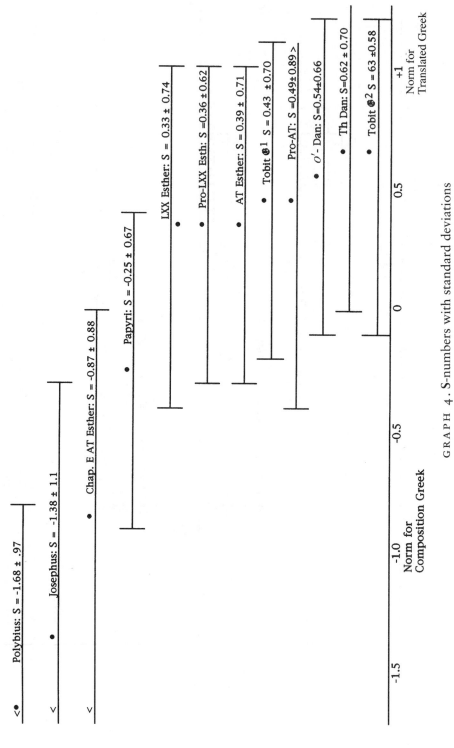

GRAPH 4. S-numbers with standard deviations

of pronouns in the Greek Pentateuch,[31] and Aejmelaeus' study of several syntactic features of the Greek Pentateuch have produced many quantitative indicators of translation technique.[32] Such quantified studies are particularly well suited to further statistical analysis that would facilitate comparison with work done by other scholars in other books of the Septuagint corpus.

Biblical scholars tend to view the use of statistics in studies of the Greek with ambivalence. Statistics may be well suited for the physical sciences and engineering, but after all, in textual studies we are handling human language, and ancient human language at that. Our interests are qualitative and intuitive, not quantitative and precise. There seems to be an unbridgeable chasm between the quantitative precision implied by the use of statistics, and the relatively inexact and qualitative methodologies of historical and linguistic research.

Therefore, a word to justify the use of statistics in the study of language is in order. Most of us are familiar with predictive statistics, which are based on probabilities being effectively used to predict outcomes by extrapolating from small, random samples of a population to inferences about the population at large. For instance, a pharmaceutical company will design drug tests using relatively small numbers of participants to test the effectiveness of the drug on the population at large. Clearly this is not the kind of statistics needed in a situation where we are not free to design the experiment. One might think of the extant Greek texts as samples of the larger population of *koine* texts that were preserved through historical happenstance. They are, therefore, 'random' samples as far as our interests in syntax are concerned, since they were chosen for preservation on theological and historical grounds, not because of any linguistic features of that text that would bias our analysis of syntax. Our interest in statistical analysis of these texts is not in *predictive* statistics, unless making predictions about that larger population of *koine* texts that have not survived is of relevance. Our interests lie with *descriptive* statistics that allow us to organize and describe a very large quantity of syntactical data in a form that is concise and convenient, and that facilitates ease of discussion about and interpretation of the syntactic data.

How can language, which by nature is qualitative, be quantified for statistical analysis? Because of the widespread use of computers it has become common to quantify a human quality – gender, for instance – with a zero or one (representing male or female), thereby allowing all sorts of other similar qualitative factors to be quantified and statistically correlated to gender.

Similarly, a Greek text can be quantified and correlated with its corresponding Hebrew *Vorlage*. For instance, the Hebrew causal כִּי (*ki*, 'for, because') can be rendered with either the Greek conjunction ὅτι (*hoti*, 'because') or γάρ (*gar*, 'for'). These translation decisions can be quantified with a zero or one and statistically described, relating the actual occurrences of each translation choice to the total number possible, that is, by the number of occurrences of כִּי in the Hebrew. Of course, more than simply two translation choices may exist, and usually do, which would require a bit more sophisticated quantification, but the point is that elements examined as criteria for characterizing translation technique and recensional activity can be quantified. And if they can be quantified, they can be statistically described. Therefore, statistical analysis of texts should be one of the tools used to enlighten our knowledge of the origin and development of the Septuagint.

TABLE 2. Translation of causal in כִּי the Pentateuch

	Total possible	ὅτι	γάρ
Genesis	155	68 (44%)	87 (56%)
Exodus	91	12 (13%)	79 (87%)
Leviticus	63	40 (64%)	23 (36%)
Numbers	75	55 (73%)	20 (27%)
Deuteronomy	137	102 (75%)	35 (25%)

Aejmelaeus is indeed correct in stating that a quantitative approach to the Greek texts has thus far not produced much fruit, if we use the computer simply to count the number of times a given syntactical feature occurs. Yet her work, and that of the Helsinki school in which she was trained, is focused on identifying syntactical features and attempting to relate those features to translation technique by counting their relative frequency in a text and comparing that count to other texts. For instance, in her effort to characterize the translation technique employed in the Pentateuch, Aejmelaeus has studied how the Hebrew conjunction כִּי, when it introduces a causal clause, has been translated in the Greek Pentateuch. She counts how many times a causal כִּי is translated by γάρ and how many times by ὅτι (Table 2).[33]

Once such data is collected, what answers about the relationships among the books can it provide? Can such data be used to determine, for instance, if the causal כִּי was handled consistently in the translation of all five books of the Pentateuch? Note that in Exodus the causal כִּי is translated by γάρ a much greater percentage of occurrences (87 per cent) than in Numbers (27 per cent). Is it likely that such variation is the result of choices made by one translator, or does such variation suggest the work of two different translators? If so, could the translation of the causal כִּי be correlated with other similar data – for instance the occurrence of possessive pronouns – to explore whether certain books or portions of books could be identified with its respective translator? Statistical analysis can help answer such questions, and many more. Such information is useful to the textual critic reconstructing either the original Greek or the Hebrew *Vorlage* by providing a characterization of the text against which individual textual critical decisions can be considered.

But counting relative frequencies and calculating percentages cannot answer our questions about the larger picture for the very reason Aejmelaeus has identified: unless we know if these percentages represent a true difference in the way the Hebrew causal כִּי was translated we have no way to evaluate the differences indicated among the books of the Pentateuch or to compare them, for instance, to the translation technique of other books in the Septuagint corpus.

A methodology that could meaningfully relate the relative frequencies of the occurrence of syntax in one book to that of another would allow many interesting questions to be probed. Does the Greek syntax of the Pentateuch suggest that all five books were translated with the same technique or not, and if not, does this imply different translators, and if so, were they working at the same time or and place or not? Do the kaige sections of Samuel-Kings share textual features with any other books of the Septuagint that could enlighten recensional history? Do the books for which two distinct textual traditions exist exhibit syntax that allows them to be grouped? For instance, does the syntax of AT Esther, OG Daniel, and one of the versions of Judges exhibit common characteristics that suggests they were produced at the same time, or by the same translation school? There is, of course, no magic formula by which one can mathematically crank out the answers to such questions, but statistical methodologies are needed to help bring the answers within reach.

There are relatively straightforward statistical tests that can compare the relative frequency of a feature found in one Greek text to the occurrence of that same feature in two or more other texts and determine whether that syntactical feature is used significantly differently among them. As more and more syntactical features are identified, counted, and compared, it will become apparent whether a group of texts share common distinctive features of syntax, and which texts comprise such a grouping. The use of statistical methods could help determine which texts share given criteria. Such information could then be used to confirm or disprove theories about the relationship of the texts.

There are dozens, if not hundreds, of statistical tests, but two will be employed here for comparing the frequency of occurrence of syntactical features in two or more texts: (1) analysis of variance, (2) the Tukey-Kramer multiple comparison test.[34] For instance, an analysis of variance helps to answer the question whether or not overall throughout all five books of the Pentateuch the translation of כִּי is handled consistently. Analysis of variance (ANOVA) may be calculated by hand (as I have done here) but it is a standard statistical method available in software such as SPSS (Statistical Package for the Social Sciences), SAS, and Cystat, which run on many different computers. Analysis of variance is used to classify observations into groups on the basis of a single property. This method could be used to group texts of the Septuagint that share any property that can be counted.

An individual translator could be expected to handle a given element of syntax in Hebrew consistently. This does not mean that he would always translate a causal כִּי with ὅτι or with γάρ, but that the number of times he chose one over the other would be relatively consistent throughout all the books he translated. When such consistency is not found, it raises the question of whether more than one translator was at work. Analysis of variance measures the variation from the mean number of times כִּי is translated by ὅτι as opposed to γάρ to determine if in any one or more of the books that ratio is beyond what would be expected for consistency.[35]

Calculation of the variance of the frequency of occurrence for the translation of the Hebrew causal כִּי by ὅτι and γάρ in the Pentateuch indicates with a confidence level of 95 per cent that the translation of כִּי was not handled consistently across the five books of the Pentateuch. Once analysis of variance has determined that there is at least one book exhibiting a significant difference among the five on this point, a further test, the Tukey-Kramer multiple comparison, can be applied to determine which book(s) of the Pentateuch handle the causal כִּי differently from the others.[36]

Such statistical testing is necessary because the percentages themselves do not unambiguously indicate significant variation. For instance, does the 31 per cent difference between the frequency of translation of the causal כִּי with γάρ in Exodus (87 per cent) compared to Genesis (56 per cent) indeed reflect a significant difference in translation technique (Table 2)? Numbers (27 per cent) and Deuteronomy (25 per cent) seem to

TABLE 3. Comparison of how causal כִּי is translated in Pentateuch

	Genesis	Exodus	Leviticus	Numbers	Deuteronomy
Genesis	——	different		different	different
Exodus	different	——	different	different	different
Leviticus		different	——		
Numbers	different	different		——	
Deuteronomy	different	different			——

TABLE 4. Comparison of how causall כִּי is translated omitting Exodus

	Genesis	Leviticus	Numbers	Deuteronomy
Genesis	——		different	different
Leviticus		——		
Numbers	different		——	
Deuteronomy	different			——

reflect a consistently infrequent translation of the causal כִּ with γάρ. Does Leviticus at 36 per cent group with Genesis or Numbers or neither? When the Tukey-Kramer multiple comparison is applied, the following pair-wise relationships emerge, with a 95 per cent level of confidence. In statistical terms this means there is a less than 5 per cent chance that two books declared 'different' with respect to this element of syntax are in fact the same, with 'different' meaning the frequency with which ὅτι versus γάρ appears in works produced by one translation technique versus some other technique (Table 3).

Even though the percentages (Table 2) indicate the relative frequency of γάρ in Genesis (56 per cent) and Leviticus (36 per cent) might be different, the Tukey-Kramer test indicates that there is no statistically significant difference between the frequency of translation of the causal כִּי by γάρ in Genesis as compared to Leviticus.

Note, however, that two other interesting patterns emerge. The handling of the causal כִּ in Exodus is clearly different from the other four books of the Pentateuch. Furthermore, Numbers and Deuteronomy are different both from Genesis and Exodus. If Exodus is omitted and the analysis of variance is recalculated, there remains a significant difference in the handling of the causal כִּי among the other four books. Tukey-Kramer analysis indicates this in Table 4.

This statistical analysis indicates that Exodus is different from the other four books of the Pentateuch in its handling of the causal כִּי, but not in the same way that Numbers and Deuteronomy are different from Genesis. There emerge at least three groupings: Exodus by itself, Numbers-Deuteronomy, and Genesis. In both tests Leviticus cannot be shown to be different from either Numbers-Deuteronomy or from Genesis. Further examination of other of its characteristics would be needed.

Does this same grouping emerge if a different feature of syntax is chosen? For instance, if the relative frequency of the repetition of possessive pronouns is examined, does Exodus again stand out from the other four? The research of Raija Sollomo

TABLE 5. Repetition of the possessive pronoun in the Greek Pentateuch

	Total possible	Pronoun repeated	Pronoun not repeated
Genesis	47	24 (51%)	23 (49%)
Exodus	50	20 (40%)	30 (60%)
Leviticus	32	24 (75%)	8 (25%)
Numbers	43	37 (86%)	6 (14%)
Deuteronomy	72	55 (76%)	17 (24%)

TABLE 6. Comparison of how possessive pronouns are translated in the Pentateuch

	Genesis	Exodus	Leviticus	Numbers	Deuteronomy
Genesis	——			different	different
Exodus		——	different	different	different
Leviticus		different	——		
Numbers	different	different		——	
Deuteronomy	different	different			——

provides a counting of the number of times the possessive pronoun, repeated in Hebrew syntax for coordinate items, is translated similarly in Greek, in violation of Greek practice (Table 5).[37]

Analysis of variance indicates with a 95 per cent confidence level that there is indeed a significant difference in the frequency of occurrence of the repetition of the pronoun in the translation of the various books of the Pentateuch. The further Tukey-Kramer multiple comparison indicates relationships among the books (Table 6).

Patterns emerge that are similar to those found for the translation of the causal כִּי. Again Exodus exhibits significant differences with three of the other books, and Numbers-Deuteronomy group together again. Leviticus is significantly different from Exodus in the way it translates the possessive pronoun, but again does not distinguish itself from Genesis. Other features of its syntax would have to be examined to see if significant differences between it and Genesis emerge.

As these few examples illustrate, statistical analysis can be used to explore the relationship between the Greek biblical books and their textual history. However, some cautions are indeed necessary. It is easy to plug numbers into a formula and crank out more numbers on a calculator or computer that are then claimed to indicate some meaningful conclusion. But the old maxim, 'garbage in-garbage out' certainly applies here. To assure meaningful conclusions, the hypothesis being tested must be framed in a way appropriate to the statistical methods being applied. Furthermore, the results indicated must not be pressed beyond what the statistical test that was employed allows. Statistics are but a tool that can help explore the characteristics of the Greek texts. There is, of course, no mathematical nor statistical methodology that could *prove* the relationship between two texts. However, when joined with traditional methodology, quantitative analysis will enlighten the question of the origin and textual history of the Greek Bible.

Karen H. Jobes

NOTES

1 Eberhard Nestle, *Septuagintastudien*, iii (Stuttgart, 1888; repr. Göttingen: Vandenhoeck & Ruprecht, 1965).

2 James Barr, 'The Typology of Literalism in Ancient Biblical Translations', MSU, 15 (1979), 279-325.

3 Barr, 294.

4 Barr, 280.

5 Emanuel Tov, *The Text-Critical Use of the Septuagint in Biblical Research*, 2nd edn (Jerusalem: Simon, 1996).

6 Tov, *Text-Critical*, pp. 20-4.

7 A more detailed description of the CATSS database may be found in John R. Abercrombie, William Adler, Robert A. Kraft, and Emanuel Tov, *Computer Assisted Tools for Septuagint Studies*, vol. 1, *Ruth* (SCS 20: Atlanta: Scholars Press, 1986); and Robert A. Kraft and Emanuel Tov, 'Computer Assisted Tools for Septuagint Studies', *BIOSCS* 14 (1981), 22-40; and John R. Abercrombie, 'Computer Assisted Alignment of the Greek and Hebrew Biblical Texts: Programming Background', *Textus* 11 (1984), 125-39.

8 Emanuel Tov and Benjamin G. Wright, 'Computer-Assisted Study of the Criteria for Assessing the Literalness of Translation Units in the LXX', *Textus* 12 (1985), 149-87.

9 Anneli Aejmelaeus, *On the Trail of the Septuagint Translators* (Kampen: Kok Pharos, 1993), pp. 1-3.

10 Aejmelaeus, *On the Trail*, p. 2.

11 Aejmelaeus, *On the Trail*, p. 3. See, for instance, 'OTI *causale* in Septuagintal Greek', ibid., pp. 15-36.

12 Aejmelaeus, *On the Trail*, p. 56.

13 For instance, see Nancy Laan, 'Stylometry and Method: The Case for Euripides', *JLLC* 10, 4 (1995), 271-8; D. L. Mealand, 'Correspondence Analysis of Luke', *JLLC* 10, 3 (1995), 171-82; and 'On Finding Fresh Evidence in Old Texts: Reflections on Results in Computer-Assisted Biblical Research', *BJRL* 74, 3 (1992), 67-87; F. Mosteller and D. L. Wallace, *Inference and Disputed Authorship: The Federalist* (Reading, MA: Addison-Wesley, 1964).

14 Ilmari Soisalon-Soininen, 'Die Infinitive in der Septuaginta', *AASF B* 132 (1965), pp. 68-75.

15 Raija Sollamo, *Repetition of the Possessive Pronouns in the Septuagint* (SCS 40: Atlanta: Scholars Press, 1995).

16 Raymond A. Martin, *Syntactical Evidence of Semitic Sources in Greek Documents* (SCS 3: Cambridge, Mass.: Scholars Press, 1974).

17 Benjamin G. Wright, 'A Note on the Statistical Analysis of Septuagintal Syntax', *JBL* 104 (1985), 111-14.

18 Karen H. Jobes, *The Alpha-Text of Esther: Its Character and Relationship to the Masoretic Text* (SBLDS 153: Atlanta: Scholars Press, 1996); also 'A Comparative Syntactic Analysis of the Greek Versions of Daniel: A Test Case for New Methodology', *BIOSCS* 28 (1995), 19-41.

19 Martin, *Syntactical Evidence* (SCS 3: Cambridge, Mass.: Scholars Press, 1974).

20 For a full mathematical description of how the relative frequencies are normalized see Jobes, *The Alpha-Text*, p. 40.

21 See Martin, *Syntactical Evidence*, pp. 6, 18.

22 For a critique of the problems and limitations of Martin's methodology see Jobes, *The Alpha-Text*, pp. 29-47.

23 The question arises of how variant readings would affect these results. For a large number of occurrences, the possibility of a variant reading for a few of them probably would not make any statistically significant difference in the profile.

24 Criterion 9 is omitted from the profile of 3 Maccabees because the text does not contain the minimum number of occurrences of καί needed for meaningful analysis. See Jobes, *The Alpha-Text*, pp. 33-4 for a list of the minimum number of occurrences required for each of the seventeen criteria.

25 Dana and Mantey's reference to the frequency with which καί was used in *koine* Greek corroborates the weakness of καί as an indicator of a Semitic *Vorlage*: 'The ordinary Hellenist, as the papyrus records reveal, had but few conjunctions in his vocabulary, and καί was the main one', *A Manual of the Greek New Testament* (Saddle River, NJ: Prentice Hall, 1955), p. 250.

26 I was faulted for not taking this subsequent step by Tim McLay, who critiqued my article 'A Comparative Syntactic Analysis of the Greek Versions of Daniel: A Test Case for New Methodology', *BIOSCS* 28 (1995), 19-41. See Tim McLay, 'Syntactic Profiles and the Characteristics of Revision: A Response to Karen Jobes', *BIOSCS* 29 (1996), pp. 15-21, and my reply in *BIOSCS* 30 (1997), 32-5.

27 Nestle, *Septuagintastudien*, iii.

28 Tov and Wright, 'Criteria for Literalness', pp. 163, 180.

29 See Jobes, *The Alpha-Text of Esther*, ch. 4.

30 Soisalon-Soininen, 'Die Infinitive in der Septuaginta'.

31 Sollamo, *Repetition of the Possessive Pronoun*.

32 Aejmelaeus, *On the Trail*.

33 Aejmelaeus, p. 26.

34 The author wishes to gratefully acknowledge Dr Russell Howell, Professor of Mathematics at Westmont College, for several conversations about which statistical methods might be of greatest relevance to this problem and for critiquing this section of the paper.

35 In statistical terms, the null hypothesis is that each sample (i.e. book) would exhibit the same relative frequencies of ὅτι and γάρ if produced by the same translator.

36 The reader is referred to a standard statistics textbook for the actual formulae used in the analysis of variance and the Tukey-Kramer test. This author referred to Jay Devore and Roxy Peck, *Statistics: The Exploration and Analysis of Data*, 3rd edn (San Francisco: Duxbury Press, 1997), pp. 513, 528.

37 Sollamo, *Repetition*, Genesis, p. 19; Exodus, p. 30; Leviticus, p. 45; Numbers, p. 51; Deuteronomy, p. 64.

THE GREEK BIBLICAL TEXTS FROM THE JUDEAN DESERT

Emanuel Tov

I. THE EVIDENCE

A. R. C. Leaney, 'Greek Manuscripts from the Judaean Desert', in *Studies in New Testament Language and Text: Essays in Honour of George D. Kilpatrick on the Occasion of His Sixty-Fifth Birthday*, ed. by J. K. Elliott (NTSup 44; Leiden: Brill, 1976), pp. 283-300; L. Greenspoon, 'The Dead Sea Scrolls and the Greek Bible', in *The Dead Sea Scrolls after Fifty Years: A Comprehensive Assessment*, ed. by P. W. Flint and J. C. VanderKam (Leiden/Boston/Köln: Brill, 1998), pp. 101-27; E. Ulrich, 'The Septuagint Manuscripts from Qumran: A Reappraisal', in *Septuagint, Scrolls and Cognate Writings: Papers Presented to the International Symposium on the Septuagint and Its Relations to the Dead Sea Scrolls and Other Writings* (Manchester, 1990), ed. by G. J. Brooke and B. Lindars (SCS 33; Atlanta, GA, 1992), pp. 49-80.

The Greek texts found in the Judean Desert constitute merely a small part of the texts found in the area, which are best known for the Hebrew and Aramaic texts, especially the texts found at Qumran. However, the Greek texts are by no means negligible, since in several sites their number equals that of the Hebrew/Aramaic texts, and in one site they even constitute the majority. Thus, while for Qumran in general the number of the Greek texts may be negligible, for cave 7 it is not, since all nineteen items found in this cave constitute Greek papyri. This cave thus witnesses activity in the Greek language, but only literary activity, since probably all the fragments found in this cave are non-documentary.

Turning now to absolute numbers of texts, a word of caution is in order. Obviously we can only refer to the numbers of the texts which have survived, but as we will turn to statistics, it should be recognized that there is no reason why Greek texts should have perished into a larger or smaller degree than the other documents. Comparative statistics of the various texts found should therefore be considered legitimate. The majority of the texts found in the Judean Desert are Semitic, mainly Hebrew, but also Aramaic. The Qumran corpus consists of remnants of some 900 compositions that were once complete. Of these some 150 are in Aramaic (including seventeen Nabatean texts), twenty-seven in Greek, and the remainder are in Hebrew (including texts written in the cryptic scripts and in paleo-Hebrew). The Greek texts in Qumran thus comprise a very small segment of the complete corpus, namely 3 per cent. This small percentage is matched only by the finds in Wadi Daliyeh, beyond the Judean Desert, while Greek texts have been found in much larger quantities at all other sites in the Judean Desert. Because of the fragmentary state of many texts, especially papyri, statistics for these sites can only be approximate (Table 1).[1]

We now turn to some detailed remarks about the Greek parchment and papyrus texts

TABLE 1. Greek Texts from the Judean Desert

Sites (North to South)	Total number of texts (leather, papyrus)	Greek texts	Percentage of total texts
Wadi Daliyeh	29	7+	24%+
Jericho	30	17+	56%+
Qumran	900	27	3%
Wadi Nar	4	2	50%
Wadi Ghweir	2	1	50%
Wadi Murabba'at	158	71	45%
Wadi Sdeir	4	2	50%
Naḥal Ḥever[2]	157+	55+	35%+
Naḥal Mishmar	3	1	33%
Naḥal Ṣe'elim	6	2	33%
Masada	48	11+	23%+

found in the Judean Desert, not counting ostraca. First, attention will be directed to sites other than Qumran, with the exclusion of the approximately fifty texts from Ḥirbet Mird because of the Byzantine date of that site.

Greek texts, most of them documentary, have been found in various places in the Judaean Desert (North to South): Wadi Daliyeh (1+ [undeciphered]), Jericho (17 and several fragments), Wadi Nar (2), Wadi Gweir (1), Wadi Murabba'at (71), Wadi Sdeir (2), Naḥal Ḥever (32 from cave 5/6; 2 from cave 8; 21, and many unidentified fragments from 'XḤev/Se' and 'Ḥev/Se?'),[3] Naḥal Ṣe'elim (2), Naḥal Mishmar (1), and Masada (remains of probably eleven texts [a few in either Greek or Latin] and several fragments).[4] The largest groups of Greek texts thus derive from Murabba'at and Naḥal Ḥever, originally wrongly denoted as 'Seiyal',[5] and involving two archives in Greek and Aramaic from Naḥal Ḥever (the archive of Salome Komaïse daughter of Levi and that of Babatha). The documentary texts found in these sites relate to such matters as marriage contracts (for example, 5/6Ḥev 18, 37), receipts (5/6Ḥev 27; XḤev/Se 12), deeds of gift (5/6Ḥev19), registration of land (5/6Ḥev 16), summons (5/6Ḥev 23, 25, 35), and letters (5/6Ḥev 52). The nature of the documents found in the locations outside Qumran thus shows that Greek was in active use among the persons who left these documents behind. That Greek was in active use beyond Qumran can also be seen from the percentage of the documentary Greek texts among the Greek texts found at the individual sites. In all sites this percentage is relatively high, but not at Qumran.

Beyond the documentary texts, a few non-documentary, that is, *literary* Greek texts, sometimes ill-defined, have been found in various sites outside Qumran, included among the statistics in Table 2: five papyri from Wadi Murabba'at, mostly of undetermined nature (*DJD* 2 [Oxford: Clarendon, 1961] 108-12), probably two from Masada (Mas 743 [Mas woodTablet gr] from 73 or 74 CE; Mas 739 [Mas papLiterary Text? gr]),[6] and one from Naḥal Ḥever (8ḤevXII gr), but none from the other localities of Wadi Gweir, Wadi Nar, Wadi Sdeir, Naḥal Ṣe'elim, and Naḥal Mishmar. The best preserved of these literary texts was found in Naḥal Ḥever, viz., the Greek Minor Prophets Scroll, 8ḤevXII gr (publication: *DJD* 8 [Oxford: Clarendon, 1990]).

In striking contrast to the texts found outside Qumran, all but one of the twenty-

TABLE 2. Documentary and Non-documentary Greek Texts
found in the Judean Desert

Sites North to South)	Total number	Doc. texts	Percentage of total number	Non-doc. texts	Percentage of total number
Wadi Daliyeh	7+		–		–
Jericho	17+	17+	100%	0	0%
Qumran	27	1	3%	26	97%
Wadi Nar	2	2	100%	0	0%
Wadi Ghweir	1	1	100%	0	0%
Wadi Murabbaʿat	71	66	93%	5	7%
Wadi Sdeir	2	2	100%	0	0%
Naḥal Ḥever	55+	54	98%+	1	2%
Naḥal Mishmar	1	1	100%	0	0%
Naḥal Ṣeʾelim	2	2	100%	0	0%
Masada	11+	9+	82%+	2	18%

seven Greek texts found in Qumran are literary, although admittedly it is hard to express certainty in the case of small papyrus fragments, viz., 4Q119-22, 126-7; 7Q1-19 (all the preserved texts of cave 7 are Greek papyri), altogether five texts on parchment and three on papyrus from cave 4, and nineteen papyri from cave 7. Almost all of these texts contain Greek Scripture texts in the wide sense of the word (including 7QpapEpJer gr). This characterization includes the literary papyri 7Q4-18, which are too fragmentary for a precise identification of their contents. The one item among the Qumran Greek texts that is not literary is the documentary text 4Q350 (4QAccount gr, written on the verso of fragment 9 of a Hebrew text, 4QNarrative Work and Prayer [4Q460]), the nature and date of which cannot be determined easily (*DJD* 26). The nature of 4QpapUnidentified Fragment gr (4Q361) cannot be defined either (see *DJD* 27, plate LXI, without transcription).

The picture emerging from an analysis of the Greek texts found in the Judean Desert is that the situation at Qumran differs totally from that of the other sites. In all sites, all the Greek texts (and in Wadi Murabbaʿat and Masada, the great majority) are documentary, showing that Greek was actively used among the persons who deposited the texts. These texts include documents showing that the administration was conducted in Greek in the Roman provinces of Syria, Arabia, and Judaea, and that letters were written in that language (see, for example, Greek letters written by Bar Kokhba's followers, found in the Cave of Letters in Naḥal Ḥever). On the other hand, there is no proof that Greek was a language in active use by the inhabitants of Qumran. It is possible that at least some of them knew Greek, since fragments of Greek Scripture were deposited in caves 4 and 7. But cave 4 probably served as a depository of some kind (not a library) in which the Qumranites placed all their written texts (mainly Hebrew and Aramaic literary works, but also *tefillin* and *mezuzot*). This depository in cave 4 contained eight Greek texts, which may signify that the person(s) who brought these texts to Qumran had used them prior to their arrival, which would imply knowledge of Greek. But it is not impossible that these texts came directly from an archive in which case no knowledge of Greek by the Qumranites needs to be assumed. Furthermore, the small number of Greek texts found at Qumran is also in striking contrast with the other sites in the Judean Desert. The difference is partly chronological (most of the sites in the Judaean Desert are from a later period than Qumran), but more so in content: the Qumran corpus is mainly religious, which at that time would involve only Greek Scripture texts, and not other compositions.

The evidence does not suggest that the Greek texts from cave 4 were read or consulted at Qumran or that they were written there. Cave 7 is a different issue. The contents of that cave which was probably used for lodging (thus R. de Vaux, *DJD* 3, 30) or as a workplace, consisted solely of Greek literary papyri, probably all Greek Scripture, and possibly all of these were brought directly to the cave from an archive outside Qumran or from a specific spot within the Qumran compound. No relation between the Greek texts of cave 4 and cave 7 need to be assumed, and there is no reason to believe that any of these texts was penned down in Qumran.

Since the documents found in Naḥal Ḥever show that Greek was used actively by the persons who left the texts behind, including a Scripture scroll, some or much use of that scroll by the persons who deposited the texts in Naḥal Ḥever may be assumed. Indeed, that Minor Prophets scroll contains a Jewish revision of the Old Greek (see below), and as such a version would have suited the freedom fighters of Bar Kochba, and was probably used by them.

The situation was completely different for the Scripture finds at Qumran, which attest to an earlier period, up till 70 CE. In the period that is attested by the settlement at Qumran, the *kaige*-Theodotian revision of the Old Greek, such as is reflected in ḤevXII gr, already existed. But neither this revision, nor similar ones, found their way to Qumran, probably not because the Qumran covenanters disagreed with the concept behind these revisions, but because they did not turn to the Bible in Greek. For them the Bible existed mainly in the source languages, and among the 220 biblical texts found at Qumran, Greek and Aramaic translations (4QtgLev, 4QtgJob, and 11QtgJob) form a very small minority indeed.

In light of this, special attention should be paid to an opisthograph, the recto of which formed fragment 9 of a Hebrew text named 4QNarrative Work and Prayer, while the verso contained a Greek documentary text, 4QAccount gr (4Q350 [see H. Cotton, *DJD* 26]). It is hard to characterize that Hebrew composition, which was described by its editor, E. Larson, as 'somewhat akin to the *Hodayot*'.[7] It may be sectarian, and in any event, its orthography and morphology suggest that it was copied (not necessarily authored) by a sectarian scribe,[8] while the verso contains a documentary Greek text. Parallels to the Greek Account from Qumran are found in various sites in the Judean Desert: Mur 8-10A, 89-102, 118-25; 1Mish 2; 34Še 5. While the evidence implies that Greek was not in active use among the Qumranites, as no documentary Greek texts have been found on the spot,[9] the Greek 4Q350 may indicate an exception, and may imply that Greek was nevertheless in use in Qumran at some stage prior to 70 CE, or that this document did not derive from Qumran.

With regard to the first possibility that Greek was in use at Qumran, and that there once was a small corpus of administrative documentary texts in Greek, attention should be directed to the documentary texts 4Q342-60 in Aramaic and Hebrew, for if documentary texts were written in Qumran in Hebrew and Aramaic, they could have been

1. Athanasius II, Patriarch of Alexandria, Dedication in Arabic, in Codex Alexandrinus. London, The British Library, Royal MS 1 D.v, f. 5 (detail).

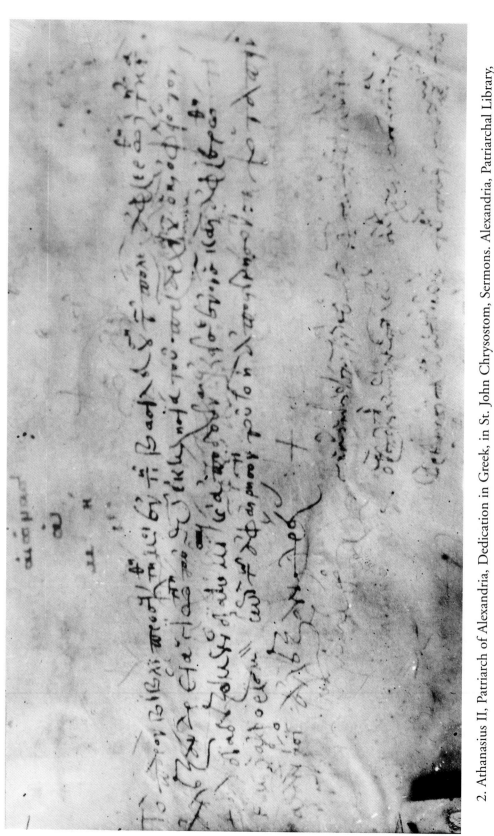

2. Athanasius II, Patriarch of Alexandria, Dedication in Greek, in St. John Chrysostom, Sermons. Alexandria, Patriarchal Library, MS 12, f. 363v.

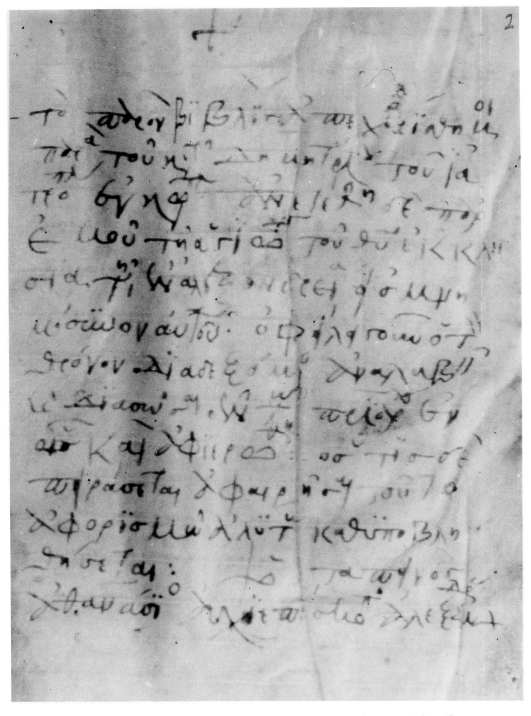

3. Athanasius II, Patriarch of Alexandria, Dedication in Greek, in St. John Chrysostom, Sermons. Alexandria, Patriarchal Library, MS 34, f. 341v.

4. Athanasius II, Patriarch of Alexandria, Dedication in Arabic, in the Minor and Major Prophets. Vatican City, Bibliotheca Apostolica, MS Ottoboni gr. 452, f. 1.

5. Athanasius II, Patriarch of Alexandria, Dedication in Arabic, in Hesychius and St John Chrysostom, Commentaries on the Psalms. Oxford, Bodleian Library, MS Roe 13, f. 224.

6. Gospel of St John 7:51-8.41, in Codex Sinaiticus. London, The British Library, Add. MS 43725, f. 252.

7. Gospel of St Matthew 27:24-52, in Codex Vaticanus. Vatican City, Bibliotheca Apostolica, MS. Vat. gr. 1209, p. 1275.

8. Acts 2:42-3:4, in Codex Bezae. Cambridge University Library, MS Nn.2.41, ff. 423v-424 by permission of the Syndics of Cambridge University Library.

written in Greek as well. However, serious doubts regarding the Qumranic origin of 4Q342-60 have been raised by A. Yardeni, *DJD* 27, 283-317.[10] Some of these texts may have derived from other, later, sites, and may have been sold to scholars as 'Qumran', possibly in order to enhance their price.[11]

We therefore resort to the assumption that 4Q350 was written on the verso of fragment 9 of the Hebrew text 4Q460 after the occupation of the site by the Qumranites when some of the documents were still laying around, and were re-used due to the scarcity of writing material. This is suggested by the following arguments: (1) Only the verso of fragment 9 of 4Q460 was inscribed, which necessarily points to a period in which that manuscript had already been torn into pieces or had partially disintegrated. (2) The writing of a documentary text on the back of a literary text is parallelled by many Greek papyri from Hellenistic Egypt (see the analysis by Gallo),[12] by Elephantine papyri,[13] and by 4QCal. Doc. C[c] (4Q324) – a documentary/literary text – which has on the verso 4QAccount C ar or heb (4Q355). Likewise, Mur papLiterary Text (Mur 112) has on its verso Mur papProceedings of Lawsuit (Mur 113). (3) As a rule, writing on the flesh side (the verso) of the parchment (4Q350 in this case) is subsequent to writing on the recto (4Q460). At the same time, it remains difficult to understand the realia of the writing on 4Q350 and 4Q460: if fragment 9 was hidden in cave 4 by the Qumran community and was indeed found in that cave, how could it have been re-used by those who were to occupy the site after the Qumran community?

The writing of the Greek text 4Q350 on the verso of the Hebrew text 4Q460, fragment 9 must have been later than the writing of the recto (4Q460), but the Greek writing could in principle have been performed within the period of the occupation of Qumran by the Qumran covenanters themselves, which seems to be a possible alternative. However, E. Larson argues that the Qumran sectarians would not have reused a scroll that contained the Tetragrammaton on the recto (4Q460 fragment 9 i 10) for such a profane use as recording a list of cereals in Greek (*DJD* 26, 369). Larson adds: 'If not, then this list could become evidence of a later occupation of the Qumran caves in the wake of the destruction of the settlement in 68 CE.' If this explanation is adapted, it may imply that this text is irrelevant to our analysis of the use of Greek within the Qumran community.

Beyond the enigmatic Greek 4Q350, the Qumran corpus bears a clearly religious character with regard to both the Hebrew/Aramaic texts and the Greek documents. Alongside the Hebrew biblical texts, the following Greek literary texts have been found, mainly containing Greek Scripture. One such text was also found in Naḥal Ḥever.

1. 4QLXXLev[a] (4Q119; Rahlfs 801)

Publication: P. W. Skehan, E. Ulrich, and J. E. Sanderson, *Qumran Cave 4.IV: Palaeo-Hebrew and Greek Biblical Manuscripts*, DJD 9 (Oxford: Clarendon, 1992), 161-5. Bibliography: P. W. Skehan, 'The Qumran Manuscripts and Textual Criticism', *VTSup*, 4 (1957), 148-60, esp. 157-60; P. Kahle, 'The Greek Bible and the Gospels: Fragments from the Judaean Desert', *SE*, 1 (TU 73; Berlin 1959), 613-21, esp. 615-18; id., *The Cairo Geniza*, 2nd edn (Oxford: Blackwell, 1959), pp. 223-6; E. Ulrich, 'The Greek Manuscripts of the Pentateuch from Qumrân, Including Newly-Identified Fragments of Deuteronomy (4QLXXDeut)', in *De Septuaginta, Studies in Honour of John William Wevers on His Sixty-Fifth Birthday*, ed. by A. Pietersma and C. Cox (Mississauga, Ont.: Benben, 1984), pp. 71-82.

Only one major fragment (fragment 1) containing Leviticus and a small unidentified fragment (fragment 2) have been preserved of this scroll (publication: *DJD* 9). Fragment 1 represents the beginning of a sheet, as the stitching on the left has been preserved. The text is written in the *scriptio continua* with occasional spaces left between the words. There are no occurrences of the divine name in this fragment. The writing was dated by Kahle, *Cairo Geniza*, 223, to the end of the second century BCE, on the authority of C. H. Roberts. P. J. Parsons, *DJD* 9, 10 suggests similarly: 'unlikely to be later than the first century BCE, or much earlier'. Skehan, 'Manuscripts', 157 dated this text to the first century CE.

This fragment probably reflects a much earlier version of the Greek translation of Leviticus than the other Greek witnesses (see section II below).

2. 4QpapLXXLev[b] (4Q120; Rahlfs 802)

Publication: P. W. Skehan, E. Ulrich, and J. E. Sanderson, *DJD* 9 (Oxford: Clarendon, 1992), 167-80. For bibliography, see 4QLXXLev[a].

Several small fragments of Leviticus 1-5 have been preserved from this scroll (publication: *DJD* 9). The more substantial ones contain 2.3-5, 3.9-13, 4.6-8, 10-11, 18-19, 26-8, 5.8-10, 16-17, 5.18-6.5. There is also a large number of unidentified fragments. The writing was dated by Skehan, 'Manuscripts', 148 to the first century BCE, and by C. H. Roberts to the late first century BCE or the beginning of the first century CE.[14] P. J. Parsons, *DJD* 9, 11 suggested likewise: '... could reasonably be assigned to the first century BCE'.

This papyrus represents an early version of Greek Scripture, as shown by several unusual renderings, including the transliteration of the Tetragrammaton as Ιαω, instead of its translation as κύριος in the later Christian manuscripts of the Septuagint. 4QpapLXXLev[b] probably reflects a version antedating the text of the main manuscript tradition of the Septuagint (LXX).

3. 4QLXXNum (4Q121; Rahlfs 803)

Publication: P. W. Skehan, E. Ulrich, and J. E. Sanderson, *DJD* 9 (Oxford: Clarendon, 1992), 181-94. Bibliography: see 4QLXXLev[a] and further: P. W. Skehan, 'The Qumran Manuscripts and Textual Criticism', *VTSup*, 4 (1957), 148-60, esp. 155-7; id., '4QLXXNum: A Pre-Christian Reworking of the Septuagint', *HThR*, 70 (1977), 39-50; J. W. Wevers, 'An Early Revision of the Septuagint of Numbers', *ErIsr*, 16 (1982), 235*-9*.

Several fragments have been preserved of this scroll, of which the most substantial are of Numbers 3.40-3 and 4.5-9, 11-16 (publication: *DJD* 9). The writing was dated by Skehan, 'Manuscripts', 155 to the first century BCE, and by Kahle, *Cairo Geniza*, 223, to the beginning of the first century CE, on the authority of C. H. Roberts. P. J. Parsons, *DJD* IX, 11 agreed to the latter dating.

This scroll may reflect a version of the Septuagint antedating the text of the known manuscript tradition of Numbers, but the evidence is not clear-cut.

4. 4QLXXDeut (4Q122; Rahlfs 819)

Publication: P. W. Skehan, E. Ulrich, and J. E. Sanderson, *DJD* 9 (Oxford: Clarendon, 1992), 195-7. Bibliography: E. Ulrich, 'The Greek Manuscripts'.

Little is known about this scroll of which only five small fragments have been preserved (publication: *DJD* 9). P. J. Parsons, *DJD* 9, 12 dated the fragments to the 'earlier second century BCE [...] mid second century BCE'.

5. 4QUnidentified Text gr (4Q126)

Published by P. W. Skehan, E. Ulrich and J. E. Sanderson, *DJD* 9, 219-21.

The nature of this text is unclear. It is dated by P. J. Parsons, *DJD* 9, 12 to the 'first century BCE or possibly the early first century CE'.

6. 4QpapParaExod gr (4Q127)

Publication: P. W. Skehan, E. Ulrich and J. E. Sanderson, *DJD* 9 (Oxford: Clarendon, 1992), 223-42. Bibliography: D. Dimant, 'An Unknown Jewish Apocryphal Work?' in *Pomegranates and Golden Bells – Studies in Biblical, Jewish, and Near Eastern Ritual, Law, and Literature in Honor of Jacob Milgrom*, ed. by D. P. Wright and others (Winona Lake, IN: Eisenbrauns, 1995), pp. 805-14.

This text, dated by P. J. Parsons, *DJD* 9, 12 to the 'first century BCE or possibly the early first century CE' was based on Greek Scripture.

7. 7QpapLXXExod (7Q1)

Publication: M. Baillet, *DJD* III, 142-3.

This text contains small fragments of Exodus 28.4-6, 7 (publication: *DJD* 9). The material is too fragmentary in order to pronounce a judgment on its content or dating. In some details 7QpapLXXExod is closer to the Masoretic Text (MT) than the main Septuagint tradition, while in other instances it is further removed from it.

8. 7QpapEpJer gr (7Q2; Rahlfs 804)

Publication: M. Baillet, *DJD* 3, 142.

This small fragment contains verses 43-4 of the Epistle of Jeremiah (publication: *DJD* 3 [Oxford: Clarendon, 1962]). Too little has survived of this scroll in order to pronounce a judgment on its nature or dating.

9. 7QpapBiblical Texts? gr (7Q3-5) and 7QpapUnclassified Texts gr (7Q6-19)

Publication: M. Baillet, *DJD* 3 (Oxford: Clarendon, 1962), 142-6. Bibliography: M. V. Spottorno, 'Nota sobre los papiros de la cueva 7 de Qumrân', *Estudios Clásicos*, 15 (1971), 261-3; J. O'Callaghan, '?Papiros neotestamentarios en le cueva 7 de Qumran?, *Biblica*, 53 (1972), 91-100, translated by W. L. Holladay, *Supplement to JBL*, 91 (1972), 2.1-14; id., 'Notas sobre 7Q tomadas en el Rockefeller Museum', *Biblica*, 53 (1972), 517-33; id., 'I Tim 3, 16: 4, 1.3 en 7Q4?', *Biblica*, 53 (1972), 362-7; id., 'Tres probables papiros neotestamentarios en la cueva 7 de Qumrân', *StudPap*, 11 (1972), 83-9; C. H. Roberts, 'On Some Presumed Papyrus Fragments of the NT from Qumran', *JTS*, n.s., 23 (1972), 446; P. Benoit, 'Note sur les fragments grecs de la grotte 7 de Qumran', *RB*, 79 (1972), 321-4; id., 'Nouvelle note sur les fragments grecs de la grotte 7 de Qumran', *RB*, 80 (1973), 5-12; A. C. Urbán, 'Observaciones sobre ciertos papiros de la cueva 7 de Qumran', *RevQ*, 8 (1973), 233-51 (Numbers 14.23-4); id., 'La identificacion de 7Q4 con Num 14, 23-24 y la restauración de textos antiquos', *Estudios bíblicos*, 33 (1974), 219-44; J. O'Callaghan, 'Sobre la identificación de 7Q4', *StudPap*, 13 (1974), 45-55; id., *Los papiros griegos de la cueva 7 de Qumrân* (Biblioteca de autores christianos 353; Madrid 1974); K. Aland, 'Neue Neutestamentliche Papyri III', *NTS*, 20 (1974), 357-581; C. P. Thiede, *Die älteste Evangelien-Handschrift? Das Markus-Fragment von Qumran und die Anfänge der schriftlichen Überlieferung des Neuen Testaments* (Wuppertal, 1986) = *The Earliest Gospel Manuscript? The Qumran Fragment 7Q5 and Its Significance for New Testament Studies* (London: Paternoster, 1992); G. W. Nebe, '7Q4: Möglichkeit und Grenze einer Identifikation', *RevQ*, 13 (1988), 629-33; S. R. Pickering and R. R. E. Cook, *Has a Fragment of the Gospel of Mark Been Found at Qumran?* (Papyrological and Historical Perspectives 1; The Ancient History Documentary Research Centre, Macquarie University, Sydney 1989); M. V. Spottorno, 'Una nueva posible identificación de 7Q5', *Sefarad, 52* (1992), 541-3 [Zachariah 7.4-5]; S. Mayer (ed.), *Christen und Christliches in Qumran?* (Eichstätter Studien 32; Regensburg 1992) [this volume contains ten essays dedicated to the fragments from cave 7]; E. A. Muro, Jr., 'The Greek Fragments of Enoch from Qumran Cave 7 (7Q4, 7Q8, & 7Q12 = 7QEn gr = Enoch 103:3-4, 7-9)', RevQ, 18 (1997), 307-12; E. Puech, 'Sept fragments grecs de la *Lettre d'Hénoch* (1 Hén 100, 103 et 105) dans la grotte 7 de Qumrân (= 7QHéngr)', *RevQ,* 18 (1997), 313-23.

Three of the unidentified papyri (7Q3-5) were designated by Baillet, *DJD* 3 as 'biblical texts?', while the other ones (7Q4-19) were described as too small for identification. Among these fragments, 7Q3-5 are slightly more substantial, but they, too, are very minute. These fragments were republished by O'Callaghan, *Los papiros griegos,* as fragments of books of the New Testament, while other scholars recognize in them fragments of LXX:

> 7Q3 = Mark 4.28
> 7Q5 = Mark 6.52-3
> 7Q8 = James 1.23-4

The following suggestions by O'Callaghan, *Los papiros griegos,* were made more hesitantly:

> 7Q4 = I Timothy 3.16-4.1,3
> 7Q6 = Acts 27.38
> 7Q7 = Mark 12.17
> 7Q9 = Romans 5.11-12
> 7Q10 = II Peter 1.15
> 7Q15 = Mark 6.48

7Q5 has been identified also as representing the following texts:

> Exodus 36.10-11 (P. Garnet, *EvQ*, 45 [1973] 8-9)
> Numbers 22.38 (G. Fee, 'Some Dissenting Notes on 7Q5 = Mark 6:52-53', *JBL*, 92 (1973) 109-12)
> II Kings 5.13-14 (C. H. Roberts, *JTS*, 23 [1972] 446)
> Matthew 1.2-3 (P. Parker, *Erbe und Auftrag*, 48 [1972] 467-69)

C. H. Roberts, *JTS,* 23 (1972), 447, suggested the following alternative identifications from LXX for the other texts:

7Q4 = Numbers 14.23-4
7Q6.1 = Psalms 34.28; Proverbs 7.12-13
7Q6.2 = Isaiah 18.2
7Q8 = Zechariah 8.8; Isaiah 1.29-30; Psalms 18.14-15; Daniel 2.43; Qoheleth 6.8

The problematic aspects of O'Callaghan's identifications are:

(1) The texts are too small for a solid identification.
(2) O'Callaghan had to amend the text of the New Testament in order to maintain the identification of 7Q5 with the New Testament.
(3) Some of the compositions identified (Acts, II Peter) were written after the dates assigned to the Qumran fragments – thus Benoit, 'Note'.
(4) In 'Nouvelle note', Benoit expressed serious doubts about some of the readings, asserting that in order to make such a major claim as finding fragments of the New Testament at Qumran, more solid evidence (such as fragments with personal names) are required.
(5) The papyrologists Pickering and Cook, *Fragment*, read some of the key letters of 7Q5 in such a way that it cannot be identified as the text of Mark.

As a result of these doubts, Aland, 'Papyri' did not include these documents in his list of New Testament papyri.[15]

G. W. Nebe, *RevQ*, 13 (1988), 629-33 suggested 1 Enoch 103.3-4 for 7Q4,1 and 1 Enoch 98.11 for 7Q4,2. This suggestion was further developed by E. A. Muro and E. Puech, who suggested to identify fragments 4, 8, 11-14 with 1 Enoch 100, 103, and 105, and to name this text 7QEn gr.

In the wake of the existence in caves 4 and 7 of texts of the Greek Pentateuch, the most likely assumption is that 7Q3-7 contain either the Septuagint text of the Pentateuch (LXX Pentateuch) or LXX Enoch.

10. 8HevXII gr (published as: 8HevXIIgr)

Publication: E. Tov with the collaboration of R. A. Kraft, *The Greek Minor Prophets Scroll from Naḥal Ḥever, (8ḤevXIIgr) (The Seiyal Collection I)* (DJD 8; Oxford: Clarendon, 1990; reprinted with corrections, 1995). Bibliography: E. Puech, 'Les fragments non identifiés de 8KhXIIgr et le manuscrit grec des Douze Petits Prophètes', *RB*, 98 (1991), 161-9; id., 'Notes en marge de 8KhXIIgr', *RevQ*, 98 (1991), 583-93; D. Barthélemy, *Critique textuelle de l'Ancien Testament* (OBO 50/3; Fribourg: Universitätsverlag/Göttingen: Vandenhoeck & Ruprecht, 1992), pp. cxl-cxliv.

8ḤevXII gr contains remnants of twenty-five columns of a Greek Minor Prophets scroll, in two different scribal hands (Jonah 1.14-Zechariah 9.5; publication: *DJD 8*) reflecting an early Jewish revision of the LXX. The date of the revision cannot be determined, but the scroll itself was copied between 50 BCE and 50 CE according to the dating of its two scribal hands. The nature of the revision, belonging to the *kaige*-Theodotion group, and reflecting distinctly Jewish hermeneutical principles, has been amply described.[16] As a Jewish revision, this text represented the Tetragrammaton in paleo-Hebrew characters.

II. COMPARISON OF THE FRAGMENTS FROM QUMRAN AND NAḤAL ḤEVER WITH THE MANUSCRIPT TRADITION OF THE LXX

Data from the preliminary editions of the Greek texts from the Judean Desert (prior to the publication of *DJD* 3, 9) were included in the critical editions of the Greek Pentateuch in the Göttingen Septuagint series,[17] while the material of ḤevXII gr has not been incorporated in that series, since the first edition of that volume appeared before that text was known.[18] Even though ḤevXII gr, as an early revision of the LXX, is not part of the manuscript tradition of the LXX itself, under normal circumstances it would have been included in one of the apparatuses of the Göttingen edition.

The following analysis describes the special features of the texts from the Judean Desert (the description of ḤevXII gr is shorter than that of the other texts, as it has been described in detail in *DJD* 8, 99-158). The elements that each text has in common with the manuscripts of the LXX are reviewed first. These common elements preclude the assumption that the manuscripts from the Judean Desert contain independent Greek versions. They are probably different forms (a revision and a more original form) of the same translation.

a. 4QLXXLev^a [19]

1. 4QLXXLev^a and the Septuagint have a common background

The two texts share several unusual renderings, establishing their common translation tradition:

Leviticus 26.5 (ὁ) σπόρος – זרע MT SP (הזרע). This equivalent recurs elsewhere only six times in LXX, while the usual LXX equivalent is σπέρμα.

Leviticus 26.5 ἄμητος = LXX^{A,B* 121 etc}] ἀλόητος LXX (= editions of Rahlfs and Wevers) – דיש MT SP. Strictly speaking this is not a case of agreement as the reading of 4QLXXLev^a is found in some of the manuscripts of LXX. ἄμητος (harvest, reaping) probably reflects the original reading, and ἀλόητος a later revision approximating to MT. Alternatively, the equivalent ἄμητος may reflect an ancient corruption common to 4QLXXLev^a and the tradition of LXX^{A,B* 121 etc} based on an early interchange of M/ΛO. In that case the reading ἀλόητος should be considered original as it reflects the general LXX vocabulary.[20] Although the equivalent ἀλόητος – דיש occurs only here in LXX, and the word itself occurs also in Amos 9.13 (MT חורש), the verb ἀλοάω occurs elsewhere four times for דיש, so that the equivalent is well-supported. The same interchange occurs also in Amos 9.13 MT חורש – ἀλόητος (LXX^{W' B-239 Q*-198 etc.} ἄμητος). The phrase used there (καὶ καταλήμψεται ὁ ἀλόητος τὸν τρύγητον) is identical to LXX Leviticus. The first explanation is preferable, as the graphical resemblance is not convincing.[21]

Leviticus 26.6 καὶ ἀ]πολῶ – והשבתי MT SP. This equivalent is unique in the Pentateuch, while it occurs elsewhere in Isaiah, Jeremiah, and Ezekiel. The regular equivalent in the Pentateuch is καταπαύω.

Leviticus 26.6 πολεμός – חרב MT SP. Elsewhere this equivalent recurs in Leviticus

26.36,37; Numbers 14.3; 20.18; Joshua 10.11; Job 5.15. The main LXX equivalents are μάχαιρα and ῥομφαία (probably also occurring in verse 8).

Leviticus 26.6 φόνῳ – לחרב MT SP. This unusual equivalent occurs elsewhere only in Exodus 5.3 and Deuteronomy 28.22.

Leviticus 26.8 διώξονται μυριάδας – רבבה ירדפו MT SP. The two texts share the reversed sequence.

Leviticus 26.11 βδελύξεται – תגעל MT SP. This equivalence occurs only here in LXX. The Greek verb usually reflects תעב, while געל is more frequently rendered by προσοχθίζω (4 x; including once in verse 15) and ἀποθέω (2 x).

Leviticus 26.13 μετὰ παρρησίας – קוממיות MT SP (קוממיות). The Hebrew *hapax* word ('with head held high') is rendered by a LXX *hapax* ('openly').

Leviticus 26.15 ἀλλά – ואם MT SP. The frequency of this unusual equivalent cannot be examined in the extant tools.

Leviticus 26.16 ψώρα – שחפת MT SP. The Hebrew recurs elsewhere only in Deuteronomy 28.27, where it is rendered by the same Greek word ('itch').

Leviticus 26.16 καὶ τὴν ψυ[χὴν ἐκτήκουσαν – ומדיבת נפש MT SP (ומדיבות). Even though the reconstruction is problematical, the syntax of the two Greek versions is similar or identical, as opposed to MT SP (note the sequence of the words).

2. 4QLXXLev^a reflects the original text of LXX, while the main LXX tradition probably reflects a revision

Evidence presented in this category reveals the main characteristics of the Qumran text, pointing to its pre-revisional nature.

2a. 4QLXXLev^a represents an unusual rendering or equivalent

Leviticus 26.4 [τὸν ὑετὸν τ]ῆι γῆι ὑμῶν] τὸν ὑετὸν ὑμῖν LXX = גשמיכם MT SP. The deviating translation of 4QLXXLev^a could have been influenced by the phrase occurring in the list of covenant blessings in Deuteronomy 28.12, 24 δοῦναι τὸν ὑετὸν τῇ γῇ σου – לתת מטר ארצך (the same exegesis may also be behind T^J מיטריא דארעכון). At the same time, a variant like גשם/מטר ארצכם is not impossible. LXX reflects an approximation to MT, while ὑμῖν reflects the pronominal suffix freely.[22]

Leviticus 26.8 πέντε ὑμῶν] ἐξ ὑμῶν πέντε LXX = מכם חמישה MT SP. The unusual sequence of 4QLXXLev^a, presenting a better construction in Greek, probably represents the original translation, for which compare ומאה מכם – καὶ ἑκατὸν ὑμῶν in the immediate context. LXX reflects an approximation to MT.

[Leviticus 26.9 [καὶ ἔσται μο]υ ἡ διαθήκη ἐν ὑμῖν[ ] καὶ στήσω τὴν διαθήκην μου μεθ' ὑμῶν LXX = והקימתי את בריתי אתכם MT SP. It is unlikely that 4QLXXLev^a reflects a variant such as והיתה בריתי בתוככם (cf. Ezekiel 37.26 ברית עולם יהיה אותם). Rather, it reflects the original free rendering (for which compare Numbers 25.13; I Kings 8.21; Malachi 2.4,5), adapted to MT in the main manuscript tradition of LXX.

Instead of the aforementioned reconstruction in *DJD* IX [καὶ ἔσται], one may also reconstruct [καὶ στήσεται], which should also be considered a free rendering. Note the Greek literary sequence μο]υ ἡ διαθήκη, for which compare the preceding and following entries.

Leviticus 26.10 ἐξοίσετ]ε μετὰ τῶν νέων] ἐκ προσώπου τῶν νέων ἐξοίσετε LXX = מפני חדש תוציאו MT SP. ἐκ προσώπου of LXX reflects a stereotyped rendering replacing the better Greek μετά of the scroll. That word reflects a more elegant Greek expression, but is probably based on a misunderstanding of the Hebrew. According to MT SP, 'you shall eat the old and then clear out (replace) the old to make room for the new'. According to 4QLXXLevª, however, 'you shall eat the old together with the new'. Note further the sequence of the words in 4QLXXLevª (compare the previous entries) which is more elegant in Greek. This sequence was corrected in the main text of LXX to MT.

Leviticus 26.12 μοι ἔθν[ος] μου λαός LXX (לי לעם MT SP). This remarkable lexical discrepancy probably best characterizes the relation between the two texts. In the vocabulary of LXX λαός usually refers to Israel (reflecting עם), while ἔθνος pertains to peoples other than Israel (also in profane Greek ἔθνη denoted 'foreign nations' prior to the time of LXX [thus LSJ]). These equivalents created the post-Septuagintal exegetical tradition (i.a. in the New Testament) that λαός refers to Israel as the chosen people, while the ἔθνη are the gentiles. 4QLXXLevª does not reflect this later standard vocabulary and therefore probably reflects the Old Greek translation. Its lexical choice is parallelled by a few verses in LXX, such as Exodus 19.6, a central verse, where עם/גוי – ἔθνος refers to Israel in the phrase ממלכת כהנים וגוי קדוש (compare also Leviticus 19.16) – in this case the Hebrew is גוי, and not עם as in Leviticus 26.12. It stands to reason that in Leviticus 26.12 also the original lexical choice preserved in 4QLXXLevª was changed in the majority tradition to accord with the vocabulary elsewhere in LXX. In another detail, however, 4QLXXLevª equals the majority LXX tradition: neither text renders the *lamed* of לעם which is not needed in Greek.

Leviticus 26.13 τὸν ζυγὸν το[ῦ δεσμοῦ = LXX^MSS] τὸν δεσμὸν τοῦ ζυγοῦ LXX^maj. text cf. MT SP מטת עלכם (SP עולכם מטות). Probably the equivalent of the earlier tradition as reflected in 4QLXXLevª and LXX^MSS was adapted in the majority manuscript tradition of LXX to the regular equivalent of על in LXX, viz., ζυγός. The earlier translation does not constitute a precise representation of MT. The two translations have in common the understanding that מטת is a singular form, probably reflecting a reading מטה. This understanding, although deviating from Ezekiel 34.27, may be supported by such verses as Jeremiah 28.10,12.

Leviticus 26.15 προστά]γμασι μου] κρίμασίν μου LXX, משפטי MT SP. The regular equivalent of משפט in LXX is κρίμα, while πρόσταγμα (4QLXXLevª) usually reflects דבר and חק (and only three times משפט in Leviticus 18.26; 19.37; 26.46). The rendering of LXX should be understood as a correction to the regular vocabulary of LXX (κρίμα – משפט, πρόσταγμα – (ה)חק). The context in which מצוה, חקה, and משפט appear may have contributed to this unusual equivalent in the scroll which probably reflects the original translation. Less likely is the assumption that προστά]γμασι reflects a variant מצותי, for which compare verse 14. Wevers, *Notes*, 445 considers the reading of the scroll a 'careless mistake'.

2b. 4QLXXLev^a probably reflects a Hebrew variant

Leviticus 26.4 τὸν ξύλινον καρφ[ ] τὰ ξύλα τῶν πεδίων (ἀποδώσει τὸν καρπὸν αὐτῶν) LXX = ועץ) השדה (יתן פריו) MT SP. The last word before the lacuna in 4QLXXLev^a cannot be read easily. It is not impossible that it represents καρπ[ὸν, in which case the scroll reflects a different reading or a change in the sequence of words. 4QLXXLev^a could reflect עץ (ה)פרי, although τοῦ καρποῦ would have been expected (for the reconstructed ועץ הפרי יתן פריו cf. Genesis 1.11). The phrase ὁ ξύλινος καρπ[ός of 4QLXXLev^a is frequently used in secular Greek (cf. LSJ, p. 1191) and may therefore reflect a free rendering. The ancient character of 4QLXXLev^a is supported by the unusual equivalent: ξύλινος is used in LXX for עץ, not only as an adjective, but also as a neuter noun (compare, for example, Deuteronomy 28.42 πάντα τὰ ξύλινα σου (כל עצך) and 1 Maccabees 10.30). In any event, the main manuscripts of LXX equal MT, with the exception of the representation of עץ in the plural.

Leviticus 26.11 βδελύξομαι = LXX^{MS126 (βδελλύζωμαι) Arab}] βδελύξεται ἡ ψυχή μου LXX = MT SP תגעל נפשי. The reading of the scroll (note the agreement with the main LXX tradition in the equivalent) may reflect an early variant אגעל, which could be original, in which case the reading of MT SP = LXX could reflect a euphemistic anti-anthropomorphic correction (for which cf. T מימרי), such as elsewhere in T. In these cases the correction adds an intermediary entity (נפש) in MT, avoiding the direct mentioning of God himself. In T *ad loc.* מימרא reflects נפש, but elsewhere it is added as an additional entity (like the addition in T of שכינתא and יקרא). Alternatively, MT SP could also represent a harmonistic change to other occurrences of this phrase in this chapter (verses 15, 43).

Leviticus 26.12 καὶ ἔσομ[αι]] καὶ ἐμπεριπατήσω ἐν ὑμῖν καὶ ἔσομαι ὑμῶν θεός LXX = והתהלכתי בתוככם והייתי לכם לאלהים MT SP. There is no room in the lacuna in the Qumran scroll for a rendering of והתהלכתי בתוככם, and these words were probably lacking in its *Vorlage*, possibly by way of *parablepsis*. Alternatively, the scroll could reflect a different sequence of the phrases.

Leviticus 26.14 τὰ/ πάντα τὰ] προστάγματα μου] + ταῦτα LXX = את כל המצות האלה MT SP. The addition of ταῦτα in LXX probably represents an approximation to MT, as האלה may have been lacking in the *Vorlage* of the scroll. At the same time, it is unclear whether the scroll reflects את כל מצותי or את כל המצות.

3. 4QLXXLev^a represents the Hebrew more closely than the 'LXX'

Leviticus 26.6 καὶ πόλεμος οὐ δι[ελε]ύσετ[αι διὰ τῆς γῆς ὑμῶν. In 4QLXXLev^a this phrase occurs at the end of verse 6 as in MT SP וחרב לא תעבר בארצכם, while LXX has the phrase at the beginning of the verse. Both sequences may be defended. In a way, the phrase follows וישבתם לבטח בארצכם in a natural way in LXX. Alternatively, also in MT SP and 4QLXXLev^a the phrase comes appropriately at the end of verse 6 before ורדפתם את איביכם. It is not impossible that one of the two sequences may have been created by a textual mishap. Note, for example, that like the phrase under consideration, verse 5 ends with בארצכם.

Leviticus 26.12 [καὶ πάλαια] = MT SP] καὶ πάλαια παλαιῶν LXX (נושן MT SP). In a conventional reconstruction there is no room in the scroll for παλαιῶν of LXX, but it could have been added in the scroll above the line. The Septuagint may represent a doublet.

Leviticus 26.12 μοι ἔθν[ος] μου λαός LXX = לי לעם MT SP. לי is more precisely rendered by μοι in 4QLXXLevᵃ than by μου in LXX.

4. Indecisive evidence

Leviticus 26.6 [ὁ]ἐκφόβων ὑμᾶς] ὑμᾶς ὁ ἐκφόβων LXX = ואין מחריד. In this phrase MT usually does not have an object, while LXX occasionally adds one, for example, Jeremiah 46 (26).27 ואין מחריד – καὶ οὐκ ἔσται ὁ παρενοχλῶν αὐτόν (thus also Zephaniah 3.13 and Ezekiel 34.28). The sequence of the words in 4QLXXLevᵃ more closely represents the usual sequence of the Hebrew (and LXX), although MT SP *ad loc.* do not have an added אתכם. The LXX is more elegant.[23]

5. Analysis

4QLXXLevᵃ and LXX reflect the same textual tradition of the Greek Leviticus (section 1), so that the differences between the two highlight their different backgrounds. There is ample evidence in favour of the assumption that 4QLXXLevᵃ reflects an earlier text (section 2), and that the other witnesses were corrected towards MT. As elsewhere in the history of LXX revisions, the revisional activity reflected in the majority manuscript tradition of LXX was neither consistent nor thorough.[24] There is very little evidence for the alternative suggestion that 4QLXXLevᵃ reflects an early revision (section 3).

b. 4QpapLXXLevᵇ²⁵

1. 4QpapLXXLevᵇ and LXX have a common background

The two texts share several unusual renderings, demonstrating their common translation tradition:

Leviticus 3.9 σὺν ταῖς]ψόα[ις – לעמת העצה MT SP

Leviticus 3.11 ὀσμ]ὴγ[εὐωδίας cf. LXX ὀσμὴ εὐωδίας – לחם MT SP

Leviticus 4.7 παρὰ τ[ὴν] βά[σιν – אל יסוד MT SP (note the preposition)

Leviticus 4.7 παρὰ τὰς θύρας – פתח (אהל מועד) MT SP

Leviticus 4.28 ἐν] αὐτῇ] om MT and 'the Three'; SP עליה = verse 14 עליה (LXX: ἐν αὐτῇ). In verse 23 בה in the same expression is likewise rendered by ἐν αὐτῇ.

Leviticus 4.28 χί]μαιρον cf. χίμαιραν LXX] + קרבנו MT SP

Leviticus 4.28 χίμαιρον (LXX: χίμαιραν) ἐξ αἰγῶν – שעירת עזים MT SP. The combination of these two nouns occurs elsewhere in Leviticus 4.29 (not in MT SP) and 5.6 (שעיר עזים).

Leviticus 4.28 θῆλει[αν ἄμωμον – תמימה נקבה MT SP. Note the reverse sequence in the Greek texts (= SP *ad loc.* and in 4.32).

Leviticus 4.28 περὶ τῆ[ς ἁμαρ]τίας – חטאתו MT SP. The two Greek versions do not represent the pronoun.

Leviticus 5.8 τοῦ σφονδύλου – ערפו MT SP. The Greek word occurs only here in LXX – the only place in Scripture mentioning the neck of an animal.

Leviticus 5.9 [τὸ δὲ κατάλοιπον] τοῦ αἵματος – והנשאר בדם MT SP. Note the representation of -ב with the Greek genetive.

Leviticus 5.9 ἁμαρτίας γάρ ἐστιν – חטאת הוא MT SP (היא). Note the addition of γάρ (cf. 5.11 כי – ὅτι LXX) and the case-ending of the noun.

Leviticus 5.19 πλημμέλη]σιν [ἔ]ναντ[ι Ιαω – אשם לה' MT SP
Leviticus 5.23 (6.4) πλημμε]λήσηι – ואשם MT SP

Leviticus 5.21 (6.2) κοιν[ωνίας – בתשומת יד MT SP. The Hebrew (meaning unclear) and Greek words occur only here.

Leviticus 5.21 (6.2) πλημμέλη]σιν [ἔ]ναντ[ι Ιαω / κυρίου – אשם ליהוה MT SP. Note both the translation equivalent and the preposition (ἔναντι is also often used elsewhere in LXX with verbs of sinning; for ἁμαρτάνω see i.a. Genesis 39.9 and Exodus 10.16).

Leviticus 5.23 (6.4) ἡ[νίκα ἄν – כי MT SP

In some instances the agreement in a particular equivalence, although occurring also elsewhere in LXX Pentateuch, cannot be coincidental.

Leviticus 2.4 ἐκ σε[μιδάλεως – סלת MT SP

Leviticus 2.4 ἄρτους ἀζύμο]υς – חלות מצת MT SP (מצות)
Leviticus 2.4 πεφυ[ραμένους – בלולת MT SP

Leviticus 2.5 πεφυραμ]ένης – בלולת MT SP

Leviticus 2.4 καὶ λά]γανα – ורקיקי MT SP

Leviticus 3.4 τῶν μηρίω[ν – הכסלים MT SP
Leviticus 3.10 τ[ὸ ἐπὶ τ]ῶν μηρίω[ν – אשר על הכסלים MT SP

Leviticus 3.5 καὶ τὸν λ]όβον – היתרת MT SP (היותרת)
Leviticus 3.10 καὶ τὸν λ]όβον[– ואת היתרת MT SP (היותרת)

Leviticus 3.9 τῆς κο]ιλία[ς – הקרב MT SP

Leviticus 4.6 τὸ]καταπετασ[μα – פרכת MT SP

Leviticus 4.27 ἀκουσίως – בשגגה MT SP

Leviticus 5.9 καὶ ῥανεῖ – והזה MT SP

Leviticus 5.18 ἧς ἠγ[νόησεν – אשר שגג MT SP

Leviticus 5.23 ἀδίκημ[α – העשק MT SP (העשוק). Other LXX equivalents are ἀδικία and ἄδικος.

2. 4QpapLXXLev[b] reflects the original text of LXX, while the main LXX tradition probably reflects a revision

Leviticus 2.5 σεμιδάλεως πεφυραμ]ένης] LXX σεμίδαλις πεφυραμένη – סלת בלולה MT SP. The main LXX reading (nominative) probably corrected the earlier genitive.

Leviticus 3.4 τὸν ἀπὸ τοῦ ἥπα[τος] LXX τὸν ἐπὶ τοῦ ἥπατος – על הכבד MT SP.

Leviticus 3.11 ὀσμ]ὴν[εὐωδίας] LXX ὀσμὴ εὐωδίας. (והקטירו הכהן המזבחה) לחם (והקטיר). The two texts reflect a different understanding of the relation between the segments in the sentence. For 4QpapLXXLev[b] this was one continuous sentence, with לחם as the object of the verb, while for LXX לחם started a nominal phrase. Since LXX reflects the Masoretic accents, possibly the scroll reflected an earlier understanding.

Leviticus 3.12 I]αω] κυρίου LXX – יהוה MT SP
Leviticus 4.27 Ιαω] κυρίου LXX – יהוה MT SP
In this discrepancy between 4QpapLXXLev[b] and the main Greek tradition, probably the most major in all the Greek Qumran scrolls, the scroll probably reflects the original text. The Qumran text transliterated the Tetragrammaton in *Greek* characters (preceded and followed by a space), a practice which is not known from other biblical manuscripts, where two alternative systems are known:[26]

(1) The writing of the Tetragrammaton in Hebrew characters, either in the paleo-Hebrew[27] or in the square Aramaic script.[28]
(2) κύριος, usually without the article, especially in the nominative, and less frequently with the article.[29]

All the texts transcribing the Tetragrammaton in Hebrew characters reflect early revisions, in which the employment of Hebrew characters was considered a sign of authenticity, even though this practice only entered the transmission of Greek Scriptures at a second stage. A parallel phenomenon took place in several Hebrew Qumran manuscripts written in the square Aramaic script, mainly non-biblical texts, in which the Tetragrammaton was written in paleo-Hebrew characters.[30] This practice, reflected in both Hebrew and Greek sources, indicates reverence for the ineffable name of God.[31]

In the reconstruction of the history of the Greek versions, the writing of the Tetragrammaton in Hebrew characters in Greek revisional texts is a relatively late phenomenon. On the basis of the available evidence, the analysis of the original representation of the Tetragrammaton in Greek Scriptures therefore focuses on the question of whether the first translators wrote either κύριος or Ιαω. According to Pietersma, the first translators wrote κύριος, mainly without the article, considered a personal name in the Greek Pentateuch, as 'the written surrogate for the tetragram'.[32] However, the internal LXX evidence offered in support of this assumption is not convincing, as all the irregularities pertaining to the anarthrous use of κύριος can also be explained as having been created by a mechanical replacement of Ιαω with κύριος by Christian scribes. On the other hand, according to Stegemann and Skehan, Ιαω reflects the earliest attested stage in the history of the LXX translation, when the name of God was represented by its transliteration, just like any other personal name in

LXX.[33] Skehan, *ibid.*, p. 29 provided important early parallels for the use of Ιαω and similar forms representing the Tetragrammaton: Diodorus of Sicily I,29,2 (first century BCE) records that Moses referred his laws to τὸν Ιαω ἐπικαλούμενον θεόν; likewise, in his commentary on Psalms 2.2, Origen speaks about Ιαη (PG 12.1104) and Ιαω (GCS, Origenes 4.53); and two onomastica used Ιαω as an explanation of Hebrew theophoric names (for full details, see Skehan). The later magical papyri likewise invoke Ιαω. In a similar vein, Stegemann gives a long list of arguments in favour of the assumption of the priority of the transliteration.[34] This transliteration reflects an unusual pronunciation of the Tetragrammaton, for which compare the form in the Elephantine papyri (יהו).

In the absence of convincing evidence in favour of any one explanation, the view of Skehan and Stegemann seems more plausible in light of the parallels provided. This argument serves as support for the view that 4QpapLXXLev[b] reflects the OG, and not a later revision/translation.

Leviticus 4.7 τῆς [καρ]π[ώσ]εως = העלה MT SP] LXX τῶν ὁλοκαυτωμάτων
Leviticus 4.10 [τῆς καρ]πώσεως = LXX; העלה MT SP
Leviticus 4.18 τῶν]καρπωσ[εών = LXX; העלה MT SP
The regular LXX equivalent for עלה is ὁλοκαύτωμα (thus Leviticus 4.7), but in 4.10,18, LXX-Leviticus used κάρπωσις (this equivalent occurs elsewhere also in Job 42.8). Therefore, probably also in 4.7 the OG contained κάρπωσις (thus 4QpapLXXLev[b]), subsequently replaced in most manuscripts with the standard LXX equivalent ὁλοκαύτωμα.

3. Indecisive evidence

Leviticus 4.4 καὶ εἰσάξ[ει] καὶ προσάξει LXX – והביא MT SP

Leviticus 4.27 οὐ πο[ιηθήσε]τα[ι] ἢ οὐ ποιηθήσεται LXX – אשר לא תעשינה MT SP. Without ἢ, probably omitted by mistake in 4QpapLXXLev[b] or its forerunner, the sentence makes little sense. The presence of this word in the main LXX tradition probably reflects the original reading, but the evidence is ambivalent.

Leviticus 5.21 (6.2)]εἰς τ[ον Ιαω] (παριδὼν παρίδῃ) τὰς (ἐντολὰς κυρίου) LXX – ומעלה מעל ביהוה MT SP

The two Greek texts differ regarding the preposition and probably also the verbs. There is no room for the added ἐντολὰς of LXX in the lacuna in 4QpapLXXLev[b]. The papyrus probably did not read παριδὼν παρίδῃ in the lacuna, as reconstructed in *DJD* IX, 176, and not occurring in LXX with εἰς, but rather ἀθετέω (used with this preposition as an equivalent of מעל in 1 Chronicles 2.7 and Ezekiel 39.23).

Leviticus 5.21 ἠδίκη]κεν] ἠδίκησεν LXX – עשק MT SP

4. Analysis

The agreements between 4QpapLXXLev[b] and the main manuscript tradition of LXX (section 1) suggest that the two sources represent different branches of the same translation. There is more evidence for the assumption that 4QpapLXXLev[b] preceded the main manuscript tradition of LXX (section 2) than for the reverse assumption. The evidence is not overwhelming, but the reverse claim that 4QpapLXXLev[b] reflects a revision of LXX can probably be made only in 5.21]εἰς τ[ον Ιαω. Probably the most convincing case for the ancient character of the Qumran text is the presentation of the divine name as Ιαω.

g. 4QLXXNum

1. 4QLXXNum and LXX have a common background

The two texts share several unusual renderings which demonstrate their common translation tradition:

Numbers 4.7 [καὶ τὰ σπονδεῖα ἐν οἷς σπέ]νδει – ואת קשות הנסך MT SP. This unusual rendering (the reconstruction is plausible) displays an important agreement between LXX and 4QLXXNum. At the same time, 4QLXXNum (probably) and some manuscripts of LXX add ἐν αὐτοῖς.

Numbers 4.8 καὶ ἐπιβάλουσιν ἐπ᾽]αὐτὴν – ופרשו עליהם MT SP

In some instances the agreement in a particular equivalence, although sometimes also occurring elsewhere in the Pentateuch, cannot be coincidental.

Numbers 4.5 τὸ[καταπέτ]ασμα = LXX – את פרכת MT SP

Numbers 4.7 τὴν τράπεζαν τὴν προ]κειμένην – שלחן הפנים MT SP. This rendering occurs elsewhere in Exodus 37.10 (38.9), 39.36 (17) LXX[B].

Numbers 4.7 τὰ τ[ρ]υβλί[α – את הקערת MT SP. This equivalence occurs also in Exodus (2 x) and Numbers (5 x).

Numbers 4.7 τ]οὺς κυαθοὺς – ואת המנקית MT SP (המנקיות). This equivalence occurs elsewhere in Exodus (3 x) and Jeremiah 52.19.

Numbers 4.8 ἐπ᾽]αὐτὴν – עליהם MT SP.

Numbers 4.12 τὰ σκ[εύη τὰ λει]τ[ουρ]γικά – כלי השרת MT SP (השרד). This equivalence recurs only in 2 Chronicles 24.14.

Numbers 4.16 καὶ τὸ θυμίαμα τῆς συνθέ]σεω[ς – קטרת הסמים MT SP.

2. 4QLXXNum reflects an earlier text

Numbers 3.40 ἀρίθμησον] ἐπίσκεψαι LXX – פקד MT SP. ἐπισκέπτομαι is the standard equivalent of פקד in the main manuscript tradition of LXX of all the books, in which ἀριθμέω is the main equivalent of מנה. On the other hand, 4QLXXNum inconsistently used both ἀριθμέω for פקד in 3.40 and ἐπισκέπτομαι in col. I, line 9 (Numbers 3.42 ἐπ[εσκέψατο).[35] The evidence suggests that 4QLXXNum reflects an earlier stage of the transmission of the translation when the equivalents of פקד had not yet been standardized. The possibility of a change in the reverse direction, suggested by Wevers, 'Early Revision', 238*[36] is less likely. Note that the two verbs are used in the same context in a description of the census in 2 Samuel 24 (ἀριθμέω verse 1 [מנה]; ἐπισκέπτομαι verses 2, 4 [פקד]), a situation that underlines their parallelism.

Numbers 4.6 [ἀ]ρτῆρας] ἀναφορεῖς LXX; בדיו MT SP
Numbers 4.8 ἀρτῆρας] ἀναφορεῖς LXX; בדיו MT SP
Numbers 4.11 ἀρτῆ[ρας] ἀναφορεῖς LXX; בדיו MT SP
Numbers 4.12 ἀρτῆρας] ἀναφορεῖς LXX; המוט MT SP

One of the two renderings systematically replaced the other, but it is hard to determine the direction of the substitution. Possibly ἀρτήρ in 4QLXXNum constitutes the original reading (it occurs in LXX only in Nehemiah 4.11 for סבל) and ἀναφορεύς the correction. This assumption is supported by the fact that ἀναφορεύς occurs in the early Greek revisions for בד in Exodus 30.4 (Th) and 39.35 (οἱ λ᾽) and for מוט in Numbers 13.23 (Aq Th). This is also the regular LXX equivalent in Exodus 25, 27, 35, Numbers 4, and 2 Chronicles 5 for בד. The reverse assumption that ἀναφορεύς is the original rendering and ἀρτήρ the correction was suggested by Skehan, '4QNumLXX', 46, and Wevers, 'Early Revision', 236*-237*. According to Wevers, the early reviser conceived of ἀναφορεύς of LXX as an agent noun, that is to say, a 'carrier' rather than 'an instrument for carrying', and he therefore replaced that word. However, this type of revision is evidenced less in the revisions of LXX which usually aim at etymological clarity vis-à-vis the Hebrew and not vis-à-vis the Greek.

Numbers 4.12 καὶ θήσουσιν] καὶ ἐμβαλοῦσιν LXX; ונתנו MT SP
The equivalent of LXX recurs in verses 10, 14, as well as elsewhere in LXX (10 x) but not elsewhere in LXX Numbers for נתן (note further elsewhere in LXX διεμβάλλω [1 x]; ἐκβάλλω [1 x]; ἐπιβάλλω [2 x]). The unusual equivalent of 4QLXXNum may point to its original character, especially since it occurs elsewhere in LXX Pentateuch (Genesis, Exodus, Leviticus); the compositum ἐπιθήσουσιν occurs also in verse 10 (MT SP ונתנו).

3. 4QLXXNum is closer to MT SP

3a. Translation equivalents

Numbers 3.43 πᾶν πρωτό]τοκο[ν ἄρσεν = כל בכור זכר MT SP] πάντα τὰ πρωτότοκα τὰ ἀρσενικά; LXX (the singular form of this noun is found also in the first part of this verse).

Numbers 4.7 ἐπ᾽ α]ὐτήν = עליו MT SP] tr LXX

3b. Possibly different Vorlage
Numbers 4.14 SP = LXX add a large plus καὶ λήμψονται ... ἐπὶ ἀναφορεῖς lacking in MT SP 4QLXXNum.

Numbers 4.9 [τὴν λυχνίαν τῆ]ς φαύσεως cf. τοῦ φωτος LXX[b]] τὴν λυχνίαν τὴν φωτίζουσαν LXX (possibly reflecting an etymologizing rendering המאיר); MT SP מנורת המאור (מנורת) SP). The rendering מאור – φαῦσις occurs elsewhere in Genesis 1.14-15; Psalms 73(74).16; Exodus 35.8 Sym; Leviticus 24.1 alius.

4. Indecisive evidence

Numbers 4.7 ὑ[α]κ̣ίνθι[νον] ὀλοπόρφυρος LXX; תכלת MT SP
The equivalent used by 4QLXXNum, ὑακίνθινος = ὑάκινθος (dark blue) usually renders תכלת, while ὀλοπόρφυρος (dark red or purple) of LXX renders once ארגמן (Leviticus 4.13).[37] Its main component, πορφύρα, renders ארגמן passim in LXX. It is unclear whether 4QLXXNum reflects an imprecise translation of תכלת or a variant ארגמן, even though the combination כליל ארגמן is not known from elsewhere (cf. בגד ארגמן Numbers 4.13; Judges 8.26).

Numbers 4.14 τὰ σπ[ονδεῖα] τὸν καλυπτῆρα LXX; המזרקת MT SP (המזרקות). καλυπτῆρα (covering) is an inappropriate equivalent, while σπονδεῖα (cups) could reflect MT SP.[38]

Analysis

4QLXXNum has much in common with the majority LXX tradition (section 1), suggesting that the two entities are branches of the same translation. At the same time, the evidence is inconclusive regarding the status of the Qumran text. Some of its equivalents give the impression of not having been adapted to the majority tradition of LXX, in which case the scroll probably reflects the OG translation (section 2). But in a few other details 4QLXXNum reflects MT more closely. Skehan, '4QLXXNum' and Wevers, 'Early Revision', support the view that in these details the scroll reflects an early revision towards MT, described as a 'pre-Christian reworking' by Skehan. However, the evidence in favour of the first assumption seems to be stronger (thus Ulrich, *DJD* 9, 189).

d. 8ḤevXII gr

When discussing the nature of 8ḤevXII gr, we are on much safer ground than in the analysis of the Qumran texts, since this scroll undoubtedly contains a revision of the OG. This text shares idiosyncratic elements with the main tradition of LXX, so that it should be considered an integral part of that tradition (see *DJD* 8, 104-6). 8ḤevXII gr thus does not represent an independent translation of LXX, or a translation that occasionally consulted the main LXX tradition. Beyond this common background, there is overwhelming evidence that this scroll reflects a revision of the OG (probably part of the *kaige*-Th group), made at an early period, before the middle of the first century BCE (when the manuscript was copied). The evidence in favour of the revisional nature of this scroll was presented in detail in *DJD* 8, 131-42. The revisional categories may be summarized as follows:[39]

1. The reviser attempted to express every element of the Hebrew with a separate Greek element, involving the addition and omission of elements vis-à-vis the OG. For example,

Habakkuk 1.15 ויגיל   – καὶ χαρήσεται ἡ καρδία αὐτοῦ LXX
                          καὶ χαρεῖται 8ḤevXII gr
Habakkuk 1.17 על כן   – διὰ τοῦτο LXX
                          εἰ διὰ τοῦτο 8ḤevXII gr

2. The reviser represented each word with an etymologically precise rendering, even if the free rendering of the OG was more elegant or contextually more appropriate. For example,

Habakkuk 1.8 וקלו   – καὶ ἐξαλοῦνται LXX
καὶ κουφ[ότεροι 8ḤevXII gr

Habakkuk 2.1 ואתיצבה   – καὶ ἐπιβήσομαι LXX
καὶ στηλώσομαι 8ḤevXII gr.

The correction is based on the equivalent מצבה – στήλη also found elsewhere in the *kaige*-Theodotion revision.

3. The reviser adhered to a single equivalent for each Hebrew word or word-group. For example,

Habakkuk 1.10 וילכדה   – καὶ κρατήσει αὐτοῦ LXX
καὶ συνλήψε[ται αὐτό 8ḤevXII gr

The correction was based on a distinction between the equivalences חזק – κρατ- and לכד – συλλαμβάνω *passim* in LXX.

Habakkuk 2.3 יתמהמה   – ὑστερήσῃ LXX
στραγ[γεύσηται 8ḤevXII gr

The correction was based on the understanding that ὑστερ- was reserved to the root אחר (cf. ὕστερος, -ον – (ון)אחר *passim*).

4. The reviser adhered to a system of formal equivalences between grammatical categories: a plural form in MT should be represented by a plural form in the translation; adverbs should be represented by adverbs; verbs by verbs, and so forth. For example,

Habakkuk 1.9 לחמס   – εἰς ἀσεβεῖς LXX
εἰς ἀδικίαν 8ḤevXII gr

Habakkuk 1.15 במכמרתו – ἐν ταῖς σαγηναῖς αὐτοῦ LXX
ἐν τῇ] σαγήνη αὐτοῦ 8ḤevXII gr

Habakkuk 2.2 ובאר   – καὶ σαφῶς LXX (cf. Deuteronomy 27.8 LXX)
καὶ ἐκφάν[ειν or ἐκφάν[ηθι 8ḤevXII gr

III. SUMMARY

Greek texts in the Judean Desert

The discovery of Greek biblical texts in caves 2, 4 and 7 at Qumran as well as in Naḥal Ḥever probably implies that these texts were owned by the persons who brought them to these sites. We do not know to what extent the scrolls were also used by them, but some comparative evidence is available regarding the use of the Greek language in the same archaeological environment. Thus, in Naḥal Ḥever many Greek documentary texts have been deposited (see *DJD* 27), showing that Greek was in active use, and hence the find of 8ḤevXII gr causes no surprise. The nature of the revision contained in this scroll fits what is otherwise known about the persons who deposited texts in Naḥal Ḥever at the time of the Second Jewish Revolt. On the other hand, active use of the Greek versions of the Pentateuch at Qumran is unlikely, as virtually no Greek documentary texts have been found there. The opisthograph 4QNarrative Work and

Prayer (4Q460) in Hebrew, with a documentary Greek text 4QAccount gr (4Q350) on the verso of fragment 9 is unique, but possibly irrelevant as the Greek text may have been written after the period of occupancy of Qumran by the Qumran community.

The fact that the Greek Scripture texts found in cave 4 in Qumran are from the Torah only may be relevant to our understanding of the distribution of that text and of the community's interest. The identity of many of the texts from cave 7 is unclear.

Greek was in active use in all sites in the Judean Desert, showing an administration conducted in Greek and letters written in that language, with the exception of Qumran. The percentages of Greek texts compared with Semitic texts found in these sites is much larger than that of the Greek texts found at Qumran.

The text of the Greek Bible

If de Lagarde's theory on the history of LXX needed any further support, it is provided by the texts from the Judean Desert. The newly-found texts share important details with the manuscript tradition of LXX known so far, so that all the known Greek texts reflect one single translation, rather than different translations, as suggested by Kahle.[40] Two of the Qumran texts probably reflect the OG better than the manuscript tradition contained in the later uncial manuscripts (4QLXXLev[a], 4QpapLXXLev[b]; the evidence for 4QLXXNum is less clear). By implication, these two texts should also share certain features, but the evidence is too limited.

The differences between the Greek texts from Qumran and Naḥal Ḥever are remarkable. Two of the texts from Qumran provide insights into the early history of LXX as they are probably better representatives of the OG than the later uncials. On the other hand, 8ḤevXII gr, an early Jewish revision of LXX, belonging to the *kaige-*Th group, represents a translation which is typologically later than the uncials and early papyri of LXX, even if the particular copy found in Naḥal Ḥever is earlier than most surviving representatives of LXX. The differences between the types of Greek text found in the two localities reflect the different nature of the groups who deposited the texts there.

The status of the Greek manuscripts from the Judean Desert thus runs parallel to that of the Hebrew manuscripts from the same area. The Hebrew manuscripts from Qumran reflect a variety of textual forms, among them proto-Masoretic texts, while those of the later sites of Naḥal Ḥever, Wadi Sdeir, Murabbaʿat, and Naḥal Ṣeʾelim (as well as the earlier site of Masada) exclusively reflect the proto-Masoretic texts (also named proto-rabbinic texts) later to be contained in MT (to be precise, the texts from the sites other than Qumran are closer to the medieval text than the Qumran proto-Masoretic texts). Similarly, at least some of the Greek texts from Qumran probably reflect an earlier form of Greek Scripture, while 8ḤevXII gr reflects a later Jewish revision deriving from proto-rabbinic Jewish circles. Both the Hebrew and Greek texts from Qumran thus reflect a community that practised openness at the textual level, without being tied down to MT, while the other sites represent Jewish nationalistic circles that adhered only to the proto-rabbinic (proto-Masoretic) text in Hebrew and the Jewish revisions of LXX towards that Hebrew text. The difference between the texts and sites derives partly from their different chronological background, but more so from their different socio-religious background.

NOTES

1 The precarious nature of statistics may be illustrated by the following: the numerous Greek fragments from what is named XHev/Se and which are grouped on two different plates (*DJD* 27, plates XLVIII and XLIX, are numbered XHev/Se 74-169 for the sake of convenience, and likewise Hev/Se? 1-57 are grouped on plates L-LIII in the same volume. It is hard to know how these collections should be accounted for in a statistical analysis. The author responsible for these texts (H. Cotton) did not want to imply that these items have to be counted as respectively 96 and 57 different compositions, and hence they should probably be counted as six different ones, although both types of accounting are imprecise. Many of the fragments in these collections will have belonged to other documents from Naḥal Ḥever published in *DJD* 27, while other fragments must have belonged to different texts, not published in the volume. The collections of fragments known as 1Q69 and 1Q70 are treated similarly. On the other hand, the manifold fragments written in the cryptic A script and recorded by S. J. Pfann as 4Q249a-z were represented by the author as no less than twenty-seven different compositions.

2 Including Ḥever/Seiyal.

3 See N. Lewis, *The Documents from the Bar Kochba Period in the Cave of Letters: Greek Papyri* (Jerusalem: Israel Exploration Society, the Hebrew University, and the Shrine of the Book, 1989).

4 See H. M. Cotton and A. Yardeni, *Aramaic, Hebrew, and Greek Documentary Texts from Naḥal Ḥever and Other Sites, with an Appendix Containing Alleged Qumran Texts (The Seiyâl Collection II)* (*DJD* 27; Oxford: Clarendon, 1997), 134-5; H. M. Cotton and J. Geiger, *Masada II, The Yigael Yadin Excavations 1963-1965, Final Reports, The Latin and Greek Documents* (Jerusalem: Israel Exploration Society and the Hebrew University, 1989); E. Tov with the collaboration of S. J. Pfann, *Companion Volume to The Dead Sea Scrolls Microfiche Edition* (Leiden: Brill, 1995).

5 See Cotton and Yardeni, *DJD* 27, 1-6.

6 See Cotton and Geiger, *Masada II*, 90.

7 E. Larson, in S. J. Pfann, *Cryptic Texts*; P. Alexander and others, in consultation with J. VanderKam and M. Brady, *Miscellanea, Part 1: Qumran Cave 4* (*DJD* 26; Oxford, 2000) 372: 'It is difficult to discern the overall character of the work in its present state of preservation. The major part of the extant fragments is given over to prayer, exhortation, and admonition. It is possible, therefore, that 4Q460 is a collection of psalms somewhat akin to the *Hodayot*. This may be suggested by the paragraphing of material which is clear on fragment 9 and is supported by the fact that the material before the *vacat* is addressed to God while that occurring after the *vacat* is addressed to Israel with little or no intervening narrative to explain the change. If this understanding of the nature of the manuscript is correct, then the person speaking in the first singular in fragment 9 i 2 is some unknown psalmist'.

8 See the arguments developed in my articles 'The Orthography and Language of the Hebrew Scrolls Found at Qumran and the Origin of These Scrolls', *Textus*, 13 (1986), 31-57; 'Hebrew Biblical Manuscripts from the Judaean Desert: Their Contribution to Textual Criticism', *JJS*, 39 (1988), 1-37.

9 The same argument cannot be used for Hebrew and Aramaic. For the Qumran community, Hebrew was *the* central language, even if they left very few documentary texts in that language (the main text showing use of this language within the community, beyond the many literary texts, is 4QRebukes Reported by the Overseer [4Q477]). No Aramaic community texts have been preserved, although the influence of the Aramaic language on the community scribes is evident in many writings.

10 In some instances Yardeni points to joins between the Qumran texts and texts which

definitely derived from Naḥal Ḥever (note especially XḤev/Se papDeed F ar [= XḤev/Se 32] which forms one document together with 4Q347). Furthermore, carbon-14 examinations point to a late date of some documents.

11 This assumption has been rejected by J. Strugnell (February 2000) who stated that the Beduin were questioned very thoroughly regarding the origin of the texts.

12 I. Gallo, *Greek and Latin Papyrology* (Classical Handbook 1; London: Institute of Classical Studies, University of London, 1986), 10; M. Manfredi, 'Opistografo', *Parola del Passato*, 38 (1983), 44-54.

13 See B. Porten and A. Yardeni, *Textbook of Aramaic Documents from Ancient Egypt*, vol. 3 (Jerusalem: Akademon, 1993). Occasionally even a biblical text was re-used, as the Greek P.Leipzig 39 of Psalms (4 CE) has a list on the reverse.

14 C. H. Roberts, *Manuscript, Society and Belief in Early Christian Egypt* (London: British Academy, 1979), 30, n. 1.

15 In his review of O'Callaghan's book (*JBL*, 95 [1976], 459), J. Fitzmyer summarised the evidence appropriately: 'So far the evidence brought forth for the identification remains too problematic and disputed, and the fragments themselves are so small and contain so few Greek letters or words that no certainty can really be arrived at about the identification of them. And so, thus far at least the proposal is unconvincing'.

16 See D. Barthélemy, *Les devanciers d'Aquila* (VTSup 10; Leiden: Brill, 1963) and Tov, *DJD* 8. For further studies, see C. Dogniez, *Bibliographie de la Septante 1970-1993* (VTSup 60; Leiden: Brill, 1995).

17 J. W. Wevers, *Leviticus, Septuaginta, Vetus Testamentum graecum auctoritate academiae scientiarum gottingensis editum*, vol. II.2 (Göttingen: Vandenhoeck & Ruprecht, 1986); id., *Numeri, Septuaginta, etc.*, vol. III.1 (Göttingen: Vandenhoeck & Ruprecht, 1982).

18 J. Ziegler, *Duodecim prophetae, Septuaginta, etc.*, vol. 13 (Göttingen: Vandenhoeck & Ruprecht, 1943; 2nd edn: 1967).

19 The text has been preserved fragmentarily. As a rule, the reconstructions of Skehan and Ulrich in *DJD* 9 are acceptable, but the following ones are in our view questionable: verse 11 [σκηνήν] (LXX: διαθήκην; MT: משכני), verse 12 [θεός] = LXX (MT לאלהים); verse 15 [αὐτοῖς] = LXX (MT בחקתי); verse 15 [ἀ[λλά] (not in MT).

20 Thus P. Walters, *The Text of the Septuagint: Its Corruptions and Their Emendation* (Cambridge: University Press, 1973), p. 226.

21 Thus J. W. Wevers, *Notes on the Greek Text of Leviticus* (SCS 44; Atlanta, GA: Scholars Press, 1997), p. 439 as opposed to his earlier text edition (see n. 12), in which ἀλόητος is adopted.

22 This rendering of LXX was probably influenced by the same factor influencing the addition of τῇ γῇ in 4QLXXLev[a], viz., the unusual phrase ונתתי גשמיכם, 'and I [God] gave their rains'. For the addition of the pronoun, cf. Jeremiah 5.24 (K) הנתן גשם ויורה – τὸν διδόντα ἡμῖν ὑετὸν πρόιμον and Ezekiel 34.26 והורדתי הגשם – καὶ δώσω τὸν ὑετὸν ὑμῖν as well as later in our chapter, Leviticus 26.20: ועץ הארץ – καὶ τὸ ξύλον τοῦ ἀγροῦ ὑμῶν.

23 Likewise, Greek enclitic pronouns, when reflecting Hebrew prepositions, such as לי, usually occur after the nouns, and only rarely before them. Cf. A. Wifstrand, 'Die Stellung der enklitischen Personalpronomina bei den Septuaginta', *Bulletin de la Société royale des lettres de Lund 1949-1950* (Lund: Gleerup, 1950), 44-70.

24 We thus adhere to the view of Ulrich, *DJD* 9, 163 (preceded by Skehan, 'Manuscripts', 158): 'Though none of these readings is accepted into the Göttingen *Leviticus*, it can be argued, on the basis not only of its antiquity but even more of its textual readings, that 4QLXXLev[a] penetrates further behind the other witnesses to provide a more authentic witness to the Old Greek translation'. On the other hand, Wevers, *Notes*, esp. 438-45 suggests that 4QLXXLev[a] reflects a later text.

25 The analysis refers only to the preserved part of the scroll, and not to the reconstructions in *DJD* 9. These reconstructions show that it is often possible to fill in the majority text of LXX, but sometimes these reconstructions are less plausible: 5.21 παριδὼν παρίδῃ (see below); ibid., τ[ὶ; 5.22 ὥστε (τοῦ is possible as well); 5.24 ἤ should possibly be inserted.

26 For a detailed analysis, see H. Stegemann, ΚΥΡΙΟΣ Ο ΘΕΟΣ ΚΥΡΙΟΣ ΙΗΣΟΥΣ: *Aufkommen und Ausbreitung des religiösen Gebrauchs von* ΚΥΡΙΟΣ *und seine Verwendung im Neuen Testament* (Habilitationsschrift, Bonn 1969), pp. 110-33, 194-228.

27 The Aquila fragments of Kings and Psalms of the 5th-6th century CE published by F. C. Burkitt (Cambridge: University Press, 1897) and C. Taylor (Cambridge, 1900); the Psalms fragments of Symmachus of the 3rd-4th century CE published, among others, by G. Mercati, 'Frammenti di Aquila o di Simmaco', *RB*, n.s., 8 (1911), 266-72; POxy. 1007 of Genesis (third century CE; double *yod*); POxy. 3522 of Job (first century CE); and both scribes of 8HevXII gr (first century BCE).

28 PFouad 266b (Rahlfs: 848) of Deuteronomy (the first scribe left spaces filled in with the tetragrammaton by a later scribe) and the Psalms fragments of the Hexapla published by G. Mercati, *Psalterii Hexapli reliquiae* (Vatican, 1958). For a detailed analysis, see Stegemann, ΚΥΡΙΟΣ.

29 Thus all the uncial manuscripts of LXX as well as POxy. 656 of Genesis (2nd century CE); P. Chester Beatty VI (Numbers-Deuteronomy). See W. W. von Baudissin, *Kyrios als Gottesname im Judentum* (Giessen, 1926-1929) and Stegemann, ΚΥΡΙΟΣ, 200-2. The anarthrous use of κύριος, as opposed to that of θεός, shows that this Greek word was probably a direct replacement of an entity without an article, either ΙΑΩ or יהוה.

30 See my article, 'The Socio-Religious Background of the Paleo-Hebrew Biblical Texts Found at Qumran', in: H. Cancik and others (eds), *Geschichte – Tradition: Reflexion, Festschrift für Martin Hengel zum 70. Geburtstag* (Tübingen: Mohr, 1996), vol. 1, pp. 353-74.

31 Origen recognized this feature when stating that the 'most accurate exemplars' of the Greek Scripture wrote the tetragrammaton in Hebrew characters (Migne, *PG*, 12, 1104 [B]).

32 A. Pietersma, 'Kyrios or Tetragram: A Renewed Quest for the Original LXX', in A. Pietersma and C. Cox (eds), *De Septuaginta, Studies in Honour of John William Wevers on His Sixty-Fifth Birthday* (Mississauga, Ont.: Benben, 1984), pp. 85-101. The quote is from p. 98.

33 Stegemann, ΚΥΡΙΟΣ, 197; P. W. Skehan, 'The Divine Name at Qumran, in the Masada Scroll, and in the Septuagint', *BIOSCS*, 13 (1980), 14-44.

34 Among other things Stegemann claims that a transliteration rather than a translation or transcription in Hebrew characters is the natural representation of this proper noun. He also claims that ΙΑΩ cannot be considered a change of an original form out of reverence to the divine name, since the use of the equivalent of יהוה in Greek does not prevent the pronunciation of God's name. The fact that this system is not encountered in later manuscripts of the Greek Bible, as opposed to the other systems, is a sign of originality rather than of its secondary nature.

35 In codex A ἀριθμέω occurs nine times in Numbers 2 as well as in Numbers 3.15, 16 for פקד where the other codices have ἐπισκέπτομαι. For exact details, see Wevers, 'Early Revision', 237*-238*. This equivalent also occurs in all manuscripts of 1 Chronicles 21.6; 2 Chronicles 17.14; 25.5; 26.11.

36 'It is a variant clarifying a Hebraic kind of Greek by a more idiomatic text'. Wevers' text edition of LXX accordingly included ἐπισκέπτομαι.

37 This rendering may be influenced by the phrase ὅλον ὑακίνθινον in Numbers 4.6 where it renders כליל תכלת.

38 Wevers, 'Early Revision', 236 suggests a different reconstruction for the scroll.

39 In this analysis, not all differences between LXX and the scroll are accounted for. Some corrections of the scroll are based on Hebrew readings differing from MT, either in

consonants or the reading tradition of the consonants.

40 The argumentation was used already by Leaney, 'Greek Manuscripts', 293 and Skehan, 'The Biblical Scrolls from Qumran and the Text of the Old Testament', *BA*, 28 (1965), 87-100, esp. 91-2.

FROM NESTLE TO THE
EDITIO CRITICA MAIOR

A CENTURY'S PERSPECTIVE
ON THE NEW TESTAMENT
MINUSCULE TRADITION

Michael W. Holmes

IN 1907 C. R. Gregory, the American-born textual critic whose name is immortalized in our enumeration system for New Testament manuscripts, expressed his conviction that

> the small letter manuscripts are likely some day to give us much information in reference to the history of the text. They are numerous, and range widely through the lands and the centuries. Their lines are likely to close quickly if we succeed in gaining a few certain connections between time and place and handwriting and text form.[1]

Over eight decades later, in 1994, Barbara Aland and Klaus Wachtel expressed their opinion that

> the external criteria of textual criticism must be improved. That is the pressing task of our discipline. [...] In this way we will be able to make up the deficiencies that continue to beset the field of textual criticism at this point. The investigation of the minuscules is for this reason a particularly crucial area of labor: its results will bind together all the manifold other branches of the NT tradition.[2]

This combination of similar tone and chronological distance arouses curiosity regarding the fate and role of the minuscule manuscripts of the New Testament in the intervening period. The publication in 1898 of the first edition of Eberhard Nestle, whose achievements this conference is celebrating, provides a fitting point of departure for a brief examination of the investigation and use of the minuscule manuscripts in New Testament textual criticism over the course of the last century.

I. THE INFLUENCE OF THE MINUSCULES
ON THE NEW TESTAMENT, 1898

It is one of the ironies of history that the minuscule manuscripts of the New Testament, which in the sixteenth century provided the basis for the first published edition of the Greek text, had by the end of the nineteenth century virtually ceased to have any effect on contemporary editions of the text.[3] As evidence of this state of affairs, we may take the first edition of the Nestle text, published in 1898. As is well known, Dr Eberhard Nestle formed his text on the basis of the published editions of Tischendorf, Westcott

& Hort, and Weymouth (replaced after 1901 by that of Bernhard Weiss). As the Alands observe, 'in effect, this purely mechanical system of a majority text summarized the results of nineteenth-century textual scholarship' in an edition that 'on the whole truly represented the state of knowledge of the time'.[4] If we examine the influence of the minuscule witnesses on the four editions utilized by Nestle, we may form some impression of the influence of this importance class of witnesses at the turn of the centuries.

Taking the source editions in reverse order, we may begin with Weiss. Metzger reports that while Weiss relied primarily upon what Hort would have termed intrinsic probability ('His procedure was to go through each New Testament book with a critical apparatus and to consider important textual variants [...] adopting the variants which he regarded as most appropriate to the author's style and theology'), 'the general complexion of Weiss's edition is remarkably similar to that of Westcott and Hort', since Weiss tended to prefer, like Westcott and Hort, readings preserved by Codex Vaticanus.[5]

Weymouth's *Resultant Greek Testament* gives, according to the title page, 'the text in which the majority of modern editors are agreed'. The primary influences on this edition were Lachmann (who used no minuscules at all), Tregelles (who lists just three minuscules, 1, 33, and 69), Tischendorf's eighth editon, Westcott and Hort, the readings of the Revised version (heavily influenced by Westcott and Hort), and commentaries by Lightfoot, Ellicott, and B. Weiss (for Matthew).[6]

Thus far, we see scarcely any influence of the minuscules, a circumstance that changes somewhat in theory but not in practice when we turn to examine the other two sources upon which Nestle drew, namely Westcott and Hort, and Tischendorf.

Hort knows of the existence of some 900 to 1000 cursives, and indicates that 'the full contents of about 150 cursives, besides Lectionaries, may be set down as practically known'.[7] Regardless, however, of how many cursives were known, a far smaller number appears to have been used with any frequency or regularity. When Hort discusses specific cursives, he mentions only seventeen manuscripts. In the Gospels these are (using Gregory's numeration) 33, four members of family 1 (1-118-131-209), four members of family 13 (13-69-124-346), 157, and 565; in Acts and the Catholic epistles, 33, 69, 81, 424, 431, 614, and 876; and in the Pauline letters, 33. Later, when Hort lists what he considers to be the 'primary documents' upon which the text is based, he mentions only two cursives: 33 (for Gospels, Acts, Catholic epistles, and Pauline epistles) and 81 (for Acts).[8] Equally revealing is what Hort writes elsewhere about the relative value of the cursives; it appears that he restricts the role of a cursive to that of giving support to an uncial reading.[9] It is difficult to avoid the conclusion that in practice the cursive manuscripts had virtually no impact on Westcott and Hort's text, which they established virtually in its entirety on the basis of uncial evidence.[10]

With regard to Tischendorf, while it is true, as Gregory says,[11] that in his eighth edition Tischendorf did not neglect the minuscules, it is also appears that they played a distinctly secondary and minor role in his text and apparatus. This is apparent first from the *Prolegomena* itself, which, after devoting over eight pages to a listing of uncial manuscripts, dismisses the minuscules in barely two-thirds of a page of generalities, with only a single manuscript being explicitly identified (Tischendorf 61 = Gregory 81); J. K. Elliott suggests that it may be the only cursive that Tischendorf ever examined.[12]

A glance at randomly chosen pages throughout the apparatus gives some feel for his use of minuscule manuscripts: in the Gospels, one finds only a small group regularly cited, mostly members of Families 1 and 13, along with 33. In Acts, there is 33 (= Tischendorf 13) and 81 (= Tischendorf 61), along with perhaps a dozen others who turn up with some frequency; in the Pauline letters one notices with some regularity 33 (= Tischendorf 17), sometimes with as many as six or eight other minuscules (none, however, cited with any discernible consistency or pattern). It is in the Catholic epistles, perhaps due to the smaller number of uncial manuscripts containing these documents, that one finds the largest number of minuscules cited, at times as many as fifteen or more. Apart, however, from the regular appearance of 33 (= Tischendorf 13), again it is difficult to observe any pattern or consistency of citation.

To be sure, Tischendorf drew upon the evidence of many more minuscules than he explicitly cites, but many of these additional minuscules are effectively hidden from recovery behind the symbols 'al.', 'al. pler.', 'al[10]', etc. Overall, even if one were to completely set aside Tischendorf's well known proclivity for Codex Sinaiticus, it is clear that his text is based virtually exclusively upon the evidence of uncial manuscripts.

Inasmuch as none of the four sources upon which Nestle drew in creating his landmark edition of the Greek New Testament gave any observable weight to the minuscule evidence, it is clear that a text formed on the basis of these sources could not have been shaped by them in any significant way. So, on the shape of the text that (in the words of the Alands quoted above) 'on the whole truly represented the state of knowledge of the time', the minuscules had no discernible influence. Moreover, they had for most users of the Greek New Testament also effectively disappeared from sight. The lack of an apparatus in the widely-used Nestle and Westcott and Hort texts hid virtually all the evidence of any sort from users, and in the only major apparatus where the evidence of more than a few minuscules might be recorded, namely Tischendorf's, much of what was reported was hidden behind abbreviations or summary numbers and therefore unrecoverable with respect to specific manuscripts.

2. FROM NESTLE[1] (1898) TO UBS[4] (1975)

Having thus been displaced from influence by the uncials, the minuscules would not soon recover from their eclipse; indeed, the uncials themselves would soon begin to be displaced somewhat by a new category of evidence then beginning to be discovered, namely the papyri.[13] But the minuscules' loss of influence on printed forms of the text in the late nineteenth century did not mean that they ceased to be of any interest to investigators. At approximately the same time as the first Nestle edition was being produced, a number of not-insignificant studies of minuscule witnesses were forthcoming.

W. H. Ferrar's study of Family 13 (famous for its Lukan placement of the *pericope adulterae*) was published in 1877 by T. K. Abbott. To Ferrar's original four members J. P. P. Martin contributed a fifth in 1886, and Abbott identified additional members of the family in an 1899 article. Meanwhile there appeared in 1893 J. R. Harris's monograph *On the Origin of the Ferrar Group*, which was followed in 1900 by *Further Researches into the History of the Ferrar Group*.[14] On other fronts, one may mention A. V. Valentine Richards, Wilhelm Bousset, H. C. Hoskier (who in 1890 contributed a detailed study of the manuscript now known as 700), and Kirsopp Lake's 1902 study of *Codex I and Its Allies*; meanwhile the report concerning 1739 had been published by von der Goltz in 1899.[15] Many of these scholars' investigations were, in the words of Kirsopp Lake, attempts 'to study groups of minuscule MSS. which were not easily to be classified either as pure Neutral or as pure Western'.[16]

The mention of von der Goltz brings us to a major project underway during the 1890s, a project so large and far-reaching that, to quote Kirsopp Lake again, 'it was generally felt that, until this undertaking had made public its results, it was relatively useless for ordinary persons to engage in detailed research. [...] For more than ten years [...] the critics were marking time'.[17] The project of which I speak, and for which von der Goltz collated 1739, is, of course, that of Hermann von Soden, whose initial volumes appeared between 1902 and 1910, with the volume of text and apparatus following in 1913.[18] The last part of his title, 'auf Grund ihrer Textgeschichte' ('on the basis of its textual history'), is worth noting: von Soden's attempt to comprehend the whole of the New Testament Greek manuscript tradition (or, more precisely, a significant and substantial part of it – about 1200 manuscripts) was a bold and ambitious undertaking, remarkable not only for seeking to provide a very full critical apparatus but at the same time a comprehensive theory with regard to the history of the New Testament text.

What is particularly notable in the present context is the weight and value von Soden gave to the minuscule witnesses in his reconstruction of the history of the text. First, there is von Soden's elevation of the *K* (= Koine) text to a level of importance equal to his *I* (= Jerusalem) and *H* (= Hesychian) texts, a move which automatically gave significant influence to the mass of Byzantine minuscules. Second, and perhaps more significant, there is the important role in the recovery of his *I* text that he accorded to manuscripts 28, 372, 565, and 700, together with the recently-discovered Koridethi codex, Θ, and, to a lesser extent, Codex Bezae, which he devalued because he thought it had been corrupted by the Latin and Syriac versions (one of the few places where the versions entered into his theories). In addition, he thought that Families 1 and 13 comprised important sub-groups of the *I* text.

Had von Soden's theories proved to be convincing, the story I am attempting to trace no doubt would have been significantly different because of the substantial role he allocated to the evidence of the minuscule manuscripts, not only for the history of the text but also for its reconstruction. But the fate of his theories and his apparatus is well known and needs no rehearsal.[19] On the one hand, the Alands rightly note that his 'studies in the Koine text constitute pioneering research [...] Many of the spectacular discoveries made in recent decades may be found anticipated in von Soden's work, sometimes in a well-developed form'. On the other hand, however, with respect to the centerpiece of his theory, the Jerusalem (*I*) text-type, the Alands conclude that 'von Soden's theories belong completely to the world of whim and fantasy'.[20] In other words, the parts of his theory that gave the most prominence and influence to minuscule witnesses proved to be the most problematic as well.

Many of the textual phenomena that von Soden associated with his Jerusalem text were by other scholars increasingly linked instead with Caesarea, especially after the publication of B. H. Streeter's *The Four Gospels*.[21] A key figure was Kirsopp Lake, who followed up a line of inquiry first broached in his 1902 volume on Family 1. He published, often in association with New and/or Blake, a number of monographs and articles on Families 1 and 13, as well as the general question of the 'Caesarean' text; the effort to establish the texts of these families was later carried on by Geerlings. Other notable contributors included Lagrange and Ayuso. In all these attempts to establish a 'Caesarean' or even 'pre-Caesarean' text-type, minuscules such as f^1, f^{13}, 28, 565, and 700[22] played an important role alongside P[45] and Θ.[23] It appears, however, that the evidence collected in the investigation of the 'Caesarean text' has proved to be more enduring that attempts to assess it. What Metzger wrote in 1963 – 'at present the Caesarean text is disintegrating' – has been confirmed by later studies.[24]

Two areas of investigation produced results of more enduring worth. With respect to the text and textual history of the Revelation, the work of H. C. Hoskier and J. Schmid must be mentioned.[25] Because there are fewer papyri and uncial witnesses to the text of the Apocalypse, the minuscules have had a correspondingly greater role in the establishment of its text. But because the textual history of the Apocalypse is unique, the achievements there do not help much in solving the textual puzzles of the rest of the New Testament.

The other area of investigation where substantial gain has occurred involves manuscript 1739. The studies of 1739 (which focused on its text of the Pauline letters) added to our knowledge, in a way that confirmed rather than altered, our understanding of the Alexandrian textual tradition, which the discovery of P[46] had illumined.[26]

If we pause to look back over the half-century or so of activity following the publication of von Soden's text, apparatus, and studies, it is clear that there was some worthwhile work done involving minuscule manuscripts, and for that we must not fail to be grateful. Having rightly expressed our gratitude, however, one may also suggest that apart from the work on the manuscripts of Revelation and on 1739, the accomplishments appear to be almost entirely a matter of accumulation of data; very little of enduring worth was achieved with respect to utilizing this data to further our understanding of the history of the text and its transmission. Even with regard to gathering data, there are some surprising *lacunae*. Leaving aside the large number of minuscules which were registered during these years, which remained almost completely unexplored, one may, for example, notice that a full collation of such an important manuscript as 565 – identified early on as a key witness to the so-called Caesarean text, and listed by Streeter as a primary witness – has never been published. Or, to take another example, manuscript 1582, one of the two oldest members of Family 1 – and like 1739 in that it too is a tenth-century manuscript containing marginal notes and comments copied from its exemplar which suggest links with a very ancient copy of the text possibly associated with Caesarea – is only now being studied in the detail it deserves.[27] The Catholic epistles, which in recent years have become the focus of considerable activity, during this time received essentially no attention at all, and the minuscule manuscripts of Acts fared only marginally better.[28]

If, as it appears, the impact of the minuscules on our understanding of the transmission of the text was only a little more than minimal in the several decades following von Soden, their impact on printed editions of the New Testament during the period we have been surveying was even less. While the thirteenth edition of Nestle (1927) added a critical apparatus, in which a few minuscule witnesses were included, the basis for the text itself remained unchanged – in fact, only at this time was Erwin Nestle finally able to conform the text fully to the majority principle adopted by his father. Although there were in subsequent editions steady improvements to the critical apparatus, the text remained virtually unchanged. Thus up through the twenty-fifth edition of Nestle in 1963 the most widely used edition of the Greek New Testament continued to present the text as established at the turn of the century. Moreover, the improvements to the apparatus should not be allowed to mislead with regard to the perceived value – more accurately, the lack of perceived value – of the minuscules. Their marginal status comes through clearly in the introduction:

the most important Papyri (P) and newly discovered fragments of Majuscules, as 0189, are taken into account; on the other hand only a few of the Minuscules (33, 614, 1 in Ap etc.), occasionally also lectionaries [...] These last witnesses, however, are not generally mentioned beside the great MSS. B, ℵ, etc. (except when all witnesses must be cited), but only where they represent *peculiar* readings' [emphasis added].[29]

The other major hand editions that appeared during this time – those by Vogels (first edition, 1920; fourth edition, 1955), Merk (first edition, 1933; eleventh edition, 1992), and Bover (first edition, 1943; fifth edition, revised by O'Callaghan, 1977) – are heavily influenced by von Soden. To the extent that their texts reflect von Soden's theories and/or influence, they can hardly be viewed as improvements over Nestle, Westcott and Hort, or Tischendorf. With respect to their apparatuses, the minuscules play at most a minimal role, the long lists of minuscules given in the introductions to each of these editions notwithstanding. For even though several hundred minuscules are listed in each edition (Vogels[4] lists 274 minuscules; Merk[9] lists 385; Bover/O'Callaghan[5] lists 360[30]), their actual use is quite uneven. Many are cited only once or a few times, and all are cited so irregularly – one almost wants to say haphazardly – that it is impossible for a user of one of these editions to form an estimation about the character of any particular witness on the basis of its citation in the apparatus.[31]

Matters might appear to have taken a different turn in 1966, when the United Bible Societies published the first edition of its *Greek New Testament*, with an entirely new text and apparatus. In contrast to earlier apparatus, which generally buried all but a few select (and very traditional) minuscules under group signs or symbols, the apparatus to this new edition listed for each variation unit a very large number of minuscules. Thus it might be possible to form an impression that the minuscules had been accorded a more significant role in the formation of this edition, with respect to both text and apparatus.

This impression, however, would be misleading for two reasons. First, the text itself, as is well known, is only a little different from that of Westcott and Hort some eight decades earlier, and the major changes from Westcott and Hort were heavily influenced by a class of evidence not available to them, namely the papyri. Thus whereas the text of the nineteenth century was dominated by the uncials, the new text was dominated by the papyri. The minuscules remained essentially without influence, five decades after von Soden and nearly seven after Nestle[1].

Second, because the edition gives no information about the manuscripts other than contents and date, it is nearly impossible for a user to form any sort of estimation of the value of the minuscule evidence presented. That is, while users are provided with a great deal of data, they are given no assistence in assessing its significance or worth.[32]

In short, this new edition, while giving the appearance of change and progress, actually does little to change matters with regard to the intelligent use of the minuscules. Furthermore, because the apparatus would (apart from alterations required by editorial changes to the text) remain essentially unchanged through the third edition in 1975 (only in the third corrected edition of 1983 would the apparatus be substantially revised), the neglect of the minuscules in popular hand editions begun before the turn of the century would continue throughout the 1970s as well.

The presentation of the minuscules in the UBS apparatus exemplifies a fundamental difficulty that has plagued our discipline throughout its history: the problem (in the words of Barbara Aland) of 'the haphazard selection of manuscripts for' – and, I would add, presentation of evidence in – 'editions of the text'.[33] Ever since Erasmus, textual critics have utilized, it seems (to quote Aland again), 'what was immediately available. [...] The selection of manuscripts, especially of minuscule manuscripts, has been determined by the limitations of [...] knowledge of these manuscripts, and therefore by chance'.[34] One consequence of this is that, as Wisse observes, 'except in von Soden's inaccurate and unused pages, the minuscules have never been allowed to speak':

Though the casual user of a critical text of the Greek New Testament has been well provided for, the expert and serious student is at the mercy of highly selective and incomplete *apparatus critici*. This situation could only be defended if the task of establishing the best possible New Testament text had been accomplished, and if the history of the transmission of that text was clear. But it is not.

At a time when, as Wisse describes it, 'lower criticism seems to have become the study of what to do when Codex Vaticanus and P[75] disagree', he rightly observes that 'a study of the minuscules could change this situation. They promise hope of discovering the several lines of textual tradition which fed into the tenth and eleventh centuries'.[35]

3. FROM NA[26] (1979) TO THE *EDITIO CRITICA MAIOR* (1997): THE MINUSCULES IN RECENT RESEARCH

Even as Wisse wrote, efforts were underway that would at least begin to change the situation he described. Indeed, Wisse himself was involved in one of them, the International Greek New Testament Project (IGNTP). The IGNTP would bear long-delayed fruit in 1984 and 1987 with the publication of its two volumes on the Gospel of Luke.[36] Here for the first time was a critical apparatus which provided the user with the full evidence of 128 minuscule manuscripts, in addition to the more familiar papyri and uncials. Moreover, the minuscules were not only well represented in this edition, in contrast to all earlier ones, but those included were for the first time the result of a comprehensive and systematic selection process, again in contrast to haphazard or ad hoc procedure of earlier editions. The Claremont Profile Method (CPM), developed by Wisse and Paul McReynolds on the basis of the pioneering work of Colwell and others, was the tool that made this reasoned and systematic selection of the minuscule evidence possible.

The shortcomings of the volume have been well-documented (sometimes unfairly so) in various reviews, and need not be rehearsed here.[37] As a thesaurus of readings, the volumes are a spectacular advance. As a means to understand the history of the text, they fall somewhat short. In part this is due to the abbreviated introduction to the volume. For each manuscript, we are informed of its present location and date, the equivalent von Soden (and occasionally Tischendorf) identification symbol, and the family to which von Soden assigned it. Beyond this, we are only told that the 128 minuscules 'have been selected by means of the Claremont Profile Method' (p. vi). Overall, the reader is given little of the kind of help for which Wisse pleaded in his monograph on the CPM.[38] Did the CPM confirm von Soden's analysis, or require a reclassification? What groups do the 128 manuscripts presented represent? We are not told; for this we must go to Wisse's monograph.[39] Thus while the minuscules have in this edition at last been given their rightful place, they have not yet been given their full voice.

The scholars associated with the IGNTP were not the only researchers giving serious attention to the minuscules. Indeed, beginning in the late 1970s, one notices a level of activity that, in comparison to the previous several decades, appears remarkable. Let us survey briefly some of this attention to the minuscules during the last two decades.

The work of J. Duplacy provided a basis for C.-B. Amphoux's 1981 dissertation and a series of articles between 1978 and 1984 (one in conjunction with Duplacy himself, and one with B. Outtier) in which Amphoux explored manuscript groupings and the textual history of the Catholic epistles.[40] In all of these investigations minuscules played a central role, especially 2138.[41] W. L. Richards, also in a dissertation and a series of articles, has given attention to the question of how to classify manuscript witnesses, especially minuscules, in the Johannine letters.[42] T. C. Geer, Jr, investigated the relationship of a dozen minuscules in his study of Family 1739 in Acts.[43] One may also mention here recent efforts to publish some form of the Byzantine textual tradition.[44]

Perhaps the most significant work involving the minuscules was underway at the Institute for New Testament Textual Research. The appearance in 1979 of the new apparatus for the twenty-sixth edition of the Nestle-Aland text offered the early fruits of efforts in Münster to isolate from the mass of Byzantine minuscules those which preserved different forms of the text. In contrast to the twenty-fifth edition (which cited only a few minuscules, and only when they represented 'peculiar readings'), the new apparatus included a small number of minuscules in the category of 'constant witnesses'.[45] Ten of these witnesses (189, 365, 1243, 1505, 1506, 1704, 1881, 1884, 2464, 2495) are not cited in hand editions outside the Nestle-Aland/UBS tradition.[46]

The changes in the minuscule evidence in the apparatus for the twenty-seventh Nestle-Aland edition are relatively modest. In the Gospels, one manuscript was dropped (1010), while three were added (579, 2427, 2452), the last two of which are not cited in hand editions outside the Nestle-Aland/UBS tradition. In Acts and the Pauline letters, none were dropped, one was downgraded (2495), and one was added (1505), while in the Catholic epistles one was upgraded (1505). The total number of minuscules not cited in hand editions outside the Nestle-Aland/UBS tradition rises to twelve. A statement in the Introduction to the twenty-seventh edition could apply to the twenty-sixth as well: 'minuscules which are of importance for the history or establishment of the text have been included among the consistently cited witnesses for the first time' (p. 47*). Here we may see a modest effort to move beyond noticing only those minuscules that agree with the great uncials.[47]

The basis for the identification of these new witnesses 'of importance for the history

[...] of the text', and perhaps this new appreciation for the value of the minuscules reflected in Nestle-Aland[27], is the work done at the Institute for the *Text und Textwert* series, the first volume of which appeared in 1987.[48] Like the CPM, the series was intended to redress the problem of the haphazard selection of manuscripts. It presents the evidence of (essentially) all the surviving Greek manuscript evidence for a particular segment of the New Testament for a selected series of test passages (98 for the Catholic epistles, 251 for the Pauline letters, 104 for Acts, and 196 for Mark). Thus it is now possible to survey systematically the minuscule evidence for substantial portions of the New Testament, and thus to begin to utilize it in more than a random and arbitrary manner. Not only does it enable researchers to identify the minority of manuscripts that differ from the Byzantine text type found in the bulk of the minuscules, but it also permits more detailed investigation of the not-insignificant variations within the Byzantine tradition itself.[49]

The series offers, as it were, raw data, presented essentially without interpretation. The real promise, however, lies in what might be learned from this raw data about the history of the text. An early and outstanding example of what can be done with this data is Barbara Aland's 1986 study of a group of minuscules (notably 2138, 1505, 1611, and 2495) that preserve a form of text closely associated with the Greek *Vorlage* of the sixth-century Harclensian Syriac version of the Catholic epistles.[50]

Now there has appeared Klaus Wachtel's major study of the history of the Byzantine text of the Catholic letters.[51] Wachtel presents in Part I the results of his investigation of the origin and spread of the Byzantine text of the Catholic epistles. It is, he argues, the result of a long process (traces of which are evident already in the earliest period) of smoothing and standardization, and reached its definitive form only in the ninth century. It is very unlikely, he continues, that its origin is the result of a formal recension of the fourth century; instead, one must reckon with a series of editorial revisions (i.e. *diorthosis*) in every epoch. His findings substantially relativize the idea of 'text types', to the extent that they are associated with recensional theories, and highlight the importance of minuscules not only for textual history but for determining the original text. Of course Wachtel does not limit himself to the minuscules in the course of his study, yet because of the considerably fewer number of papyri and uncials available in the Catholic epistles, the minuscules necessarily play a substantial role in his study, and indeed, at times provide decisive evidence. Here we have an outstanding example of how the minuscules can contribute to a fuller understanding of the history of the transmission of the New Testament text.

The *Text und Textwert* series, together with the many other specialized projects sponsored by the Institute, while of undoubted value in their own right, are at the same time means towards a more overarching goal, the production of a major critical edition of the New Testament. It was thus with no small degree of anticipation that the first fascicle of the *Novum Testamentum Graecum, Editio Critica Maior*, or ECM, as it quickly came to be referred to, appeared in 1997.[52] By and large, it has lived up to its expectations; with respect to the clarity, usability, and appearance of its layout, it has perhaps exceeded them.

Of particular interest to us is its coverage of the manuscript tradition. The edition presents the evidence in full of 182 continuous-text manuscripts (9 papyri, 25 majuscules, 148 minuscules), an unprecedented degree of coverage, the more so as the chosen 182 provide representative coverage of all 522 complete manuscripts and larger fragments of the Catholic epistles. Equally impressive is its presentation of textual variants. The ECM offers, for example, in James 2.1-11 sixty-nine variation units (where Nestle-Aland[27] has twenty-two and UBS[4] one); in James 3.13-18, the count is ECM thirty-nine, Nestle-Aland[27] twelve, and UBS[4] none.

Even more astonishing, however, is the claim that the method of selection utilized in choosing these witnesses – a process involving the use of ninety-eight text passages in the Catholic letters, in conjunction with full collations to verify the initial results – 'guarantees reliably that the critical apparatus contains all the known readings which have appeared in the history of the text from its earliest beginnings through the formation and final establishment of the Byzantine text'.[53] Even if this claim is perhaps just the least bit optimistic,[54] it is nonetheless essentially accurate.

We must not miss the significance of what has been achieved by the IGNTP/Luke and especially the ECM/James volumes. Here, for the first time, for parts of the New Testament at least, our discipline is finally beginning to accomplish what is generally regarded as the basic first step of textual criticism: a full examination of the surviving evidence.

4. WHY BOTHER WITH THE MINUSCULES?

What value is it to us and to the discipline, one might ask, to achieve this particular goal? The question becomes the more pointed when it is observed that the tremendous work and data involved in the production of the ECM has resulted in the publication of a critical text that differs from Nestle-Aland[27] at only two minor points (both of which mark a return to the text of Westcott and Hort). As one reviewer put it, instead of 'an excitingly different new text', there was only 'a damp squib – merely a very modest revision'.[55] So why bother, some may ask, especially as there is such an apparent consensus today with respect to the printed text, and in view of our rich resources in terms of early papyri and uncials?

Of the points that might be touched on in response to this question, one has already been mentioned: the need for a comprehensive and persuasive history of the text. This remains to be written for much of the New Testament. Wachtel has shown what such an effort might look like, and has demonstrated the critical role the minuscules must play in such an endeavor. A second point is suggested by Aland and Wachtel: utilizing the history of the text to improve the external criteria used to assess readings.[56]

For now, let me suggest and develop another point, one that starts with the claim of apparent consensus regarding the printed text, and the wealth of papyri and uncial resources. This apparent consensus is deceptive, because it is not fully grounded in a persuasive and fully-developed history of the New Testament text. Indeed, regarding the history of the text there is no consensus today, only competing hypotheses. This is not to say that our widespread preference for one particular textual tradition is wrong, but it is to remind us that the basis upon which that preference rests is seriously incomplete, and will remain so until we have been more successful at reconstructing the history of the transmission of the text.

In doing so, the minuscules will play a key role. This is because – and here we come to the other point I alluded to above – the apparent 'richness' of our resources 'is in part illusory', to quote J. Neville Birdsall, who reminds us of how many minuscules can be linked into families or groups, each of which can be traced back to an uncial ancestor.[57] We have, however, virtually no extant manuscripts which correspond to these ancestors: the expected links are missing. In short, the minuscules remind us of how incomplete is our knowledge of the early and later centuries with respect to the history of the text. This is a point often denied by ignoring it. We are unable to link the minuscule families and groups with extant manuscripts, but we nonetheless put forth hypotheses that suggest direct connections and thus protect and preserve both the status of those extant manuscripts and the present theory that there are only a few major textual traditions, a theory congenial to our printed texts. But suppose, as an alternative, that there are *not* direct connections, as the absence of connecting links could suggest? This would imply that the missing ancestors of these minuscule groups would be not descendents of existing textual traditions, but parallel lines of descent. That this hypothesis is not merely hypothetical is indicated by instances such as Matthew 27.16-17 involving the variant 'Jesus Barabbas', preserved in Θ, Family 1, and a handful of other minuscule and versional witnesses (notably the Curetonian Syriac).

In a sense, the question here is analogous to the debate within the biological community about how to envision evolution, whether in terms of a tree (in which the many small twigs and branches are all linked to the central trunk through a small number of main branches) or a bush (in which most of the many branches connect directly with the root stem).[58] At the present time in New Testament textual criticism, we seem to work with the 'tree' model: the many small twigs and branches (i.e. individual manuscripts and small families, represented primarily by the minuscules) connect through a small number of main branches (the three or four main textual traditions, represented by the major uncials and papyri) to the central trunk (i.e. the archetype). In contrast, the 'bush' model suggests the image of a much larger number of branches (i.e. individual manuscripts, families, and other small groupings), not all of which will have survived, springing up almost directly from the root stem (i.e. the archetype). The 'tree' model not only fits well with, but also (in a bit of potentially circular argumentation) contributes to, our present hypotheses. However, the 'bush' model relativizes matters somewhat. If there were more lines of descent than have survived among the papyri and early uncials, then the authority and influence we have granted to those papyri and uncials must be reconsidered. The minuscules both force us and help us to do this. And for these reasons, we must, as we seek to learn the history of the New Testament text, give due weight to what have for too long been neglected resources, the minuscule manuscripts of the New Testament.

NOTES

1 Caspar René Gregory, *Canon and Text of the New Testament* (New York: Charles Scribner's Sons, 1907), p. 371.
2 Barbara Aland and Klaus Wachtel, 'The Greek Minuscule Manuscripts of the New Testament', in *The Text of the New Testament in Contemporary Research: Essays on the Status Quaestionis*, ed. by Bart D. Ehrman and Michael W. Holmes, SD, 46 (Grand Rapids: Eerdmans, 1995), pp. 43-60 (p. 58).

3 To be sure, the Textus Receptus continued to be reprinted (for example, the British and Foreign Bible Society did not abandon it until 1904). The focus of this essay, however, is on new editions of the text, and thus reprints of existing editions fall outside its scope.

4 Kurt Aland and Barbara Aland, *The Text of the New Testament: An Introduction to the Critical Editions and to the Theory and Practice of Modern Textual Criticism*, trans. by Erroll F. Rhodes, 2nd edn (Grand Rapids: Eerdmans; Leiden: Brill, 1989), p. 20.

5 Bruce M. Metzger, *The Text of the New Testament: Its Transmission, Corruption, and Restoration*, 3rd edn (New York and Oxford: Oxford University Press, 1992), pp. 136-7; cf. Aland and Aland, *Text*, pp. 26, 103.

6 Richard Francis Weymouth, *The Resultant Greek Testament*, 3rd edn (London: James Clarke, 1905), pp. ix-xii.

7 Brook Foss Westcott and Fenton John Anthony Hort, *The New Testament in the Original Greek*, 2 vols (Cambridge: Macmillan, 1881; 2nd edn, 1896), [II]: *Introduction* [and] *Appendix*, pp. 76, 77.

8 Westcott and Hort, *Introduction*, pp. 154-5, 192.

9 Westcott and Hort, *Introduction*, pp. 253-6.

10 Furthermore, while Hort writes that the 'large amount of present ignorance respecting the contents of cursives is much to be lamented', inasmuch as 'valuable texts may lie hidden among them', nevertheless it was his opinion that 'nothing can well be less probable than the discovery of cursive evidence sufficiently important to affect present conclusions in more than a handful of passages, much less to alter present interpretations of the relations between the existing documents' (Westcott and Hort, *Introduction*, p. 77).

11 Constantinus Tischendorf, *Novum Testamentum Graece, editio octava critica maior*, 3 vols (Leipzig: Giesecke & Devrient, and Hinrichs, 1869-94), III: *Prolegomena*, by Casper Renatus Gregory (1894), p. 33.

12 J. K. Elliott, *A Bibliography of Greek New Testament Manuscripts* (Cambridge: University Press, 1989), p. 90.

13 The manuscript identification system of von Soden, for all its difficulties or faults (for example, reifying as part of a manuscript's identification number a feature subject to debate, namely its date), did have an often-overlooked advantage: it was neutral with regard to script and writing material, in a way that the Gregory system is not. The style of writing, or the kind of material used for a manuscript, are not automatic indicators of its significance, either for the recovery or the history of the text.

14 W. H. Ferrar, *A Collation of Four Important Manuscripts of the Gospels*, ed. by T. K. Abbott (Dublin: Hodges, Foster, and Figgis; London: Macmillan, 1877); J. P. P. Martin, *Quatre manuscrits du N.T. auxquels on peut ajouter un cinquième* (Paris: Maisonneure et Cie, 1886); K. Lake, 'Some New Members of the "Ferrar Group" of MSS of the Gospels', *JTS*, 1 (1899), 117-20; J. Rendel Harris, *On the Origin of the Ferrar Group* (London, C. J. Clay, 1893); J. Rendel Harris, *Further Researches into the History of the Ferrar Group* (London: C. J. Clay, 1900).

15 The work of Valentine-Richards was published posthumously: *The Text of Acts in Codex 614 (Tisch. 137) and its allies*, with an introduction by J. M. Creed (Cambridge: University Press, 1934); Wilhelm Bousset, *Textkritische Studien zum Neuen Testament*, Texte und Untersuchungen, 11.4 (Leipzig: J. C. Hinrichs, 1894); H. C. Hoskier, *A Full Account and Collation of the Greek Cursive Codex Evangelium 604* (London: Nutt, 1890); Kirsopp Lake, *Codex I of the Gospels and its Allies*, Texts and Studies, 7/3 (Cambridge: University Press, 1902); E. von der Goltz, *Eine Textkritische Arbeit des zehnten bezw. sechsten Jahrhunderts*, Texte und Untersuchungen, 2.4 (Leipzig: J. C. Hinrichs, 1899).

16 K. Lake, *The Text of the New Testament*, 6th edn, revised by Silva New (London: Rivingtons, 1928), p. 77.

17 Lake, *Text*, pp. 77-8.

18 Hermann von Soden, *Die Schriften des Neuen Testaments in ihrer ältesten erreichbaren Textgestalt hergestellt auf Grund ihrer Textgeschichte*, Part I: *Untersuchungen*, 3 vols (Berlin, 1902-10; 2nd edn, Göttingen: Vandenhoeck & Ruprecht, 1911); Part II: *Text mit Apparat* (Göttingen: Vandenhoeck & Ruprecht, 1913).

19 For a full description (as well as incisive criticisms) of von Soden's textual theories, see Lake, *Text*, pp. 77-84; also Frederik Wisse, *The Profile Method for Classifying and Evaluating Manuscript Evidence*, Studies and Documents, 44 (Grand Rapids: Eerdmans, 1984), pp. 9-18; Metzger, *Text*, pp. 139-43; Aland and Aland, *Text*, pp. 22-3.

20 Aland and Aland, *Text*, pp. 23, 66.

21 Burnett Hillman Streeter, *The Four Gospels: a Study of Origins* (London: Macmillan, 1924).

22 These manuscripts are listed by Streeter as primary and secondary witnesses; in addition, he mentions 1424, 544, 157, 1071, and 1604 (*Four Gospels*, p. 108). Note also B. H. Streeter, 'Codices 157, 1071 and the Caesarean Text', in *Quantulacumque, Studies Presented to Kirsopp Lake*, ed. by Robert P. Casey, Silva Lake, and Agnes K. Lake (London: Christophers, 1937), pp. 149-50; J. N. Birdsall, '406, a Neglected Witness to the Caesarean Text', in *Studia Evangelica*, ed. K. Aland and others, Texte und Untersuchungen, 73 (Berlin: Akademie-Verlag, 1959), pp. 732-6; M. M. Carder, 'A Caesarean Text in the Catholic Epistles?', *NTS*, 16 (1969-70), pp. 252-76 (who utilized manuscript 1243 as a collating base).

23 For bibliography on the search for the 'Caesarean' text, see Bruce M. Metzger, 'The Caesarean Text of the Gospels', in *Chapters in the History of New Testament Textual Criticism*, by Bruce M. Metzger, New Testament Tools and Studies, 4 (Grand Rapids: Eerdmans; Leiden: Brill, 1963), pp. 42-72; Larry W. Hurtado, *Text-Critical Methodology and the Pre-Caesarean Text: Codex W in the Gospel of Mark*, SD, 43 (Grand Rapids: Eerdmans, 1981).

24 Metzger, 'The Caesarean Text of the Gospels', p. 67; cf. Hurtado, *Text-Critical Methodology*, pp. 43-5, 83, 88-9.

25 H. C. Hoskier, *Concerning the Text of the Apocalypse*, 2 vols (London: B. Quaritch, 1929); J. Schmid, *Studien zur Geschichte des griechischen Apokalypse-Textes*, 3 vols (Munich: Zink, 1955-6).

26 See Otto Bauernfeind, *Der Römerbrieftext des Origens*, Texte und Untersuchungen, 14.3 (Leipzig, 1923); Kirsopp Lake, J. de Zwaan, and Morton S. Enslin, 'Athos, Laura 184 [B'64] (Greg. 1739; von Soden α78), Acts, Catholic Epistles, Paul', in *Six Collations of New Testament Manuscripts*, ed. by Kirsopp Lake and Silva New, Harvard Theological Studies, 17 (Cambridge, Mass.: Harvard University Press; London: Oxford University Press, 1932), pp. 141-219; G. Zuntz, *The Text of the Epistles: a Disquisition upon the Corpus Paulinum*, The Schweich Lectures of the British Academy, 1946 (London: British Academy, 1953); K. W. Kim, 'Codices 1582, 1739, and Origen', *JBL*, 69 (1950), pp. 167-75; J. Neville Birdsall, 'A Study of Ms. 1739 of the Pauline Epistles and its Relationship to Mss. 6, 424, 1908, and M' (unpublished doctoral thesis, University of Nottingham, 1959); J. N. Birdsall, 'The Text and Scholia of the Codex von der Goltz and its Allies, and their Bearing upon the Texts of the Works of Origen, especially the Commentary on Romans', in *Origeniana, premier colloque international des études origeniennes*, Quarderni di 'Vetera Christianorum', 12 ([Bari]: Istituto di Letteratura Cristiana Antica, Università di Bari, 1975), pp. 215-22; W. J. Elliott, 'An Examination of von Soden's I b2 Group of MSS' (unpublished master's thesis, University of Birmingham, 1969) [includes collations of 1739, 2298, 323, 322, 440, 216, 1872, 1149, 491, 35, 935]; W. J. Elliott, 'The Relationship between 322 and 323 of the Greek New Testament', *NTS*, 14 (1968), pp. 271-81.

27 See Amy S. Anderson, 'Codex 1582 and family 1 of the Gospels: the Gospel Of Matthew' (unpublished doctoral thesis, University of Birmingham, 1999).

28 Collations of eight manuscripts were published by Kenneth W. Clark, *Eight American Praxapostoloi* (Chicago: University of Chicago Press, 1941).

29 Nestle-Aland, *Novum Testamentum Graece*, 25th edn (Stuttgart: Württembergische Bibelanstalt, 1963), 'Introduction', p. 70*.

30 The numbers are those given by J. K. Elliott, *A Survey of Manuscripts Used in Editions of the Greek New Testament*, Supplements to Novum Testamentum, 57 (Leiden: Brill, 1987), pp. xxi, xxviii, xxx.

31 These observations apply as well (*mutatis mutandis*) to the apparatus of both A. Souter's edition of the New Testament (1st edn, 1910; 2nd edn, 1947) and S. C. E. Legg's volumes on Mark (1935) and Matthew (1940).

32 Cf. Wisse: 'the reader is left completely in the dark as to what value he should attach to the minuscule evidence. Listing witnesses with variants in this way is confusing rather than enlightening' (*Profile Method*, p. 15 note 25; cf. Appendix III, pp. 134-40).

33 Aland and Aland, *Text*, p. 317.

34 Aland and Aland, *Text*, p. 317. See earlier K. Aland, 'The Present Position of New Testament Textual Criticism', in *Studia Evangelica*, ed. by K. Aland and others, Texte und Untersuchungen, 73 (Berlin: Akademie-Verlag, 1959), pp. 717-31 (pp. 724-6).

35 Wisse, *Profile Method*, p. 5.

36 *The New Testament in Greek III: The Gospel According to St. Luke*, ed. by the American and British Committees of the International Greek New Testament Project, 2 vols (Oxford: Clarendon Press, 1984, 1987).

37 Cf. William L. Peterson, in *JBL*, 107 (1988), pp. 758-62; J. H. Petzer, 'The Oxford Greek New Testament: A Review Article', *Neotestamentica*, 23 (1989), pp. 83-92; Barbara Aland, in *JTS*, 42 (1991), pp. 201-15.

38 See Wisse, *Profile Method*, pp. 138-40, esp. point 6.

39 See Wisse, *Profile Method*, pp. 47-90 (Chapter V, 'The Classification of 1385 Lucan Manuscripts on the Basis of the Profile Method') and pp. 91-116 (Chapter VI, 'The Manuscript Groups and Clusters').

40 For details see Léon Vaganay, *An Introduction to New Testament Textual Criticism*, 2nd edn, rev. and updated by Christian-Bernard Amphoux, trans. by Jenny Heimerdinger, English edn amplified and updated by Amphoux and Heimerdinger (Cambridge: University Press, 1991), pp. 23, 35, 71-3, 97.

41 Manuscript 2138 is one of a family of about twenty manuscripts, three of which (614, 1505 and 2495) are among the 'consistently' or 'frequently' cited witnesses in the Catholic letters in NA[27]. For the status of these witnesses in NA[26], see its 'Introduction', p. 53*.

42 W. L. Richards, *The Classification of the Greek Manuscripts of the Johannine Epistles*, Society of Biblical Literature Dissertation Series, 35 (Missoula, MT: Scholars Press, 1977); W. L. Richards, 'Textual Criticism on the Greek Text of the Catholic Epistles: A Bibliography', *Andrews University Seminary Studies*, 12 (1974), pp. 103-11; W. L. Richards, 'The Present Status of Text Critical Studies in the Catholic Epistles', *Andrews University Seminary Studies*, 13 (1975), pp. 261-72; W. L. Richards, 'The New Testament Greek Manuscripts of the Catholic Epistles', *Andrews University Seminary Studies*, 14 (1976), pp. 301-11; W. L. Richards, 'Gregory 1175: Alexandrian or Byzantine in the Catholic Epistles?', *Andrews University Seminary Studies*, 21 (1983), pp. 155-68.

43 Thomas C. Geer, Jr, *Family 1739 in Acts*, SBL Monograph Series, 48 (Atlanta, GA: Scholars Press, 1994).

44 Zane C. Hodges and Arthur L Farstad, *The Greek New Testament According to the Majority Text* (Nashville: Thomas Nelson, 1982; 2nd edn, 1985); Maurice A. Robinson and William G. Pierpont, *The New Testament in the Original Greek According to the Byzantine/Majority Textform* (Atlanta: Original Word Publishers, 1991).

45 In the Gospels these are f^1 and f^{13} plus eight others (28, 33, 565, 700, 892, 1010, 1241, 1424); in Acts, nine manuscripts (33, 81, 323, 614, 945, 1175, 1241, 1739, 2495), with eleven others cited occasionally; in the Pauline epistles, twelve MSS (33, 81, 104, 365, 630, 1175, 1241, 1506, 1739, 1881, 2464, 2495), with seven others cited occasionally; in the Catholic epistles, eight manuscripts (33, 81, 323, 614, 630, 1241, 1739, 2495), with eleven others cited occasionally.

46 According to the information presented in Elliott, *Survey*.

47 Cf. Wisse, *Profile Method*, p. 2, note 2.

48 Kurt Aland and others, *Text und Textwert der griechischen Handschriften des Neuen Testaments, I: Die Katholischen Briefe*, 3 vols, ANTF, 9-11 (Berlin and New York: De Gruyter, 1987); *II: Die Paulinischen Briefe*, 4 vols, ANTF, 16-19 (Berlin and New York: De Gruyter, 1991); *III: Apostelgeschichte*, 2 vols, ANTF, 20-1 (Berlin and New York: De Gruyter, 1993); *IV: Die Synoptischen Evangelien, 1. Das Markusevangelium*, 2 vols, ANTF, 26-7 (Berlin and New York: De Gruyter, 1998).

49 For a more detailed description see Aland and Aland, *Text*, pp. 317-37.

50 In Barbara Aland, *Das Neue Testament in syrischer Überlieferung I: Die grossen Katholischen Briefe*, ANTF, 7 (Berlin and New York: De Gruyter, 1986), pp. 41-90.

51 Klaus Wachtel, *Der byzantinische Text der katholischen Briefe: eine Untersuchung zur Entstehung der Koine des Neuen Testaments*, ANTF, 24 (Berlin and New York: De Gruyter, 1995).

52 *Novum Testamentum Graecum Editio Critica Maior, Vol. IV: Catholic Letters. Installment 1: James. Part 1: Text; Part 2: Supplementary Material*, ed. by Barbara Aland and others for the Institute for New Testament Textual Research (Stuttgart: Deutsche Bibelgesellschaft, 1997).

53 *Novum Testamentum Graecum Editio Critica Maior*, 'Introduction', p. 12*.

54 In response to a query from Bart Ehrman, Klaus Wachtel admitted that the claim 'might have been formulated a bit more carefully'. He rightly points out, however, 'that the tradition of the first millennium is adequately represented, because all known witnesses relevant for the study of this epoch are included in the apparatus'. See Klaus Wachtel, 'Response to Four Reviews of the James Volume of the Editio Critica Maior', *TC: A Journal of Biblical Textual Criticism* [http://shemesh.scholar.emory.edu/scripts/TC], 3 (1998), paragraph 6; Bart D. Ehrman, 'Novum Testamentum Graecum Editio Critica Maior: An Evaluation', *TC: A Journal of Biblical Textual Criticism* [http://shemesh.scholar.emory.edu/scripts/TC], 3 (1998), paragraph 9.

55 J. K. Elliott, in *Novum Testamentum*, 50 (1998), pp. 195-204 (p. 198).

56 Barbara Aland and Klaus Wachtel, 'The Greek Minuscule Manuscripts of the New Testament', p. 56.

57 J. N. Birdsall, 'The New Testament Text', in *The Cambridge History of the Bible*, vol. 1: *From the Beginnings to Jerome*, ed. by P. R. Ackroyd and C. F. Evans (Cambridge: University Press, 1970), pp. 308-77 (pp. 316, 315).

58 See, for example, Stephen Jay Gould, *Wonderful Life: The Burgess Shale and the Nature of History* (New York and London: W. W. Norton, 1989), pp. 35-8.

THOROUGHGOING
ECLECTICISM

J. K. Elliott

ALL MODERN PRINTED critical editions of the Greek New Testament are eclectic editions, that is to say, their editors have selected the text from a number of manuscripts at their disposal. No single manuscript is followed throughout. The printed text thus produced is the creation of the modern editors and does not reproduce in its entirety the actual wording of any one particular manuscript.

In most cases the text in our printed editions follows the reading of the majority of extant manuscripts; where variation occurs certain manuscripts are commonly relied on, typically Codex Sinaiticus and Codex Vaticanus together with other early witnesses. When these favourite manuscripts are divided over a particular variant, most editors have to resort to principles based on internal evidence or intrinsic probability before reaching their decision on what to print.

The *Textual Commentary*, edited by Bruce Metzger to accompany the third edition of the United Bible Societies' *Greek New Testament*[1] and, later, revised for the fourth edition, gives us an insight into the decision-making process in only a small part of the Greek New Testament (NT), but at least this shows us how its committee functioned. We see that the editors, although basically wedded to the originality of the Westcott and Hort type of text, nonetheless had to cope with several difficult textual problems. Sometimes the text printed is described in the *Commentary* as the 'least unsatisfactory reading'.

What has been said so far shows how the majority of textual critics grudgingly apply principles of intrinsic probability to text-critical problems only when their preferred external evidence is unhelpful or ambiguous. 'Thoroughgoing eclecticism', by contrast, operates the other way round, that is to say, the initial questions asked when variants need to be resolved are: Which reading is in accord with our author's style or language or theology? and Why and how did the alternative readings occur?

'Thoroughgoing eclecticism' is one of the names given to the procedure for dealing with textual variation that prefers to debate each and every variant wherever these arise and to reach a decision not only on the reading most likely to represent the original words of the original author but also on the motives why the variant(s) arose. These decisions are reached largely independently of the manuscript support for the variants.

Thoroughgoing eclecticism is not the only term used to define this process. 'Rational criticism' was once used,[2] but it gives the unfortunate impression that alternatives are less than rational! 'Radical eclecticism' is another way of describing the process, but again that may be unfortunate in implying that it is irresponsible and extreme. 'Rigorous criticism' has also been coined. In recent years this methodology has been associated with the name of G. D. Kilpatrick, in whose footsteps I proudly walk. Kilpatrick himself preferred the term 'consistent eclecticism' and that has much to commend it. It means that there is a consistent application of text-critical principles based on internal criteria and intrinsic probability.

Kilpatrick stands in a line of text critics such as C. H. Turner, A. C. Clark and A. E. Housman and others. Although we are seemingly in a minority among text-critics (itself a minority discipline within biblical studies), many modern scholars seem to respect or follow, sometimes unconsciously, the position we uphold and promote. Many biblical scholars inevitably find themselves confronted with textual variation in their studies. Those who write commentaries regularly address such matters. I note that the recent International Critical Commentaries on Matthew[3] and Acts[4] pay due attention to matters text-critical and in many instances adopt a reading at variance with current printed Greek Testaments and in favour of a reading preferred on internal grounds.

Thoroughgoing eclecticism applies certain criteria to assist its decision-making process. It is not subjective, as some detractors might erroneously suppose. The criteria are generally principles known to and applied (when forced to do so) by most textual critics. They are indeed the principles that editors look at when a cult of the best manuscripts founders if their favourites disagree. Even the majority text adherents have to look to other solutions to variants when the majority itself is divided. Thoroughgoing critics would broadly support lists of principles such as those found in the *Textual Commentary*[5] and in many handbooks on textual criticism.[6] I have set out the working principles on several occasions including the 1995 Metzger *Festschrift*.[7] These include a recognition of the following: that parablepsis can cause the accidental shortening of the text being copied; that scribes were often prone to harmonize parallel texts which seemed to be divergent; and that scribes tended to improve upon perceived breaches of acceptable standards of language.

All such criteria are usually hedged around with qualifying comments such as 'other things being equal'. For instance, I often wish to defend the principle (at variance with that found in many of the textbooks) that a reading giving the *longer* text is more likely to be original than a shortened version, and this is based on the argument that scribes often accidentally, but sometimes deliberately, reduced the text that they were copying. Such a principle would not be applied mechanically. One would not defend the originality of a longer reading if its language or style or theology were at odds with the context. (Examples of the reverse – the lengthening of a text – can of course also be found where it seems that a gloss has been incorporated into the text being copied, or that there has been harmonizing to a longer parallel.)

We may ask what is it that makes thoroughgoing critics differ from others who are prepared to recognize the validity of internal principles? Put simply, it is that the thoroughgoing critic applies the criteria in a consistent, thoroughgoing (but not doggedly mechanical) way. In theory, this means that if the arguments on style, usage and other internal criteria point to a reading that may be supported by only a few manuscripts, then that reading should nonetheless be accepted. In practice I must now admit that one feels more comfortable with the favoured reading if it is not found only in a solitary late minuscule or in only a versional witness.[8] We may note, however, that certain readings lacking the support of normally favoured manuscripts are to be found even in the critical editions themselves. For example, in UBS[4] one may note at random the text printed at Acts 4.33 (supported by P[8] maj.); at Hebrews 7.1 (C* maj.); at Hebrews 12.3 (the reflexive with A P 104 *pc*); and at Revelation 18.3 (with 1006[c] and 2329 virtually alone). See also Hodges and Farstad's Majority Text edition[9] – especially in Revelation. The UBS text still persists in printing a conjecture at Acts 16.12 supported (perhaps) by some versional evidence.[10]

If the arguments based on accepted principles lead to the apparent originality of an allegedly weakly attested reading, so be it; I would still like that reading to be given a fair hearing. Furthermore, in these days when an increasingly larger representation of Byzantine minuscules are being collated and these collations published,[11] a reading once thought to be read only by a single minuscule may find itself supported now by other manuscripts.

Thoroughgoing textual criticism has been accused of betraying a cavalier attitude to manuscripts, of treating manuscripts as mere carriers of variants or of not appreciating the history of the text. Such criticisms are unjustified. Thoroughgoing eclecticism is alert to the maxim that knowledge of manuscripts must precede knowledge of readings. We would be unwilling to accept the originality of a reading found in a manuscript whose known proclivities made certain of its readings improbable as the original text of the New Testament author. For example, a manuscript with a proven track record for expanding the divine names with a liturgical formula would be an unreliable witness in favour of a variant giving a longer, as opposed to a shorter, form of a divine name. Similarly, a manuscript whose scribe was regularly erratic in its spelling or another whose scribe exhibited conspicuous carelessness in word order would not be relied on when supporting, perhaps uniquely, an orthographical variant or a reading offering a changed sequence of words, even where in other circumstances such a variant might be seen as theoretically acceptable as the original.

We are also alert to the history of the text. Kilpatrick in particular made great play of the history of the Greek language in the early Christian centuries. He was ready to argue that scribes, influenced by stylistic guidelines about what was and what was not considered acceptable standards of Greek (such as those published by the neo-Atticists), would adjust elements in New Testament manuscripts whose Greek did not conform to these standards. He was also fond of recalling Vogels' observation that all the genuine (i.e. meaningful) variants in our *apparatus* were known from before AD 200 – in other words, virtually the whole fund of our known variants was in existence prior to the date of the overwhelming number of extant manuscripts. This is in a sense a negative fact, in that it denies the validity of attempts to seek a purer text in older existing witnesses, the bulk of which are not earlier than the fourth century, and it renders external evidence of secondary importance to internal evidence, but it is nonetheless a position that does pay due attention to verifiable observations concerning the history of the text. Kilpatrick too was prepared to accept the broad lines of textual divisions, Alexandrian, Western, Byzantine and the like, because these are largely irrelevant to attempts to seek the original text. Codex Washingtoniensis or Codex Bezae are sometimes the bearers of the original text; likewise the Byzantine text is sometimes correct against the Alexandrian tradition.

I am nevertheless aware of problems in the method. To express it at its crudest: thoroughgoing eclectic critics when confronted by a variant look at all the appearances of the feature (grammatical, linguistic, theological, stylistic and so on) as appropriate;

J. K. Elliott

they then sort out the non-conformist items with the aid of the *apparatus*; they finally produce a generalized statement concerning the writer or the problem. The snag is that conformity is recognized in firm examples, and one needs to be aware that hitherto unknown variants can suddenly be produced that make firm instances into new variation units. But, in reality, the principles seem to yield results. One example I regularly cite is at Mark 10.1 where our critical texts print συμπορεύονται ... ὄχλοι thereby giving a unique instance of the plural of ὄχλος in Mark against forty or so firm instances of the singular. While exegetes dependent on the printed text may seek possible reasons for this unexpected plural, thoroughgoing critics will note from a full apparatus the variant συνερχεται ... ὁ ὄχλοι and will accept it as the original reading here because it is a text consistent with Mark's practice, perhaps arguing that the aberrant plural noun was introduced as a harmonization to the Matthaean parallel. The manuscripts reading the plural (Sinaiticus, Vaticanus and the bulk of Byzantine witnesses) and the manuscripts reading the singular (mainly 'Western') are of marginal importance in the editing of Mark 10.1 if the premises are consistently applied by thoroughgoing critics.

The oft-heard criticism of deductions such as the above is that the opposite could also occur, namely that authors are not necessarily consistent and that Mark, in this example, was as capable of writing a plural as a singular. In other words, the argument goes that it is conceivable that scribes, alert to an author's prevailing characteristics, restored to his text a rigidity not originally there if he noted that the manuscript being copied moves away from the author's habitual style. For this to be put into effect requires our acceptance of a great perspicacity on the part of a copyist, who, unlike modern scholars, would not have access to concordances, statistical word lists and grammars which allow us to identify and monitor features of the biblical authors' styles. I find such reasoning improbable not only in relation to the example given in Mark 10.1 but to other comparable places, although I concede that it is a counter-argument which needs to be kept in one's sights.

Another example I have used elsewhere[12] is at Mark 6.41 where Metzger's *Commentary* tells us that μαθητής is more likely to be followed by a dependent genitive than not, and that when variation occurs between the inclusion and exclusion of the possessive, the former is likely to be original. With that reasoning I agree, because various groups and individuals in the Early Church had their own disciples, but as Christianity developed, the word 'disciples', unless further distinguished, tended to mean *Jesus*' disciples. Scribes, finding what they would consider to be redundant possessives after the word 'disciples' when referring to Jesus' disciples, often felt able to delete the pronoun, a practice consistent with a general tendency to restrict the allegedly excessive use of post-positional possessives in Koine Greek. There is thus much variation in our manuscripts in this matter. As far as αὐτοῦ with μαθηταὶ is concerned, variants occur at, among other places, Matthew 8.21; 15.36; 16.5; 17.10; 19.10; 20.17; Luke 12.22; 20.45; John 20.30. The UBS committee was unprepared to follow its own principle at Mark 6.41 or at these other verses. There the UBS text either omits or brackets the possessive, often because the characteristic brevity of the Alexandrian text commended itself to the committee.

Jakob van Bruggen's plea in the present volume that the Byzantine text-type be allowed an unprejudiced hearing when one is assessing textual variation is welcomed by thoroughgoing eclecticism. As far as his examples are concerned, I accept his arguments in favour of the longer text at Luke 24.42. I am less convinced by his arguments at Luke 2.33, 43 where he is favourably disposed to the originality of the readings found in the majority text. (I would consider it more likely – and in accord with the development of the virgin birth tradition – that Luke's glaringly conspicuous references to Jesus' father at 2.33, and to Jesus' parents at 2.27, 41,[13] 43 are original, and that all the variants at these verses are secondary, even if scribes were not always consistent in eliminating other, less obvious, references to Joseph as Jesus' father elsewhere in the context.) Again we are confronted by questions of who is likely to be the more consistent – Luke or the scribes; again, I prefer to grant that a creative author rather than a mere copyist will demonstrate the greater degree of stylistic consistency. However, the important point to note is that van Bruggen agrees with the principles of thoroughgoing textual criticism in assessing the variation units along the lines of Lukan style and scribal tendencies. His argument is not predetermined by a defence of a particular text-type; his conclusions merely confirm his observations that the Byzantine text-type may sometimes support the original reading, and that therefore its voice and contribution are worthy of being listened to. I may beg to disagree with some of van Bruggen's textual decisions – but open debate is encouraged by thoroughgoing eclecticism.

Perhaps I have been too defensive – even negative – about thoroughgoing eclecticism in the light of misgivings that have been readily expressed about the method. I should now end by indicating just five of its positive benefits:

(1) It looks at textual problems independently of the manuscript support, which can be refreshingly open and instructive.
(2) It identifies an author's style, or first century usage, and can help us catalogue distinctive linguistic features, as C. H. Turner did with Mark.[14] Such approaches sit comfortably with more recent investigations into narrative and audience-reception theories.
(3) It takes seriously transcriptional probability. It makes readers aware of the reasons why and how scribes altered the texts they were copying.
(4) It not merely seeks the original text – a will o' the wisp, according to some like Amphoux – but, perhaps more importantly, it also tries to find likely motives for the perceived changes throughout the tradition, a view compatible with Ehrman's[15] or Parker's[16] recent views on the validity of *all* variants as part of the living text.
(5) Evidence is produced before conclusions are drawn over a variation unit.

Even text-critics unsympathetic to thoroughgoing eclecticism recognize that such investigations enhance our knowledge and understanding of the language and style of the biblical authors, and of the pressures on scribes that encouraged their changing the text of their exemplars, even if these critics are unwilling to accept the text-critical conclusions to which such investigations logically lead them.

J. K. Elliott

NOTES

1 Bruce M. Metzger, *A Textual Commentary on the Greek New Testament* (London and New York: United Bible Societies, 1971; 2nd edn, Stuttgart: Deutsche Bibelgesellschaft and the United Bible Societies, 1994).

2 Following M.-J. Lagrange, *Introduction à l'étude du Nouveau Testament Deuxième partie: Critique textuelle II: La critique rationnelle* (Paris: Gabalda 1935), but what he was advocating is not what is now understood by thoroughgoing criticism.

3 W. D. Davies and Dale C. Allison Jr., *The Gospel according to St. Matthew*, 3 vols (Edinburgh: T. & T. Clark, 1988-97).

4 C. K. Barrett, *The Acts of the Apostles* 1 (Edinburgh: T. & T. Clark, 1994).

5 Bruce M. Metzger, *A Textual Commentary on the Greek New Testament*, 2nd edn, pp. 12*-14*.

6 Keith Elliott and Ian Moir, *Manuscripts and the Text of the New Testament* (Edinburgh: T. & T. Clark, 1995), esp. ch. 3; Bruce M. Metzger, *The Text of the New Testament* (New York and Oxford: University Press, 1992), pp. 195-206; Josep O'Callaghan, *Introducció a la Crítica Textual del Nou Testament* (Barcelona: Claret, 1997), esp. ch. 6.

7 'Rational Criticism and the Text of the New Testament', *Theology*, 75 (1972), 338-43. 'Can We Recover the Original New Testament?', *Theology*, 77 (1974), 338-53. 'Plaidoyer pour un éclecticisme intégral appliqué à la critique textuelle du Nouveau Testament', *RB*, 74 (1977), 5-25. 'In Defence of Thoroughgoing Eclecticism in New Testament Textual Criticism', *Restoration Quarterly*, 21 (1978), 95-115. 'An Eclectic Textual Commentary on the Greek Text of Mark's Gospel', in *New Testament Textual Criticism: Its Significance for Exegesis* (Essays in Honour of Bruce M. Metzger), ed. by E. J. Epp and G. D. Fee (Oxford: Clarendon Press, 1981), pp. 47-60. 'Textkritik Heute', *Zeitschrift für die Neutestamentliche Wissenschaft*, 82 (1991), 34-41; 'Thoroughgoing Eclecticism in New Testament Textual Criticism', in *The Text of the New Testament in Contemporary Research: Essays on the* Status Questionis. *A Volume in Honor of Bruce M. Metzger*, ed. by Bart D. Ehrman and Michael W. Holmes, SD 46 (Grand Rapids: Eerdmans, 1995), pp. 321-35.

8 C. Landon, *A Text Critical Study of the Epistle of Jude*, JSNT Supplement 135 (Sheffield: Academic Press, 1996), is prepared, on grounds of thoroughgoing textual criticism, to promote as original several readings in Jude that have only meagre external attestation.

9 Zane C. Hodges and Arthur L. Farstad, *The Greek New Testament according to the Majority Text* (Nashville, Camden, New York: Nelson, 1985).

10 Thoroughgoing critics see no reason to resort to conjectures. That the original text has survived in our 5,000 extant Greek manuscripts and in the numerous versional manuscripts is a cornerstone of the method. Conjectures seldom achieve scholarly consensus. They are a free rewriting of the New Testament and thoroughgoing critics would not resort to conjecture as a way of removing firm examples of, say, a grammatical feature that appears to sit uncomfortably within an otherwise coherent feature in the corpus being examined. By contrast, G. D. Fee, a onetime vehement opponent of thoroughgoing criticism, is prepared to argue in his *New International Commentary* on I Corinthians (Grand Rapids: Eerdmans, 1987) that the verses commonly numbered I Corinthians 14.34-5 are not original to Paul's letter, but were added later – and that in the face of the fact that there is no manuscript evidence in favour of the shorter text. (But now see C. Niccum, 'The Voice of the Manuscripts on the Silence of Women: the External Evidence for I Corinthians 14.34-5', *NTS*, 43 (1997), 242-55.)

11 For example in the occasional series *Text und Textwert der griechischen Handschriften des Neuen Testaments* (Berlin and New York: De Gruyter).

12 J. K. Elliott, '*Mathetes* with a Possessive in the New Testament', *Theologische Zeitschrift*, 35 (1979), 300-4.

13 Van Bruggen does not discuss the variants in these two verses.

14 In his 'Notes on Markan Usage', in *JTS*, recently reprinted in J. K. Elliott (ed.), *The Language and Style of the Gospel of Mark* (Leiden: Brill, 1993) = *Novum Testamentum Supplements* 71.

15 Bart D. Ehrman, *The Orthodox Corruption of Scripture* (New York and Oxford: University Press, 1993).

16 D. C. Parker, *The Living Text of the Gospels* (Cambridge: University Press, 1997).

THE MAJORITY TEXT
WHY NOT RECONSIDER ITS EXILE?

Jakob van Bruggen

I GREW UP with a Bible translation based on the Nestle-Aland text; as a theological student I was educated with that same text. At first I based my work as a New Testament scholar and teacher on the newest editions of this new textus receptus, and together with my students I use this edition even today as the most important available scientific collection of textual materials.

It was not until 1975 that I found time for an independent investigation of the issue concerning the NT text. During the preparation of my lecture on the Ancient Text of the New Testament[1] I retained my admiration and respect for the Nestle text, but I lost my confidence in the theory behind the earlier editions and in the theory behind the decisions of the UBS committee that moulded the later form of the Nestle text.

At that moment I knew nothing about the American defenders of the Majority Text.[2] Later on I met them, and as a continental scholar I succeeded in convincing Zane C. Hodges and Arthur L. Farstad that their edition had to be compatible with the reigning Nestle text. A special second critical apparatus was added to their edition to make visible *all* the differences with that text and thus keeping the door open for discussion and dialogue.

From 1980 onwards I was involved in the publication of commentaries on the Gospels. I decided to give the Majority readings a fair chance among other readings. I became more and more convinced of the non-secondary character of those readings, and at the same time came to understand that neither harmonization nor conflate readings can be used as a criterion in evaluating manuscripts.[3]

The notion that the Byzantine Text has exclusive characteristics is coming under greater criticism. Klaus Wachtel concludes that we can find harmonizations and readings that make the text easier in every sort of manuscript, although not always on the same scale.[4]

Why then is there such a strong tendency to discredit the Majority Text? Our knowledge of the text before the fourth century is based on a small and arbitrary cluster of heterogenous (fragmentary) manuscripts that survived.[5] Scientifically, we have no decisive materials for or against the Majority Text in the first three centuries, just as we have no decisive materials from those centuries for any text-type, assuming that we can actually speak about *types* of text.[6] Things would be different if the existence of a Lucian recension could be proved, but that recension is in effect only an axiom. Kobus Petzer concluded that there must have been such a recension,[7] but his argument is dependent on proving that the Byzantine Text was really based upon a recension, but at this point his reasoning is circular. Although Kurt Aland defended the idea of an

Antiochean (Lucian) recension in the book *Text*,[8] this idea is no longer defended in the edition of the Catholic Epistles.[9] Wachtel's study denies the influence of such textual recensions completely.[10] If, then, the Byzantine Text is not the product of a later recension, there is reason to reconsider its exile.

We find the Majority Text to be more elaborate and explicit in less relevant semantic details, such as the possessive pronoun or the more abundant use of the titles of God and Jesus. These details cannot be mapped in a systematic way, neither can they be explained by the hypothesis of redaction: perhaps this phenomenon can more easily be understood in reverse: philologians inadvertently brought more consistency to the Egyptian text by skipping explicit details which, on account of a preference for a smoother text, were better omitted.[11]

But what about its *versteintes* (petrified) character[12] as Kurt Aland typified it? Aland's choice of words is suggestive. The Majority Text has many internal differences, albeit on a smaller scale than the Egyptian Text, but what does 'petrified' mean? Can one throw away the Nestle text because within a hundred years it proved to be a 'petrified' text compared with the Majority edition? Let us look at things from a different viewpoint. In the first three centuries the Greek New Testament was a living, modern part of the liturgy in Greek-speaking churches. Hence it underwent the mishaps of a bible translation that is in use in churches. Many smaller changes crept in because people felt that some words were antiquated. We can therefore expect the text of the New Testament to change more during the first centuries, when it was read in the churches as a living, modern text, than in the later centuries when it was already experienced as an ancient, antiquated text with its own distinctive characteristics at a linguistic level. After two or three centuries the distance between the original text or translation has become too wide for small modernizations and then we see a far more precise and conservative maintenance of text and translation. The bible translation prepared by Martin Luther underwent many changes in the printed editions of the first centuries of its existence: today, however, Luther's translation is either printed in its original state, or modified to form, a quite new edition, no longer advertised as the original Luther translation. What else can we expect in the first three centuries, in Greek-speaking areas, than a text that is at first less constant than later on?

Are there doctrinal influences? Although it is not so difficult to choose a few examples of variants to prove that the text underwent doctrinal influences in the first centuries, it cannot be proven when we take the whole set of variants in the surviving manuscripts. There have been doctrinally edited manuscripts,[13] but their influence clearly was not so great. In my opinion there is perhaps one exception: due to the spread of the Marcionite manuscripts in combination with the existence for a certain time of a Marcionite liturgy, it is possible that this resulted in incidental damages to other manuscripts of Luke (the Lord's Prayer[14] and the Ascension story). Those damages were mostly repaired later on by corrections in the damaged manuscripts.[15]

Can we use the criteria for evaluating variants to prove that the Byzantine Text is secondary?

Firstly, to do so we have to take the whole set of comparable variants. For example: when at certain points the Byzantine Text has a longer reading, it is not yet proven that this text in comparable situations always has a longer reading. When we take negative selection criteria (harmonization, lectio facilior, and so on) and apply them to the

Byzantine Text, we can certainly illustrate that the Byzantine Text is wrong at many points. However, when we do the same with other texts, we have a comparable result, and when we repeat this process with positive criteria (shorter readings, more difficult readings, and so on) we again get the same results.

Secondly, the set of criteria that we have cannot systematically and scientifically be applied.[16] We always have to make a choice between criteria that lead to contradictory results in the process of evaluation when applied at the same time. For example: a longer reading is sometimes more difficult; a reading that seems to be harmonizing externally (comparing three gospels) is sometimes disharmonizing internally (within the pericope of that specific gospel), and so on. We see in the report of the decisions of the UBS committee that the scarcely hidden decisive factor behind the choice of applied criteria is always at the external level (older, better manuscripts against the later and more deteriorated manuscripts).

Thirdly, the variant that can best explain the origin of all the other variants is the best one. Due to the above-mentioned problems it is difficult to execute this rule in practice, but when we take the text-type as a whole, it is a well-known fact that the easiest way to organize a collation of manuscripts is to start with the Byzantine Text.[17] Why deny that this text as a whole gives the best answer to the first maxim of modern criteria for selection of variants?

The whole issue of textual criticism depends upon how wide or narrow one's viewpoint is. The huge volumes of materials coming from Münster are impressive and I admire with thankfulness the results that are of use to everyone. It is, however, clear that the choice against the Byzantine Text already had been made before the materials were investigated.[18] The thousand *Teststelle* were formulated to continue the exile of the Byzantine Text and not to reconsider it. In fact they obscure a view of the true character of many Byzantine readings by sending all variant readings, without a single exception, into exile simply because *some* of its variant readings, a thousand or so, are condemned.

I have experienced that there are so-called Majority readings which have the stamp of originality right on their foreheads. Let me give only two examples:

1. Luke 2.33. Most manuscripts have the reading 'Joseph and his mother' (Ἰωσὴφ καὶ ἡ μήτηρ αὐτοῦ). This expression is philologically incorrect because it is ambiguous in meaning: it is unclear whether the mother of Jesus or the mother of Joseph himself is meant. In a number of manuscripts the expression is correct: 'his father and his mother' (ὁ πατὴρ αὐτοῦ καὶ ἡ μήτηρ). At the same time the expression 'Joseph and his mother' in 2.43 (most manuscripts) has a philologically more correct and unambiguous variant 'his parents' (οἱ γονεῖς). Those more correct variants can be found in the more ancient manuscripts and they are considered to be original by modern textual criticism. The reasoning is that the majority reading ('Joseph and his mother') has a doctrinal background: it tries to avoid the impression that Joseph should be the real father of Jesus ('his father and his mother'; 'his parents'). Petzer[19] discusses Luke 2.33 twice in his book, and he sees the majority readings as protecting the (later) doctrine of the virgin birth of Jesus. Looking only to the two places that attract attention when starting from the Nestle text, this seems a reasonable explanation. However, looking somewhat further in this passage and coming from another viewpoint, this explanation can be

falsified completely. Nearly all the manuscripts maintain in Luke 2.27, 41 the expression 'his parents' (οἱ γονεῖς) and in Luke 2.48 Mary (!) speaks to Jesus (in all the manuscripts) about 'your father and I' (ὁ πατήρ σου κἀγω). It is not reasonable to suppose that scribes took away two doctrinally problematic readings and maintained another three in the same passage! On the other hand, the two variants are the only two places in this passage where the expression is semantically somewhat ambiguous ('Joseph and his mother') and invites philological clarification. The readings of the majority of the manuscripts in Luke 2.33 and 2.43 bear the stamp of originality against the corrections in some older manuscripts.

2. Luke 24.42. In a limited number of manuscripts and in many modern translations we miss the words that are found in most of the manuscripts 'and [a piece] of a honey-comb' (καὶ ἀπὸ μελισσίου κήριου). It is very difficult to suppose that those words were added by some scribes. Which reason would they have had to do something as unusual as adding a completely new element to the text? Nor can it be a gloss that crept into the text, because it cannot be a meaningful gloss in the margin of the shorter verse 42. It is, however, easy to understand that twenty-one letters were unintentionaly skipped in the copying of a manuscript where they formed one line (καὶ ἀπὸ μελισσίου κήριου καὶ λαβὼν ...), because of homoioarcton.[20] In the *Textual Commentary* on the UBS Greek New Testament[21] we find at this point an example of the circular reasoning which is so frequently used in the modern establishment of the text. At first the possibility of homoioarcton is passed over in silence. Without comment we find the remark that it must be an 'obvious interpolation': 'for it is not likely that [these words] would have fallen out of so many of the best representatives of the earlier text-types'. Once the best, always the best, it would seem. But how is one to explain this rather strange inter-polation? The *Textual Commentary* says: 'Since in parts of the ancient church honey was used in the celebration of the Eucharist and in the baptismal liturgy, copyists may have added the reference here in order to provide scriptural sanction for liturgical practice.' However, Luke 24.42 is not about the eucharist or baptism at all! The disciples present to the Lord 'a piece of broiled fish'. How is it possible that copyists, reading about broiled fish, had an association with Eucharist or Baptism? And supposing that they did make this strange association, why did they introduce the honey into the text and not the broiled fish into the liturgy of the Eucharist? The honey that inadvertently dripped away in some early manuscripts is nevertheless spared in the majority of the manuscripts and provides sufficient flavour to reconsider their exile!

Sometimes the return of the Majority Text is seen as a threat.[22] Why be afraid? Why not respect the whole of the tradition? If only the voice of the Majority Text were allowed to sing again in the chorus of text-types! I am not pleading for solo performance. I am sure that the voice of this text, when heard freed from a hundred years of prejudice, will be strong enough to regain appreciation. It is time to end this cold war against a type of text that has been in exile for too long.

NOTES

1 Jakob van Bruggen, *De tekst van het Nieuwe Testament* (Groningen: De Vuurbaak, 1976); translation: *The Ancient Text of the New Testament* (Winnipeg: Premier, 1976).
2 See for a survey of the revival of the Majority Text: Daniel B. Wallace, 'The Majority-Text

Theory: History, Methods and Critique', *Journal of the Evangelical Theological Society*, 37 (1994), 185-215. Also Daniel B. Wallace, 'The Majority Text and the Original Text: are They Identical?', *Bibliotheca Sacra*, 148 (1991), 151-69; Daniel B. Wallace, 'Historical Revisionism and the Majority Text Theory: the Cases of F. H. A. Scrivener and Herman C. Hoskier', *NTS*, 41 (1995), 280-5; and Daniel B. Wallace, 'The Majority Text Theory: History, Methods, and Critique', in *The Text of the New Testament in Contemporary Research. Essays on the Status Quaestionis: A Volume in Honor of Bruce M. Metzger*, ed. by B. D. Ehrman and M. W. Holmes, SD 46 (Grand Rapids: Eerdmans, 1995), pp. 297-320. See also Gordon D. Fee, 'The Majority Text and the Original Text of the New Testament', in *Studies in the Theory and Method of New Testament Textual Criticism*, SD 45, ed. by Eldon Jay Epp and Gordon D. Fee, SD 45 (Grand Rapids: Eerdmans, 1993), pp. 183-208.

3   W. Franciscus Wisselink, *Assimilation as a Criterion for the Establishment of the Text: A comparative Study on the Basis of Passages from Matthew, Mark and Luke* (Kampen: Kok, 1989). Wilbur N. Pickering, 'Conflation or Confusion', in *The Identity of the New Testament Text*, rev. edn (Nashville: Nelson, 1980), pp. 171-200.

4   Klaus Wachtel, *Der byzantinische Text der katholischen Briefe. Eine Untersuchung zur Entstehung der Koine des Neuen Testaments*, ANTF, 24 (Berlin: De Gruyter, 1995), p. 87.

5   The papyri, although mostly found in Egypt, are nevertheless representative for the textual situation in the whole church in the 2nd century according to Eldon Jay Epp, 'The Significance of the Papyri for Determining The Nature of the New Testament Text in the Second Century: A Dynamic View of Textual Transmission', in *Gospel Traditions in the Second Century. Origins, Recensions, Text, and Transmission*, ed. by William L. Petersen (Notre Dame: University of Notre Dame Press, 1989), pp. 71-103. He therefore complains that the New Testament Text in the twentieth century has not considerably changed after the publication of the papyri: E. J. Epp, 'The New Testament Papyrus Manuscripts in Historical Perspective', in *To Touch the Text: Biblical and Related Studies in Honor of Joseph A. Fitzmyer*, ed. by Maurya P. Horgan and Paul J. Kobelski (New York: Crossroad, 1989), pp. 261-88. Barbara Aland rejects this complaint: Barbara Aland, 'Das Zeugnis der frühen Papyri für den Text der Evangelien', in *The Four Gospels 1992: Festschrift Frans Neirynck*, ed. by F. Van Segbroeck et al., Bibliotheca Ephemeridum Theologicarum Lovaniensium 100, vol. 1 (Leuven: Peeters, 1992), pp. 325-35. Philip Wesley Comfort, *The Quest for the Original Text of the New Testament* (Grand Rapids: Baker, 1992), p. 142, tries to substantiate the programme of Epp by proposing many changes to the Aland text. One of his examples is Luke 23.34a (according to Comfort this passage has to be omitted because it is missing among others in P^{75}). However, it is precisely this passage which Joël Delobel ('Luke 23.34a: A Perpetual Text-Critical Crux?', in *Sayings of Jesus: Canonical & Non-Canonical. Essays in Honour of Tjitze Baarda*, ed. by William L. Petersen et al. (Leiden: Brill, 1997), pp. 25-36) defends as authentic.

6   Doubts about the concept of text types are also expressed by Barbara Aland, 'Neutestamentliche Textforschung, eine philologische, historische und theologische Aufgabe', in *Bilanz und perspektiven gegenwärtiger Auslegung des Neuen Testaments: Symposion zum 65. Geburtstag von Georg Strecker*, ed. by Friedrich Wilhelm Horn, Beihefte zur Zeitschrift für die neutestamentliche Wissenschaft, 75 (Berlin: De Gruyter, 1995), pp. 7-29 (esp. 10-15).

7   Kobus Petzer (= J. H. Petzer), *Die Tekst van die Nuwe Testament. 'n Inleiding in die basiese aspekte van die teorie en praktyk van die tekskritiek van die Nuwe Testament*, Hervormde Teologiese Studies, suppl. 2 (Pretoria: Universiteit van Pretoria, 1990), pp. 76-8.

8   K. Aland and B. Aland, *Der Text des Neuen Testaments. Einführung in die wissenschaftlichen Ausgaben sowie in Theorie und Praxis der modernen Textkritik* (Stuttgart: Deutsche Bibelgesellschaft, 1982), pp. 74-5.

9 Kurt Aland (ed.), *Text und Textwert der griechischen Handschriften des Neuen Testaments. I. Die katholischen Briefe*, ANTF 9-11, 3 vols, in Verbindung mit Annette Benduhn-Mertz und Gerd Mink (Berlin: De Gruyter, 1987), II.1, pp. VII-VIII.

10 See also B. Aland, 'Neutestamentliche Textforschung', pp.23-4.

11 Peter M. Head, 'Observations on Early Papyri', *Biblica*, 71 (1990), 247 agrees with the conclusions of E. C. Colwell and J. R. Royse that 'omission is the more common scribal habit. If early scribes were more likely to omit words and phrases from their texts (for whatever reasons) it follows that we should not prefer the shorter reading, but rather prefer the longer reading (other factors being equal)'.

12 See K. Aland, *Die katholischen Briefe*, II.1, pp. VII-VIII.

13 See Eusebius, *Historia Ecclesiastica* 5, 28.17.

14 The hypothesis of J. W. Burgon, *The Revision Revised* (London: John Murray, 1883), J. Van Bruggen, 'Abba, Vader! Tekst en toonhoogte van het Onze Vader', in *De Biddende kerk*, ed. by C. Trimp (Groningen: Vuurbaak, 1979), pp. 9-42, and C.-B. Amphoux, 'La révision Marcionite du "Notre Père" de Luc (11,2-4) et sa place dans l'histoire du texte', in *Recherches sur l'histoire de la bible Latin*, ed. by R. Gryson and P.-M. Bogaert, Cahiers de la RTL, 19 (Louvain-la-Neuve: Univ. Fac. Théologie, 1987), pp. 105-21, that the shorter form of the Lord's Prayer in Luke 11 was produced by Marcion is denied by J. Delobel, 'The Lord's Prayer in the Textual Tradition', in *The New Testament in Early Christianity*, ed. by J. M. Sevrin, Bibliotheca Ephemeridum Theologicarum Lovaniensium, 86 (Leuven: Peeters, 1989), 293-309 and by T. Baarda, 'Een marcionitische corruptie?', *Nederlands Theologisch Tijdschrift*, 44 (1990), 273-87.

15 The influence of marcionite readings is minimalized through the study of John J. Cableaux, *A Lost Edition of the Letters of Paul. A Reassessment of the Text of the Pauline Corpus Attested by Marcion* (Washington: The Catholic Biblical Association of America, 1989). See for Marcion also Ulrich Schmid, *Marcion und sein Apostolos. Rekonstruktion und Historische Einordnung der marcionitischen Paulusbriefausgabe*, ANTF, 25 (Berlin: De Gruyter, 1995).

16 In my opinion this situation offers a partial explanation for the instability of the variant letter-ratings in the successive editions of the *UBS Greek New Testament*. Regarding that instability Kent D. Clarke, *Textual Optimism. A Critique of the United Bible Societies' Greek New Testament*, JSNT SS 138 (Sheffield: Sheffield Academic Press, 1997).

17 T. R. Ralston, 'The "Majority Text" and Byzantine Origins', *NTS*, 38 (1992), 122-37, argues for taking the Majority Text and not the textus receptus as a collation base.

18 Klaus Wachtel investigates the character of the Byzantine Text, but at the same time he sets out with the intention of proving that this text has a *secondary* character. The decision is already made before the start of the investigation! He writes (Wachtel, p. 8): 'Ein Ziel dieser Arbeit ist daher der Nachweis, dass (1.) eine Lesart, mit der die Mehrheit der jüngeren Handschriften von den ältesten und besten Textzeugen abweicht, in der Regel nicht die ursprüngliche ist, und dass (2.) typische Mehrheitslesarten dieser Art auch schon in alten Handschriften belegt sind, aber gleichwohl als sekundär gelten müssen.' ('One of the purposes of this study is to prove that 1. readings in the majority of the later manuscripts that deviate from the older and better witnesses, normally not belonging to the original readings, and that 2. such typically majority readings can be found already in ancient manuscripts, but nevertheless must be considered to be secondary.)

19 Petzer, pp. 62-3 and 216.

20 G. D. Kilpatrick, 'Luke 24:42-43', *Novum Testamentum*, 28 (1986), 306-8.

21 Bruce M. Metzger, *A Textual Commentary on the Greek New Testament* (London: United Bible Societies, 1971), pp. 187-8.

22 Kurt Aland (ed.), *Text und Textwert der griechischen Handschriften des Neuen Testaments. II. Die paulinischen Briefe*, ANTF, 16-19, 4 vols, in Verbindung mit Annette Benduhn-Mertz, Gerd Mink und Horst Bachmann (Berlin: De Gruyter, 1991), 1, 163 ('eine besondere Herausforderung, wenn nicht Gefährdung …') ('a special challenge, if not danger …').

THE USE OF THE CHURCH FATHERS IN NEW TESTAMENT TEXTUAL CRITICISM

Bart D. Ehrman

THE IMPORTANCE OF patristic witnesses for establishing the text of the New Testament has been recognized since the earliest days of the discipline.[1] At the turn of the eighteenth century, John Mill examined not only Greek manuscripts but also the writings of the Church Fathers while constructing the groundbreaking critical apparatus for his edition of the Greek New Testament.[2] As is well known, the apparatus included some 30,000 variant readings that he discovered, a number that caused quite a stir. One outspoken proponent of the Textus Receptus, Daniel Whitby, declared that Mill has been 'laboring to prove the text of Scripture precarious'.[3] Reasoning of this sort drew the eminent classicist Richard Bentley into the fray to point out the Mill had not *invented* these 30,000 readings, but only observed them. With his interest piqued, Bentley set himself to the task of reconstructing the text of the New Testament as it was known to the Fathers of Orthodoxy who had reigned at the Council of Nicea. Patristic evidence figured significantly in the venture. Bentley reasoned that Jerome had chosen the best Greek manuscripts from which to produce his Vulgate, and that the readings of these manuscripts would most likely be preserved in the oldest surviving copies of the Latin text, as opposed to the printed Latin texts based on medieval manuscripts. By happy coincidence, Bentley's test probes in the Pauline epistles revealed that these older Latin texts invariably agreed with the oldest Greek manuscripts, especially Codex Alexandrinus. He concluded that congruity of this kind revealed the New Testament text as available to the Church Fathers of the fourth century, and proposed that these champions of orthodoxy had themselves chosen the best copies available at the time, those, no doubt, representing the text as known to the greatest exegete and textual critic of the *pre*-Nicene Age, Origen of Alexandria.[4]

The leaps in Bentley's logic may seem painfully obvious to those of us who stand as beneficiaries to the accumulated wisdom of nearly three centuries of intensive research produced in his wake. All the same, it bears noting that patristic sources were recognized for their inherent significance at the outset. Much like the International Greek New Testament Project and the *Editio Critica Maior* of these latter days, Bentley's *Proposals for Printing* advertised that his edition would present every patristic citation of the text from the first five centuries of the Church.

For much of the period since, scholars have recognized that patristic sources provide an unparalleled kind of specificity for the tasks of textual analysis. Unlike most of the Greek manuscripts and versions, the scriptural quotations in these sources can be pinpointed with relative precision in both time and space; for the most part, we know when and where the Fathers wrote. For this reason, through a careful examination of their citations of Scripture, we can say with correspondingly relative certainty what the text must have looked like at certain moments in the history of transmission.[5]

Despite this obvious advantage of precision, throughout the history of the discipline patristic evidence has been (1) normally discussed with worrisome imprecision by practitioners in the field, and (2) relegated to a distant third place among the kinds of evidence traditionally cited for establishing the text. These two phenomena are not unrelated. They both signal the complexity of these materials and the unique problems attendant to their analysis.

The unique problems involved in evaluating the patristic data – indeed, even of recognizing whether and where there are data to be evaluated – have been tackled in significant ways in recent years, leading to major methodological advances that now make it possible to learn a good deal from our surviving sources. These methods may benefit from further refinement, but by no stretch of the imagination can they be ignored. Gone are the days when a Father's text can be described in loose and impressionistic terms. In this field of study in particular, methodological rigour is required and the requisite methods are now in place.

At the same time, I should stress that even though we have better access than ever to patristic data for the New Testament text, the ultimate significance of these data has not always been self-evident or fully recognized, even to those working on them – let alone to others trying to plough through the fruits of their labour.

The remainder of this essay will consider these two aspects of the field. First, and briefly, I will lay out the procedures that have now been devised for establishing this kind of evidence; second, of somewhat broader interest, I will discuss ways in which these data have proved useful for other tasks of the discipline, and thereby suggest several aspects of their ultimate significance.

ESTABLISHED PROCEDURES

A major pioneer in this field has been Gordon Fee, whose methodological proposals merit careful study.[6] These proposals are reflected in procedures strictly followed in the SBL series, *The New Testament in the Greek Fathers*, started by Fee and edited now by Michael Holmes. Here I will simply summarize the salient points.

(1) For the study of patristic sources, only critical editions of a Father can be used. Study after study has shown that earlier printed editions of the Fathers, by and large based on late medieval manuscripts, are not reliable in the presentation of their biblical citations. As I discovered for my dissertation on Didymus the Blind, Rod Mullen for his on Cyril of Jerusalem, and John Brogan for his on Athanasius, Migne's *Patrologia* is unusable for this kind of study. This in itself has vitiated most of the patristic analyses done prior to the late 1970s, nearly all of which need to be completely redone.[7] In many instances, we continue to be handicapped in this area, as anyone, for example, tempted to work on the text of Chrysostom understands full well. Patristics scholars should be urged to continue to produce solid critical editions if we hope to make further advances.

Church Fathers in New Testament Textual Criticism

(2) It is important to learn the habits of citation of the Father. Some ancient authors wrote the way some pious Christians pray, using biblical language in every breath, making it hard to know where they were making allusions in their own minds; others made characteristic kinds of changes, for example, condensing texts or modifying certain kinds of syntactical constructions; others gave precise or nearly precise wordings whenever appealing to a text. For obvious analytical reasons, it helps to know who did what.

(3) Relatedly, it has become increasingly clear that quotations of texts and allusions to texts are very different things and should not be confused in trying to establish what a Father's manuscripts look like. Allusions need to be labelled as such and treated very gingerly when trying to reconstruct a text. At the same time, scriptural allusions and paraphrases should not be ignored, since they sometimes provide just the kind of evidence that is needed – for example, when an author is clearly referring to a passage and happens to mention, even in a paraphrase, a clause or verse that is absent from some witnesses. The key is to know how the manuscript tradition reads at every point, and to see whether an allusion provides any evidence for one reading over another. In all such instances, of course, a *case* has to be made on the basis of a full analysis.

(4) Oddly enough, some of the earlier attempts at studying a specific Father's texts were uniformly casual about ascertaining the *source* of his biblical quotations. Some rather well-known studies of Mark's text in the Fathers, for example, ignored the circumstance that most of Mark is also found in Matthew and/or Luke, and proceeded to evaluate quotations as if they were naturally drawn from the second Gospel when in fact there was no reason to think so.[8] No one can get away with this kind of sloppiness anymore, but anyone who supervises a dissertation in this area knows how shocking it is for students to realize for the first time that what they thought was a huge pile of data is in fact whittled down considerably by the circumstance that precise Synoptic parallels are found in the tradition. This applies, of course, not only to the 'original' forms of the Synoptics, but also to their transmitted forms; if a Father does not specify where he drew the long form of the Lord's Prayer, then it is impossible to say whether he got it from Matthew *or* Luke, or, possibly even more likely in this case, somewhere else. Moreover, as I found in my study of Didymus, sometimes a Father gets his sources confused, even when he *does* indicate what they are.[9]

(5) It is important to consider the extenuating circumstances of a Father that may have had some impact on his citations of the text. Well known, of course, is the issue of Origen's relocation from Alexandria to Caesarea, prior to the publication of most of his extant works. Did he take his manuscripts with him? Did he use locally-produced manuscripts wherever he was? I am not sure that the problem has been completely solved yet. What about Athanasius's exiles? An even more obvious problem cropped up in my dissertation on the readings of Didymus's manuscripts, since Didymus himself was blind and couldn't *read* any manuscripts. Every Father has peculiarities of his own that need to be dealt with.[10]

(6) It is now obvious that a presentation of a Father's text must provide *all* of the surviving data. It is not good enough simply to indicate places of variation. We need all the texts reproduced in their entirety. Otherwise, the data are nearly impossible to track down and evaluate, and the analysis cannot be checked. Open access is the key to progress in this area.

(7) It is extremely useful in this kind of study to provide an apparatus indicating places of variation among leading representatives of the relevant textual groupings. Only clear and certain readings of the Father, based on a careful assessment of the relative accuracy of his citations, are relevant for these collations.

(8) The resultant data need to be analyzed carefully and methodically by the application of both a quantitative and profile analysis. The quantitative method devised by Ernst Colwell and used to good effect by Fee and others has proved itself repeatedly.[11] It can probably be improved, and I think it is being improved by people who are more statistically apt, including Jean-Francois Racine, who is now completing work on his dissertation at the University of Toronto on the quotations from Matthew in the writings of Basil the Great.

In my judgement, anyone who is *still* suspicious of a statistical approach to classification of manuscripts has not come to terms with what it means to classify witnesses according to textual groupings. To put a manuscript in a group means that it is judged to relate more closely with that group of witnesses than with others. This is a necessarily quantitative evaluation, which requires, by its very nature, a statistical demonstration. No longer can we classify a witness on the basis of some impressionistic judgements of readings that happen to strike our eye, for example, to call a witness Western because it happens to have some readings shared by other Western witnesses. Overall agreement in all genetically significant variation is obviously the key.

At the same time, raw statistics provide only part of the picture. In order to take into account unique agreements in readings shared by all of a group's members, or by most of them, or by members of one group but not members of other groups, etc., a clearly reasoned group profile method is needed. I developed a set of comprehensive profiles of this sort that worked to good effect on Didymus, and they appear to have worked as well for the studies of Mullen, Brogan, Darrell Hannah (on I Corinthians in Origen) and others.[12]

It evidently never occurred to most of the earlier practitioners in this field that once all the patristic data have been collected and analyzed, the job is still not done. Only after we have this kind of information do the really interesting and important questions begin. That is to say, it is not enough to conclude that 'Athanasius is therefore an Alexandrian witness'. *Of course* he is an Alexandrian witness; he lived in Alexandria. Even worse is the conclusion, found with disheartening frequency in a large number of earlier studies, especially unpublished dissertations, that 'This or that Father is mainly Alexandrian, but with some leaning towards the Byzantine text'. What does that mean exactly, and why does it matter? You would think that anyone who had devoted a couple of years of his or her life to a project would want to think, if just for a moment, about its significance – at least to the discipline. How does analyzing these texts help us in the broader tasks of textual criticism?

THE POTENTIAL SIGNIFICANCE OF THE STUDY

Let me say at the outset that the importance of these data is almost never self-evident – one has to *look* for it. One of the keys is knowing what to look for. Recent studies have succeeded in establishing significance in the following areas:

Church Fathers in New Testament Textual Criticism

The History of Transmission in Specific Places

Most people in our field would probably agree that our single greatest desideratum is a full and convincing account of the history of transmission. We will make no more progress towards establishing the oldest form of the text until we have a persuasive reconstruction of the course of its subsequent modification. This reconstruction must be done locally. It is no good to talk in broad sweeping generalities about what happened to the text. We need to know the forces that were involved in its modification, where they asserted themselves, and when. And the only way to know what happened locally is through the kinds of evidence provided for us by the Church Fathers.

We can imagine being ready, I think, to write the history of the transmission of the text in Alexandria. Already in hand are full analyses of the Gospel texts of Didymus and Athanasius. We also have a full analysis of the quotations of I Corinthians in Origen by Darrell Hannah, and the complete data of Origen's text of John. Moreover, we have a study yet to be published of Cyril of Alexandria's text of the Gospels, by Arthur Cunningham, a dissertation completed at the University of Manchester.[13] Urgently needed are studies of the remaining portions of all these Fathers. There are several dissertations here just begging to be done.

Even with these incomplete data, we have already made some significant progress. Let me cite just one example, as it relates to my study of Didymus the Blind and what it revealed about the nature of the Alexandrian Text. Hort's distinction between a Neutral and an Alexandrian text has lived on in the still commonplace division of the Alexandrian witnesses into Early Alexandrian and Late Alexandrian. This more common set of terms circumvents some of the well-known idiosyncrasies of Westcott and Hort's system, but creates other problems of its own. In an earlier foray into the quotations of Didymus, for example, Carlo Martini noted that readings distinctive to the Late Alexandrian witnesses are sometimes found in Early Alexandrian witnesses; on these grounds, he proposed that the revision of the early form of the text into the later happened not sometime in the late third or early fourth centuries, as commonly imagined, but at about the same time as the production of the earliest surviving Alexandrian witnesses themselves.[14]

In my study of Didymus, I realized that even this more nuanced understanding of the text in Alexandria is problematic.[15] In terms of purely quantitative alignments, Didymus is more closely connected with the so-called Early Alexandrian witnesses than the Late Alexandrians. However, when one examines readings that characterize the two groups, Didymus shares more of the Late Alexandrian readings than the Early, and is further removed from the Early Alexandrians than even some of the clearly Late Alexandrians. If his closest ties are to the Early Alexandrians rather than the Late Alexandrians, yet there are other Late Alexandrians that stand closer to the characteristic readings of the Early Alexandrians than does he, what are we to make of these data?

This question opened up a new vista for me, and made me realize that our understanding of the Alexandrian text was erroneous. There were not two forms of text in Alexandria, one relatively pristine and the other a later and less pure revision. To be sure, the so-called later Alexandrians do diverge significantly from the so-called earlier Alexandrians, but they do not, as a rule, diverge in the same *places*. In fact, most of them appear to have closer quantitative ties with the P⁷⁵-B line of text than with each other, even though individually they all relate at about the same levels of agreement with that more pristine line of text.

Thus we do not have Early and Late forms of the Alexandrian text, we have Primary and Secondary witnesses to this text. That is to say, there was one dominant form of the text in Alexandria, and different witnesses attest it in varying degrees of purity. Rather than referring then to Early and Late Alexandrian texts we should speak of Primary and Secondary Alexandrian witnesses.

These conclusions, I should add, were convincingly supported by Brogan's study of Athanasius.[16]

The Textual Character and History of Specific Manuscripts

The data derived from a study of a Father's quotations, of course, are quite limited in comparison with what one finds in continuous text manuscripts. Occasionally, though, this kind of study can point to significant issues of classification for the manuscripts themselves. In my study of Didymus, I was able to isolate 163 units of genetically significant variation in his quotations of Matthew. Codex Alexandrinus is lacunose for most of this material, sharing only twenty of these units. It did strike me as odd, though, that in those twenty readings, Alexandrinus, which is normally classified as Byzantine in the Gospels, agreed over 80 per cent of the time with Didymus and over 90 per cent of the time with Codex Vaticanus. I decided that the data were too sparse to draw any conclusions, but my interest was at least piqued. At the same time, it is striking to note that in Brogan's study of Athanasius, similar results were obtained. Of the seventy-six units of variation found in Athanasius's text of Matthew, Alexandrinus attests only twelve, but the manuscript agrees with Athanasius in eleven of these. Is it possible that Alexandrinus in fact had a strongly Alexandrian form of Matthew, even though its textual alignments shift in the other Gospels?[17]

The obverse could be posited for the minuscule 1241, often cited as a secondary Alexandrian witness. In my study of Didymus, I found the text of 1241 to be *so* far removed both from Didymus and the other Alexandrian witnesses used for my apparatus, that I became immediately suspicious of its overall textual character, which has been established, as far as I can tell, on impressionistic grounds by earlier investigators struck by its occasionally interesting readings, rather than via statistical analysis. Strikingly, my suspicions appear to have been confirmed by subsequent patristic analyses by Jean-Francois Racine and John Brogan, where similar caveats are raised.[18]

In a different vein, but still relating to individual manuscripts, I should here say a brief word about Brogan's study of Athanasius in relationship to the correctors of Codex Sinaiticus. Rather than provide all the details of his analysis, here I need only summarize his startling results: in the units of genetically significant variation in the Gospel quotations of Athanasius, the early correctors of Sinaiticus differ from the first hand in twenty-five instances. Of these instances, Athanasius agrees with the correctors in six instances out of six in Matthew, two out of three in Luke, and fifteen out of sixteen in John, a total of twenty-three out of twenty-five possible times (six of these are by scribes A and B, contemporaries with Athanasius; nineteen are by C, a century or two later). Brogan plausibly conjectures that at least in a couple of instances, the form of text that Athanasius himself promoted affected subsequent scribes in Alexandria.[19]

The Oldest Form of Specific Passages

Probably the most widely recognized value of patristic citations of the New Testament involves their utility for establishing the earliest form of the tradition. This appears to have been the motivation behind the inclusion of such sources in Mill's edition in 1707 and Bentley's proposed inclusion some thirteen years later, as well as for their presence in apparatus ever since. Determining which form of a text a Father used is not always a simple matter, as the original IGNTP committee learned to its chagrin. Still, a cautious use of the Fathers for individual texts is absolutely critical if we are to proceed toward the goal of establishing the earliest form of the tradition. Since this is widely acknowledged, I will simply provide a single illustrative example.[20]

One of the most intriguing textual variants of Luke's Gospel occurs early on, in the account of Jesus' baptism, where according to Codex Bezae and a number of ecclesiastical writers from the second century onwards, the voice from heaven is said to proclaim, 'You are my Son, today I have begotten you' (Luke 3.22). There are solid grounds for thinking that this in fact is the original text of Luke, and that orthodox scribes who could not abide its adoptionistic overtones 'corrected' it into conformity with the parallel in Mark, 'You are my beloved Son, in you I am well pleased' (Mark 1.11).

The strongest support for the reading of Codex Bezae derives from transcriptional and intrinsic probabilities, but its external attestation should not be discounted as quickly as it normally is. Granting that the reading does not occur extensively after the fifth century, it cannot be overlooked that in witnesses of the second and third centuries, centuries that have not provided us with any superfluity of Greek manuscripts, it is virtually the only reading that survives. Not only was it the reading of the ancestor of Codex Bezae and the Old Latin text of Luke, it appears also to have been the text known to Justin, Clement of Alexandria, and the authors of the Gospel according to the Hebrews and the Didascalia. It is certainly the text attested by the Gospel according to the Ebionites, Origen, and Methodius. Somewhat later it is found in Lactantius, Hilary, Tyconius, Augustine, and several of the later Apocryphal Acts. I should stress that except for the third-century manuscript P[4], there is no certain attestation of the other reading, the reading of our later manuscripts, in this early period. The reading of Codex Bezae, then, is not an error introduced by an unusually aberrant witness, as sometimes claimed. This manuscript is in fact one of the last witnesses to preserve it. Nor is it a 'Western' variant without adequate attestation. Among sources of the second and third centuries, it is virtually the only reading to be found; down to the sixth century it occurs in witnesses as far-flung as Asia Minor, Palestine, Alexandria, North Africa, Rome, Gaul, and Spain.

How can we account for a textual situation of this sort? The best attested reading of the early period, a reading known throughout the entire Christian world, virtually disappears from sight, displaced by a reading that is both harmonized to that of another Gospel and less offensive doctrinally. I think there is every reason to suspect that here we are dealing with an original reading that has been displaced for theological reasons, and the patristic evidence plays a key role in making that determination.

This leads me now to a fourth area of significance for the Patristic evidence.

The Scribal Alteration of the Text

As we have just seen, it is a relatively small step from establishing the earliest form of the text to noting the various modes of its subsequent alterations; from there, though, it is a somewhat large leap into the dark to establish plausible historical factors that affected the scribes who made these changes. Even though these factors must have been very real to the scribes themselves, they necessarily remain hypothetical to us, given the constraints of our evidence. It would be nice to have published exit interviews with scribes who left their scriptoria, but we do not even know who these people *were* (although Kim Haines-Eitzen's recent study will be of some considerable use toward this end).[21]

One of the best ways of thinking about what affected the otherwise unknown Christian scribes is by seeing what affected their otherwise known Christian contemporaries, especially the authors whose works we still have. This kind of pointer to intent is not foolproof, of course, but in specific instances, the patristic sources go some considerable way in helping us posit 'motivation' with at least a modicum of probability.

Consider another example drawn from Luke's Gospel, this time near the end, in the scene in the Garden immediately before Jesus' arrest. The account of the bloody sweat has long intrigued scholars, and I do not need to go into all the intricacies of the recent discussions. There are excellent reasons for thinking that the account has been interpolated into the text by scribes who were impressed with its portrayal of a very human, non-docetic, Jesus undergoing such intense suffering that an angel came and ministered to him and his sweat became like great drops of blood, falling to the ground.[22] In any event, whether these verses were added to the account, which originally lacked them, or deleted from the account, which originally had them, patristic sources show the text was changed by the mid-second century. The verses were known already to Justin, but were absent from the text known to Clement of Alexandria.

This was a period, of course, of intense Christological debate among various Christian groups. What is particularly striking is that when these verses *do* begin to be cited, they are in every instance used to counter any notion that Jesus was not a real flesh and blood human being. Thus Justin observes that Jesus' 'sweat fell down like drops of blood while He was praying', and claims that this shows 'that the Father wished His Son really to undergo such sufferings for our sakes', so that we 'may not say that He, being the Son of God, did not feel what was happening to Him and inflicted on Him' (*Dial.*, 103). So too Irenaeus, in an attack on the docetic aspects of the Ptolemaic Christology, argues that if Jesus were not really a man of flesh, he would not 'have sweated great drops of blood', for this is a token 'of the flesh which had been derived from the earth' (*Adv. Haer.*, III, 22,2).

My point is that we do not need to hypothesize the usefulness of these verses for an anti-docetic polemic; we know that the verses were put to precisely this use during the period of our concern. Second-century heresiologists used Jesus' 'bloody-sweat' to attack Christians who denied his real humanity.

Similar results can be obtained by means of detailed considerations of the citations of a particular Father, as demonstrated by Brogan's nuanced analysis of some of Athanasius's citations of the Gospels. In particular, he showed how the precise theological point that Athanasius wanted to make affected the way he cited his text, sometimes in subtle ways.[23] Subtlety has sometimes been lost in previous analyses on patristic evidence. Brogan provides a model that other studies should follow. In particular, he highlights the significance of the form of a text for the patristic *interpretation* of the text.

The Relationship of Text and Interpretation

This is an area that has been almost completely overlooked, not only by textual scholars but also by historians interested in the polemical conflicts of early Christianity. In point of fact, there are numerous instances in which the form of an author's biblical text affected his interpretation of it, and for us to fail to understand this relationship is to misconstrue the historical situation.

An obvious example comes from Origen's conflict with Celsus, where in response to the charge that Jesus was nothing more than a blue-collar construction worker (my paraphrase of 'tekton'), Origen insists that the Gospels never *call* Jesus a 'tekton'. Scholars sometimes maintain that Origen was either being duplicitous or forgetful here, given the text of Mark 6.3. But, of course, that text has a variant, and Origen may have known it in its alternative form. One could plausibly argue, as my student Wayne Kannaday in fact is doing in his dissertation, that just such an apologetic context is what led scribes to change the text in the first place.

An even more fruitful area to explore involved the detailed wrangling over texts between Christians. This can be seen, for example, in the case of Heracleon and Origen. We can reconstruct portions of Heracleon's text of the Fourth Gospel with some degree of confidence from Origen's quotation of it (our only access to it); moreover, when we do so, it becomes clear that it differed from Origen's text in significant ways. What is most striking is that in a number of instances, the different interpretations that Origen and Heracleon advanced over the passages in question were directly affected by the form of the texts available to them.[24]

The raw data are these: in the surviving fragments Heracleon cites the Gospel of John nearly fifty times. In more than one out of five instances (11/49 total) Heracleon appears to attest a different form of the text from that known to Origen. Of these, over half (6/11) are instances in which their different interpretations of the text depend to some extent on the variant forms of its wording. Thus in almost one out of every eight verses cited by Heracleon, the divergent wording of the text has played some role in the exegesis.

Just by way of one quick example, I might mention Origen's interpretation of John 1.21. Origen objects to Heracleon's construal of this verse by claiming that he had not attended closely to its wording. As it stands, the objection appears odd, given Heracleon's remarkable attentiveness to textual details elsewhere. Nonetheless, according to Origen, when John the Baptist answers the Levites and Priests that he is neither the Christ nor the prophet, Heracleon fails to observe the repetition of the article and so mistakenly thinks that John denied being 'a' prophet rather than 'the' (messianic) prophet. This disregard for the words of the text, maintains Origen, is what leads to Heracleon's fantastic explanation of why Jesus elsewhere calls John a prophet when the Baptist himself denies it.

It is interesting to note that Origen cites this passage a total of eight times in his extant writings, seven times with the article. The only exception is the paraphrase of Heracleon's position. What must not escape our attention, however, is that there is a stream of the New Testament textual tradition that also lacks the article. In this instance, of course, the Latin witnesses (lacking an article) are of no assistance; moreover, and regrettably, one of the two leading representatives of the Western tradition (Codex Bezae) happens to be lacunose in this part of John. However, Codex Sinaiticus, the other leading Western witness, is extant; remarkably, it stands virtually alone against all other witnesses in reading the shorter form of the text. Heracleon's textual affinities are strongly Western, as full quantitative and profile analyzes show beyond any doubt. Thus Origen may well have attacked Heracleon for failing to observe an article that was not present in his text of John.

Other examples like this could be multiplied, but this one should suffice to make my basic point.

CONCLUSION

My thesis can be summed up tersely. The study of patristic citations must proceed with extreme methodological rigour, but they must proceed. They provide us with the best hope for reconstructing the history of (a) the textual tradition of the New Testament, on a local basis, (b) the textual background of individual manuscripts, and (c) the pedigree of individual variants. In addition, they can inform us of the motivation behind scribal alterations of the text, and reveal the closely-knit relationship between text and exegesis in the history of interpretation.

NOTES

1 I would like to express my appreciation to the organizers of the Hereford Conference for their invitation to me to participate. Although I have revised this piece for publication, principally through adding documentation, I have chosen not to remove all traces of its origin as an oral presentation.

2 For a fuller account, see Adam Fox, *John Mill and Richard Bentley: A Study in the Textual Criticism of the New Testament 1675-1729* (Oxford: Blackwell, 1954).

3 See his *Examen Variantium Lectionum J. Milii* (London, 1710).

4 For a brief statement of Bentley's critical procedure, see his *Proposals for Printing a New Edition of the Greek Testament and St. Hieron's Latin Version* (London: J. Knapton, 1721), pp. 16-27. For a study, see Fox, *John Mill and Richard Bentley*.

5 See my discussion in 'The Use and Significance of Patristic Evidence in New Testament Textual Criticism', in *New Testament Textual Criticism, Exegesis, and Church History: A Discussion of Methods*, ed. by Barbara Aland and J. Delobel (Kampen: Kok Pharos, 1994), pp. 118-35.

6 See especially his overview, 'The Use of the Greek Fathers for New Testament Textual

Criticism', in *The Text of the New Testament in Contemporary Research: Essays on the Status Quaestionis*, ed. by Bart D. Ehrman and Michael W. Holmes (Grand Rapids: Eerdmans, 1995), pp. 191-207, and the literature he cites there.

7 Bart D. Ehrman, *Didymus the Blind and the Test of the Gospels*, SBLNTGF, 1 (Atlanta: Scholars Press, 1986); Roderic L. Mullen, *The New Testament Text of Cyril of Jerusalem*, SBLNTGF, 7 (Atlanta: Scholars Press, 1997); John J. Brogan, *The Text of the Gospels in the Writings of Athanasius*, SBLNTGF, 8 (Atlanta: Scholars Press, forthcoming).

8 See the discussion in Gordon Fee, 'The Text of John and Mark in the Writings of Chrysostom', *NTS*, 26 (1980), 325-47.

9 Ehrman, *Didymus*, p. 9, n. 16.

10 See my discussion in *Didymus*, pp. 21-2.

11 For an overview of the methods, see Bart D. Ehrman, 'Methodological Developments in the Analysis and Classification of New Testament Documentary Evidence', *Novum Testamentum*, 29 (1987), 22-45, and idem, 'The Use of Group Profiles for the Classification of New Testament Documentary Evidence', *JBL* (1987), 465-86.

12 See Ehrman, *Didymus*; Ehrman, 'Group Profiles'; Mullen, *Cyril of Jerusalem*; Brogan, *Athanasius*; and Darrell C. Hannah, *The Text of I Corinthians in the Writings of Origen*, SBLNTGF, 4 (Atlanta: Scholars Press, 1997).

13 For Origen on John, see Bart D. Ehrman, Gordon D. Fee and Michael E. Holmes, *The Text of the Fourth Gospel in the Writings of Origen*, SBLNTGF, 3 (Atlanta: Scholars Press, 1992).

14 'Is There a Late Alexandrian Text of the Gospels?', *NTS*, 24 (1977-8), 285-96.

15 For what follows, see Ehrman, *Didymus*, pp. 262-7.

16 Brogan, *Athanasius*, ch. 7.

17 Ehrman, *Didymus*, pp. 190-2; Brogan, *Athanasius*, ch. 5.

18 Ehrman, *Didymus*, pp. 192-3; Mullen, *Cyril of Jerusalem*.

19 Brogan, *Athanasius*, ch. 7.

20 For a fuller discussion of this variant, see Bart D. Ehrman, *The Orthodox Corruption of Scripture: The Effect of Early Christological Controversies on the Text of the New Testament* (New York: Oxford University Press, 1993), pp. 62-7.

21 *Guardians of Letters: Literacy, Power, and the Transmitters of Early Christian Literature* (New York: Oxford University Press, 2000).

22 For a fuller discussion, see Ehrman, *Orthodox Corruption*, pp. 187-94.

23 Brogan, *Athanasius*, ch. 7.

24 For the data and their interpretation, see my two articles, 'Heracleon and the "Western" Textual Tradition', *NTS*, 40 (1994), 465-86, and 'Heracleon, Origen, and the Text of the Fourth Gospel', *VC*, 47 (1993), 105-18.

WHY SO MANY HOLES IN THE PAPYROLOGICAL EVIDENCE FOR THE GREEK NEW TESTAMENT?

Stanley E. Porter

I. INTRODUCTION TO THE PAPYRI AND THEIR IMPORTANCE

THE TEXTUAL EVIDENCE for the Greek New Testament, as this collection of papers makes clear, consists of a range of types of documents. What are called the papyri in New Testament text-critical circles constitute but one part of that evidence, and have gone through a long process of discovery. Between the sixteenth and eighteenth centuries, a few travellers came upon the curiosity of papyrus scraps; in the mid to late eighteenth century, several major papyrus documents came to light, and a number of scrolls were offered for sale. Apart from the Herculaneum papyri (the first portions of which were published in the late eighteenth and nineteenth centuries), the first publications of papyri (even into the nineteenth century) were largely a disappointment, and failed to satisfy the great anticipation that the knowledge of the Egyptians would finally be revealed. This process of discovery was only haphazard until about the middle of the nineteenth century, but became much more intense from about the 1870s onwards.

It was at this time that the foundations of the great papyrological collections were laid, and the field was literally invented by a new generation of scholars who had access to these primary documents for the first time – Wessely, Wilcken, Kenyon, Grenfell and Hunt, to name but a few. At the same time, and often in conjunction with one of the major holdings, papyrological publications began to appear, such as the Mittheilungen aus der Sammlung der Papyrus Erzherzog Rainer (1887-97, now replaced by its new series), the Berliner Griechische Urkunden (1892-), and, of course, the Oxyrhynchus Papyri (1898-).[1] In terms of the larger picture of papyrological research (I will return to some of this terminology below), there are now well over 100,000 papyrus documents, many of them fragmentary, that are a part of the total body of finds. Approximately half of these have been published,[2] with the other half being worked on slowly and to varying degrees by a dedicated but very small group. The International Association of Papyrologists only totals about 350 members worldwide, so the numbers of scholars involved in this endeavour is limited.

Among these 100,000 plus papyri are now about 108 New Testament Greek papyri in published form (at the time of writing; the number has increased since).[3] I say 'about', because there is some dispute about how this number should be arrived at, since what might be classified as two texts may actually be two fragments of the same text. I will return to the question this grouping raises in the next section, because it has some wider implications. In any case, the number of New Testament Greek papyri remains relatively small, when one considers the significance of the New Testament for a major world religion such as Christianity.

This group of papyri form part of the New Testament text-critical discussion.[4] Minuscules formed the basis of what became known as the Textus Receptus.[5] At least some of the ancient versions of course had been known for centuries, even if their significance for New Testament textual criticism had not been fully realized.[6] Even though the great codices, Sinaiticus and Vaticanus, were either not discovered or not integrated into New Testament textual criticism until the late nineteenth century,[7] the first New Testament biblical papyrus (P[11]), published by Constantine Tischendorf in 1868, was the only one to precede Tischendorf's own monumental eighth edition of the Greek New Testament (1869, 1872) and Westcott and Hort's edition, with accompanying discussion of the principles of textual criticism (1881).[8] Before 1898, four more papyri were published (P[3] by Wessely, P[7] and P[8] by Gregory, and P[14] by J. Rendel Harris),[9] but because they were fragmentary and some relatively late (fourth-seventh century), they did not generate the enthusiasm that was to accompany the papyri in later years. Even in the light of later, significant New Testament papyrological discoveries, there are a number of statements by significant early paleographers and New Testament scholars to the effect that the papyri were not as important as other documents, such as the major codices. Someone as important to the discipline as Kenyon states in his *Handbook to the Textual Criticism of the New Testament* that the papyri fragments, 'interesting as they are as examples of what the soil of Egypt may yet be holding for us, are for the most part so slight in themselves as barely to deserve mention'.[10] It was only with the further discovery of a number of other papyri, especially those published in the Oxyrhynchus collection, the so-called Chester Beatty papyri, and the Bodmer papyri, that the biblical papyri began to assume a position of pre-eminence.[11] Due especially to the early date of many of these papyri, a significant shift in emphasis was the final result. In 1953, Günther Zuntz, rather than using the major codices as his collating base, utilized P[46], the oldest manuscript of Paul's letters, as the basis for evaluating the Pauline textual tradition.[12] In 1966, with the publication of the *UBSGNT[1]*, a printed edition finally collated all of the known papyri in an edition of the Greek New Testament, with all of the previous printed editions using significantly fewer than the number available.[13] As the situation now stands, of the 108 papyri, approximately fifty-three of them have been dated to as early if not earlier than the earliest extant codices, Sinaiticus and Vaticanus (fourth century).

Having defined and placed the papyri in this context, in which they are thought by many scholars to hold a place of pre-eminence regarding New Testament textual criticism, I wish now to raise a number of questions regarding the papyri, and how it is that they are defined and used in the text-critical task.

2. TERMINOLOGY

The first set of questions revolves around basic terminological distinctions. New Testament textual critics usually classify their documents according to four categories:

papyri, uncials, minuscules, and lectionaries.[14] This is a mixed bag of terms. The first refers to the *medium*, the second and third to forms of *handwriting* (even though the first and fourth also required some form of handwriting), and the fourth to a perceived *use* of the document.[14]

The terms are also misleading. For example, as 'uncials' refers to what amounts to a kind of capital letters, one would presume that the papyri must be written in something other than some form of capital letters. That is not the case. Apart from a few instances of ligatures, the New Testament papyri treated here are all in uncial or, perhaps better, majuscule letters. In addition, many lectionaries (defined as non-continuous text designed for liturgical use) are also written in majuscules and also could have been written on papyrus.[15] Neglected in this categorization are other writing surfaces, such as parchment and paper. In terms of handwriting, there should be two major categories of New Testament documents, majuscules and minuscules.[16]

There have been several results of this kind of classification. Firstly, the lectionary has been bracketed out of importance. Apart from the early lectionaries, dated to the fourth to sixth centuries (*l*1604, *l*1403, *l*1276, *l*1347, *l*1354), most lectionaries are dated significantly later, around the eighth to eleventh centuries, and hence are not considered as valuable in the text-critical endeavour. Secondly, there has been a loss of perceived recognition of the relation between papyri and uncials, focused more on the nature of the surface on which they are written than the handwriting that is used, with the possibility of confusion over the perceived development of the materials used in transmission of the New Testament text. It appears that for biblical manuscripts, papyrus was used before parchment (not a category used to identify manuscripts),[17] and continued to be used until the eighth century, even though parchment was in significant use by the fourth century. A further distinction lost by these divisions is the languages in which these texts are written. Greek is the primary language, but other languages are represented on these texts as well. For example, there are a number of Graeco-Coptic papyri, in which both languages are written side by side in parallel columns, as well as occasionally with one page having Greek and the other Coptic (Graeco-Coptic papyri include P[41], P[42], and P[96]). However, the same kind of bi-lingualism is also found in some of the uncials (for example, Codex Bezae with Greek and Latin) and lectionaries (*l*1435 with Greek and Coptic). E. J. Epp says that the papyri 'have been placed in a separate category due to their early date and greater significance, and also for historical reasons' related to their recent discovery,[18] but as mentioned earlier, only about half have a date as early or earlier than the major codices on parchment.

Thus, in New Testament studies, the term 'papyrus' is used to refer to the material on which these documents in majuscule hand and of continuous biblical text are written.

Another form of potential terminological confusion is found in relation to how the term papyrus is used outside the area of New Testament textual criticism. New Testament textual criticism as a discipline is a part of what is variously called theology, or more particularly New Testament studies, since it is concerned with the establishment of the text that is studied in the area of New Testament criticism. However, these same papyri used in New Testament textual criticism are also a part of the field of papyrology. In the earliest days of their discovery and publication, there was no distinction made between a papyrologist of non-New Testament and New Testament documents. It is true, the first person to publish a biblical papyrus was Constantine Tischendorf, the man who edited more early biblical documents than any other. After the few initial publications, however, the publication of even biblical papyri came to be dominated by papyrologists such as Grenfell and Hunt, who together edited twenty-one New Testament papyri. The field of papyrology was, to a large extent, invented by Wessely, who went on to edit many other biblical documents, besides the thousands of other documents that he deciphered, approximately 30,000 in all, written in a variety of languages (Greek, Latin and Coptic), on a number of surfaces (such as papyrus, parchment, and others).[19] In fact, the term 'papyrus' is used in papyrology:

> to represent a class of written artifacts, not all actually involving papyrus as a material. The ancient societies that used papyrus also used pieces of broken pottery [...] parchment, wooden tablets and labels, and bone for the same kinds of purposes for which papyrus was employed. What these materials generally have in common is that they were used for written artifacts with no particular pretensions to permanence.[20]

Documents intended as a permanent record were inscribed on bronze and stone. In papyrology, as defined by papyrologists, the vast majority of documents that fall within their scope are considered 'documentary', as opposed to 'literary'. The Egyptian documentary papyri contain records of a variety of day-to-day activities, such as business transactions, public testaments such as wills, official documents such as census returns, and private accounts such as letters between friends and families. The New Testament papyri fall into the category of literary texts. These texts include those in which various literary authors have been preserved on various surfaces, some of the authors and works known from later medieval documents, such as Homer and Aristotle, and others known only from these papyri, such as the Oxyrhynchus Historian (POxy. 842). There are both similarities and differences between these sets of documents and the resulting scholarly handling of them. The common factors include the fact that they have survived more through accident than intention, and the resultant need for restoration, preservation and decipherment of the documents concerned. However, there are also a number of differences. For example, the reasons and motivations for the original production of the documents may be widely divergent. A letter from a worker in Alexandria to his home in Oxyrhynchus may have been written hastily, simply to convey information of importance only in the immediate situation. A text of Homer, or a letter of Paul, may have been relatively carefully copied to provide a lasting record of this revered author. As a result, documentary and literary papyri may require different skills for decipherment, have differing types of access to templates for comparison (such as other texts of an ancient author or a contract or letter), and even relatively different levels of completeness (an entire letter of about ten lines compared to a few verses of a biblical book of several chapters).

One must appreciate the complexity of this situation, and where the New Testament papyri fit within this larger field of papyrological research. For example, in one of the standard handbooks to New Testament textual criticism, the author notes that several small fragments of the famous Chester Beatty codex 'have turned up in a collection of papyri at Vienna'.[21] Surprisingly, it is not noted that this collection in Vienna possesses forty-five New Testament documents, including eleven of the approximately 108 papyri.[22] More importantly, it was the first major papyrological collection, and is still probably the world's largest, in terms of the number of documentary holdings, with approximately 60,000 in total. This shifts the priorities completely, it seems to me. From a New Testament textual perspective, the Chester Beatty papyri are highly important, and, with the Bodmer papyri, arguably the most important papyri that we have, and for that reason loom large for New Testament textual criticism. Their relative significance diminishes, however, when it is realized that they are documents that fit within a much larger set of manuscripts that are one of our primary means of knowledge and reconstruction of the ancient world, of which the New Testament was a part.

This potential confusion regarding the papyri is to a large extent perpetuated by the use of the Gregory-Aland numbers.[23] Most New Testament textual critics, and certainly most New Testament scholars, know the documents that are used in New Testament textual criticism by a set of numbers that are given to the texts according to the categories mentioned above: papyri, uncials, minuscules, and lectionaries. However, all of these documents also have other designating numbers, usually including a number that corresponds to the collection in which they are published (the most well-known probably being the Oxyrhynchus collection), and the accession number of the library or museum in which they are held. It would seem to be a self-evident process by which a text receives a Gregory-Aland number and thereby enters into the ranks of the texts that are used in the establishment of the text of the New Testament. I am not privileged to the inner workings of this process, but my impression is that it is not as straight-forward as it might at first seem.

I merely wish to suggest here that there are advantages and disadvantages to the Gregory-Aland system. One disadvantage is that there is a certain restriction of data by means of the classification system. For example, if a document is not assigned a Gregory-Aland number, and hence is not included in the catalogue of New Testament papyri, it will not be accorded the same status as those that are included, even if it has some bearing on the issue of New Testament textual criticism. Some of the Apocryphal Gospel papyri are assigned fairly early dates, putting them among the earliest papyri that reflect the text of the New Testament (for example, PEgerton 2/PLond.Christ. 1 is assigned a date of the second century). They have not been assigned Gregory-Aland numbers, and are referred to simply as the Apocryphal Gospels by many scholars, lumping together a number of disparate texts that range over several centuries. The effect of the numbering system is that some scholars are adamant that these papyri have no place in New Testament textual criticism since they are clearly later composite texts that draw upon the various canonical Gospels and other New Testament texts, including even Paul's writings.[24] Others wish to assert their priority, so much so that they are seen to be even earlier than the canonical texts.[25] As a result, their potential significance, on an individual basis, for chronicling the emergence of different variants, or helping to arbitrate variants in the Synoptic Gospels, has not been appreciated. I cannot help but think that some of this strongly polarized thinking has been exacerbated by the firm line drawn between assigning a text a Gregory-Aland number and not. A certain status – whether that is high or low status is dependent upon the group examining the evidence – is conveyed by the classification. This kind of disjunction was not found in the ancient world, since it has been shown that the scribes in what appears to have been a scriptorium in ancient Oxyrhynchus worked on a variety of manuscripts (for example, the copyist of P^{22} is also apparently that of POxy. 654 (Gospel of Thomas).[26] Although a different kind of volume, with different purposes (and its own limitations), the catalogue of biblical papyri compiled by van Haelst in some ways overcomes some of these difficulties by bringing all of the evidence together in one volume and its own numbering system, while recognizing different relative status for the documents involved.[27] In the Gregory-Aland system, if a text is classified as a papyrus it will be handled in a different way than if it is classified as a lectionary, and its place and importance in textual criticism will be largely decided on that basis.

This is not to suggest that the Gregory-Aland system should be eliminated, since some system is desirable (and this one is probably better than most). What I am saying is that it is important to see these documents within their larger context and not to let the Gregory-Aland numbers create an artificial barrier around their understanding. The New Testament papyri are, in at least one sense, just like other papyri of the ancient world, now housed in various collections around the world. The reliance upon the Gregory-Aland numbers tends to isolate them artificially in a way that precludes useful comparisons with other New Testament texts, and with other non-biblical yet even Christian texts. The formative and shaping influence of the Gregory-Aland system is seen in the fact that often texts have been joined together under the same Gregory-Aland number that are classified with different numbers in a given collection (e.g. P^{41}) or are housed in separate places (e.g. P^{45}). Is it *always* wise to join these separate fragments together, overlooking the fact that a P number may consist of any possible number of individual pieces? Such a classification may lead to confusion, for example when one realizes that P^{58} is now a part of P^{33}, but that perhaps simply corrects an earlier mistake made by the classifiers. In many instances these classifications are unproblematic and uncontroversial, such as including one of the Vienna papyri as part of P^{45}. More controversial, however, are some of the classificatory categories themselves.

New Testament textual critics deal with these documents in terms of their Gregory-Aland numbers, referring to them by such numbers as P^{45} and P^{46}, P^{66}, and P^{52}. However, when one wishes to actually use these texts in a major collection (something that is not done that often by biblical scholars) one must request them using the accession numbers of the institution involved, which may include publication numbers. This further emphasised the point I was making above, that the New Testament Greek papyri are but a relatively small part of the broader field of papyrological studies. Their importance may be great because of the text that they enshrine, but the documents themselves are simply a few over 100 out of well over 100,000 such documents. The larger complex of papyrological studies must always be considered; there is much more to the field of New Testament research into the papyri than simply categorizing and debating the merits of these particular texts on the basis of published editions. It is important for those who deal with these documents to have first-hand exposure to them as much as is possible.[28] Even working from good photographs is subject to numerous limitations that can only be clarified by first-hand examination. Of course, there are limitations upon access to some of the papyri: some have disappeared, and some have restricted access. When first-hand examination is not possible, it should be made clear that one is working from photographs, photocopies or earlier editions, or whatever is being used. I know from experience that what are sometimes represented as new editions of papyri are not actually 'new' editions (for example, when I have discovered that the editor was never in fact in the library).

The conventions of New Testament textual criticism, especially in the way that it refers to its documents such as the papyri, have in some distinct ways distorted the field of papyrological research. The use of the categories of classification have overlooked a number of problems with how one even talks about and classifies the texts involved. The over-reliance upon the Gregory-Aland numbers has artificially restricted the corpus of manuscripts available for discussion in New Testament textual criticism, and has made the problems of being a New Testament textual critic seem smaller than they really are.

3. EXTENT AND NATURE OF THE PAPYRI

Virtually all of the papyri of the Greek New Testament are thought to come from codices.[29] All but four of these texts have another part of the biblical text written on the other side. Whereas scrolls usually have writing on one side of the papyrus only, the codex, like the modern book, has writing on the front and back, since the individual sheets of papyrus were folded over and bound together.

A few observations must be made about this evidence, however, beginning with the extent of the finds. One hundred and eight papyri, according to the Gregory-Aland system, may seem like a large number, and so it is when compared to what we had access to even fifty or especially 100 years ago. It must also be noted, however, that two-thirds of these papyri are a single folio, that is two pages (front and back), and most of these fragmentary. Of those that are as early as or earlier than the major codices, only about ten extend to more than two pages. Of all the papyri, only about nine of them contain portions of more than one biblical book. In fact, according to the current Gregory-Aland list, not even all of the canonical New Testament is represented by the papyri, with 1 and 2 Timothy lacking. A number of books are represented by only one or two papyri (to give only two examples, 2 Corinthians (P^{34}, P^{46}), and Galatians (P^{46}, P^{51})). For several books P^{74} constitutes a major witness, but P^{74} is dated to the seventh century.[30] Thus there is not the equivalent of an entire New Testament represented by the papyri, and far less of it is to be found that is as early as the major codices.[31] Even though there are several instances where several papyri bear witness to the same biblical passage, 1 and 2 Peter and Jude are the only complete books of the New Testament represented by the papyri. Many of the books represented are missing major sections. For example Matthew is missing chapters 6-9, 15-16 and 22, Mark chapters 1, 3, 10 and 12-16, Luke chapters 19-21, Romans chapter 7, 1 Thessalonians chapter 3, 2 Thessalonians chapters 2 and 3, and Revelation chapters 4, 7, and 18-22.[32] Thus, a major problem in the use of the New Testament Greek papyri is their fragmentary nature.[33]

A further difficulty with the papyri is how they are classified for usage as evidence in New Testament textual criticism. One method is by text-type. The Alexandrian text is widely represented in the papyri, especially in some of the major papyri, such as P^{46}, P^{66} and P^{75}, which are especially close to Codex Vaticanus (though not all in the same way). Several of the papyri, however, represent other text-types, such as the Western text (P^{5} P^{19} P^{25}), or a mix of text-types, such as P^{45}, said by Epp to fall between the codices

Vaticanus and Bezae,[34] or P², said to be a mix of Alexandrian and Western texts. The Alands have also introduced a system of categorization of the papyri according to their value. About half are listed as category I, which is defined in one place as:

Manuscripts of a very special quality which should always be considered in establishing the original text [...] The papyri and uncials through the third/fourth century also belong here automatically, one may say, because they represent the text of the early period.[35]

Apparently this very special quality is that they follow what is 'presumably the original' Alexandrian text, 'before the tradition was channeled into types'.[36] A few texts are classed as category II, defined as: 'Manuscripts of a special quality, but distinguished from manuscripts of category I by the presence of alien influences (particularly of the Byzantine text), and yet of importance for establishing the original text'.[37] Others are category III, 'Manuscripts of a distinctive character with an independent text, usually important for establishing the original text, but particularly important for the history of the text'.[38] A couple of papyri are categorized as category IV, which follows the D text.

One can see from this that there is a significant variation in the perceived role and reliability of the various papyri for establishing the text of the New Testament. One could look more closely at this system of categorization, including the means of dating the manuscripts, the calculation used – which posits as a working hypothesis that the twenty-sixth edition of the Nestle-Aland is the 'original text'[39] – and the fact that one is actually only looking at the Egyptian textual tradition,[40] but I think that I have pointed out enough to show that dealing with the papyri is perhaps more complex than is often realized.

Epp describes the papyri in this way: 'All of the papyri are continuous-text MSS, that is, MSS containing (originally) at least one NT writing in continuous fashion from beginning to end',[41] and then contrasts the papyri from lectionaries on this basis. Do we really know that much about all of the papyri to make such a sweeping statement? We do know that some of the papyri represent continuous-text manuscripts, especially those that have more than one book represented in canonical order, or some variation of it. However, the number of manuscripts with more than one book is surprisingly small. Only ten papyri have the text of more than one book, and only eleven have more than ten folios. I am not as confident that we can make the same determination from those manuscripts that only have one text. The argument appears to be that the verso of the papyrus represents the continuation of the text occurring on the recto, and on the basis of the relative length between texts, the size of the codex can be determined. But does this necessarily mean that the manuscript is not a lectionary? Perhaps it is simply that all that we have is quotation of one text at this particular place in the codex; we may well have more lectionary texts among the papyri than we think.

This sounds rather speculative, however, there are several pieces of evidence that might shed further light on the situation. Firstly, the pre-eighth century lectionary texts do not have lexical systems of pericopes that agree with the normal Greek lectionary,[42] therefore a very small text, such as may be written on only two sides of a small papyrus, may well be a portion of a reading. The problem is that we do not have a means of checking simply on the basis of this small text. Secondly, we find indications that destroyed portions of papyri may have had more than simply the biblical text, or at least simply continuous biblical text. For example, two papyri in the Vienna collection (P⁵⁵, P⁷⁶) have portions of John's Gospel on them, but at the bottom of the fragment is the word *hermeneia*, 'translation' or 'interpretation'. On one of the papyri below *hermeneia* there is a paraphrase of some Johannine-sounding language.

What are we to make of these and similar texts (P⁶⁰, according to Metzger)⁴³ – should they be reclassified as lectionaries or commentaries? It is difficult to consider these continuous texts in the same way as a text that clearly contains only the biblical text. It seems to me to be continuous text in the way that a modern commentary, such as one by Lightfoot, has commentary below the Greek text. The translation or interpretation implies that this text had a liturgical purpose, and thus was not simply an edition of the biblical text. A manuscript that might also be helpful in illustrating the fluid boundaries between these categories is PVindob. G. 29831. Greg Horsley contends that this document, which was originally published as a biblical amulet with John 1.5-6 on it, constitutes the rejected pages of a miniature codex.⁴⁴ Whether Horsley's conclusions are accepted or not is beside the point,⁴⁵ but what these examples do show is that attempts to rigidly define the difference between a true biblical text and another text, such as a lectionary text, are problematic.

As a result, the lectionary text has been greatly neglected, since it was thought not to be continuous text but a text designed for liturgical use. I would be intrigued to discover which copies of the Greek New Testament were not used in early Christian worship and liturgy in some way. How can we know? The presumption would seem to be that at least the vast majority of these documents were copied within a Christian community, and designed for reading and study within that context. It was thought that lectionaries were of lesser quality because less care was taken in their copying, but this has now been shown to be false in the light of their ostensible use and consistency one to another, even if many represent what is called the Byzantine text.⁴⁶

The definition of continuous text also requires further clarification. How much continuous text is necessary for the text to qualify? As noted above, so many of the texts have so little text that it cannot be determined that they are continuous or not. Some of the lectionaries have a significant amount more continuous text than the papyri that we have. For example, papyri with five or fewer verses include P², P⁷, and P¹² (with a single verse!) – these papyri are given the benefit of the doubt as being continuous. On the other hand, *l*1043 alone includes in Greek Matthew 3.7-17, 4.23-5.12, 7.13-20, 10.37-42, 9.35, Mark 6.18-29, Luke 2.1-20, 11.27-32, 24.36-8 and John 20.1-18 and 24-7.

Aland and Aland admit that there is institutionalized confusion regarding which texts have been included in the list of papyri:

Among the ninety-six [now roughly 108] items which now comprise the official list of New Testament papyri there are several which by a strict definition do not belong there, such as talismans (P⁵⁰ [fourth-fifth century], P⁷⁸ [third-fourth century]), lectionaries (P² [sixth century], P³ [sixth-seventh century], P⁴⁴ [sixth-seventh century]), various selections (P⁴³ [sixth-seventh century], P⁶² [fourth century]), songs (P⁴² [seventh-eighth century]), texts with commentary (P⁵⁵ [sixth-seventh century], P⁵⁹ [seventh century], P⁶⁰ [seventh century], P⁶³ [500], P⁸⁰ [third century]), and even writing exercises (P¹⁰ [fourth century]) and occasional notes (P¹² [third century]).⁴⁷

Several other papryi should be included in the list of problematic documents as well. These include P⁷ (third-fourth century), which Aland and Aland consider questionable as being a patristic fragment,⁴⁸ P²⁵ (fourth century), which may well be a fragment of the Diatessaron, and P^{76} (sixth century), which has the words *hermeneia*, as noted above. Thus, by this reckoning, eighteen of the approximately 108 papyri are problematic, almost half of these are early documents. The Alands' explanation of these phenomena is also worth noting: 'The presence of lectionaries may be explained as due to a structural flaw in the overall system, the inclusion of commented texts to the lack of an adequate definition for this genre [...] and the other examples are due to the occasionally uncritical attitude of earlier editors of the list.'[49]

Each of these explanations merits brief comment. Taking the third explanation first, nine of the papyri listed above were apparently included under Kurt Aland's tenure as caretaker of the list.[50] The first and second explanations support what I have asserted above, that the system has flaws with regard to lectionaries.

What possible solutions are open to us? One would be to restrict the classificatory definitions severely, and exclude the texts now seen to be wrongly included. Another would be to expand the definitions, and include texts that have probably wrongly been excluded. The Alands' solution is found in their conclusion: 'But these peculiarities are on the whole negligible.'[51] I am not entirely convinced. Eighteen of 108 instances is one in six, or just under 17 per cent of the total, hardly negligible. A re-thinking of the categories regarding the papyri would seem to be in order. As a consequence of discussion at the conference when this paper was first presented, I would like to propose that there be two lists of New Testament manuscripts. One of the lists would be given to those documents for which there is little or no doubt regarding their being New Testament manuscripts. The other would include those documents for which there is some doubt, such as the papyri noted above (including lectionaries), the Apocryphal Gospels, as well as some other manuscripts noted further below. These should be included in discussion of the text of the New Testament, but should not be relied upon as being continuous text.

The analysis above also has several direct implications for New Testament textual criticism, in which the standard printed editions represent what are called eclectic editions. These editions are, so far as I can determine, supposedly based upon the four major codices (Sinaiticus, Vaticanus, Bezae and Washingtonianus), along with the fourth-century and earlier papyri and the four earliest parchment (majuscule) documents.[52] I wonder how wise it is to rely so heavily upon the papyri, in the light of the evidence marshalled above. The exact nature of some of these texts is unknown, in the sense that one is not certain of their nature, composition or use. There is so little extant text that to put much stock in them at all would seem to be unwise, since no sort of scribal tendencies can be established. In fact, it may be that little attention has been paid to them. Epp notes that modern critical editions, including the twenty-fifth edition of the Nestle-Aland text, are not significantly different from the edition of Westcott and Hort, which did not have access to any papyri. He therefore concludes that the papyri have not been incorporated in a significant way into New Testament textual criticism. He sees this as a shortcoming.[53] Even the more radically revised twenty-sixth edition the Nestle-Aland (identical to the twenty-seventh edition) is only changed in 176 places, rejecting 980 possible instances where the earliest papyri have another reading, including a number from P^{45}, P^{46}, and P^{66}.[54] I would suggest that we recognize what tacitly is the case and move away from an idealized eclectic text that never existed in any Christian community back to the codices that still form the basis of our modern textual tradition. We certainly should re-evaluate the hypothesis that the Nestle-Aland text is tantamount to the original text,[55] unless it agrees with one of the major codices. These codices represent the Bible for a given Christian community, and while they may not represent the text as it came penned from the author, this is probably as early as we can get while still preserving the integrity of the New Testament. This would bring New Testament textual criticism into line with that of the Hebrew Bible, as well as much classical textual criticism.[56] Furthermore, in the light of what we know about canonical formation,[57] it is difficult to talk with certainty about the shape and transmission of the New Testament before the fourth century, therefore some of the texts usually excluded from New Testament textual criticism should probably be given Gregory-Aland numbers, or at least have their status shifted so that such things as lectionaries, commentaries, and possibly even so-called apocryphal Gospels are included in the text-critical discussion.

4. DO ALL OF THE NEW TESTAMENT PAPYRI COME FROM EGYPT?

One of the distinguishing features of the New Testament Greek papyri is that, as Epp says, they all come from Egypt. However, the wider field of papyrological studies has provided useful information that has helped New Testament scholars to be able to understand more of the process of textual transmission, on the basis of what is known of Egypt. Thus Epp states,

we may reasonably assert, although not yet easily prove, that the various textual complexions evident in our very earliest manuscripts, the Egyptian papyri, very possibly and quite plausibly represent texts from that *entire Mediterranean region* (including, of course, forms of text that might have originated in Egypt itself). Thus, in contrast to the common view that the papyri represent only the text of provincial Egypt, it is much more likely that they represent an extensive textual range (if not the full textual spectrum) of earliest Christianity.[58]

As noted above, even the papyri of Egypt represent a range of texts,[59] and the possibility must be left open that findings from elsewhere may affect the textual picture. We know that papyrus was widely used throughout the Mediterranean world as a common writing material. Due to its physical properties, including its biodegradable composition, it has not been found in the same quantities outside of Egypt, but instructive examples have been discovered, nevertheless. For example, one of the earliest finds of texts was from Herculaneum, buried by the eruption of Vesuvius in AD 79. These carbonized documents included many texts from the philosopher Philodemus, as well as others.[60] There have been other finds as well, including some documents from Greece, Dura-Europas, and even Palestine.[61] The Palestinian documents have been the most instructive since they include a range of items. The Babatha archive and related finds have included documentary papyri very similar to those found in Egypt, chronicling the personal affairs of a woman involved in a variety of legal and financial transactions regarding her family and estate.[62] There have also been found various texts of the Old Testament, for example, in the Dead Sea region.[63]

Many papyri are still to be deciphered. Some may be New Testament Greek papyri, although it is not likely that many more New Testament papyri from Egypt will be found (short of new archival discoveries), since when the papyri were first discovered efforts were made to scan them quickly to see if any of them were of special significance for Christianity. That is the reason that such texts as the Sayings of Jesus were published as POxy. 1,[64] and a fragment of Matthew's Gospel as POxy. 2, and that P³ (PVindob. G. 2323, 1884) was followed so closely by publication of the Fayyum fragment (PVindob. G. 2325).[65] Many of the papyri that remain are much later Byzantine documents, and while they have intrinsic value in illuminating the ancient world of that time, they do not have the same significance as earlier texts, and certainly not the attraction of the biblical texts.

A fragment of a New Testament Greek text could emerge from a new discovery of papyri at some other site in the ancient world besides Egypt. One could argue that it is simply an accident of history that one has not been found (and it would be highly desirable to do so), since we know that Christianity early on had at least a foothold throughout Palestine, Asia Minor, Greece and Italy, as attested by no less than the Pauline letters and the traditions that they relate. Therefore, it should not be particularly surprising if a fragment were to be identified, even if tentatively, as a fragment of a New Testament text from outside of Egypt. The most likely place for such a fragment to be found, not on the basis of the spread of Christianity but on the basis of where other papyri have come to light, is in the Roman Near East, especially around the Dead Sea.[66]

This, in fact, is what has been claimed. Joseph O'Callaghan tentatively, followed by several others, most recently Carsten Thiede more vigorously, has argued that a portion of 1 Timothy and a portion of Mark have been discovered in Qumran cave 7 (a cave that had exclusively Greek documents, now numbered 1-19), besides possibly some other New Testament books.[67] In the light of what I have observed above, it strikes me as being very odd that there has been such a strong outcry against their suppositions. I do not have time to discuss the texts from cave 7 in depth here,[68] but I would say this: although we are far from establishing the certainty of New Testament documents as having been found as a part of the Qumran archives, in the light of the papyrological evidence, and the nature of papyrological studies, we should reconsider whether a simple dismissal of the two fragments found in cave 7 – 7Q4 and 7Q5 – is the most responsible way of handling the evidence. Should these fragments be given Gregory-Aland numbers? If the amulet that Horsley suggests is a discarded page of a codex is given a number (perhaps in the second list introduced above), and if the papyri that appear to be lectionaries and the like are placed in the second list, then I suggest that these two papyri should be given a place in the second list (introduced above) and not prematurely dismissed.

5. STEPS FORWARD IN PAPYROLOGICAL RESEARCH

Papyrological research as a whole has been stymied in a number of ways. The sheer number of texts to be restored, edited, reconstructed and published with informative notes is almost overwhelming in itself. Phenomenal progress has been made, but, as noted above, at the most half of the discovered papyri have been published, even though probably most of them have been known now for almost one hundred years. As most papyrologists know, there are entire collections still untouched. For example, I have been in contact with one major library that has over nine large file boxes full of Byzantine papyri, virtually unedited and unstudied, last apparently looked at (before I opened the boxes) in the early 1970s. The same situation does not hold for New Testament papyri, although there is always the possibility that some important New Testament document will be found in one of these archives. The second restriction is that there has been a methodological limitation on papyrological research. The documentary papyri have been seen to provide one of the best sources of knowledge of incidental data regarding the financial, economic, personal, and religious realities of the inhabitants of the ancient world. In other words, they have been used as sources for historical information and reconstruction, and much more should be made of how the papyri can figure into methodological revision of the historical method.[69] The next stage after the texts have been deciphered is to understand what they imply regarding the world from which they emerged, teasing out the implications of the significant contextual details contained within the papyri. The literary papyri have been primarily examined as support for the traditional concerns of philology, that is, establishing the texts of the best-read authors of the ancient world.

Whereas Bagnall has raised the very important issue of the role that the papyri can and should play in historical research, the linguistic side remains neglected, despite the huge quantities of linguistic data that have been generated. Greg Horsley and Paul van Minnen at the international papyrological conference in Copenhagen in 1992 issued a challenge to explore the usage of modern linguistic methodology for the study of the papyri.[70] Among other issues that he notes for further attention, Horsley specifically addresses the issues of verbal aspect, bilingualism, the dating of texts, responsibility in restoring fragmentary texts to be used in linguistic study, the place of koine and the issue of dialect, the study of particles, the use of quotations, the issue of register, the role of sociolinguistics, translation and word order. I could not agree more that such areas have been neglected, not only in much papyrological study, but especially in the role that they might play in analyzing the papyri (as well as other documents) that bear on New Testament textual criticism. As van Minnen states,

> The study of phonology, morphology, and syntax, the three parts of traditional grammar, are badly in need of an update. Beyond that, no one has attempted to apply text grammar, discourse analysis, and sociolinguistics to Greek papyri. And yet, Greek papyri represent a thousand years in the study of the Greek language and, moreover, a bilingual culture that was apparently able to cope somehow with the problems inherent in such a culture.[71]

For example, there has been little study of variants in terms of Greek verbal structure, after having determined a given biblical author's linguistic tendencies. These tendencies could be cross-checked against what is known of frequency of verbal occurrence in order to establish or check dates of individual papyri. Word order has only recently begun to receive the kind of attention that it should in the study of the Greek New Testament. Once inaccurate estimations of word order have been exposed, it will be possible to evaluate variants in terms of what constitutes marked and unmarked word order. Similar kinds of studies need to be done regarding particles, as well as other types of words and structures. The issue of register, in conjunction with a greater attention to sociolinguistic factors, could prove insightful for analysis of the context of situation of a given New Testament document, as well as various fragmentary papyri.[72] Variants could well point to different contexts of situation in which these texts were copied and used.

As important as these various linguistic topics are for general study of the Greek of the New Testament, and in particular for textual criticism, an area that has only recently been explored is that of discourse analysis and textual criticism. Discourse analysis is a complex linguistically-based set of methods, involving not only traditional areas of linguistic analysis such as lexicography, semantics, syntax, and pragmatics, but more recent areas such as corpus-based techniques and complex statistical analysis – all of which would need to be applied at different linguistic levels.[73] These should include analysis of extant whole documents before fragments are studied. Textual criticism has long had as one of its principles that any variant unit should be evaluated in the light of the author's style.[74] However, the concept of style has rarely been adequately defined in linguistic arenas, to say nothing of text-critical circles, and has only made serious progress recently when integrated into a discourse framework. The utilization of discourse analysis to establish and evaluate discourse tendencies as a means of testing variants would seem to be a natural and needed methodological step forward in New Testament textual criticism of the papyri. The book of Acts is one place where there has been significant work on style in terms of comparing texts.[75] Similarly, the only discourse analytical textual criticism to date that I am aware of has studied Codex Bezae and the book of Acts.[76] Much more can and must be done in these areas.

CONCLUSION

Papyrology is an exciting and ever-changing and developing field, in which new documents are brought to light, published and discussed for the insight they give into the ancient world in which Christianity developed and in which its texts were written and disseminated. However, New Testament scholars have tended to focus upon textual criticism, perhaps at the expense of being papyrologists first and text-critics second. The result has been, as I hope to have shown, some distortion of the nature of the textual situation with regard to the papyri. Perhaps one of the greatest problems is that extra-palaeographical concerns have, it seems to me, interfered with this discussion. The introduction of two lists of manuscripts might well go some of the way toward alleviating some of these difficulties. If we are able to take a step back and approach some of the same New Testament papyrus fragments, as well as other documents, from a broader and more innovative papyrological perspective, we will perhaps arrive at fewer certainties, but lay a better foundation for the few that we do find.

NOTES

1 See E. G. Turner, *Greek Papyri: An Introduction* (Oxford: Clarendon Press, 1968), pp. 17-41, for a good history of the discovery and publication of the papyri. An early account by one of those at the forefront is found in F. G. Kenyon, *The Palaeography of Greek Papyri* (Oxford: Clarendon Press, 1899), esp. pp. 34-55, with plates. For a checklist of the major papyrological publications, see J. F. Oates et al., *Checklist of Editions of Greek Papyri and Ostraca*, BASPSup, 4, 3rd edn (Atlanta: Scholars Press, 1985).

Why so Many Holes in the Papyrological Evidence?

2 See P. van Minnen, 'The Century of Papyrology (1892-1992)', *BASP*, 30 (1993), 5-18, for a brief history, but I think that his statistics are inaccurate.

3 See E. J. Epp, 'Textual Criticism in the Exegesis of the New Testament, with an Excursus on Canon', in *Handbook to Exegesis of the New Testament*, ed. by S. E. Porter, NTTS, 25 (Leiden: Brill, 1997), 65.

4 For discussion of the history of the New Testament Greek papyri, see E. J. Epp, 'The Papyrus Manuscripts of the New Testament', in *The Text of the New Testament in Contemporary Research: Essays on the Status Quaestionis*, ed. by B. D. Ehrman and M. W. Holmes, SD, 46 (Grand Rapids: Eerdmans, 1995), esp. pp. 4-6.

5 See B. Aland and K. Wachtel, 'The Greek Minuscule Manuscripts of the New Testament', in *The Text of the New Testament* (ed. Ehrman and Holmes), pp. 43-60; cf. K. Aland and B. Aland, *The Text of the New Testament*, trans. by E. F. Rhodes, 2nd edn (Grand Rapids: Eerdmans, 1989), pp. 128-58, with plates.

6 These are surveyed in B. M. Metzger, *The Early Versions of the New Testament: Their Origin, Transmission, and Limitations* (Oxford: Clarendon Press, 1977).

7 On Tischendorf and the discovery of Codex Sinaiticus, see S. E. Porter, *The Grammarian's Rebirth: Dead Languages and Live Issues in Current Biblical Study* (London: Roehampton Institute London, [1996]), pp. 7-10, with bibliography p. 23; cf. J. Bentley, *Secrets of Mount Sinai: The Story of the Codex Sinaiticus* (London: Orbis, 1985). On Codex Vaticanus, and Tischendorf's involvement in its publication, see F. G. Kenyon, *The Text of the Greek Bible*, ed. by A. W. Adams, 3rd edn (London: Duckworth, 1975), pp. 87-8.

8 C. Tischendorf, *Novum Testamentum Graece*, 2 vols, 8th edn (Leipzig: Giesecke & Devrient, 1869, 1872); B. F. Westcott and F. J. A. Hort, *The New Testament in the Original Greek*, 2 vols (Cambridge and London: Macmillan, 1881). Cf. K. Aland, 'The Significance of the Papyri for Progress in New Testament Research', in *The Bible in Modern Scholarship*, ed. by J. P. Hyatt (London: Carey Kingsgate, 1966), pp. 325-7.

9 PVindob. G. 2323, Kiev Centr. Nauc. Bibl. F. 301 (KDA) 553 p, PBerol. 8683, PHarris 14.

10 (London: Macmillan, 1926), 21.

11 The first publication of the Oxyrhynchus collection dates to 1898. See P¹ (POxy. I 2), P⁵ (POxy. II 208), P⁹ (POxy. III 402), P¹⁰ (POxy. II 209), P¹³ (POxy. V 657), P¹⁵ (POxy. VII 1008), P¹⁶ (POxy. VII 1009), P¹⁷ (POxy. VIII 1078), P¹⁸ (POxy. VIII 1079), P¹⁹ (POxy. IX 1170), P²⁰ (POxy. IX 1171), P²¹ (POxy. X 1227), P²² (POxy. X 1228), P²³ (POxy. X 1229), P²⁴ (POxy. X 1230), P²⁶ (POxy. XI 1354), P²⁷ (POxy. XI 1355), P²⁸ (POxy. XIII 1596), P²⁹ (POxy. XIII 1597), P³⁰ (POxy. XIII 1598), P³⁹ (POxy. XV 1780), P⁵¹ (P.Oxy. XVIII 2157), P⁶⁹ (POxy. XXIV 2383), P⁷¹ (POxy. XXIV 2385), P⁷⁷ (POxy. XXXIV 2683), P⁷⁸ (POxy. XXXIV 2684), P⁹⁰ (POxy. L 3523), plus those cited above. The Chester Beatty papyri were published from 1933 to 1937 (P⁴⁵ P⁴⁶ P⁴⁷) and the Bodmer papyri in the mid-1950s (P⁶⁶ P⁷² P⁷⁴ P⁷⁵, with P⁷³ being published in 1990).

12 G. Zuntz, *The Text of the Epistles: A Disquisition upon the Corpus Paulinum*, Schweich Lectures 1946 (London: British Academy, 1953).

13 Epp, 'Papyrus Manuscripts', pp. 11-13.

14 Epp, 'Textual Criticism', p. 65.

15 Epp, 'Textual Criticism', p. 65. Cf. C. D. Osburn, 'The Greek Lectionaries of the New Testament', in *The Text of the New Testament* (ed. Ehrman and Holmes), p. 62.

16 The terminological inexactitude is continued even among those who attempt to correct it. After rejecting the use of uncial to refer to what he calls majuscule manuscripts, confining the term to particular Latin manuscripts, Parker says the following: 'With regard to the class of MS of the Greek NT with which we are concerned, a MS must satisfy three criteria if it is to be included: script, material, and contents: majuscule in script, parchment as to material, and with a continuous text rather than lections [...] If a MS in a majuscule hand is written on

papyrus, then it is classified among the papyri; if it is a lectionary as to contents, then it should be classified among the lectionaries [...] Because of these three criteria, one could argue that the designation "uncial" refers not to the script so much as to the whole character of the book in question. This usage is so common as to be almost universal. Nevertheless, it is palaeographically inexact, and we must learn to do without it. The term *majuscule* will be employed throughout the present study.' Of course, by his own definition, the term majuscule is just as imprecise as uncial. See D. C. Parker, 'The Majuscule Manuscripts of the New Testament', in *The Text of the New Testament* (ed. Ehrman and Holmes), p. 22.

17 See M. L. Bierbrier (ed.), *Papyrus: Structure and Usage* (London: British Museum, 1986).

18 Epp, 'Textual Criticism', p. 65.

19 See C. Wessely, *Prolegomena ad Papyrorum Graecorum Novam Collectionem Edendam* (Vienna: Gerold, 1883); cf. his *Aus der Welt der Papyri* (Leipzig: Haessel, 1914).

20 R. Bagnall, *Reading Papyri, Writing Ancient History* (London: Routledge, 1995), pp. 9-10.

21 B. M. Metzger, *The Text of the New Testament: Its Transmission, Corruption, and Restoration* (New York: Oxford University Press, 1968), p. 37.

22 All of these are to be issued in a new edition in S. E. Porter and W. J. Porter (eds), *New Testament Greek Papyri and Parchments: New Editions*, MPER, ns 28 (Vienna: Austrian National Library, forthcoming).

23 See Aland and Aland, *Text of the New Testament*, pp. 72-5.

24 See, for example, J. H. Charlesworth and C. A. Evans, 'Jesus in the Agrapha and Apocryphal Gospels', in *Studying the Historical Jesus: Evaluations of the State of Current Research*, ed. by B. Chilton and C. A. Evans, NTTS, 19 (Leiden: Brill, 1994), pp. 491-532.

25 See, for example, R. J. Miller (ed.), *The Complete Gospels* (San Francisco: HarperCollins, 1994).

26 See P. W. Comfort, *The Quest for the Original Text of the New Testament* (Grand Rapids: Baker, 1992), p. 60; cf. E. G. Turner, 'Scribes and Scholars of Oxyrhynchus', in *Akten des VIII. Internationalen Kongresses für Papyrologie Wien 1955*, ed. by H. Gerstinger, MPER, ns 5 (Vienna: Rohrer, 1956), pp. 141-6.

27 J. van Haelst, *Catalogue des Papyrus Littéraires Juifs et Chrétiens*, Université de Paris IV Paris-Sorbonne série 'Papyrologie', 1 (Paris: Publications de la Sorbonne, 1976).

28 For example, W. J. Elliott and D. C. Parker (eds), *The New Testament in Greek. IV. The Gospel According to St John, Volume 1: The Papyri*, NTTS, 20 (Leiden: Brill, 1995).

29 There are four papyri which may not come from codices, each of which is problematic (P^{12} P^{13} P^{18} P^{43}). There are peculiarities with several of these papyri, some of them being opistographs. For example, P^{12} has Hebrews 1.1 on the recto but Genesis 1.1-5 on the verso; P^{13} (which is actually two sets of fragments, POxy. V 657 and PSI 1292) has portions of Hebrews written on a papyrus with a text of Livy on the other side; P^{18} is written on the verso of a papyrus with another text on the other side; P^{43} has portions of Revelation on each side, but in different hands with radically different line lengths. Nevertheless, P^{18} and P^{22} (which has a blank recto side) are considered scrolls by L. Vaganay, *An Introduction to New Testament Textual Criticism*, rev. by C.-B. Amphoux, trans. by J. Heimerdinger, 2nd edn (Cambridge: University Press, 1991), p. 11; contra Aland and Aland, *Text of the New Testament*, p. 102.

30 Cf. Aland and Aland, *Text of the New Testament*, p. 85, who consider this a reliable text.

31 See the chart in Aland and Aland, *Text of the New Testament*, p. 85, for dating of papyri in relation to the books of the New Testament.

32 I am grateful to J. Chapa for his paper, 'Fragments from a Papyrus Codex of the Book of Revelation', delivered at the XXII Congresso Internazionale Di Papirologia, Florence, 23-29 August 1998, bringing information regarding Revelation up to date. His text of this papyrus is published now as POxy. LXVI 4499.

Why so Many Holes in the Papyrological Evidence?

33 See Fee, 'Papyrus Manuscripts', p. 11; cf. Aland and Aland, *Text of the New Testament*, pp. A-C.

34 Epp, 'Papyrus Manuscripts', p. 14.

35 Aland and Aland, *Text of the New Testament*, p. 106.

36 Aland and Aland, *Text of the New Testament*, pp. 159, 335.

37 Aland and Aland, *Text of the New Testament*, p. 106; cf. p. 335.

38 Aland and Aland, *Text of the New Testament*, p. 106; cf. pp. 335-6.

39 Aland and Aland, *Text of the New Testament*, p. 333. The Introduction to the twenty-seventh edition of the Nestle-Aland (e.g. 45*-46*) seems to back away from this position.

40 K. W. Clark, 'Today's Problems with the Critical Text of the New Testament', in *Transitions in Biblical Scholarship*, ed. by J. C. Rylaarsdam, Essays in Divinity, 6 (Chicago: University of Chicago Press, 1968), pp. 163-4.

41 Epp, 'Papyrus Manuscripts', p. 5.

42 See Aland and Aland, *Text of the New Testament*, p. 167; cf. Osburn, 'Greek Lectionaries', p. 63.

43 See Metzger, *Text of the New Testament*, p. 253; idem, 'Greek Manuscripts of John's Gospel with "Hermeneiai"', in *Text and Testimony: Essays on New Testament and Apocryphal Literature, in Honour of A. F. J. Klijn* (Kampen: Kok, 1988), pp. 162-9. Cf. H. Quecke, 'Zu den Joh-Fragmenten mit "Hermeneiai"', *Orientalia Christiana Periodica*, 40 (1974), 407-14; 43 (1977), 179-81; B. Outtier, 'Les *prosermeneiai* du Codex Bezae', in *Codex Bezae: Studies from the Lund Colloquium June 1994*, ed. by D. C. Parker and C.-B. Amphoux, NTTS, 24 (Leiden: Brill, 1996), pp. 74-8.

44 G. H. R. Horsley, 'Reconstructing a Biblical Codex: The Prehistory of MPER n.s. XVII. 10 (*P. Vindob*. G 29 831)', in *Akten des 21. Internationalen Papyrologenkongresses Berlin, 13.-19.8.1995*, ed. by B. Kramer, W. Luppe, H. Maehler, and G. Poethke, 2 vols (Stuttgart: Teubner, 1997), I, pp. 473-81.

45 I am not convinced that these pages were ever part of a biblical text, lectionary or otherwise, since Horsley's major argument, that the biblical passage on the pages is not of an amulet sort, still holds even if it originated as a blotted copy of a codex.

46 Other examples include P^{18} P^{71} P^{73} P^{76} P^{78} P^{80} P^{93} P^{96}, POxy. LXIV 4402 and 4446. Oburn, 'Greek Lectionaries', p. 61, citing D. W. Riddle, 'The Use of Lectionaries in Critical Editions and Studies of the New Testament Text', in *Prolegomena to the Study of the Lectionary Text of the Gospels*, ed. by D. W. Riddle and E. C. Colwell, SLTGNT, 1 (Chicago: University of Chicago Press, 1933), pp. 74-5; Aland and Aland, *Text of the New Testament*, p. 169. Cf. also Epp, 'Textual Criticism', pp. 66-7.

47 Aland and Aland, *Text of the New Testament*, p. 85. Cf. Vaganay, *Introduction to New Testament Textual Criticism*, p. 24, who lists P^3 P^4 and P^{44}. But is this correct? Cf. L. Vaganay, *An Introduction to the Textual Criticism of the New Testament*, trans. by B. V. Miller (London: Sands, 1937), p. 33, where a typographical error seems to have created a new papyrus number as a lectionary.

48 Aland and Aland, *Text of the New Testament*, p. 96.

49 Aland and Aland, *Text of the New Testament*, p. 85.

50 According to Aland and Aland, *Text of the New Testament*, p. 74, the papyri reached P^{14} under Gregory, and P^{48} under von Dobschütz, with subsequent numbers Kurt Aland's responsibility.

51 Aland and Aland, *Text of the New Testament*, p. 85.

52 The four earliest parchment (majuscule) documents are 0189 0220 0162 0171; cf. 0212. Epp, 'Textual Criticism', p. 66; Aland and Aland, *Text of the New Testament*, p. 104.

53 Epp, 'Papyrus Manuscripts', pp. 13-14. Cf. also his 'The Twentieth-Century Interlude in New Testament Textual Criticism', repr. in E. J. Epp and G. D. Fee, *Studies in the Theory*

and Method of New Testament Textual Criticism, SD, 45 (Grand Rapids: Eerdmans, 1993), 84-5.

54 See Comfort, *Quest for the Original Text*, pp. 123, 125.

55 See Aland and Aland, *Text of the New Testament*, pp. 24, 333.

56 Cf. C. M. Martini, 'Eclecticism and Atticism in the Textual Criticism of the Greek New Testament', in *On Language, Culture, and Religion: In Honor of Eugene A. Nida*, ed. by M. Black and W. A. Smalley (The Hague: Mouton, 1974), pp. 149-56. For another alternative, relying upon the earliest papyri, see Comfort, *Quest for the Original Text*, pp. 129-34.

57 For discussion of this issue, see F. F. Bruce, *The Canon of Scripture* (Glasgow: Chapter House, 1988), esp. pp. 115 ff.; L. M. McDonald, *The Formation of the Christian Biblical Canon*, 2nd edn (Peabody: Hendrickson, 1995), esp. pp. 195 ff. Cf. T. C. Skeat, 'Early Christian Book-Production: Papyri and Manuscripts', in *The Cambridge History of the Bible. II. The West from the Fathers to the Reformation*, ed. by G. W. H. Lampe (Cambridge: University Press, 1969), pp. 54-79; C. H. Roberts and T. C. Skeat, *The Birth of the Codex* (London: British Academy, 1983); T. C. Skeat, 'The Origin of the Christian Codex', *ZPE*, 102 (1994), 263-8; H. Y. Gamble, *Books and Readers in the Early Church* (New Haven: Yale University Press, 1995), *passim*.

58 Epp, 'Textual Criticism', p. 58.

59 See Clark, 'Critical Text of the New Testament', p. 165.

60 On the earliest published Herculaneum texts, see Turner, *Greek Papyri*, p. 171. Publication continues, as evidenced in the series *Ricerche sui Papiri Ercolanesi* (Naples: Giannini, 1969-), and in various other collections of papyri, such as articles by M. Capasso, D. Delattre, M. Gigante, G. Indelli, K. Kleve, F. Longo Auricchio, in *Akten des 21. Internationalen Papyrologenkongresses*.

61 On the Derveni papyrus (PDerveni), the earliest literary papyrus found, and one of the few from Greece, see A. Laks and G. W. Most (eds), *Studies on the Derveni Papyrus* (Oxford: Clarendon Press, 1996); on the papyri of Dura-Europas, see G. D. Kilpatrick, 'Dura-Europas: The Parchments and the Papyri', *GRBS*, 5 (1964), 215-25; and on the papyri of the Roman near east, including Palestine, see H. M. Cotton, W. E. H. Cockle and F. G. B. Millar, 'The Papyrology of the Roman Near East: A Survey', *JRS*, 85 (1995), 214-35.

62 See N. Lewis, *The Documents from the Bar Kokhba Period in the Cave of Letters: Greek Papyri* (Jerusalem: Israel Exploration Society, Hebrew University of Jerusalem, Shrine of the Book, 1989); H. M. Cotton and A. Yardeni, *Aramaic, Hebrew and Greek Documentary Texts from Naḥal Ḥever and Other Sites (The Seiyâl Collection II)*, DJD, 27 (Oxford: Clarendon Press, 1997), esp. 133-279.

63 See E. Tov, *The Greek Minor Prophets Scroll from Naḥal Ḥever (8HevXIIgr)*, DJD, 8 (Oxford: Clarendon Press, 1990); 4QLXXLevᵃ, 4QLXXLevᵇ, 4QLXXNum, 4QLXXDeut, all in P. W. Skehan, E. Ulrich and J. E. Sanderson, *Qumran Cave 4. IV. Palaeo-Hebrew and Greek Biblical Manuscripts*, DJD, 9 (Oxford: Clarendon Press, 1990).

64 Published independently as B. P. Grenfell and A. S. Hunt (eds), Λογια Ιησου: *Sayings of Our Lord from an Early Greek Papyrus* (London: Frowde, 1897).

65 See C. Wessely, 'Evangelien-Fragmente auf Papyrus', *Wiener Studien*, 4 (1882), 198-214; idem, 'Analekten. 1. Neue Evangelien-Fragmente auf Papyrus,' *Wiener Studien*, 7 (1885), 69-70; G. Bickell, 'Ein Papyrusfragment eines nichtkanonischen Evangeliums', *ZKT*, 9 (1885), 498-504, followed by many other editions and re-editions.

66 See S. E. Porter, 'The Greek Papyri of the Judaean Desert and the World of the Roman East', in *The Scrolls and the Scriptures: Qumran Fifty Years After*, ed. by S. E. Porter and C. A. Evans, JSPSup, 26, RILP, 3 (Sheffield: Academic Press, 1997), pp. 293-316, for discussion of the linguistic character of the Roman near east.

67 See J. O'Callaghan, '¿Papiros neotestamentarios en la cueva 7 de Qumrân?', *Biblica*, 53

(1972), 91-100; idem, '¿1 Tim 3,16; 4,1.3 en 7Q4?', *Biblica*, 53 (1972), 362-67; *idem*, 'Tres probables papiros neotestamentarios en la cueva 7 de Qumrân', *StudPap*, 11 (1972), 83-9; idem, 'Sobre la identificación de 7Q4', *StudPap*, 13 (1974), 45-55; idem, 'Sobre el papiro de Marcos en Qumran', *FN*, 5 (1992), 191-8; for several of his major publications. He is followed by C. P. Thiede, *The Earliest Gospel Manuscript? The Qumran Fragment 7Q5 and its Significance for New Testament Studies* (Exeter: Paternoster, 1992), *passim*; and idem, *Rekindling the Word: In Search of Gospel Truth* (Leominster: Gracewing, 1995), pp. 158-204, whose work I rely upon here. For bibliography up to 1990 of both O'Callaghan, and his supporters and detractors, see J. A. Fitzmyer, *The Dead Sea Scrolls: Major Publications and Tools for Study*, SBLRBS, 20 (Atlanta: Scholars Press, 1990), pp. 168-72; to be supplemented by G. N. Stanton, *Gospel Truth? New Light on Jesus and the Gospels* (London: HarperCollins, 1995), pp. 20-32, 197-8; and E. Tov, 'The Greek Biblical Texts from the Judean Desert', in this volume. One of the few New Testament scholars to weigh seriously O'Callaghan's proposals is W. L. Lane, *The Gospel According to Mark*, NICNT (Grand Rapids: Eerdmans, 1974), pp. 18-21.

68 For further reading on the issues involved, see A. R. C. Leaney, 'Greek Manuscripts from the Judaean Desert', in *Studies in New Testament Language and Text: Essays in Honour of George D. Kilpatrick on the Occasion of his Sixty-Fifth Birthday*, ed. by J. K. Elliott, NovTSup, 44 (Leiden: Brill, 1976), pp. 292-300, who gives serious consideration to O'Callaghan's proposals, while finally rejecting them. The texts were published in M. Baillet, J. T. Milik and R. de Vaux (eds), *Les 'Petites Grottes' de Qumrân*, DJD, 3 (Oxford: Clarendon Press, 1962). The unique character of the cave has been pointed out by C. M. Martini, 'Note sui papiri della grotta 7 di Qumran', *Biblica*, 53 (1972), 101-4, who thinks it may even have been used by Christians. For discussion of recent findings regarding the Qumran community, see C. Hempel, 'Qumran Communities: Beyond the Fringes of Second Temple Society', in *The Scrolls and the Scriptures*, ed. by S. E. Porter and C. A. Evans, pp. 43-53. For discussion of the issues of dating of books of the New Testament, see L. M. McDonald and S. E. Porter, *Early Christianity and its Sacred Literature* (Peabody: Hendrickson, 2000), chs 8 and 10. See also P. Benoit, 'Nouvelle note sur les fragments grecs de la grotte 7 de Qumrân', *RB*, 80 (1973), 5-12; C. H. Roberts, 'On Some Presumed Papyrus Fragments of the New Testament from Qumran', *JTS*, 23 (1972), 446-7; W. Schubart, *Palaeographie. I. Griechische Palaeographie* (Munich: Beck, 1925), pp. 111-17; F. Dunand, 'Papyrus grecs biblique (P.F. Inv. 266). Volumina de la Genèse et du Deuteronome (avec 15 planches)', *Études de Papyrologie*, 9 (1971), 81-150; H. Hunger, '7Q5: Markus 6,52-53-oder? Die Meinung des Papyrologen', in *Christen und Christliches in Qumran?*, ed. by B. Mayer, Eichstätter Studien, 32 (Regensburg: Pustet, 1992), pp. 33-56; S. R. Pickering and R. R. E. Cook, *Has a Fragment of Mark been Found at Qumran?* (Sydney: The Ancient History Documentary Research Centre, Macquarie University, 1989); C. H. Roberts, *An Unpublished Fragment of the Fourth Gospel in the John Rylands Library* (Manchester: University Press, 1935); and V. Spottorno, 'Una nueva posible identificación de 7Q5', *Sefarad*, 52 (1992), 541-3, cited and critiqued in Thiede, *Rekindling the Word*, pp. 189-94.

69 As Bagnall has shown in his recent work, Bagnall, *Reading Papyri, Writing Ancient History*, *passim*. His methodological statements have been applied in his *Egypt in Late Antiquity* (Princeton: University Press, 1993).

70 G. R. H. Horsley, 'Papyrology and the Greek Language: A Fragmentary Abecedarius of Desiderata for Future Study', in *Acta of the 20th International Congress of Papyrology held in Copenhagen in August 1992*, ed. by A. Bulow-Jacobsen (Copenhagen: Museum Tusculanum, 1994), pp. 48-70; van Minnen, 'Century of Papyrology', p. 17.

71 Van Minnen, 'Century of Papyrology', p. 17. One of the few to attempt such studies recently is J. K. Elliott, *Essays and Studies in New Testament Textual Criticism*, EFN, 3 (Córdoba:

Ediciones El Almendro, 1992), pp. 79-111, although not from a modern linguistic perspective.

72 See S. E. Porter, 'Dialect and Register in the Greek of the New Testament: Theory' and 'Register in the Greek of the New Testament: Application with Reference to Mark's Gospel', in *Rethinking Context, Rereading Texts: Contributions from the Social Sciences to Biblical Interpretation*, ed. by M. Daniel Carroll R. (Sheffield: Academic Press, 2000), pp. 190-208, 209-29.

73 See S. E. Porter and M. B. O'Donnell, *Discourse Analysis and the New Testament* (forthcoming), esp. ch. 6.

74 Epp, 'Textual Criticism', p. 63.

75 See J. H. Petzer, 'The History of the New Testament – Its Reconstruction, Significance and Use in New Testament Textual Criticism', in *New Testament Textual Criticism, Exegesis and Church History: A Discussion of Methods*, ed. by B. Aland and J. Delobel (Kampen: Kok Pharos, 1994), esp. pp. 20-1.

76 J. Heimerdinger, 'Word Order in Koine Greek: Using a Text-Critical Approach to Study Word Order Patterns in the Greek Text of Acts', *FN*, 9 (1996), 139-80; idem, *The Contribution of Discourse Analysis to Textual Criticism: A Study of the Bezan Text of Acts*, JSNTSup (Sheffield: Academic Press, forthcoming).

THE LIFE AND WORK OF EBERHARD NESTLE

Warren A. Kay

INTRODUCTION

In 1898 the Würtemberg Bible Society in Stuttgart published anonymously a pocket edition of the Greek New Testament. Within a few years the anonymous editor was identified on the title page of a new edition as Eberhard Nestle, a specialist in ancient languages, who was at the time at the height of his career. This new text gained great popularity and went through many editions; by 1950 more than half a million copies had been sold.[1] The edition became such a standard that the name of its editor has become transformed into a *terminus technicus* for the book itself. Even today the mention of the name 'Nestle' carries associations with this particular edition of the Greek New Testament rather than with the historical individual.[2]

Something of the character and achievement of Eberhard Nestle can be seen by comparing him with Constantine Tischendorf, the prominent nineteenth-century textual critic and discoverer of the Codex Sinaiticus. We know a good deal about Tischendorf, partly because he wrote a number of substantial autobiographical pieces,[3] but as we will see below, the sources for a biography of Nestle are limited, and Nestle was very hesitant to write about himself. Tischendorf travelled, visiting the great libraries of Europe and exploring Egypt and Palestine in search of Greek and Latin manuscripts. Eberhard Nestle did very little travelling outside a small area of Germany except for a two year stay in England.[4] Tischendorf received many honours and cared much for titles and awards, but Nestle cared little for them.[5] Tischendorf succeeded at most things he engaged in, becoming professor at the University of Leipzig at the age of twenty-five. Nestle struggled for academic teaching posts and never received a permanent appointment at a university. Tischendorf had little trouble with money and was always able to raise money for his many projects. Nestle had money difficulties throughout his life which limited his attendance at conferences and often motivated his publishing.[6] Nevertheless, few people, except those involved in the study of the history of the Greek Bible, know the name 'Tischendorf', but there is hardly a German theologian of his generation whose *name* is so well known today as Nestle.[7] Even though the name of Nestle is known today, it is almost exclusively as a technical term for the lineage of Greek New Testament editions that he founded in 1898. The purpose of this paper is to shed more light on this person, Eberhard Nestle.

Warren A. Kay

The sources for a biography of the life of Eberhard Nestle are meagre. Two world wars have destroyed much of the physical evidence, including written sources. In 1951 Eberhard Nestle's son Erwin published a selection of letters written by his father under the title 'Aus Briefen von Eberhard Nestle'[8] and in an opening paragraph he relates how many of his father's letters were lost during World War II. There are two substantial biographical essays, one written as an obituary several years after Nestle's death in 1916, and another essay written by Erwin Nestle for the centenary of the birth of his father in 1951. However, with these and a small number of personal letters and scattered autobiographical comments, the basic facts of Nestle's life can be recounted with little difficulty.

Christof Eberhard Nestle was born on 1 May 1851 in Stuttgart. His father, Gottlieb Nestle, held the position of court administrator (Obertribunalprokurator) in Stuttgart. His mother died on 11 September 1855 when Eberhard was only four years of age.[9] When he was old enough, he followed what others have called 'the normal educational training of a Swabian theologian'.[10] From 1865 to 1869 he studied in the cloister school at Blaubeuren (one of the four old cloister schools in Württemberg), and from 1869 he studied at the theological seminary (Stift) of Tübingen University.[11]

In 1870 he interrupted his studies to serve as a volunteer hospital orderly in the Franco-Prussian War. The crowded living conditions and the sanitary problems typically associated with field hospitals in time of war resulted in Nestle contracting typhus while serving near Sedan in northeast France. According to a long-time colleague Heinrich Holzinger, this illness permanently damaged Nestle's previously strong constitution.[12] However, by the end of February 1871 he was able to resume his theological studies at Tübingen University where he had a particular interest in Middle Eastern (oriental) languages.

In 1872 Nestle completed a prize-winning essay on the relationship of the Hebrew and Greek texts of Ezekiel for which he received his doctorate in 1874.[13] After passing his first examination, in 1874 he worked for a short but fruitful period as *Stadtvikar* to Ravensburg, but in summer moved again to Tübingen University to take an appointment as a substitute Seminary librarian. Here he was the recipient of a further prize, for his essay *Israelite Personal Names According to Their Religious-Historical Meaning*.[14]

Having been awarded his doctorate, Nestle continued his orientalist research in Leipzig and Berlin (for a short time), then served two years as tutor and substitute German pastor in London.[15] Both in Berlin and more significantly in England, Nestle was influenced by the preaching of Robert Pearsall Smith.[16] Smith was one of the leaders of the North American and European revivalist movement of the later nineteenth century. Early in 1875 Smith travelled through Germany and Switzerland, and Nestle heard Smith preach when he was in Berlin. Nestle's first impression was not enthusiastic, but when he heard Smith again in Brighton in 1875, the Evangelistic meetings made a strong impression on the young Nestle. He came to question the value of his studies, and doubted if God wanted him to engage in such academic pursuits. In June 1875 he wrote to his family:

My wish is simply this, that God would now show me the way that I should go to best serve His

Kingdom. I don't yet see which way it is, but I am at peace and wait for God's leading. But this much seems clear to me, that I cannot continue in the studies in which I have been engaged. That was all only attempts to avoid the call of God and to seek my own honor, even though I pretended to want to serve the cause of truth.[17]

Nestle's father was understandably shocked by this news. Wishing to encourage his son to continue his biblical studies Gottlieb Nestle wrote back:

We thank dear God with you, that he has revealed your own heart to you. But [...] as godliness is useful in all things, so I can not imagine what the cause and basis of this change of heart could be, that you would give up your orientalist studies. These studies are not un- or anti-Christian, with which a pious Christian sensibility could not be harmonized. It is just that now you must continue your studies in another way. If the desire for human honor has been the motivation so far, then in the future you will conduct these studies for the honor of God. This is certainly the right way if you have developed your God-given talents as far as you are able. To wait for another way that God might show to you now appears to me misguided.[18]

In the end, Eberhard Nestle followed his father's advice, but as his son Erwin pointed out, 'much more than the dogmatic questions, personal piety remained close to his heart'.[19]

During his two years in England Nestle spent most of his time in London, where he studied Syriac paleography in the British Museum. The value of Syriac for studies of the Greek biblical texts was beginning to be realized, and the British Museum had in the 1840s acquired a large number of Syriac manuscripts from Nitrian monasteries in Libya.[20] Among these manuscripts was one containing considerable portions of the Gospels, which had been published in 1858 by William Cureton.[21] Nestle was able to use his knowledge of Syriac in his own textual studies of the Old and New Testaments throughout his life, and he served frequently as a resource for others who were conducting research in Syriac manuscripts.[22] However, the most immediate result of Nestle's work in Syriac was the publication of a Syriac grammar in 1881.[23]

After his return to Germany Nestle served briefly as vicar in Schnait, and in the summer of 1877 became tutor at the theological seminary in Tübingen, lecturing on Semitic languages and Old Testament themes. This did not develop into a permanent academic position, and in 1880 he accepted another ecclesiastical post as deacon in Münsingen. Here he 'started his household' by marrying Clara Kommerell,[24] the daughter of a professor of mathematics and rector of the Tübingen Realschule.[25] Nestle took his duties as pastor very seriously, but he continued to pursue his academic interests as well. Even his young wife learned to read Greek in order to help with the collation of Greek manuscripts. On 22 May 1883 Clara Nestle gave birth to their first child, Erwin[26] who would go on to study theology and continue the work of his father. Later that year, Nestle was called to be a teacher at the *Gymnasium*[27] in Ulm. There he taught, among other things, religion, English, Hebrew, German and Greek. Besides his teaching duties, Nestle became involved in a study of the Septuagint textual witnesses that had become famous in the nineteenth century. The results of his research were published in 1886 as a collection of essays, *Septuagintastudien*.[28] The textual study of the Septuagint continued as a life-long interest for Nestle, and he went on to publish five more volumes of *Septuagintastudien* over a period of twenty-five years, the last published just two years before his death.

A severe personal blow came in 1887 when Nestle lost his wife to cancer.[29] A letter to an English friend two years later contains a tender, albeit scholarly, reference to his wife: 'My boy is, I am thankful to say, always well and a great comfort to me. How my עֵזֶר כְּנֶגְדִּי would have shared my joy.'[30] This Hebrew reference quotes from Genesis 2.18 (with a change in the pronomial suffix), and can be translated as 'helper partner'. In 1890 he remarried to Elisabeth Aichele, the daughter of a minister from Bernstadt near Ulm. From this marriage came five daughters and a son.

Only three years after the death of his first wife, Nestle had to endure in the fall of 1890 what was, according to his own words, 'the most painful experience of my academic life'.[31] The effects of these events may best be appreciated by noting that in spite of Nestle's general reluctance to reveal autobiographical details, he wrote bitterly and explicitly about these events in at least two places.[32] The basic facts are quite straightforward: Nestle was called to Tübingen in order to fill a vacant professorship, and an invitation by letter from the ministry of culture enabled him, with a leave of absence from his post at the *Gymnasium*, to take over the teaching assignment. Privately, Nestle was assured that he would get the permanent appointment. In the end he was not appointed to the chair, so that Nestle had to return to Ulm in 1893, bitterly disappointed.[33] Apparently, the uncertain nature of this position became apparent to him quite early, because he began inquiring about other possible positions. In 1892, while still expecting the response from Tübingen, Nestle wrote the following to Rendel Harris:

I must wait again, but I can do so more quiet than before and write to you to-day to return on your kind question whether you should not write to Chicago for a Semitic place there. At some time I was inclined to answer in the affirmative and to ask you to do so. But now I think better not: in my age (41) the change would be too great, especially when I think of my family. If I can not find a place at a University, God will find another one for me, perhaps one not as conspicuous as a university but a place where I may be useful, a blessing for others and blessed myself.[34]

This last sentence proved to be prophetic, as we shall shortly see.

While still at Ulm, Nestle's research on the Greek New Testament continued: he wrote an introduction to the textual criticism of the Greek New Testament (published in 1896)[35] and completed his edition of the Greek New Testament, published anonymously in 1898.[36] In that same year Nestle moved to the small town of Maulbron in Württemberg, where he had been appointed professor at the Theological Seminary.[37] This teaching post at Maulbron was the longest and most satisfying of Nestle's career, although he often complained of the difficulties of keeping up-to-date with scholarship in such an isolated place.[38] The Seminary honoured Nestle in 1912 by making him director (Ephorus).

Soon after receiving this honour, Eberhard Nestle was admitted to Katharinen Hospital in Stuttgart where he underwent two operations for gallstones. Due to unforeseen complications following the second operation, Nestle died on 9 March 1913, less than two months before his sixty-second birthday. Rendel Harris, biblical scholar and orientalist whose friendship with Nestle went back to 1883, visited Maulbron from England, and reported the following about the passing of Eberhard Nestle:

When the long illness in the hospital at Stuttgart appeared to be drawing towards health, and the two operations that he passed through were supposed to have been successful, I thought of nothing so inspiring for him as to point out a mistake in his printed Gospel of Luke. His family were preparing garlands for his house-door and home in expectation of his return, my welcome was to point out one more of the very few errors into which he had fallen. And then came the news of his relapse and passing away, and that the garlands had been laid upon his bier.[39]

Eberhard Nestle was buried in the churchyard of the seminary in Maulbron and his simple epitaph consisted of one word, 'Pax'.[40]

RELIGIOUS INFLUENCES AND PERSONAL LIFE

Nestle grew up in a culture that at the time was predominantly pietistic, and it was said of him that throughout his life he remained close to the older Württemberg Pietism, in which the efforts to raise the standard of theological education was very evident.[41] In contrast to North-German Pietism, whose adherents were mostly members of the nobility, in Württemberg Pietism the adherents were found predominantly among the clergy, and in the middle classes in the towns and rural districts, which ensured a greater popularity for the movement. In Württemberg, moreover, Pietism enjoyed a distinct advantage through its intimate sympathy with academic and scientific theology, the resultant combination being exemplified by the New Testament critic and exegete Johann Albrecht Bengel who constantly sought to unite the two.[42] One of the main characteristics of Pietism was the fact that it claimed to be founded exclusively on the Bible.[43] This Pietism, as we have already observed, dominated Nestle's adult life and had a profound influence on his academic career. It is with this background in mind that we can best understand Nestle's fondness for quoting the following words from Bengel: 'Te totum applica ad textum, rem totam applica ad te' (Apply your whole self to the text, apply the whole thing to yourself).[44]

In addition to the general influence of Pietism, during his time as a student Nestle was attracted to *Vermittlungstheologie* (theology of mediation) which was, with Liberalism and traditional Lutheran confessional theology, the most influential theological stream in mid-nineteenth century Germany.[45] *Vermittlungstheologie* found original expression in the journal founded by Schleiermacher in 1828 entitled *Theologische Studien und Kritiken* and attempted to serve 'true mediations' (wahren Vermittlungen) between the modern scientific consciousness and the idea of Christianity.[46] It claimed that a simple biblical faith and the scientific spirit should both be simultaneously valid. The members of this school sought a variety of ways to combine traditional Protestantism of the confession with modern science, philosophy and theological scholarship.[47] Nestle himself admits the influence of *Vermittlungstheologie* in a letter to his family in 1873,[48] and a brief article on Nestle in *The New Schaff-Herzog Encyclopedia of Religious Knowledge* (1908) also indicates that he was an adherent of the 'mediating school of theology'.[49]

In numerous places Nestle refers to his work as scientific (wissenschaftlich), and for him, as with others in the nineteenth century, the term 'science' (Wissenschaft) described those academic disciplines that developed and followed strict methodologies. The natural sciences (Naturwissenschaften) additionally have empirically demonstrable facts as their object.[50] Theology was considered scientific only so long as it employed acceptable, systematic methodology. Textual criticism has to do with texts, and possesses a definite methodological approach to their evaluation. Thus when Nestle referred to his own work as scientific, it was very much in line with the natural sciences (Natur-wissenschaften). When we consider Nestle's background in Pietism, as well as the influence of *Vermittlungstheologie*, the mediation of biblical faith with a scientific spirit, we can begin to understand the motivation for his scientific work on the text of the Bible.

In the course of his work, Eberhard Nestle developed a large circle of friends in the academic community. In a valuable essay written in 1916, one of Nestle's colleagues made the following comments: 'Anyone who asked him for some kind of information could count on his willingness to help. Nestle sacrificed much time to others and was from time to time well used, particularly by English and Americans.'[51] In addition to Rendel Harris, noteworthy among his English friends were the twin sisters Agnes Lewis and Margaret Gibson, discoverers of the Sinaitic Syriac palimpsest.[52] The sisters visited Nestle at his home in an old monastery in Maulbron, and it was following such a visit that Margaret Gibson wrote the following words which give us a little insight into the Nestle family life:

It was sweet to see them all gathered round the breakfast table; and what I especially admired was the way in which they said grace. First the father offered up a petition, then Mrs. Nestle another then his son Erwin, then each of the girls in turn according to their age; not one was left out, even a tiny voice being heard at the close from the mother's knee.[53]

NESTLE'S PUBLISHING CAREER

The bibliography of Nestle's book-length publications includes about forty entries.[54] He also wrote numerous articles for some of the most important reference works of his day, including the *Realencyklopädie für protestantische Theologie und Kirche*,[55] James Hastings' *Dictionary of the Bible*,[56] and *The Encyclopædia Biblica*,[57] as well as writing articles for scholarly journals. His son Erwin correctly states that Nestle produced 'a vast number' of small articles in all sorts of German, English, and even American journals. The impression Erwin gives is, however, misleading: for example, when he states that in the year 1905 his father produced 225 publications, and between 1908 and 1912 that Eberhard Nestle wrote no fewer than 743 articles.[58] It must be pointed out that many of these articles are small notes, like the following:

The Sod Bible.
The Oxford University Press is renowned for the beauty and accuracy of its Bibles, and that with full right. Yet this time it has added a new specimen to the odd Bibles already produced. In 1717 it produced the 'Vinegar Bible' (Lk 20, 'vinegar' for 'vineyard'); 1801, the 'Murderer Bible' (Jude 16, 'murderers' for 'murmurers'); 1807, the 'Ears to Ear Bible' (Mt 13:43, 'ears to ear'); 1810, the 'Wife-hater's Bible' (Lk 14:26, 'wife' for 'life'); and now the 'Sod Bible' (Dt 32:15, 'SOD' for 'GOD'); see *The Companion Bible*, being the Authorized Version of 1611, with the Structures and Notes, Critical, Explanatory, and Suggestive. Part I., The Pentateuch, with 52 Appendices—Henry Frowde: Oxford University Press (no date! but end of 1909).
Eb. Nestle.[59]

I have provided here the entire text, and although this is not a lengthy article, it does show Nestle's concern for detail, as well as his sense of humour.

The Life and Work of Eberhard Nestle

In 1881 Oscar von Gebhardt published a Greek and Greek-German New Testament. His reason for doing so was to try to counteract the practice of the British and Foreign Bible Society to circulate in Germany nothing but reprints of the *textus receptus* which dated back to Erasmus' edition of 1519.[60] From 1805 to 1895, the British and Foreign Bible Society distributed more than 351,495 copies of the *textus receptus*. In 1894 alone they printed 12,200 copies, and went on to circulate about 1,600 copies each year in Germany and Switzerland.[61] Oscar von Gebhardt's editions, however, were not cheap enough to compete against the *textus receptus* editions.

It became necessary to make a more decided effort against this practice. To this end the Württembergische Bibelgesselschaft at Stuttgart published the Nestle pocket edition of the Greek New Testament in 1898.[62] The advantage of this edition was that it was not only well produced, but it was as cheap as any reprint of the *textus receptus*. It was Nestle's intention to offer the current results of the scientific investigation of the Greek text of the New Testament. He did not want to give a reading of the text subjectively based on his own critical examination of the different versions. Instead, he collated the great editions of the nineteenth century: Tischendorf[63] and Westcott and Hort.[64] In order to get a majority in those cases where these two editions differed, he used the edition of Weymouth.[65] Nestle included any reading supported by at least two of the three editions, and in the event that all three differed, he gave a 'mean reading'. All other readings were relegated to footnotes. From the third edition onwards, Nestle used the recently published edition of Bernhard Weiss[66] instead of Weymouth.

Shortly after the anonymous publication in 1898 of Nestle's Greek New Testament, a very positive review of the work was published in the *Expository Times*. It praised the book for (among other things) overcoming the supremacy of the *textus receptus*, and for being a modern critical edition with manuscript evidence in footnotes. The review concludes by saying: 'It would be the best reward for the great expense which the Bible Society of Stuttgart has spent on this undertaking, if other Societies would make a large use of it.'[67] This glowing review of the anonymous Greek New Testament was written by none other than Nestle himself.[68]

Nestle, however, had no illusions about the quality of his work or the work of the others upon whom his work was based. While there can be no question that Nestle's editions produced a text corresponding far more closely to the 'original' than that contained in the *textus receptus*, Nestle himself knew that much research remained to be done in New Testament textual criticism. He wrote:

Just as archaeologists, who undertake the excavation of ruined temples in Olympus or Delphi, see in the broken fragments at least the spirit of their ancient glory, even so, much work remains to be done till all the building stones are re-collected and the plan determined which will permit the restoration of the sanctuary of New Testament Scriptures to its original form.[69]

Although Eberhard Nestle is best remembered for his work on the Greek New Testament, he had a life-long interest in the Septuagint, dating back to his doctoral dissertation on Ezekiel (1872) and his *Septuagintastudien*. Even before he produced his Greek New Testament, Nestle was interested in producing an edition of the Septuagint, and as early as 1895 he was negotiating with a publisher for such a task as is evidenced in the following selection from a letter to Rendel Harris:

The news about an edition of the LXX, to be prepared by myself is rather too early. A Berlin publisher wishes me to make one; Strack is interested in the matter, but it is not even in the state of preliminaries. [...] It would be a wonderful task; but I am everywhere hindered by want of books.[70]

At the request of the Württembergische Bibelgesellschaft, Nestle eventually began work on a pocket edition of the Greek Old Testament, but he was unable to complete the work before his death. Heinrich Holzinger reports that when Nestle realized his end was near, the great biblical scholar lamented that he would not be able to complete his plans for an edition of the Septuagint.[71] Thus Nestle's observation concerning the death of Paul de Lagarde could be said of Nestle himself: 'When I die, I hope to die while on the way.'[72] Nestle's son, Erwin, in collaboration with Johannes Dahse, published the edition of the book of Jeremiah (with parallel Greek and Hebrew Texts) that Eberhard Nestle had nearly completed before his death.[73]

CONCLUSION

This essay was written to explore some of the major aspects of the life and work of Eberhard Nestle. The character that has emerged from this study is one of deep personal piety, great education, erudition, and a love of learning, but also it is a person who experienced disappointment and tragedy. His accomplishments were formidable, and he has left his mark on Christianity and the communication of the Gospel like few others. Nestle's close friend, Rendel Harris, had these words to say about the impact of Eberhard Nestle on Christendom:

Quite recently, as I was driving through a town in the heart of Asia Minor (I think it was the ancient Philomelium, from which the church of the place once sent to Smyrna for details of Polycarp's martyrdom), I passed a colporteur who was engaged in the arduous and often thankless task of the circulation of the Scriptures. I stopped the carriage and bought from him a Romaic Greek Testament and a copy of the older Greek in Nestle's latest edition. Nor did I miss the opportunity of writing to him in his last sickness to tell him how I had come across his book in an out-of-the-way place, where Christianity lies very low, and will some day revive again: when it does, it will owe its new vitality in part to the circulation of the Scriptures in such editions as Nestle spent the best part of his life to produce.[74]

When Eberhard Nestle died, his final plans for an edition of the Septuagint went unfulfilled, but his legacy to future generations was secure, for his edition of the Greek New Testament was already in its ninth edition.

NOTES

1 'Man bedenke, was es heißt daß die Württ. Bibelanstalt bis heute mindestens eine halbe Million Exemplare verbreitet hat!' Johannes Herrmann, 'Der "Nestle"', *Evangelisch-lutherische Kirchenzeitung*, 5 (1951), 302.

2 As a prominent example of this, in the standard book on the various editions of the Greek New Testament, Kurt and Barbara Aland consistently refer to 'Der "Nestle"' (the 'Nestle') when referring to the editions of the Greek New Testament descending from Eberhard Nestle's original edition of 1898: '[Wenn man] über die Ausgaben des Neuen Testaments im 20. Jahrhundert berichtet werden soll, eingangs zu sagen hat, daß hier der 'Nestle' eine absolut dominierende Stellung einnahm', Kurt and Barbara Aland, *Der Text des Neuen Testaments: Einführung in die wissenschaftlichen Ausgaben und in Theorie wie Praxis der modernen Textkritik* (Stuttgart: Deutsche Bibelgesellschaft, 1981), p. 30.

3 Constantine Tischendorf wrote a number of books describing large portions of his life. See, for example, *Reise in den Orient*, 2 vols (Leipzig: Bernhard Tauchnitz Jr., 1846), and *Die Sinaibibel: Ihre Entdeckung, Herausgabe und Erwerbung* (Leipzig: Giesecke & Devrient, 1871). A twentieth-century biography of Tischendorf was written by Hildegard Behrend, *Auf der Suche nach Schätzen: Aus dem Leben Constantin von Tischendorfs*, 5th edn (Berlin: Evangelischer Verlag, 1956).

4 Nestle wanted to travel, but was prevented from doing so because of financial limitations, family responsibilities, and health: 'Truly this was my wish, when I was in England, that I might find some one, whom I might accompany to the Holy Land, but I did not and now I am 10 years older and no more what I used to be.' Letter to Rendel Harris dated 10 Nov. 1889. The letters of Eberhard Nestle to Rendel Harris are a part of the 'James Rendel Harris Papers', housed in the Orchard Learning Centre of Selly Oak Colleges, Birmingham. All further references to Nestle's letters to Rendel Harris are taken from this collection and were originally written in English.

5 On 10 Aug. 1894 Nestle wrote the following to Rendel Harris: 'Do you know, that Königsberg at the occasion of their University-Jubilee gave me DD as Halle did Robinson? I don't care for titles, but it was and is sunshine.'

6 Thus Nestle wrote in a letter to Rendel Harris dated 10 Aug. 1894: 'The work is attractive for me and to earn some money is a thing which I must take on even more than I am by nature inclined to do. If I were to die early, my wife and children would be in very straight circumstances.'

7 'Der Nestle', p. 301.

8 'Aus Briefen von Eberhard Nestle', ed. by Erwin Nestle, *Blätter für württembergische Kirchengeschichte*, 51 (1951), 143-50.

9 Some helpful information about the family was found in the 'Familien-Chronik' ('Family Chronicle') in the Nestle family Bible, which is part of the Nestle Library at the Scriptorium in Grand Haven, Michigan.

10 Erwin Nestle, 'Eberhard Nestle. Zu seiner 100. Geburtstag', *Für Arbeit und Besinnung*, 5 (1951), p. 194; *Württembergische Nekrolog für 1913* (1916), 50.

11 The system of education at German universities in the nineteenth century is quite different from that of present-day Great Britain and America. A very readable description of the universities and higher education in mid-nineteenth century Germany, written by a contemporary, is: Philip Schaff, *Germany: Its Universities, Theology, and Religion* (Philadelphia: Lindsay and Blakiston, 1857).

12 *Württembergische Nekrolog*, p. 51.

13 Heinrich Holzinger, *Über das Verhältnis des von den Septuaginta benutzten Textes des Ezechiel zu der heute rezipierten masoretischen Redaktion*. Unpublished.

14 Eberhard Nestle, *Die israelitischen Eigennamen nach ihrer religionsgeschichtlichen Bedeutung. Ein Versuch* (Haarlem: n.p., 1876).

15 Johannes Herrmann, 'Der "Nestle"', p. 301.

16 For general information about Smith, see: M. Schmidt, 'Smith, Robert Pearsall', *Die Religion in Geschichte und Gegenwart. Handwörterbuch für Theologie und Religionswissenschaft*, 3rd edn, ed. by Hans Freiher von Campenhausen and others (Tübingen: J. C. B. Mohr [Paul Siebeck], 1960), vol. 6, col. 112.

17 Letter to his family dated 5 June 1875, 'Aus Briefen von Eberhard Nestle', pp. 145-6 (my translation).

18 Letter from his father dated 12 June 1875, 'Aus Briefen von Eberhard Nestle', p. 146 (my translation).

19 'Aus Briefen von Eberhard Nestle', p. 144. In a similar vein, H. Holzinger noted that Nestle 'held himself back from systematic-theological questions'. Holzinger further notes that Nestle

remained throughout his life a decidedly *Christian* theologian, since for him everything centred on the Gospel (cf. *Württembergische Nekrolog*, p. 78).

20 Philip Schaff, *Theological Propaedeutic: A General Introduction to the Study of Theology*, 7th edn (New York: Charles Scribner's Sons, 1907), p. 117.

21 *Remains of a Very Ancient Recension of the Four Gospels*, ed. by William Cureton (London: John Murray, 1858).

22 Both Rendel Harris and Agnes Lewis (among others) relied on Nestle for occasional assistance with questions on Syriac.

23 This grammar was originally published in Latin under the title *Brevis linguae syriacae grammatica* (Berlin: Reuther, 1881); German trans., *Syrische Grammatik mit Litteratur, Chrestomathie und Glossar*, 2. vermehrte und verbesserte Auflage (Berlin: Reuther, 1888); English trans. of 2nd edn by R. S. Kennedy, *Syriac Grammar with Literature, Chrestomathy and Glossary* (London: Williams & Norgate, 1889).

24 His wife Clara Kommerell was born in Tübingen on 30 Dec. 1852, and they were married on 22 June 1880, 'Familien-Chronik'.

25 *Württembergische Nekrolog*, p. 52.

26 Erwin Nestle was born in Münsingen on 22 May 1883, 'Familien-Chronik'.

27 There is no real functional equivalent to the Gymnasium in the United States. Philip Schaff provides a very helpful description of the Gymnasium as a German educational institution in chapter IV of *Germany: Its Universities, Theology, and Religion* (cf. pp. 44-55). Schaff states that 'students of the [German] university must have passed through a regular preparatory course of nine or ten years in a gymnasium, which is generally divided into nine or ten classes [...] comprising a methodological tutorial instruction in ancient and modern languages, mathematics, natural sciences, geography, history and philosophy' (p. 49).

28 *Septuaginastudien* I, 'Beilage zum Program des Gymnasiums Ulm' (Ulm: Wagner, 1886); a second instalment of these brief studies was published in Ulm in 1896; four more *Septuaginastudien* were published as 'Beilage zum Program des Seminars Maulbronn' (Stuttgart: Stuttgarter Vereins-Buchdruckerei, 1899, 1903 1907 and 1911).

29 Clara Nestle died in Ulm on Monday, 3 Oct. 1887, 'Familien-Chronik'.

30 Letter to Rendel Harris dated 10 Nov. 1889.

31 Eberhard Nestle, *Einführung in das griechische Neue Testament*, 3. umgearbeitete Auflage (Göttingen: Vandenhoeck & Ruprecht, 1909), p. vi.

32 Nestle outlines the main facts in the 'Vorrede' of *Marginalien und Materialien* (Tübingen: J. H. Heckenhauer'sche Buchhandlung, 1893), pp. v-vi; a brief reference is also made in *Einführung in das griechische Neue Testament* (3rd edn), p. vi.

33 *Württembergische Nekrolog*, p. 55.

34 Letter dated 17 Sept. 1892. As late as 1894 Nestle was still seeking a position at a university and applied for the vacant chair of Arabic at the University of Cambridge. Cf. letter to R. Harris, 7 May 1894.

35 Eberhard Nestle, *Einführung in das griechische Neue Testament* (Göttingen: Vandenhoeck & Ruprecht, 1897); 2nd revised and enlarged edn, 1899; 3rd revised edn, 1909. English trans. of 2nd edn: *Introduction to the Textual Criticism of the Greek New Testament*, trans. by William Edie, ed. with a preface by Allan Menzies (London: Williams and Norgate 1901).

36 *Novum Testamentum Graece* (Stuttgart: Württembergische Bibelanstalt, 1898).

37 Maulbron lies about 23 miles north-west of Stuttgart. Made famous by the Cistercian monastery founded there in 1138, Maulbron has a long and very interesting history, with significant events taking place there during the Protestant Reformation. Cf. H. Fausel, 'Maulbron', *Die Religion in Geschichte und Gegenwart*, vol. 4, col. 811. Also worthy of note is the fact that Nestle wrote the article on Maulbron for the *Realencyklopädie für protestantische Theologie und Kirche*, ed. by Albert Hauck, vol. 12 (Leipzig: J. C. Hinrichs,

1896), pp. 441-5 (hereafter cited as *PRE*).

38 For example, in the preface to his *Einführung in das griechische Neue Testament* (3rd edn), p. v, Nestle writes: 'Soweit es an einiem Orte wie Maulbron möglich ist, habe ich seither den Gang der neutestamentlichen Forschung verfolgt'.

39 Rendel Harris, 'Eberhard Nestle,' *Expository Times*, 24 (1912-13), p. 450.

40 Erwin Nestle, 'Eberhard Nestle', p. 198.

41 *Württembergische Nekrolog*, p. 78.

42 It is no accident that Nestle wrote an essay on Bengel: 'Bengel als Gelehrter: Ein Bild für unsre Tage', *Marginalien und Materialien* (Tübingen: Heckenhauer, 1893).

43 The standard work on pietism is still Albrecht Ritschl, *Geschichte des Pietismus*, 3 vols (Bonn: A. Marcus, 1880-6).

44 Nestle, *Einführung in das griechische Neue Testament*, p. 19. The Latin sentence also stood as a motto at the beginning of the 'Erläuterungen zum Griechischen Neuen Testament', of Nestle's *Novum Testamentum Graece* for many editions and was only omitted in the 27th edn of 1993, when the introduction was completely rewritten by Kurt and Barbara Aland.

45 The only monograph written on *Vermittlungstheologie* is by Ragnar Holte, *Die Vermittlungstheologie: Ihre theologischen Grundbegriffe kritisch untersucht* (Uppsala: University of Uppsala, 1965). Of particular interest for our study is ch. 1, 'Das Wissenschaftliche Program der Vermittlung', pp. 24-47. Also important is Emanuel Hirsch, 'Vermittlungstheologie und Konfessionalismus unter der Einwirkung Hegels und Schleiermachers', *Geschichte der neuern evangelischen Theologie im Zusammenhang mit den allgemeinen Bewegungen des europäischen Denkens* (Gütersloh: Gütersloher Verlagshaus Gerd Mohn, 1949), vol. 5, pp. 364-430. Cf. also: Paul Tillich, *Perspectives on 19th and 20th Century Protestant Theology*, ed. with introduction by Carl E. Braaten (New York: Harper & Row, 1967), pp. 208-23; E. Schott, 'Vermittlungstheologie', *Die Religion in Geschichte und Gegenwart* (Tübingen: J. C. B. Mohr [Paul Siebeck], 1962), vol. 6, 1362.

46 Emanuel Hirsch, *Geschichte der neuern evangelischen Theologie im Zusammenhang mit den allgemeinen Bewegungen des europäischen Denkens* (Gütersloh: Gütersloher Verlagshaus Gerd Mohn, 1949), vol. 5, p. 375.

47 E. Hirsch, *Geschichte der neuern evangelischen* Theologie, 5, p. 375.

48 Letter dated 15 June 1873, 'Aus Briefen von Eberhard Nestle', p. 144.

49 It is interesting that in the article on Eberhard Nestle appearing in *The New Schaff-Herzog Encyclopedia of Religious Knowledge* (ed. by Samuel Macauley Jackson [New York: Funk & Wagnalls Company, 1908], vol. 8, p. 119) the unnamed author notes in passing that 'theologically [Nestle] is an adherent of the mediating school'. However, nowhere in this encyclopaedia is there an explanation of what the 'mediating school' of theology is. Further, in the preface to volume 1, the editor writes that the encyclopaedia 'contains hundreds of sketches of living persons derived in almost every instance from matter furnished by themselves' (p. x). From this we can conclude that Nestle probably provided the information for the entry on himself and therefore that he is providing personal confirmation from a period later in life that he was an adherent of *Vermittlungstheologie*.

50 Günther Keil, *Philosophie Geschichte*, vol. II, *Von der Aufklärung bis zur Gegenwart* (Stuttgart: Verlag W. Kohlhammer, 1987), p. 160.

51 *Württembergische Nekrolog*, p. 54.

52 There is very little available on the lives and careers of these two sisters. The discovery of the manuscripts is described by M. D. Gibson in *How the Codex Was Found: A Narrative of Two Visits to Sinai, from Mrs. Lewis's Journals, 1892-93* (Cambridge: Bowes & Macmillan, 1893). Rendel Harris tells of the discovery of the manuscript and its value in 'The New Syriac Gospels', *Contemporary Review*, 66 (1894), 654-73.

53 Margaret D. Gibson, 'Professor Nestle', *Expository Times*, 24 (1912-13), 380.

54 There is to date no complete bibliography of the works of Eberhard Nestle. *Württembergische Nekrolog* contains a bibliography of Nestle that is primarily a list of his booklength publications, although a number of his encyclopaedia articles are also included. Surprisingly, the secondary literature on Nestle often cites this bibliography as a complete (*vollständig*) bibliography. However the article itself clearly describes the bibliography in the following words: 'Von Nestles wissenschaftlicher Arbeit und Art gibt einen Begriff schon die nachfolgende Zusammenstellung seiner Veröffentlichungen von der Hand seines Sohnes. Dabei ist übrigens sofort festzustellen, daß die Liste eine sehr *unfollständige* ist' [my emphasis], *Württembergische Nekrolog*, p. 56.

55 Nestle was a contributor to the 2nd edn of *Realencyklopädie für protestantische Theologie und Kirche* (ed. by J. J. Herzog [Leipzig: J. C. Hinrichs,1880]) and the 3rd edn (ed. by Albert Hauck [Leipzig: J. C. Hinrichs, 1896]).

56 James Hastings, *Dictionary of the Bible* (Edinburgh: T. & T. Clark, 1898).

57 *The Encyclopædia Biblica*, ed. by T. K. Cheyne and J. Sutherland Black (London: Adam and Charles Black, 1899).

58 Erwin Nestle, 'Eberhard Nestle', p. 197.

59 *Expository Times*, 21 (1909-10), 329.

60 Oscar von Gebhardt, *Novum Testamentum Graece et Germanice: Das neue Testament griechisch nach Tischendorfs letzter Recension und Deutsch nach dem revidierten Luthertext* (Leipzig: Tauschnitz, 1881). In the preface Gebhardt explicitly states his motivation for producing this edition (cf. p. v).

61 Nestle, *Einführung in das griechische Neue Testament* (2nd edn), p. 16. The 3rd edn contains a table detailing the various editions of the *textus receptus* for the first 100 years of the British and Foreign Bible Society (p. 16).

62 Accounts of his method of creating a majority text are well known and can be found in his own words in *Novum Testamentum Graece cum apparatu critco curavit Eberhard Nestle novis curis elaboraverunt Erwin Nestle et Kurt Aland Editio vicesima quinta* (Stuttgart: Württembergische Bibelanstalt, 1927, 1968), p. 59. Cf. also Kurt Aland and Barbara Aland, *Der Text des Neuen Testaments: Einführung in die wissenschaftlichen Ausgaben und in Theory wie Praxis der modernen Textkritik* (Stuttgart: Deutsche Bibelgesellschaft, 1982), pp. 29-30 (English edn: *The Text of the New Testament*, trans. by Erroll F. Rhodes [Grand Rapids: Eerdmans, 1989], pp. 19-20); Bruce Manning Metzger, *The Text of the New Testament: Its Transmission, Corruption and Restoration*, 3rd edn (New York: Oxford University Press, 1992), p. 144.

63 *Novum Testamentum Graece, editio octava critica maior*, ed. by Constantinus Tischendorf (Leipsig: Hermann Mendelssohn, vol. I 1868, vol. II 1872, vol. III with *Prolegomena* ed. by C. R. Gregory 1894).

64 *The New Testament in the Original Greek*, ed. by Brook Foss Westcott and Fenton John Anthony Hort, 2 vols (Cambridge/London: Macmillan and Company, 1881).

65 R. F. Weymouth, *The Resultant Greek Testament* (London: Elliot Stock, 1886).

66 Bernhard Weiss, *Das Neue Testament*, Handausgabe, 3 vols (Leipzig: Hinrischs, 1894-1900).

67 Eberhard Nestle, '"The Greek Testament" of the Bible Society of Stuttgart', *Expository Times*, 9 (1897-98), 420.

68 Eberhard Nestle, '"The Greek Testament" of the Bible Society of Stuttgart', p. 419.

69 Nestle, *Einführung in das griechische Neue Testament* (2nd edn), p. 27 (my translation).

70 Letter to Rendel Harris dated 23 Aug. 1895.

71 According to Holzinger, Nestle's actual words were: 'Meine Septuaginta ist nun auch hinunter', *Württembergische Nekrolog*, p. 55.

72 Nestle quoted this Persian saying while noting the projects left unfinished at the death of de Lagarde, 'Paul Anton de Lagarde', *PRE*, vol. 11, p. 213.

73 As the publisher notes in a foreword to the work first published in 1924, the edition was ready to be published in 1914, but World War I delayed publication. Difficulties after the war further delayed publication until the book was brought to completion by J. Dahse and Erwin Nestle (*Das Buch Jeremia, Griechish und Hebräisch* [Stuttgart: Privilegierte Württembergische Bibelanstalt, 1924], p. iii). The Württembergische Bibelgesellschaft did not give up the idea of an edition of the Greek Old Testament and in 1917-18 Alfred Rahlfs, who was already involved in producing a large critical edition of the Septuagint at the 'Gesellschaft der Wissenschaften' in Göttingen, was asked to take over the task. Because of many problems following World War I, a small 'specimen' section of this small edition was not published until 1922 ('Das Buch Ruth griechisch, als Probe einer kritischen Handausgabe der Septuaginta herausgegeben von Alfred Rahlfs') and an edition of Genesis was published in 1926. A change in plans gave Vandenhoeck & Ruprecht rights to publish the large critical edition of the Septuagint and once more the Württembergische Bibelgesellschaft undertook to publish a pocket edition that was finally released in two volumes in 1935. *Septuaginta*, ed. by Alfred Rahlfs, 2 vols (Stuttgart: Württembergische Bibelanstalt, 1935), Editor's Preface, pp. LIV-LV.

74 Rendel Harris, 'Eberhard Nestle', *Expository Times*, 24 (1912-13), 449-50.

THE FUTURE OF
NEW TESTAMENT
TEXTUAL STUDIES

Bruce M. Metzger

W HEN I WAS INVITED to deal with the subject 'The Future of New Testament Textual Studies' my first impulse was to protest, echoing the words of Amos to the priest Amaziah, 'I am no prophet, nor the son of a prophet' (Amos 7.14). After further thought, however, it struck me that perhaps what was wanted was the consideration of several pressing problems that need to be addressed by future investigators of the Greek New Testament. Before calling attention to such matters, it seems appropriate to discuss an aspect of contemporary education and culture that bodes ill for the future of Greek studies in general.

I. THE DECLINE OF INTEREST IN THE CLASSICS[1]

During the past three or four generations, there has been a decreasing number of institutions in the United States that offer courses in Greek and Latin. As would be expected, there has also been a decreasing number of students who elect to study the classical languages. At the close of the nineteenth century, a considerable number of high schools offered both Greek and Latin. It was possible, for example, for Luther Weigle, who later became Dean of Yale Divinity School and chairman of the committee of translators of the Revised Standard Version of the Bible (1952), to enrol for several years of both Latin and Greek in the high school of Harrisburg, Pennsylvania.

At the beginning of the twentieth century practically every university and most colleges in North America offered instruction in the Classics, and not a few required some knowledge of Latin for admission to the institution. At that time, the study of Classics was popular because it was seen as a practical passport to the professions. Students who hoped for a political life studied Demosthenes and Cicero as models of eloquence, those aiming for the ministry learned Greek, and the upper classes sought a grounding in the Classics as a sign of refinement.

In the 1960s, high schools experimented with looser requirements, and Latin was among the first casualties of the new pedagogical freedom. Between 1962 and 1976 public school enrolments in Latin withered, dropping from more than 700,000 to 150,000. This decrease was followed by an ongoing decline in college-level enrolments. Between 1971 and 1991, the number of majors in Classics dropped by 30 per cent, as did Greek enrolments in the decade from 1977 to 1986. Of more than one million BAs awarded in 1994, only six hundred were granted in Classics. At Yale University, among more than 1500 students in the class of 1994, there were only nine who had concentrated in Greek and Latin.[2]

The highly market-orientated nature of the American education system renders its institutions especially vulnerable. Administrators are finding themselves less able – and less willing – to sustain 'inefficient' areas of study. Similar considerations have also begun to alter the offerings of universities in the United Kingdom. In 1987 when Margaret Thatcher's Conservative government passed the Education Reform Act, the departments of Latin and Greek in the University of Aberdeen, founded in 1497, were discontinued as 'unproductive'.[3] During the debate in Parliament, Lord Jenkins, the Chancellor of Oxford University, predicted that by the year 2000 Britain would have no first-rate university. He pointed out that universities are like trees: they take a long time to grow, but are quickly chopped down.[4]

In 1982 a national survey in the USA found that Classics had fewer doctoral programmes than any of the other thirty-two disciplines surveyed, and produced the fewest PhDs. Even worse, the Classics professorate had one of the poorest rates of employment of any discipline – not to mention the second lowest salaries in the Humanities. Those who consider these statistics have been moved to compare classicists to endangered species like whooping cranes and pandas.[5]

Classics is in danger of becoming – like alchemy – a part of the history of the West rather than a discipline in its own right. Ancillary studies involving linguistics, papyrology, palaeography, and textual criticism attract fewer and fewer students because of the decline in Greek and Latin. Each generation knows the languages less well than the preceding one. 'In 1864,' Professor William M. Calder, III, of the University of Illinois reminds us, 'Wilamovitz's classics master dictated Xenophon in Greek to schoolboys who took him down in Latin. I could not possibly do what those schoolboys did, and I wonder whether any American classicist can.'[6]

Despite the generally gloomy statistics of diminishing interest in the Classics, during the past few years an occasional article on the study of Latin in American schools and colleges paints a brighter picture. Most recently, Richard A. LaFleur, head of the Classics Department at the University of Georgia and editor since 1979 of *Classical Outlook*, provided encouraging information concerning a modest growth of interest in Latin in American schools and colleges.[7] On the basis of data collected by the American Council on the Teaching of Foreign Language, between 1990 and 1994 public secondary school Latin enrolments increased by more than 15 per cent, and evidence suggests a similar rise in private schools and continuing growth through 1997. Greek enrolments, while much lower than Latin, appear to have stabilised since 1990 in secondary schools and even (after declining steadily for twenty years) in the nation's colleges and universities.

Clearly, for teachers of classical languages and for their students, LaFleur's good news is welcome. After a disastrous decline, Greek continues to hold its own, and Latin's star is rising at a quickening pace, from the elementary grades straight through to university level.[8]

Gaudeamus igitur – but at the same time let us be mindful too. Latin is still studied by fewer than 2 per cent of America's high school pupils, and college Greek and Latin, while relatively stable in terms of raw numbers, continue to decline as a percentage of the total college and university population.

The Future of New Testament Textual Studies

Realistically, one must acknowledge that teachers of Latin and Greek will always be a minority group and therefore, as LaFleur concludes his article in *Classical Outlook*, 'We must continue and intensify our efforts in developing and employing new, livelier, and more effective methods and resources, in constantly reinterpreting the Classics for an ever-changing audience'. This will not be easy, but it is along such lines that Victor D. Hanson and John Heath conclude their impassioned discussion entitled *Who Killed Homer?: The Decline of Classical Education and the Recovery of Greek Wisdom.*[9]

II. ITEMS AND TOPICS THAT AWAIT INVESTIGATION

Apart from various assessments of the state of the health of classical studies, there is no diminution of problems and investigations in the area of New Testament textual studies that urgently clamour for attention. Some have to do with the proper methodology to be followed in assessing variant readings (eclecticism or local genealogical analysis), and others with the identification of family relationships among manuscripts. Before attempting, however, to solve such basic questions, it is more sensible to focus at the outset on topics that will extend and clarify the range of information to be derived from individual manuscripts. As additional Greek manuscripts of the New Testament come to light, there is pressing need to assess the character of their text. Since the publication in 1994 of the second edition of Kurt Aland's *Kurzgefasste Liste der griechischen Handscriften des Neuen Testaments* (2nd edn, Berlin: De Gruyter, 1994), sixteen additional papyrus fragments from Oxyrhynchos, ranging from the second to the fifth centuries, have been identified. Each is a fragment of a single page, chiefly of the gospels. They extend Aland's enumeration of papyri from P^{100} to P^{115}.

Three more uncial manuscripts now bring the total to 0309. Of these additional manuscripts, two are small fragments, but 0307 from the seventh century preserves seven pages of text from the three Synoptic Gospels.

Six more miniscule manuscripts have been assigned numbers, from 2857 to 2862. One of these manuscripts was recently acquired by The Scriptorium, in Grand Haven, Michigan, where it is identified as VK MS 901. It dates from the eleventh century, and contains 196 pages of the four Gospels.

Finally, nine additional Greek lectionary manuscripts now bring the total to 2412.[10]

Lectionaries

The mention of Greek lectionaries reminds one that the study of such witnesses to the New Testament has been given only sporadic attention over the years. In fact, some scholars, including Hermann von Soden, deliberately excluded them from otherwise comprehensive studies. Even the last edition of the Nestle-Aland *Novum Testament Graece* (27th edition) lists only seven lectionary manuscripts from the more than 2400 thus far catalogued.

The most concentrated effort to collect evidence from Greek lectionaries was undertaken earlier this century at the University of Chicago. Under the leadership of Donald W. Riddle and Ernest C. Colwell, along with their students, a beginning was made in the scientific research of this body of evidence. The International Greek New

Testament Project, under the guidance of Allen Wikgren, provided significant data from lectionaries for inclusion in the critical apparatus of two volumes entitled *The New Testament in Greek: The Gospel According to St Luke* (Oxford: Clarendon Press, 1984, 1987).

At the present time, under the supervision of Carroll D. Osburn at Abilene, Texas, work is going forward in the study of Greek lectionaries that contain portions of the Acts of the Apostles. The standard lectionary system presents some 647 verses of the 1006 verses in Acts. Another project involving the study of Greek lectionaries is underway at the University of Thessaloniki under the supervision of Iannis Karavidopoulos.

For the future, two desiderata that are crying out for attention are: a) a full history of the Greek lectionary text, based on adequate data from both uncial and miniscule texts; and b) a critical edition, based on full collations of both synaxaria and menologia, in order to replace the Greek text edited near the beginning of the last century by B. Antoniades under the authority of the Ecumenical Patriarchate of the Orthodox Church (Constantinople: 1904).

Unavailable Manuscripts

The discovery of additional manuscripts is of no use if they are not made available for study. In was in September of 1975 that the Minister of Culture and Sciences at Athens was informed by monks from the Monastery of St Catherine on Mount Sinai that a large number of manuscripts had been found in an old storage room at the monastery. The first notice in western Europe of the discovery appeared on 3 April 1978 in the *Frankfurter Allgemeine Zeitung*, which reported that a sensational find at Sinai had brought to light forty-seven boxes of icons and manuscripts, many in fragmentary form.[11] The fullest description is the résumé of an inventory made by N. Nikolopoulos.[12] These include: ten nearly complete parchment codices and a great number of quaternions and isolated folios of at least fifty other codices, dating from the fourth to the tenth or eleventh centuries. Among minuscule manuscripts, there are 210 items on parchment and 433 items on paper – most of the latter are detached folios.

Surprisingly, there is an impressive number of rolls, thirteen with uncial script and eighty with minuscule script. Finally, the inventory includes a considerable number of oriental manuscripts: 120 Arabic, 96 Syriac, 56 Armenian, and others in Georgian, Slavonic, Amharic, and Hebrew.

Physical Aspects

Besides the collation of the text of New Testament manuscripts, it is also necessary for scholars to examine carefully all aspects of the physical make-up of the documents. Such codicological examination involves a painstaking study of the preparation of the parchment, the ruling pattern, the gatherings and sewing of the codex, as well as detailed palaeographical analysis. Only a very few manuscripts have received such minute scrutiny. After Codex Sinaiticus was acquired by the British Museum in 1933, Milne and Skeat subjected it to a rigorous examination that resulted in the publication of a valuable monograph.[13] The most recent such codicological examination of a New

Testament manuscript is the magisterial study by Parker of Codex Bezae.[14] Many more New Testament manuscripts are deserving of similar analysis in future years.

Apart from the obvious features of size and format, state of the preservation of the handwriting, and similar details, attention also deserves to be directed toward such features as the presence of other documents that may be included in the manuscript. One of the unusual and often overlooked features of a considerable number of Greek manuscripts of the book of Revelation is the presence of other texts of a miscellaneous character. Of the more than 5600 New Testament manuscripts in the catalogue kept by the Münster Institute, only about 300 preserve the book of Revelation. There are a few, comparatively a very few (about sixty), Greek manuscripts which contain our whole New Testament (that is to say, the other books and the Revelation), but in most cases the books are commonly copied off without the Revelation. The other side of this circumstance is the fact that Revelation not infrequently stands in the middle of volumes that have no other biblical content. Several of the manuscripts that contain only Revelation are the quires containing Revelation taken out of the middle of some general theological book.

The following manuscripts, identified by Gregory-Aland number and by date, present the Revelation in company with a variety of non-biblical texts:

Uncial MS 046, x; and miniscule MSS 2015, xv; 2016, xv; 2017, xv; 2018, c. 1300; 2020, xv; 2022, xiv; 2023, xv; 2024, xv; 2025, xv; 2027, xiii; 2030, xii; 2038, xvi; 2042, xiv; 2048, xi; 2049, xvi; 2050, 1107; 2051, xvi; 2052, xvi; 2054, xv; 2055, xv; 2056, xiv; 2059, xi; 2060, 1331; 2069, xv; 2070, 1356; 2074, x; 2077, 1685; 2078, xvi; 2083, 1560; 2196, xvi; 2329, x; 2428, xv; 2434, xiii; 2436, 1418; 2493, xiv; 2663, 1540.

The following manuscripts, arranged in chronological order, will give some indication of the variety of documents that are presented along with the text of the book of Revelation (no account is taken here of manuscripts that present a commentary on the book of Revelation).

The uncial MS 046 comprises 326 folios, of which twenty contain the Revelation and the rest present writings of Gregory of Nyssa.

MS 2059 contains the works of Dionysius the Areopagite.

MS 2030 contains works of Basil, Gregory of Nyssa, and Peter of Alexandria.

MS 2027 contains works of Basil, Theodoret, and Maximus.

MS 2060 contains the homilies of Chrysostom on the Gospel of John.

MS 2070 contains several treatises of Isaac the Syrian, the Song of Songs with the commentary of Psellus.

MS 2056 contains extracts from various ecclesiastical writers.

MS 2023 contains the orations of Gregory of Nazianzus.

MS 2025 begins with the book of Job, is followed by Justin Martyr's *Exhortation to the Greeks*, and concludes with Revelation.

MS 2055 contains the works of Dionysius the Areopagite, Basil's *Contra Eunomium*, and various treatises on chronology.

MS 2054 contains a life of St Elias and a life of St Gregory the Armenian.

MS 2078 contains treatises of Chrysostom and John of Damascus.

MS 2196 contains miscellaneous treatises.

MS 2049 contains lives of saints, the Acts of Thomas, and several theological treatises, with Revelation standing between the life of Euphrosyne and Basil's essay on love to God.

The preceding specimens show the wide variety of authors among whom scribes have included a copy of Revelation. What should be deduced from such diversified codices? First, we must keep in mind that, though Eastern Orthodox theologians, beginning with Athanasius in AD 367, have included the book of Revelation in list of the canonical books of the New Testament, and although Revelation has been commented on by several Greek ecclesiastical writers,[15] the book has never had a place among the Bible lessons of the Greek lectionary system – past or present. Consequently, as we have seen earlier, relatively few copies of the Greek New Testament contain all twenty-seven books.

Future investigators of manuscripts of Revelation should consider what may be the significance that a sizeable number of copies have had a history which was independent of Church 'use', and which, as Hoskier put it, 'owe their freedom from Ecclesiastical standardization to their transmission apart from the documents collected as our "New Testament"'.[16]

Other Problems

In addition to investigations of codicological features of New Testament manuscripts, attention should be given to various other problems that relate to the text of the Greek New Testament. Among larger and smaller tasks that still await future investigations are the following:

(1) 'There is room for a monograph on the question of variations in the size of letters in different manuscripts by the same scribe.'[17]
(2) What can be learned about ancient scribes from artistic evidence?
(3) Collect and analyse biblical quotations in Christian and Jewish inscriptions.
(4) Trace the presence of Atticizing tendencies in Greek manuscripts.
(5) Collect passages in Patristic writers that shed light on the history of the transmission of the text, such as specific mention of the existence of variant readings.[18]
(6) Collect from the Greek Fathers all references to the Syriac language and literature.
(7) Study the orthography of Semitic proper names in Greek manuscripts of the Old and New Testaments.

Lists of other such tasks have been drawn up by Hermann von Soden,[19] by James H. Ropes,[20] and by the present writer.[21] Some of the tasks have, of course, been investigated already, but many others mentioned in the lists still await attention by textual scholars in the future.

> The harvest is plentiful,
> but the labourers are few.

The Future of New Testament Textual Studies

NOTES

1 *Classics: A Discipline and Profession in Crisis?*, ed. by Phyllis Culham and Lowell Edwards (Lanham, MD: University Press of America, 1989).

2 David Damrosch, 'Can Classics Die?', *Lingua Franca: The Review of Academic Life*, 5, no. 6 (Sept/Oct, 1995), 61-6.

3 In 1988 F. F. Bruce included the following dedication in his book, *The Canon of the New Testament* (Glasgow: Chapter House): 'To the Departments/of Humanity [=Latin and Greek/ in the University of Aberdeen/ Founded 1497/ Axed 1987/ With Gratitude for the Past/ and with Hope/ of their Early and Vigorous Resurrection'.

4 Richard Janko, 'Dissolution and Diaspora', in *Classics: A Discipline and Profession in Crisis?*, pp. 325-9.

5 Susan G. Cole, 'Taking Classics into the Twenty-first Century: A Demographic Portrait', in *Classics: A Discipline and Profession in Crisis?*, pp. 15-23.

6 Quoted by Damrosch, 'Can Classics Die?', p. 65.

7 Richard A. LaFleur, '*Latina Resurgens*: Classical Languages Enrollments in American Schools and Colleges', *Classical Outlook*, 74 (1997), 125-30.

8 Articles proclaiming, and analysing, Latin's resurgence appear occasionally in the popular media, for example: Lawrence Hardy, 'Latin's Study Undergoes a Scholarly Revival', *USA Today*, July 19, 1995, section 4D; and Julie Flaherty, 'In America's Schools, Latin Enjoys a Renaissance', *New York Times*, Nov. 27, 1998, p. A25.

9 (New York: Simon & Schuster, 1998). See also the somewhat similar discussion in Glenn W. Most's wide-ranging article, '"With Fearful Steps Pursuing Hopes of High Talk with the Departed Dead"', in *Transactions of the American Philological Association*, 128 (Atlanta: Scholars Press, 1998), 311-24, esp. 318-19.

10 Brief descriptions of all the previously mentioned manuscripts are given in *Bericht der Hermann Kunst-Stiftung zum Förderung der neutestamentlichen Textforschung für die Jahre 1995 bis 1998* (Münster, Westfalen).

11 Subsequently, similar announcements were made by S. Agourides and James Charlesworth in *BA*, 46, 1 (1978), 29-31; 42, 3 (1979), 174-9; and 43, 1 (1980), 26-34.

12 The inventory is the basis of an article by Linos Politis, 'Nouveau manuscrits grecs découverts au Mont Sinaï', *Scriptorium*, 34 (1980), 5-17. Official sigla have been assigned to the biblical items by Aland (see the second edition of his *Liste*), namely, uncials 0278-0290, minuscules 2797-2801, and lectionaries *l*2212-*l*2257.

13 H. J. M. Milne and T. C. Skeat, *Scribes and Correctors of the Codex Sinaiticus* (London: British Museum, 1938).

14 David C. Parker, *Codex Bezae: An Early Christian Manuscript and its Text* (Cambridge: University Press, 1992).

15 In the sixth century by Oecumenius, bishop of Tricca in Thessaly, later that century by Andreas, metropolitan of Cappadocian Caesarea, followed in the ninth century by Arethas, a successor of Andreas in the see of Caesarea. For further information see Josef Schmid, *Studien zur Geschichte des griechischen Apocalypse-Textes* (Münich: Karl Zink, 1955).

16 H. C. Hoskier, *Concerning the Text of the Apocalypse* (London: Quaritch, 1929).

17 Kirsopp and Silva Lake, *Family 13* (London, 1941), p. 12, n. 11.

18 See, for example, the author's articles: 'Explicit References in the Works of Origen to Variant Readings in New Testament Manuscripts', *Historical and Literary Studies* (Grand Rapids, MI: Eerdmans, 1968), pp. 88-103; and 'St. Jerome's Explicit References to Variant Readings in Manuscripts of the New Testament', in *New Testament Studies* (Leiden: Brill, 1980), pp. 199-210.

19 *Die Schriften des Neuen Testaments*, I, iii (Berlin: Verlag von Arthur Glaue, 1910), partly

summarized by Alexander Souter, *The Text and Canon of the New Testament* (London: Duckworth, 1913), pp. 144-5, revised by C. S. C. Williams (London: 1954), pp. 131-3.

20 *The Text of Acts* (London: Macmillan, 1926), pp. cccii-cccvi.

21 *Chapters in the History of the New Testament Textual Criticism* (Leiden: Brill, 1963), pp. 39-41 and 68-72.

THE FUTURE OF SEPTUAGINT TEXTUAL STUDIES

John William Wevers

I MUST BEGIN with a confession. I have never worn or coveted a prophetic mantle, nor have I ever attempted prophecy. The best that I can do is to treat my assignment as *in spe*. I can indicate on the basis of a long association with the Septuagint text (LXX) certain directions which I hope Septuagint text criticism may take in the coming decades.

It might not be amiss to begin by calling attention to a fundamental difference between LXX and New Testament (NT) text criticism. The task which the LXX text critic faces is the recovery of a translation, not of an original writing. A closer parallel to NT text critical work would be that of my close friend and colleague, Emanuel Tov, both in his *Textual Criticism of the Hebrew Bible*,[1] and in his current position as Editor-in-chief of the Qumran texts, i.e. of the *Discoveries in the Judean Desert* volumes which are now appearing with regularity under his gentle prodding.

In line with my Dutch Calvinist background, I intend to make *three* statements: I. The Göttingen LXX and its prospects; II. Concerning new patterns which are emerging for editing LXX volumes; and III. Some new approaches to LXX text criticism.

I. The Göttingen Septuaginta. The urge to create critical editions based on examination of manuscripts waited on the invention of movable type in the fifteenth century by Johannes Gutenberg. The first such attempt was sponsored by Cardinal Ximenes de Cisneros – the Complutensian Polygot, printed in 1514-17, though not issued until 1520-22.[2] According to the preface, a large number of manuscripts were used, mainly Spanish, but including some on loan from the Vatican. Unfortunately, the resulting LXX text cannot always be relied on, since corrections based on the Hebrew text rather than on Greek manuscripts do occur. Contemporary to the Complutensian was the Aldina under the editorship of Andreas Asolanus; this edition was based on manuscripts from the Biblioteca Marciana of Venice, and appeared in 1518-19. Pride of place, however, must be given to the Sixtine edition under the editorship of Cardinal Antonio Carafa, officially called 'Sixtina' since it was sponsored by Pope Sixtus V.[3] It appeared in 1587. The text was primarily based on that of Codex B, an excellent fourth-century text, though it was supplemented by a number of cursives from the Vatican Library as well as from other libraries (mainly in Italy).[4] What made the Sixtina so remarkable was the inclusion of readings from Aq, Sym and Theod as well from the Fathers provided by P. Morinus at the end of chapters, and in supplements by F. Nobilius. The Sixtina became exceedingly popular, supplanting almost all others and was reprinted again and again under various editors well into the nineteenth century,[5] though the edition of J. E. Grabe (1707-20) based on Codex A (fifth century) did gain some acceptance.[6]

Modern approaches to LXX textual studies may be represented by two nineteenth-century scholars. The first of these was Zacharias Frankel, a very important and innovative scholar, whose work was almost completely neglected. His *Vorstudien zu der Septuaginta* appeared in 1841. By 'Septuaginta' he meant the Greek Pentateuch, to which the term Septuagint was originally applied. In this volume he set out his principles of LXX text criticism. A decade later, in his *Über den Enfluss der palästinischen Exegese auf die alexandrinische Hermeneutik*, he worked out these principles for the five books of the Pentateuch.[7] His largely forgotten work is desperately in need of rediscovery by today's Septuagint scholar.

Much more influential was the second scholar, Paul de Lagarde, a younger contemporary of Frankel, whose work he completely disregarded. Lagarde based his work on the *trifaria varietas* of Jerome. In Jerome's *Praefatio in lib. Paralip.*, he stated:

Alexandria and Egypt attribute the authorship of their Greek O.T. to Hesychius. From Constantinople as far as to Antioch the rendering of Lucian the Martyr holds the field; while the Palestinian provinces in between these adopt those codices which, themselves the production of Origen, were promulgated by Eusebius and Pamphilus. And so the whole world is in conflict with itself over this threefold variety of text.[8]

The reference to the promulgation by Eusebius and Pamphilus is to their having made fifty copies of the fifth column of Origen's Hexapla at Constantine's behest. Lagarde maintained that the entire manuscript tradition was a lineal descendant of a single UrSeptuaginta, and that this could actually be recovered by ridding the LXX text of all the recensional elements to be found in the *trifaria varietas*. The first task of the critic, then, was to establish the text of each recension, and he himself published a first volume of the so-called Lucianic, i.e. that text which according to Jerome held the field in Syria. This volume was a disaster, both premature and misguided, and remains to this day a curious monument to industry, but without any scientific value.[9]

Lagarde died in 1891 without having achieved what he wanted. He left a single scholarly heir, the devoted Alfred Rahlfs, who remained loyal to his gifted master by continuing his work towards the recovery of the original LXX, though by no means faithful to all the means which Lagarde had proposed.

Rahlfs was recognized by his colleagues at Göttingen as a true master of Septuagint, and they supported his work by interceding on his behalf for financial support. This intercession was spearheaded by Rudolf Smend (d. 1913) and aided by the Orientalist Julius Wellhausen and the Classicist Eduard Schwyzer, all members of der Königliche Gesellschaft der Wissenschaften zu Göttingen [now known as the Akademie der Wiss. zu Göttingen]. By 1908 they had succeeded in establishing the Septuaginta Unternehmen as a project of the Gesellschaft, with secure funding under the Leiter-schaft of Alfred Rahlfs, which office he occupied until his death in 1935.[10]

Meanwhile in Great Britain an ambitious LXX project was also under way. It had been established somewhat earlier, and was a less ambitious project than the Göttingen one, since it was to create a careful collation of a well-chosen group of manuscripts to a diplomatic text, viz. that of Codex B, and where B was not extant, to Codex A. The first fascimile appeared in 1906,[11] and the last one in 1940, after which the project was discontinued, and has since been abandoned.

It was Rahlfs who made the LXX Unternehmen what it became. He was its inspiration and its chief executive. He hired some assistants not only for collation work, but also to engage in preparatory studies; he himself undertook the preparation of a catalogue of extant manuscripts,[12] which appeared in 1914. Furthermore photographs of manuscripts from libraries, museums, and monasteries throughout the world had to be purchased and brought together to Göttingen. Rahlfs himself prepared an *editio minor* of the Psalter.[13] The first *editio maior* did not appear until a year after Rahlfs died; *I Maccabaeorum* was prepared by Rahlfs' successor as Leiter, Werner Keppler, who was killed during the Second World War. Meanwhile Josef Ziegler had been assigned to edit *Isaias* which appeared in 1939. Ziegler was to be the chief (and only) editor for decades, and he produced in masterful fashion all the prophetic books, the Wisdom of Solomon, the Wisdom of Jesus ben Sirach, as well as Job. The last-named appeared in 1982. Two major editors have worked as editors with and after Ziegler: Robert Hanhart, who served as fourth Leiter of the Unternehmen, edited most of the deuterocanonical books plus Esther and Ezra-Nehemiah (II Esdras), and finally myself as editor of the books of the Pentateuch.

As to prospects for the future of the Göttingen Septuaginta, the following volumes have been assigned to editors: Ruth and Joshua to U. Quast; Daniel (revision only of the o' text) O. Munnich; Regnorum I et II (i.e. 1 and 2Sam) A. Aejmelaeus, and Ecclesiastes P. Gentry. Other volumes for which the collations are completed and revised are I et II Chronicles, Judges, and Regnorum III et IV. IV Maccabees was finished long ago, was assigned at least twice to editors, but now awaits reassignment, and may need some new collations as well. Currently collations are being made for the Psalter; it has been estimated that these will take at least a decade to complete. No collations at all have been begun for Song of Songs nor for Proverbs. No assignments have been made for any of these, and the Kommission is seeking possible editors, though none has as yet been found.

As to the staffing at the Unternehmen, the Leiter is Prof. Aejmelaeus, who is also Assoc. Professor ('Ausserplanmässig') of Old Testament in the Theologische Fakultät of the University. Long-time staff (i.e. over thirty years) are Udo Quast and Detlef Fraenkel; both will reach retirement age within a decade. Not only is it difficult to imagine the Unternehmen without these two professionals, but the Unternehmen has been officially advised that its current funding will terminate in the year 2015. The future for the Unternehmen is bleak on three fronts: editors, staff and funding. I can envision no greater tragedy for the future of LXX studies than the closure of the Septuaginta Unternehmen.

II. My second observation deals with the actual work of the editor, more particularly with ways in which this could be improved. It might be helpful to describe in some detail precisely how an edition is made. This statement is in large part autobiographical.

Collations of manuscripts are the responsibility of the Unternehmen. Only after all the manuscripts have been collated does the work of 'Revidierung' take place. This is a tedious but important checking of each manuscript by two experienced palaeographers, but it is imperative to ensure that the collations are accurate. When the *Revidierung* process is finished for the volume, one can see at a glance whether any manuscript numbers remain without underlining – and such readings are then rechecked. For the Pentateuch there were somewhat over one hundred manuscripts to be collated and revised. Only after this procedure is completed does the editor receive the collation books.

The editor then receives all this raw material – in my case my first assignment was the book of Genesis, six collation *Hefte,* containing 1208 double pages! As an introduction to the work, it took at least three reviews of the contents, by which I mean a careful comparison, word by word of the collation books with the Hebrew text. By the time that I had finished going through the 1208 pages three times certain numbers seemed to cluster in support of variants. For example, the numbers 44-106-107-125-610 often came together in support of a variant text. Some variants were supported only by 19-108-118-314 and 537. Gradually text groups began to emerge out of the chaos. By the time that I had gone through this comparison three times, I was fairly sure of the text history, and in due course there appeared eleven text families, with two such being further divided with one or two sub-groups.

The next major task was the collation of all the papyri evidence. Since papyri are often fragmentary, this is left to the editor to collate. If possible, one does this on the basis of photographs, though some editors of papyri provided no such, and one had to rely on their transcriptions. For Genesis there was a total of twenty-nine papyri, of which three were substantial, large texts. These were 911, the so-called Berliner Genesis, from the late third century, containing materials from the first thirty-five chapters, and published by H. A. Sanders and C. Schmidt.[14] The other two major witnesses were both Chester Beatty manuscripts published by F. G. Kenyon; 961 was a fragmentary text from the fourth century containing text from chapters 9-44, and 962 from the third century with text from chapters 8-46.[15] A further twenty-six papyri were obtained, some only a single page with parts of two or three verses, but each one had to be carefully collated, since most of these were old witnesses, ranging from the middle of the first century BCE to the ninth century of our era.

Once the evidence of the papyri was all recorded in the collation books, one had to turn to the evidence of the versions. I was fortunate that my earlier training had included an introduction to some of the languages involved, viz. Latin, Syriac, Arabic and Ethiopic, but I knew no Coptic nor Armenian, and I had to spend considerable time teaching myself the elements of these languages. Fortunately, I have always loved languages, had a good background in modern linguistics, particularly in Applied Linguistics, but nonetheless a lot of hard work was involved. (For Coptic I was fortunate in having two Egyptologists as Departmental colleagues in Toronto, who were always ready to answer my queries, but for Armenian there was no Armenologist about. I was able to consult a couple of priests of the Armenian Orthodox Church, but what I needed was Classical Armenian. In due course, I managed to 'crack the code' and started to read the biblical text.) I usually spent considerable time in reading the text of a daughter version in comparison with the Greek before doing any collating. So I read at least five or six chapters of the Zohrabian text of the Armenian before putting pen to paper. I will admit that when I was really stuck I would see how the Cambridge editors had handled the Armenian, and this would give me a clue as to what to look for in the Armenian Dictionaries.

Each succeeding daughter version presented its own challenges. Some were rather free renderings; others were more isolated in character; such was the case with the Syrohexaplar, which one could easily retrovert word for word into its parent Greek Text. Some of these versions were extant in a number of manuscripts. Thus the Sahidic was extant in twenty-one partially extant texts, all of which had to be collated.

The Vetus Latina constituted a special problem. Fortunately, the text of B. Fischer's *Die Reste der altlateinische Bibel* II. *Genesis* was available.[16] For the other volumes of the Pentateuch one spent time at the Vetus Latina Institut housed in the Benedictine Monastery in Beuron, where its facilities were generously placed at my disposal, and those in charge were always ready to extend their expert help to me. The problem with the Vetus Latina is, as everyone knows, that the Latin Fathers, being literate, also knew Greek, and were familiar with the LXX text, and could make their own renderings into Latin. Thus the Latin evidence is bewilderingly multifaceted. Fischer had, however, done a masterful job of sorting all this out into strands of the Old Latin. For later books, I simply cited the Fathers individually. Thus the integrity of Latin quotations was often questionable. Fortunately, most of the Latin text was available in manuscript form as well.

I consider the collation of the daughter versions extremely important, but it does represent the weak link in the preparation of the Göttingen editions, and ways to improve this are being suggested.

What still remains for the editor to collate is the least satisfactory part of an editor's responsibilities, viz. the patristic quotations of LXX text. Here one faces two unfortunate difficulties. The first is the widespread lack of critical editions, which then makes one largely dependent on Migne's *Patrologia,* which often present an inferior text. Furthermore, most of these are not indexed, though a number of patristic sources have now been analyzed by the Centre d'Analyse et de Documentation Patristiques in Strassburg, and its indices were made available to me through the Unternehmen.

A second difficulty concerns the Church Fathers themselves. Most of them cited passages from memory. For some Fathers (for example, Chrysostom) I found it almost hopeless to do anything with their citations. Paging through thousands of pages of the eighteen volumes of Migne which contain text attributed (sometimes falsely) to Chrysostom is a thankless task, at times yielding as many as four or five different forms of a popular passage.

Finally, the critical text had to be set up, the text history written, the Apparratuses prepared, and particular problems of text elucidated. Here simple justice demands that I give due recognition to the devoted help of both Udo Quast who was always ready to check any readings which were in doubt, and who read every line of proof, both in galleys and in page proof, with utmost care, and to Detlef Fraenkel whose expertise in Catena texts and in hexaplaric readings was always at my disposal. Without these two professionals, my volumes would have been unthinkable.

It is fully clear from the above that the one area where change is both possible and needed is the work on the daughter versions. Only an expert in the Ethiopic text is able to assess whether for a given passage the version supports a particular Greek reading or is simply Ethiopic. Only a professional Armenologist can state whether an Armenian rendering supports a subjunctive or a future indicative, since the two use the same inflection in Armenian. Or suppose a variant text articulated θεός, how does one treat the Old Latin which only in the earliest form, the North African texts, actually on occasion uses a demonstrative pronoun to render Greek articulation?

Robert Hanhart, the Leiter Emeritus of the Unternehmen, and I often discussed the problem of the daughter versions in connection with the Psalter, but it remained for his successor to do something about it. At the Cambridge meeting of IOSCS in the summer of 1995, Anneli Aejmelaeus invited a number of specialists to discuss her proposal of a symposium on the Greek Psalter to be held two years from that date, i.e. in July 1977 in Göttingen. She invited not only the old editors of the Unternehmen, but also experts on the Greek Psalter, and on the Vetus Latina, the Coptic (i.e. the Sahidic), the Ethiopic, the Syriac, the Arabic, the Armenian, the Georgian and the Catena and hexapla, as well as people working on the Qumran Psalter remains to take part in a symposium with papers invited on their specialties; these papers are being prepared for publication by the Unternehmen. This symposium was a resounding success, and it has been proposed that for the Greek Psalter a principal editor should have associates at least in the major daughter versions who would collate these versions.

I would hope that this bodes well for other volumes as well. I suspect that this would have a side benefit in that new prospective editors might not find the task of editing a volume quite as daunting as hitherto. The work is, as I have indicated, more than can reasonably be expected of a single individual. So I would present my second hope for the LXX future that editors for the remaining volumes would be strengthened by associate editors for some of the daughter versions.

III. My third point concerns the art of text criticism itself. Since the time of Lagarde many text critics have tried to follow Lagarde in his attempt to apply the *trifaria varietas* to the text tradition of particular books. Probably two of the finest LXX scholars of the twentieth century illustrating this trend are my own academic grandfather, James A. Montgomery, in his ICC commentary on Daniel,[17] and Max Margolis' edition of the Greek Joshua.[18]

It will be recalled that the Lagardian programme called for the identification of these three ancient recensions (along with their publication) before the recovery of the original LXX could be made by the elimination of all recensional elements. Lagarde himself was never able to put this ambitious and wildly impractical scheme into practice, nor did his successor try to, though respecting and honouring his memory throughout his life, as his monograph on Lagarde's scientific life's work in the context of his biography fully demonstrates.[19] Both Montgomery and Margolis were convinced of the correctness of the Lagardian programme, and attempted to carry it out by applying the *trifolia varietas* to the text history of the volumes on which they worked. Its most consistent application was that by Margolis, who spent much of his scholarly life on his edition of the Greek Joshua. He classified his evidence under six headings, of which the first five dealt with direct evidence. His first group was called *E*, i.e. the Egyptian recension, which consisted of Codex B[20] plus manuscripts 55, 82 (in part), 120, 129, an Oxyrhynchus papyrus fragment, the Coptic versions and the Ethiopic. This presumably would be his identification of the Hesychian recension.

The Future of Septuagint Textual Studies

The second group he called the *S* or the Syriac recension, better known as the Lucianic recension. Margolis subdivided this group into two group S_a and S_b subgroups. The former was the primary Syrian group, and consisted of Codex K plus five cursive manuscripts [54, 75, 118, 127 and 314], along with the seventh century Lyons Vetus Latina manuscript.[21] He found the secondary S group to contain seven manuscripts [44, 74, 76, 106, 107, 134 and 610] plus an Oxford lectionary text.[22]

The third group he called *P,* or the Palestinian recension, subdivided into the Hexapla, i.e. P_1 and the Tetrapla or P_2. The Hexapla consisted of Codex G, three cursive manuscripts [19, 108 and 376] as well as the Complutensian Polyglot and Lagarde's edition.[23] For Margolis the Tetrapla was represented by manuscript 426, the Syrohexaplar, and the Onomastika Sacra of Eusebius/Jerome.[24]

Group no. 4 or *C* stood for the Constantinopolitan recension, which was presumably based on the fifty copies ordered by Constantine to be made by Eusebius and Pamphilus for use in his capitol.[25] This consisted of Codices A M V[1] W along with eight cursive manuscripts [29, 59, 68, 71, 82 (in part only), 121 and 122], together with the Armenian.

The remaining witnesses, seventeen manuscripts[26] he designated as *M*, i.e. as mixed texts. His final group, no. 6, consisted of Church Fathers, viz. Eusebius, Justin Martyr, Origen and Theodoret. In summary, then, there are four recensions, the Egyptian, Syrian, Palestinian, and the Constantinopolitan, along with a Mixed group, which is hardly a recension.

Rahlfs never tried to force the manuscript evidence into such preordained recensions in his semicritical editions,[27] though he did retain the notion of the hexaplaric and Lucianic recensions. What Rahlfs did was to start with the raw evidence of the witnesses, rather than with a preconceived schema into which the materials somehow were made to fit. This was clearly the case with his Genesis edition, which was based not on new collations, but on the evidence of the Cambridge Septuagint. To a great extent, my own analysis of the much larger amount of evidence (in fact three times as large and recollated by the Göttingen Unternehmen), confirms Rahlfs' grouping almost entirely as fitting the evidence. A few adjustments did have to be made in view of the greater amount of evidence at my disposal, but I was surprised how far Rahlfs had anticipated my conclusions.

I would say that the textual tradition in the future should abandon in large part the attempt to adapt Jerome's *trifaria varietas* to the analysis of textual witnesses. Admittedly, for large parts of the LXX the hexaplaric text is identifiable through the presence of the Aristarchian signs which Origen used in his hexapla, and must be retained, though this should be limited to the texts which were translated from a Hebrew parent text. But even here this is not always possible, as, for example, for the books of Paralipomenon, where as far as I know a hexaplaric text is not identifiable as extant. I would also question the relevance of the so-called Lucianic text for the LXX outside the books of the Former Prophets. For much of what some critics have called 'L' for Lucianic text, it would be better simply to call it a Byzantine text, that text which was used in the liturgy of the Byzantine Church.[28]

And finally, I would comment on possible new approaches to the recovery of the original text. I might say parenthetically that I am under no illusion that it is possible to recover the autographon. What the modern text critic does is to strive to come as closely as possible to that text. This is, I would venture to suggest, what the Göttingen Septuaginta has as its ideal.

In the past, inordinate stress has been placed on the evidence of the oldest uncial texts, more particularly on Codices B, ℵ and A, respectively from the fourth, the fifth and the late fifth centuries. These are certainly important witnesses, but Codex Vaticanus, excellent text though it certainly is, was not copied until almost 600 years had elapsed since the autographon was written. It is not original LXX, but is an eclectic text as all manuscripts are.[29] What a truly critical text intends is to rid the text of the eclectic, i.e. to restore the original text as closely as possible. To call a critical text such as the Göttingen Septuaginta an eclectic text is a serious misnomer. But I do believe that we have relied too much on external text criticism, viz. reliance on such criteria as age of a manuscript, the uncial nature of its script, etc. rather than on internal criteria.

It is in this connection that an important step forward has been made by Ilmari Soisalon-Soininen of Helsinki and his students. What the Finns have done is to analyze how translators of the Hebrew have dealt with grammatical matters of the parent texts. How are the conjunctions καί and δέ distributed; how are pronominal suffixes dealt with by the various translators, how are the semiprepositions ἔναντι, ἔναντίον and ἐνώπιον differentiated, are questions which they have asked and dealt with. They have called this 'translation technique'. The questions asked are excellent, but in my opinion these must be considerably extended. I would also ask: What kinds of patterns of translation does a particular translator use? How does he approach his text? Does it make a difference that the text he is translating is a 'holy' or a 'sacred' text? Does he approach his text word for word with relative disregard for the context, or is he contextually determined? In other words, what I am pleading for is to consider the translator as a person, an individual, who somehow has characteristics of his own, one who has identifiable ways of putting things, who has a conception of what he is doing, and whose grammatical sense may differ from that of his fellows. In short, what I believe we as Septuagint text critics must learn to do is to think like the translator. We must become so familiar with the translator's work that one can predict how he might render a text.

What this means is that we must learn to ask not just for the external criteria of what textual support a given reading might have, but also to investigate how the person translating operates in such a context.

Let me give a few examples of what I mean. A comparison of Numbers and Deuteronomy with respect to the relative clauses in the two works reveals a fundamentally different grammatical conception of the relation of the relative pronoun to its antecedent. In Deuteronomy the translator tended to make the pronoun agree in inflection with the antecedent. One could expect the relative pronoun of a structure such as 'in the field which contained grain' to read ἐν τῷ ἀγρῷ ᾧ ... In Numbers I could only find two cases in which the pronoun agreed with its antecedent; usually the Numbers translator inflected the pronoun according to its use in the clause, in other words, would read ἐν τῷ ἀγρῷ ὅς ... This might well mean that, should Codices A and B read the pronoun as dative, but others read the nominative pronoun, that the critical scholar would probably have to choose to disregard the uncial texts in favor of ὅς. Or to give another example: both Leviticus and Numbers refer to the אשה sacrifice, but Numbers always renders it by κάρπωμα, whereas Leviticus uses a series of different

Greek nouns, including κάρπωμα. On the other hand, the word חטאת can mean either 'sin' or 'a sin offering', and only the context can distinguish which meaning is intended. Leviticus created a neat rendering. For 'sin' he used the usual ἡ ἁμαρτία, but when it meant 'sin offering' he created a new Greek structure; not only did he put the word into the genitive, as τῆς ἁμαρτίας, but he rendered it by τὸ περὶ (τῆς) ἁμαρτίας. Numbers did borrow the Leviticus rendering on occasion, but often simply used the genitive when the sacrifice was meant.

Close attention to the person of the translator and his attitudes may identify some of his theological prejudices. Both Deuteronomy and Numbers avoid rendering מלך by βασιλεύς when the word pertains to Israel's ruler. This is particularly clear in Deuteronomy, who does use βασιλεύς for non-Israelite kings, but for Israel's monarch it, as well as Numbers, uses ἄρχων, but never βασιλεύς. Numbers' attitude towards Balaam is decidedly negative. That he should be a prophet of Yahweh was a repugnant notion, and he usually substitutes τοῦ θεοῦ for the normal κυρίου. Similarly the angel of Yahweh who intercepts him on the way is only once rendered by ἄγγελος κυρίου; otherwise it is always the ἄγγελος τοῦ θεοῦ. The exception only comes when Balaam confesses his sin before the 'angel of Yahweh'. Each translator must be closely examined to discover his attitudes, points of view, and even his prejudices. I believe that this is the direction in which the text criticism of the Septuagint must and will go in the future.

In summary, I have made three major statements in anticipating the future of Septuagint textual studies. First of all, I hope that the Göttingen Septuaginta may in due course be completed, but that work on recovering the original Septuagint text may never languish. Secondly, I hope that editors in the future may receive assistance from experts in the collation of versions, and that more and more of the Fathers who quote the Old Testament text may be published in critical editions. And finally, that text criticism may expand to include not only exterior criteria, but begin to treat translators as real people who should be understood as such. I hope that text criticism may become full-fledged, by which I mean that both external and internal text criticism may be practiced by the critic.

NOTES

1 Mineapolis and Assen: Fortress, 1992.
2 A most useful review of the earliest editions of the Septuagint is that of *Urtext und Übersetzungen der Bibel in übersichtlicher Darstellung*, a reprint of the article 'Bibeltext und Bibelübersetzungen' from the third edition of the *Realencyklopädie für protestantische Theologie und Kirche* (Leipzig, 1897). Particularly relevant is the section on 'Die alexandrinische Übersetzung des Alten Testaments' by Eberhard Nestle, pp. 62-84.
3 See especially Eberhard Nestle, *Septuaginta Studien* (Ulm, 1886). Also relevant is vol. 2 (Ulm, 1896).
4 The Sixtine edition is based principally on the text of Codex B, though its editor, Cardinal Antonio Carafa, is known to have also consulted a number of other manuscripts, not only from the Vatican library itself, but also from other libraries, principally from Italy. Which manuscripts were used is not recorded.

Unfortunately, Codex B had lost the opening leaves containing the text of Genesis 1.1-46.28, its text beginning with the last four words of the verse. The text which was lacking was supplied by a fifteenth century suppletor, who copied the text from MS 19 (Chigi R.VI 38), a twelfth-century manuscript housed in the Vatican Library. Thus only from 46.28

onward is the Sixtine based on Codex B, as a survey of these final chapters immediately makes clear. Even unique readings of B are almost all attested in Sixt as well. In fact, the designation '=Sixt' occurs only four times for a non-B reading in the final chapters of Genesis.

I was sufficiently curious as to the sources of the Sixtine text in the major part of Genesis for which the B text was not extant to make a rough and ready collation of Sixt for these chapters, based simply on the occurrence of '=Sixt' in Apparatus I of the Göttingen text. This is of course methodologically inadequate as evidence, since only deviation from the critical text is noted by such a collation. Nor will I vouch for the accuracy of my collation, since scanning an apparatus will hardly guarantee finding all instances where '=Sixt' obtains. But my collation did consist of 420 instances. Most of these were, however, popular variants, and so I divided the total into two categories, placing in a separate list those variant readings which had no more than six supporters.

I did allow, however, one of the six supporters to consist of a single text family. Since the source of the suppletor text (B^s) was a member of the *b* text which consisted of five manuscripts which rather consistently read the same text and could be said to be a single witness, *b* was allowed as the equivalent of one supporter.

This was also allowed for the *z* group, consisting of four manuscripts, two of which were used as basis for the Aldine edition. It should also be noted that the Complutensian edition's main source was from the above-mentioned *b* group as well.

The results of this examination were not overly significant. For MS 31 (Vienna, Nat. Bibl., theol. gr. 7), which was the major source used by the Aldine editor, Andreas Asolanus, the support in the shorter list was 89 (out of a total of 198) cases, i.e. 45 per cent of the shorter list, or 21.2 per cent of 420. For MS 122 (Venice, Bibl. Marc., gr. 4), also used by Asolanus, the support was 71 (out of 162) cases, i.e. 44 per cent vs 17.9 per cent. The only other significant support was that by the *b* group, which supported the text of the Sixtine in 48 (out of 128) cases, i.e. 37.5 per cent vs 11.4 per cent.

I suspect that what all of this means is that the editor made used of B^s, i.e. the suppleted text added to B, or possibly simply the Complutensis itself on the one hand, and the Aldine, on the other, both of which being available to the editor.

5 For editions of the Sixtina, see especially the reference to Ebernard Nestle in note 2 above.
6 For the four octavo volumes, published in Oxford, as well as for its editors after Grabe's death, see Eberhard Nestle, 'Die alexandrinische Übersetzung des Alten Testaments' 62; see note 2 above.
7 See J. W. Wevers, 'An Apology for Septuagint Studies', BIOSCS XVIII (1985), 19-21.
8 Translation found in S. Jellicoe, *The Septuagint and Modern Study* (Oxford: Clarendon, 1968), p. 134. Jerome's text reads: 'Alexandria et Aegyptus in Septuaginta suis Hesychium laudat auctorem; Constaninopolis usque Antiochiam Luciani Martyris exemplaria probat; mediae inter has provinciae Palestinae codices legunt, quos ab Orignene elaboratos Eusebius et Pamphilus vulgaverunt: totusque orbis hac inter se trifaria varietate compugnat.'
9 *Librorum Veteris Testamenti Canonicorum Pars Prior Graece* (Göttingen, 1883). Fortunately, no second volume was prepared.
10 The present Chairman of the Kommission is the grandson of Rudolf Smend, also named Rudolf; he has written a fascinating account of the work of his grandfather in connection with the establishment of the Unternehmen in 'Der geistige Vater des Septuaingta-Unternehmens', MSU, 20 (Festschrift R. Hanhart) (Göttingen, 1990), pp. 332-44.
11 *The Old Testament in Greek: According to the text of Codex Vaticanus, supplemented from other uncial manuscripts, with a critical apparatus containing the variants of the chief ancient authorities for the text of the Septuagint*, ed. by A. E. Brooke and N. McLean, Vol. 1, Part I (Cambridge: University Press, 1906). The last fascicule was Volume 3, Part I. *Esther, Judith, Tobit*. For Volumes 2 and 3,1 a third editor was added, H. St J. Thackeray.

12 *Verzeichnis der griechischen Handschriften des Alten Testaments*, für das Septuaginta-Unternehmen aufgestellt. *Nachrichten v.d. Königlichen Gesellschaft d. Wissenschaften zu Göttingen.* Philol.-hist. Kl. 1914 (Berlin, 1914). A revision of the Verzeichnis has been assigned to D. Fraenkel of the Unternehmen.

13 *Psalmi cum Odis* (Göttingen, 1931).

14 *The Minor Prophets in the Freer Collection and the Berlin Fragment of Genesis. Univ. of Michigan Studies.* Humanistic Series XXI (New York, 1927).

15 Both papyri were published by F. G. Kenyon, *The Chester Beatty Biblical Papyri*, fasc. 4 (London: Emery Walker, 1934). Facsimile edition of 961 appeared in 1935, and of 962 in 1962.

16 Freiburg, 1951-4.

17 *A Critical and Exegetical Commentary on the Book of Daniel ICC* (Edinburgh: T. & T. Clark, 1927). See also his commentary on the Books of Kings in the same series, ed. by H. S. Gehman (New York, 1951).

18 *The Book of Joshua in Greek According to the Critically Restored Text with an Appendix Containmg the Variants of the Principal Recensions and of the Individual Witnesses*, ed. by Max L. Margolis. Parts 1-4 (comprising 1:1 to 19:38) (Paris, 1931-8); Part 5 (19:39-24:33; with a Preface by Emanuel Tov) (Philadelphia, 1992). All the parts were sustained by the Alexander Kohut Foundation.

19 *Paul de Lagardes wissenschaftliches Lebenswerk im Rahmen einer Geschichte seines Lebens dargestellt.* MSU 4, 1 (Berlin, 1928).

20 For convenience I have changed his idosyncratic symbols into their equivalences in Rahlfs *Verzeichnis.*

21 For bibliographical details, see my *SEPTUAGINTA: Vetus Testamentum Graecum Auctoritate Academiae Scientiarum editum.* III,2. *Deuteronomium* (Göttingen: Vandenhoek & Ruprecht, 1977), p. 20, sub. no. 100.

22 Oxford, Bodleian Library, MS Laud gr. 36.

23 *Librorum Veteris Testamenti Canonicorum.* Pars Prior Graece Pauli de Lagarde edita (Göttingen, 1883). This constituted the edition of what he considered to be the Lucianic recension. It was based on manuscripts 19 and 108; what Lagarde did not realize was that the parents of these two manuscripts had changed after Deuteronomy to a hexaplaric text.

24 E. Klostermann (ed.), *Das Onomastikon der biblischen Ortsnamen, GCS* 11,1 (1904).

25 See Eusebius, Vita Const. iv, 35-7.

26 These are 15, 18, 52, 53, 56, 57, 58, 64, 72, 85, 128, 130, 343, 344, 407, 509, 661 and 730.

27 *Das Buch Ruth, griechisch als Probe einer kritischen Handausgabe der Septuaginta* (Stuttgart, 1922); *SEPTUAGINTA: Societatis Scientiarum Gottingensis auctoritate.* I. *Genesis* (Stuttgart, 1926); idem. X. *Psalmi cum Odis* (Göttingen, 1931).

28 For Genesis I was able to identify the Byzantine text by collating the Lectionary texts used in the Byzantine liturgy, on the basis of *Monumenta Musicae Byzantinae*: Vol. 1 *Prophetologium* ediderunt Carsten Høeg et Günther Zuntz (Copenhagen: Einar Munksgaard, 1939-70).

29 See Lagarde's *Anmerkungen zur griechischen Übersetzung der Proverbien* (Leipzig, 1863), p. 3. His first axiom is worth quoting. It reads: 'die manuscripte der griechischen übersetzung des alten testaments sind alle entweder unmittelbar oder mittelbar das resultat eines eklektischen verfahrens: darum muss, wer den echten text wiederfinden will, ebenfalls eklektiker sein. sein maasstab kann nur die kenntniss des styles der einzelnen übersetzer, sein haupthilfsmittel muss die fähigkeit sein, die ihm vorkommenden lesarten auf ihr semitischen original zurückzuführen oder aber als original-griechische verderbnisse zu erkennen'.

ABBREVIATIONS

ANTF	Arbeiten zur neutestamentlichen Textforschung
BA	*Biblical Archaeologist*
BASP	*Bulletin of the American Society of Papyrologists*
BEThL	Bibliotheca ephemeridum theologicarum Lovaniensium
BJRL	*Journal of the John Rylands Library*
DJD	*Discoveries in the Judaean Desert*
GRBS	*Greek, Roman and Byzantine Studies*
HThR	*Harvard Theological Review*
JBL	*Journal of Biblical Literature*
JJS	*Journal of Jewish Studies*
JRS	*Journal of Roman Studies*
JSNT	*Journal for the Study of the New Testament*
JTS	*Journal of Theological Studies*
MSU	Mitteilungen des Septuaginta-Unternehmens
NTGF	The New Testament in the Greek Fathers
NTS	*New Testament Studies*
NTTS	New Testament Tools and Studies
RB	*Revue biblique*
RevQ	*Revue de Qumran*
SBL	Society of Biblical Literature
SCS	Septuagint and Cognate Studies
SD	Studies and Documents
VC	*Vigiliae Christianae*
VT	*Vetus Testamentum*
ZKT	*Zeitschrift für katholische Theologie*
ZPE	*Zeitschrift für Papyrologie*

BIBLIOGRAPHY

Abercrombie, John R., 'Computer Assisted Alignment of the Greek and Hebrew Biblical Texts: Programming Background', *Textus*, 11 (1984), 125-39

Abercrombie, John R., William Adler, Robert A. Kraft, and Emanuel Tov, *Computer Assisted Tools for Septuagint Studies*, vol. 1, *Ruth*, SCS, 20 (Atlanta: Scholars Press, 1986)

Aejmelaeus, Anneli, *On the Trail of the Septuagint Translators* (Kampen: Kok Pharos, 1993)

Agourides, S., and James Charlesworth, 'A New Discovery of Old Manuscripts on Mt Sinai: A Preliminary Report', *Biblical Archaeologist*, 41, 1 (1978), 29-31

Aland, Barbara, Review of 'The New Testament in Greek: The Gospel According to St Luke', Oxford, 1984, 1987, *JTS*, 42 (1991), 201-15

Aland, Barbara, *Das Neue Testament in syrischer Überlieferung I: Die grossen Katholischen Briefe*, Arbeiten zur Neeutestamentlichen Textforschung, 7 (Berlin and New York: De Gruyter, 1986), 41-90

Aland, Barbara, 'Das Zeugnis der frühen Papyri für den Text der Evangelien', in *The Four Gospels: Festschrift Frans Neirynck*, ed. by F. Van Segbroeck and others, Bibliotheca Ephemeridum Theologicarum Lovaniensium 100. vol. 1 (Leuven: Peeters, 1992), pp. 325-35

Aland, Barbara, 'Neutestamentliche Textforschung, eine philologische, historische und theologische Aufgabe', in *Bilanz und perspektiven gegenwärtiger Auslegung des Neuen Testaments*, Symposion zum 65. Geburtstag von Georg Strecker, Beihefte zur Zeitschrift für die neutestamentliche Wissenschaft 75, ed. by Friedrich Wilhelm Horn (Berlin: De Gruyter, 1995), pp. 7-29

Aland, Barbara, and others, *Novum Testamentum Graecum Editio Critica maior, Vol. IV: Catholic Letters, Installment 1: James. Part 1: Text: Part 2: Supplementary Material*, edited for the Institute for New Testament Textual Research (Stuttgart: Deutsche Bibelgesellschaft, 1997)

Aland, Barbara, and Klaus Wachtel, 'The Greek Minuscule Manuscripts of the New Testament', in *The Text of the New Testament in Contemporary Research: Essays on the Status Quaestionis*, ed. by Bart D. Ehrman and Michael W. Holmes, SD, 46 (Grand Rapids: Eerdmans, 1995), pp. 43-60

Aland, K., 'The Present Position of New Testament Textual Criticism', in *Studia Evangelica*, ed. by K. Aland and others, Texte und Untersuchungen, 73 (Berlin: Akadamie-Verlag, 1959), pp. 717-31

Aland, K., 'The Significance of the Papyri for Progress in New Testament Research', in *The Bible in Modern Scholarship*, ed. by J. P. Hyatt (London: Carey Kingsgate, 1966), 325-27

Aland, Kurt, 'Neue Neutestamentliche Papyri III', *NTS*, 20 (1974), 357-581

Aland, K. (ed.), *Repertorium der griechischen christlichen Papyri I: Biblische Papyri …* (Berlin/New York: De Gruyter, 1976)

Aland, Kurt (ed.), *Text und Textwert der griechischen Handschriften des Neuen Testaments*, I: *Die Katholischen Briefe*, 3 vols, ANTF 9-11 (Berlin and New York: De Gruyter, 1987); II: *Die Paulinischen Briefe*, 4 vols, ANTF 16-19 (Berlin and New York: De Gruyter, 1991); III: *Apostelgeschichte*, 2 vols, ANTF 20-1 (Berlin and New York: De Gruyter, 1993); IV: *Die Synoptischen Evangelien, I. Das markus evangelium*, 2 vols, ANTF 26-7 (Berlin and New

Bibliography

York: De Gruyter, 1998)

Aland, Kurt and Barbara Aland, *Der Text des Neuen Testaments: Einführung in die wissen-schaftlichen Ausgaben und in Theorie wie Praxis der modernen Textkritik*, (Stuttgart: Deutsche Bibelgesellschaft, 1982), English edition, *The Text of the New Testament: An Intro-duction to the Critical Editions and to the Theory and Practice of Modern Textual Criticism*, trans. by Erroll F. Rhodes, 2nd edn (Grand Rapids: Eerdmans; Leiden: Brill, 1989)

Alexander, P. and others, in consultation with J. VanderKam and M. Brady, *Miscellanea, Part 1: Qumran Cave 4*, DJD 36 (Oxford: Clarendon Press, 2000)

American and British Committees of the International Greek New Testament Project (eds), *The New Testament in Greek III: The Gospel According to St Luke*, 2 vols (Oxford: Clarendon Press, 1984, 1987)

Amphoux, C.-B., 'La révision Marcionite du "Notre Père" de Luc (11, 2-4) et sa place dans l'histoire du text', in *Recherches sur l'histoire de la bible Latin*, ed. by R. Gryson and P.-M. Bogaert, Cahiers de la RTL, 19 (Louvain-la-Neuve: Univ. Fac. Théologie, 1987), 205-21

Amphoux, C.-B., 'Schéma d'Histoire du Texte grec du Nouveau Testament', *New Testament Textual Research Update*, 3/3 (1995), 41-6

Anderson, A. S., 'Codex 1582 and Family 1 of the Gospels: the Gospel of Matthew' (unpublished doctoral thesis, University of Birmingham, 1999)

Arckenholz, Johann, *Mémoires concernant Christine, reine de Suède, pour servir d'éclaircisse-ment à l'histoire de son règne et principalement de sa vie privée, et aux évenemens de l'histoire de son tems civile et littéraire*, 4 vols (Amsterdam/Leipzig, 1751-60)

Auwers, J.-M., 'Le texte latin des Évangiles dans le Codex de Bèze', in Parker and Amphoux, *Codex Bezae*, pp. 183-216

Baarda, Tjitze, 'Een marcionitische corruptie?', *Nederlands Theologisch Tijdschrift*, 44 (1990), 273-87

Baber, H. H., *Vetus Testamentum Graecum, e codice MS. Alexandrino asservatur, typis ad similitudinem ipsius codicis scripturae fideliter descriptum*, 3 vols (London: Richard Taylor, 1816-1821)

Bagnall, R., *Egypt in Late Antiquity* (Princeton: University Press, 1993)

Bagnall, R., *Reading Papyri, Writing Ancient History* (London: Routledge, 1995)

Baillet, M., J. T. Milik and R. de Vaux, *Les 'Petites Grottes' de Qumrân*, DJD 3 (Oxford: Clarendon Press, 1962)

Barr, James, 'The Typology of Literalism in Ancient Biblical Translations', MSU, 15 (1979), 279-325

Barrett, C. K., *The Acts of the Apostles 1* (Edinburgh: T&T Clark, 1994)

Barthélemy, D., *Les devanciers d'Aquila* (VTSup 10; Leiden: Brill, 1963)

Barthélemy, D., *Critique textuelle de l'Ancien Testament* (OBO 50/3; Fribourg: Universitäts-verlag/Göttingen: Vandenhoeck und Ruprecht, 1992)

Bauernfiend, Otto, *Der Römerbrieftext des Origens*, Texte und Untersuchungen, 14.3 (Leipzig: J. C. Hinrichs, 1923)

Behrend, Hildegard, *Auf der Suche nach Schätzen: Aus dem Leben Constantin von Tischendorfs*, 5th edn (Berlin: Evangelischer Verlag, 1956)

Benoit, P., 'Note sur les fragments grecs de la grotte 7 de Qumran', *RB*, 79 (1972), 321-4

Benoit, P., 'Nouvelle note sur les fragments grecs de la grotte 7 de Qumran', *RB*, 80 (1973), 5-12

Bentley, J., *Secrets of Mount Sinai: The Story of the Codex Sinaiticus* (London: Orbis, 1985)

Bentley, Richard, *Proposals for Printing a New Edition of the Greek Testament and St. Hierom's Latin Version* (London: J. Knapton, 1721)

Bericht der Hermann Kunst-Stiftung zum Förderung der neutestamentlichen Textforschung für die Jahre 1995 bis 1998 (Münster, Westfalen)

Bickell, G., 'Ein Papyrusfragment eines nichtkanonischen Evangeliums', *ZKT*, 9 (1885), 498-504

Bibliography

Bierbrier, M. L. (ed.), *Papyrus: Structure and Usage* (London: British Museum, 1986)

Birdsall, J. N., '406, a Neglected Witness to the Caesarean Text', in *Studia Evangelica*, ed. by K. Aland and others, Texte und Untersuchungen, 73 (Berlin: Akadamie-Verlag, 1959), pp. 732-6

Birdsall, J. Neville, 'A Study of Ms. 1739 of the Pauline Epistles and its Relationship to Mss. 6, 424, 1908, and M' (unpublished doctoral thesis, University of Nottingham, 1959)

Birdsall, J. N., 'The Bodmer Papyrus of John', *The Tyndale New Testament Lecture for 1958* (London: Tyndale Press, 1960)

Birdsall, J. N., 'The New Testament Text', in *The Cambridge History of the Bible*, vol. 1: *From the Beginnings to Jerome*, ed. by P. R. Ackroyd and C. F. Evans (Cambridge: University Press, 1970), pp. 308-77

Birdsall, J. N., 'The Text and Scholia of the Codex von der Goltz and its Allies, and their Bearing upon the Texts of the Works of Origen, especially the Commentary on Romans', in *Origeniana, premier colloque international des études origeniennes*, Quarderni di 'Vetera Christianorum', 12 ([Bari]: Instituto di Letteratura Cristiana Antica, Università di Bari, 1975), pp. 215-22

Birdsall, J. Neville, 'Rational Eclecticism and the Oldest Manuscripts: A Comparative Study of the Bodmer and Chester Beatty Papyri of the Gospel of Luke', in J. K. Elliott (ed.), *Studies in New Testament Language and Text* (Leiden: Brill, 1976), pp. 39-51

Birdsall, J. N., 'The Geographical and Cultural Origin of the Codex Bezae Cantabrigiensis: A Survey of the *Status Quaestionis*, mainly from the Palaeographical Standpoint', *Studien zum Text und zur Ethik des Neuen Testaments* (F/S H. Greeven), ed. by W. Schrage (Berlin: De Gruyter, 1986), 102-14

Birdsall, J. N., 'The Recent History of New Testament Textual Criticism (from Westcott and Hort, 1881, to the present)', *Aufstieg und Niedergang der römischen Welt (Teil 2, Bd. 26.1)* (Berlin/New York: De Gruyter, 1992), pp. 99-198

Birdsall, J. N., 'After Three Centuries of the Study of Codex Bezae: the *Status Quaestionis*', in Parker and Amphoux, *Codex Bezae*, pp. xix-xxx

Bousset, Wilhelm, *Textkritische Studien zum Neuen Testament*, Texte und Untersuchungen, 11.4 (Leipzig: J. C. Hinrichs, 1894)

Bowman, Alan K., *Egypt after the Pharaohs, 332 BC-AD 642, from Alexander to the Arab Conquest* (London: British Museum Press, 1986)

Brogan, John J., 'The Text of the Gospels in the Writings of Athanasius' (doctoral dissertation, Duke University, 1997)

Brogan, John J., *Athanasius and the Text of the Gospels: Transmitter and Transformer of the Alexandrian Text*, SBLNTGF (Atlanta: SBL, forthcoming)

Brooke, A. E., and N. McLean (eds), *The Old Testament in Greek: According to the text of Codex Vaticanus, supplemented from other uncial manuscripts, with a critical apparatus containing the variants of the chief ancient authorities for the text of the Septuagint*, vol. 1 (Cambridge: University Press, 1906)

Browning, Robert, *Medieval and Modern Greek* (2nd edn, Cambridge: University Press, 1983)

Bruce, F. F., *The Canon of Scripture* (Glasgow: Chapter House, 1988)

Buonocuore, M. (ed.), *Bibliografia dei fondi manoscritti della Biblioteca Vaticana (1968-1980)*, 2 vols, *Studi e Testi*, vols 318, 319 (1986)

Burgon, J. W., *The Revision Revised* (London: J. Murray, 1883)

Burkitt, F. C., 'The Date of Codex Bezae', *JTS* 3 (1902), 501-13

Burkit, F. C., *Evangelion da-Mepharresche* (Cambridge: University Press, 1904)

Burkit, F. C., *The Gospel History and its Transmission*, 3rd edn (Edinburgh: T. & T. Clark, 1911)

Burkitt, F. C., and C. Taylor, *Fragments of the Books of Kings according to the translation of Aquila* (Cambridge: University Press, 1897)

Bibliography

Callahan, A. D., 'Again: the Origin of the Codex Bezae', Parker and Amphoux, *Codex Bezae*, pp. 56-64

Campenhausen, Hans Freiher von and others (eds), *Die Religion in Geschichte und Gegenwart. Handwörterbuch für Theologie und Religionswissenschaft*, 3rd edn, ed. by Hans Freiher von Campenhausen and others, 7 vols (Tübingen: J. C. B. Mohr [Paul Siebeck], 1956-65)

Canart, P. and V. Peri (eds), *Sussidi Bibliografici per i manoscrith greci della Biblioteca Vaticana*, Studi e Testi, 261 (Vatican: 1970)

Carder, M. M., 'A Caesarean Text in the Catholic Epistles?', *NTS*, 16 (1969-70), 252-76

Cavallo, Guiglielmo, *Ricerche sulla maiuscola biblica*, Studi e testi di papirologia 2 (Florence: Le Monnier, 1967)

Cavallo, Guglielmo, 'Libro e pubblico alla fine del mondo antico', in *Libri, editori e pubblico nel mondo antico: Guida storica e critica*, ed. by Guglielmo Cavallo (Rome/Bari: Editori Laterza, 1975), pp. 83-132

Cavallo, Guglielmo, 'Iniziale, scritture distinctive, fregi: morfologie e funzioni', in *Libri e documenti d'Italia: dai Longobardi alla rinascita della città*, ed. by Cesare Scalon (Udine: Arti grafici friulane, 1996), pp. 15-33

Ceresa, M. (ed.), *Bibliografia dei fondi manoscritti della Biblioteca Vaticana (1981-1985)*, Studi e Testi, 342 (Vatican: 1991)

Chantraine, P., *Grammaire Homérique*, 2 vols (Paris: Klincksieck, 1958-63)

Chapa, J., 'Fragments from a Papyrus Codex of the Book of Revelation', paper delivered at the XXII Congresso Internazionale di Papirologia, Florence, 23-29 August 1998

Charitakis, G., 'Katalogos tôn chronologêmenôn kôdikôn tês patriarchês vivliothêkês Kaïrou', *Epeteris Hetaireias Vyzantinôn Spoudôn*, 4 (1927), 109-210

Charlesworth, J. H., 'St Catherine's Monastery: Myths & Mysteries', *BA*, 42, 3 (1979), 174-9

Charlesworth, J. H., 'The Manuscripts of St Catherine's Monastery', *BA*, 43, 1 (1980), 26-34

Charlesworth, J. H. and C. A. Evans, 'Jesus in the Agrapha and Apocryphal Gospels', in *Studying the Historical Jesus: Evaluations of the State of Current Research*, ed. by B. Chilton and C. A. Evans, NTTS, 19 (Leiden: Brill, 1994), 491-532

Charlier, C., 'Les Manuscrits personnels de Florus de Lyon et son activité littéraire', *Mélanges E. Podechard* (Lyons: 1948), 71-84

Cheyne, T. K. and J. Sutherland Black (eds), *The Encyclopædia Biblica*, 4 vols (London: Adam and Charles Black, 1899)

Clableaux, John J., *A Lost Edition of the Letters of Paul: A Reassessment of the Text of the Pauline Corpus Attested by Marcion* (Washington: The Catholic Biblical Association of America, 1989)

Clark, Kenneth W., *A Descriptive Catalogue of Greek New Testament Manuscripts in America* (Chicago: University Press, 1937)

Clark, Kenneth W., *Eight American Praxapostoloi* (Chicago: University of Chicago Press, 1941)

Clark, K. W., 'Today's Problems with the Critical Text of the New Testament', in *Transitions in Biblical Scholarship*, ed. by J. C. Rylaarsdam, Essays in Divinity, 6 (Chicago: University of Chicago Press, 1968), 157-69

Clarke, Kent D., *Textual Optimism: A Critique of the United Bible Societies' Greek New Testament*, JSNT, supp. ser., 138 (Sheffield: Academic Press, 1997)

The Codex Alexandrinus (Royal MS 1 D.v-viii) in Reduced Photographic Facsimile, 5 vols (London: British Museum, 1909-57)

Cole, Susan G., 'Taking Classics into the Twenty-first Century: A Demographic Portrait', in *Classics: A Discipline and Profession in Crisis?*, ed. by Phyllis Culham and Lowell Edwards (Lanham, MD: University Press of America, 1989), pp. 15-23

Comfort, Philip Wesley, *The Quest for the Original Text of the New Testament* (Grand Rapids: Baker, 1992)

Bibliography

Cotton, H. M., W. E. H. Cockle and F. G. B. Millar, 'The Papyrology of the Roman Near East: A Survey', *JRS*, 85 (1995), 214-35

Cotton, H. M. and J. Geiger, *Masada II, The Yigael Yadin Excavations 1963-1965, Final Reports, The Latin and Greek Documents* (Jerusalem: Israel Exploration Society and the Hebrew University, 1989)

Cotton, H. M. and A. Yardeni, *Aramaic, Hebrew, and Greek Documentary Texts from Naḥal Ḥever and Other Sites, with an Appendix Containing Alleged Qumran Texts (The Seiyâl Collection II)* (DJD 27; Oxford: Clarendon Press, 1997)

Cowper, B. H. (ed.), *Codex Alexandrinus. Novum Testamentum Graece* (London: Williams & Norgate, 1860)

Culham, Phyllis, and Lowell Edwards (eds), *Classics: A Discipline and Profession in Crisis?* (Lanham, MD: University Press of America, 1989)

Cureton, William (ed.), *Remains of a Very Antient Recension of the Four Gospels* (London: John Murray, 1858)

Damrosch, David, 'Can Classics Die?', *Lingua Franca: The Review of Academic Life*, 5, no. 6 (Sept./Oct., 1995), 61-6

Dana, H. E. and Mantey Julius R., *A Manual of the Greek New Testament* (Saddle River, NJ: Prentice Hall, 1955)

Davey, Colin, 'Fair Exchange? Old Manuscripts for New Printed Books', in *Through the Looking Glass: Byzantium through British Eyes*, ed. by Robin Cormack and Elizabeth Jeffreys (Aldershot: Aldgate, 2000), pp. 127-34

Davies, W. D. and Dale C. Allison Jr, *The Gospel according to St. Matthew*, 3 vols (Edinburgh: T&T Clark, 1988-97)

Davis, Stephen J., *The Cult of Saint Thecla: A Tradition of Women's Piety in Late Antiquity* (Oxford: University Press, 2001)

Delobel, Joël, 'The Lord's Prayer in the Textual Tradition', in *The New Testament in Early Christianity*, ed. by J. M. Sevrin, Bibliotheca Ephemeridum Theologicarum Lovaniensium 86 (Leuven: Peeters, 1989), pp. 293-309

Delobel, Joël, 'Luke 23:34a: A Perpetual Text-Critical Crux?', in *Sayings of Jesus: Canonical & Non-Canonical: Essays in Honour of Tjitze Baarda*, ed. by William L. Petersen and others (Leiden: Brill, 1997), pp. 25-36

Devore, Jay, and Roxy Peck, *Statistics: The Exploration and Analysis of Data*, 3rd edn (San Francisco: Duxbury Press, 1997)

Dimant, D., 'An Unknown Jewish Apocryphal Work?', in *Pomegranates and Golden Bells: Studies in Biblical, Jewish, and Near Eastern Ritual, Law, and Literature in Honor of Jacob Milgrom*, ed. by D. P. Wright and others (Winona Lake, IN: Eisenbrauns, 1995), pp. 805-14

Dogniez, C., *Bibliographie de la Septante 1970-1993* (VTSup 60; Leiden: Brill, 1995)

Dunand, F., 'Papyrus grecs biblique (*P.F.* Inv. 266). Volumina de la Genèse et du Deuteronome (avec 15 planches)', *Études de Papyrologie*, 9 (1971), 81-150

Easterling, Patricia, 'Before Palaeography: Notes on Early Descriptions and Datings of Greek Manuscripts', in *Texte und Untersuchungen zur Geschichte der altchristlichen Literatur*, 124 (1977), pp. 179-87

Easterling, Patricia, 'From Britain to Byzantium: the Study of Greek Manuscripts', in *Through the Looking Glass: Byzantium through British Eyes*, ed. by Robin Cormack and Elizabeth Jeffreys (Aldershot: Aldgate, 2000), pp. 107-20

Ehrman, Bart D., *Didymus the Blind and the Test of the Gospels*, SBLNTGF, 1 (Atlanta: Scholars Press, 1986)

Ehrman, Bart D., 'Methodological Developments in the Analysis and Classification of New Testament Documentary Evidence', *Novum Testamentum*, 29 (1987), 22-45

Ehrman, Bart D., 'The Use of Group Profiles for the Classification of New Testament Documentary Evidence', *JBL* (1987), 465-86

Ehrman, Bart D., Gordon D. Fee and Michael E. Holmes, *The Text of the Fourth Gospel in the Writings of Origen*, SBLNTGF, 3 (Atlanta: Scholars Press, 1992)

Ehrman, Bart D., 'Heracleon, Origen, and the Text of the Fourth Gospel', *VC*, 47 (1993), 105-18

Ehrman, Bart D., *The Orthodox Corruption of Scripture: The Effect of Early Christological Controversies on the Text of the New Testament* (New York: Oxford University Press, 1993)

Ehrman, Bart D., 'Heracleon and the 'Western' Textual Tradition', *NTS*, 40 (1994), 465-86

Ehrman, Bart D., 'The Use and Significance of Patristic Evidence in New Testament Textual Criticism', in *New Testament Textual Criticism, Exegesis, and Church History: A Discussion of Methods*, ed. by Barbara Aland and J. Delobel (Kampen, The Netherlands: Kok Pharos, 1994), pp. 118-35

Ehrman, Bart D., 'Novum Testamentum Graecum Editio Critica Maior: An Evaluation', *TC: A Journal of Biblical Textual Criticism* [http://shemesh.scholar.emory.edu/scripts/TC], 3 (1998)

Elliott, J. K., 'Rational Criticism and the Text of the New Testament', *Theology* 75 (1972), 338-43

Elliott, J. K., 'Can We Recover the Original New Testament?', *Theology*, 77 (1974), 338-53

Elliott, J. K., 'Plaidoyer pour un éclecticisme intégral appliqué à la critique textuelle du Nouveau Testament', *RB* 74 (1977), 5-25

Elliott, J. K., 'In Defence of Thoroughgoing Eclecticism in New Testament Textual Criticism', *Restoration Quarterly* 21 (1978), 95-115

Elliott, J. K., '*Mathetes* with a Possessive in the New Testament', *Theologische Zeitschrift*, 35 (1979), 300-4

Elliott, J. K., 'An Eclectic Textual Commentary on the Greek Text of Mark's Gospel', in *New Testament Textual Criticism: Its Significance for Exegesis* (Essays in Honour of Bruce M. Metzger), ed. by E. J. Epp and G. D. Fee (Oxford: Clarendon Press, 1981), pp. 47-60

Elliott, J. K., *A Survey of Manuscripts used in Editions of the Greek New Testament*, Supplements to Novum Testamentum, 57 (Leiden: Brill, 1987)

Elliott, J. K. (ed.), *The Principles and Practice of New Testament Textual Criticism: Collected Essays*, BETL, 96 (Leuven: Peeters, 1990)

Elliott, J. K., 'Textkritik Heute', *Zeitschrift für die Neutestamentliche Wissenschaft* 82 (1991), 34-41

Elliott, J. K., *Essays and Studies in New Testament Textual Criticism*, EFN, 3 (Córdoba: Ediciones El Almendro, 1992)

Elliott, J. K., 'Thoroughgoing Eclecticism in New Testament Textual Criticism', in *The Text of the New Testament in Contemporary Research: Essays on the* Status Questionis: *A Volume in Honor of Bruce M. Metzger*, ed. by Bart D. Ehrman and Michael W. Holmes, SD, 46 (Grand Rapids: Eerdmans, 1995), pp. 321-35

Elliott, J. K., *A Bibliography of New Testament Manuscripts*, Society for New Testament Studies, monograph series, 62 (Cambridge: University Press, 1989; 2nd edn 2000)

Elliott, Keith and Ian Moir, *Manuscripts and the Text of the New Testament* (Edinburgh: T&T Clark, 1995)

Elliott, W. J., 'The Relationship between 322 and 323 of the Greek New Testament', *NTS*, 14 (1968), 271-81

Elliott, W. J., 'An Examination of von Soden's I b2 Group of MSS' (unpublished master's thesis, University of Birmingham, 1969)

Elliott, W. J. and D. C. Parker (eds), *The New Testament in Greek. IV. The Gospel According to St John, Volume 1: The Papyri*, NTTS, 20 (Leiden: Brill, 1995)

Epp, E. J., 'The New Testament Papyrus Manuscripts in Historical Perspective', in *To Touch the Text: Biblical and Related Studies in Honor of Joseph A. Fitzmyer*, ed. by Maurya P. Horgan,

Bibliography

and Paul J. Kobelski (New York: Crossroad, 1989), pp. 261-88

Epp, E. J., 'The Significance of the Papyri for Determining The Nature of the New Testament Text in the Second Century: A Dynamic View of Textual Transmission', in *Gospel Traditions in the Second Century: Origins, Recensions, Text, and Transmission*, ed. by William L. Petersen (Notre Dame: University of Notre Dame Press, 1989), pp. 71-103

Epp, E. J., 'The Twentieth-Century Interlude in New Testament Textual Criticism', repr. in E. J. Epp and G. D. Fee, *Studies in the Theory and Method of New Testament Textual Criticism*, SD, 45 (Grand Rapids: Eerdmans, 1993), 83-108

Epp, E. J., 'The Papyrus Manuscripts of the New Testament', in *The Text of the New Testament in Contemporary Research: Essays on the Status Quaestionis*, ed. by B. D. Ehrman and M. W. Holmes, SD, 46 (Grand Rapids: Eerdmans, 1995), 3-21

Epp, E. J., 'Textual Criticism in the Exegesis of the New Testament, with an Excursus on Canon', in *Handbook to Exegesis of the New Testament*, ed. by S. E. Porter, NTTS, 25 (Leiden: Brill, 1997), 45-97

Everett Green, Mary A. (ed.), *Calendar of State Papers, Domestic: The Commonwealth*, 13 vols (London, 1875-1886)

Failler, Albert, 'Le séjour d'Athanase II d'Alexandrie à Constantinople', *Revue des études byzantines*, 35 (1977), 43-71

Faivre, Jules, 'L'église Saint-Sabas et le martyrium de Saint-Marc à Alexandrie', *Bulletin de l'Association des amis de l'art copte*, 3 (1937), 60-74

Fausel, H., 'Maulbron', *Die Religion in Geschichte und Gegenwart* (Tübingen: J. C. B. Mohr [Paul Siebeck], 1960), vol. 4, col. 811

Fee, Gordon D., 'The Text of John and Mark in the Writings of Chrysostom', *NTS*, 26 (1980), 325-47

Fee, Gordon D., *New International Commentary on I Corinthians* (Grand Rapids: Eerdmans, 1987)

Fee, Gordon D., 'The Majority Text and the Original Text of the New Testament', in *Studies in the Theory and Method of New Testament Textual Criticism*, ed. by Eldon Jay Epp and Gordon D. Fee, SD, 45 (Grand Rapids: Eerdmans, 1993), pp. 183-208

Fee, Gordon D., 'The Use of the Greek Fathers for New Testament Textual Criticism', in *The Text of the New Testament in Contemporary Research: Essays on the* Status Quaestionis, ed. by Bart D. Ehrman and Michael W. Holmes, SD, 46 (Grand Rapids: Eerdmans, 1995), pp. 191-207

Feron, E. and F. Battaglini, *Codices manuscripti graeci Ottoboniani Bibliothecae Vaticanae descripti* (Vatican City: Vatican Press, 1893)

Ferrar, W. H., *A Collation of Four Important Manuscripts of the Gospels*, ed. by T. K. Abbott (Dublin: Hodges, Foster, and Figgis, 1877)

Finegan, Jack, *Encountering New Testament Manuscripts: A Working Introduction to Textual Criticism* (London: SPCK, 1975)

Fitzmyer, J., 'Los papiros griegos de la Cueva 7 de Qumran', *JBL*, 95 (1976)

Fitzmyer, J. A., *The Dead Sea Scrolls: Major Publications and Tools for Study*, SBLRBS, 20 (Atlanta: Scholars Press, 1990)

Flaherty, Julie, 'In America's Schools, Latin Enjoys a Renaissance', *New York Times*, November 27, 1998, p. A25

Foss, Clive, *Ephesus after Antiquity: A Late Antique, Byzantine and Turkish City* (Cambridge: University Press, 1979)

Fox, Adam, *John Mill and Richard Bentley: A Study in the Textual Criticism of the New Testament 1675-1729* (Oxford: Blackwell, 1954)

Fraenkel, D., U. Quast, and J. W. Wevers (eds), *Studien zur Septuaginta – Robert Hanhart zu Ehren*, MSU 20 (Göttingen: Vandenhoeck & Ruprecht, 1990)

Bibliography

Gallo, I., *Greek and Latin Papyrology*, Classical Handbook, 1 (London: Institute of Classical Studies, University of London, 1986)

Gamble, Harry Y., *Books and Readers in the Early Church: A History of Early Christian Texts* (New Haven/London: Yale University Press, 1995)

Gamillscheg, Ernst and Dieter Harlfinger, *Repertorium der griechischen Kopisten 800-1600*, Band 1: Handschriften aus Bibliotheken Grossbrittaniens (Vienna: 1981); Band 2: Frankreichs (1989), Band 3: Roms mit dem Vatikan (1997).

Geer, Jr, Thomas C., *Family 1739 in Acts*, SBL Monograph Series, 48 (Atlanta, GA: Scholars Press, 1994)

Gibson, M. D., *How the Codex Was Found: A Narrative of Two Visits to Sinai, from Mrs. Lewis's Journals, 1892-93* (Cambridge: Bowes & Macmillan, 1893)

Gibson, Margaret D., 'Professor Nestle', *Expository Times*, vol. 24 (1912-13), pp. 379-80

Gould, Stephen Jay, *Wonderful Life: The Burgess Shale and the Nature of History* (New York and London: W. W. Norton, 1989)

Greenspoon, L., 'The Dead Sea Scrolls and the Greek Bible', in *The Dead Sea Scrolls after Fifty Years: A Comprehensive Assessment*, ed. by P. W. Flint and J. C. VanderKam (Leiden/Boston/Köln: Brill, 1998), 101-27

Gregory, C. R., *Textkritik des Neuen Testamentes* (Leipzig: J. C. Hinrichs, 1900-1909)

Gregory, Caspar René, *Canon and Text of the New Testament* (New York: Charles Scribner's Sons, 1907)

Grenfell, B. P. and A. S. Hunt (eds), Λογια Ιησου: *Sayings of Our Lord from an Early Greek Papyrus* (London: Frowde, 1897)

Guineau, B., L. Holtz and J. Vezin, 'Étude comparée des tracés à l'encre bleue du ms. Lyon, B.M. 484 et du fol. 384v du Codex de Bèze', in Parker and Amphoux, *Codex Bezae*, pp. 79-94

Haas, Christopher, *Alexandria in Late Antiquity: Topography and Social Conflict* (Baltimore: Johns Hopkins University Press, 1997)

Haines-Eitzen, Kim, *Guardians of Letters: Literacy, Power, and the Transmitters of Early Christian Literature* (New York: Oxford University Press, 2000)

Halkin, François, 'Manuscrits galésiotes', *Scriptorium*, 15 (1961), 221-7

Hannah, Darrell C., *The Text of I Corinthians in the Writings of Origen*, SBLNTGF, 4 (Atlanta: Scholars Press, 1997)

Hanson, Victor D. and John Heath, *Who Killed Homer?: The Decline of Classical Education and the Recovery of Greek Wisdom* (New York: Simon & Schuster, 1998)

Hardy, Edward R., *Christian Egypt: Church and People. Christianity and Nationalism in the Patriarchate of Alexandria* (New York: Oxford University Press, 1952)

Hardy, Lawrence, 'Latin's Study Undergoes a Scholarly Revival', *USA Today*, July 19, 1995, section 4D

Harris, J. Rendel, *On the Origin of the Ferrar Group* (London: C. J. Clay and Sons, 1893)

Harris, Rendel, 'The New Syriac Gospels', in *Contemporary Review*, 66 (1894), pp. 654-73

Harris, J. Rendel, *Further Researches into the History of the Ferrar Group* (London: C. J. Clay and Sons, 1900)

Harris, J. R., *The Annotators of the Codex Bezae (with some notes on Sortes Sanctorum)* (London: C. J. Clay and Sons, 1901)

Harris, Rendel, 'Eberhard Nestle', *Expository Times*, 24 (1912-13), pp. 449-50

Hastings, James, *Dictionary of the Bible*, 5 vols (Edinburgh: T&T Clark, 1898)

Head, Peter M., 'Observations on Early Papyri', *Biblica*, 71 (1990), 240-7

Heimerdinger, J., 'Word Order in Koine Greek: Using a Text-Critical Approach to Study Word Order Patterns in the Greek Text of Acts', *FN*, 9 (1996), 139-80

Heimerdinger, J., *The Contribution of Discourse Analysis to Textual Criticism: A Study of the Bezan Text of Acts*, JSNTSup (Sheffield: Academic Press, forthcoming)

Bibliography

Hempel, C., 'Qumran Communities: Beyond the Fringes of Second Temple Society', in S. E. Porter and C. A. Evans (eds), *The Scrolls and the Scriptures: Qumran Fifty Years After*, JSPSup, 26, RILP, 3 (Sheffield: Sheffield Academic Press, 1997), pp. 43-53

Hering, Gunnar, *Ökumenisches Patriarchat und europäische Politik, 1620-1638* (Wiesbaden: Franz Steiner, 1968)

Herrmann, Johannes, 'Der "Nestle"', *Evangelisch-lutherische Kirchenzeitung* 5 (1951), pp. 301-2

Heubeck, A. and others (eds), *A Commentary on Homer's Odyssey*, 3 vols (Oxford: Clarendon Press, 1988-92)

Hirsch, Emanuel, *Geschichte der neuern evangelischen Theologie im Zusammenhang mit den allgemeinen Bewegungen des europäischen Denkens* (Gütersloh: Gütersloher Verlagshaus Gerd Mohn, 1949)

Hodges, Zane C. and Arthur L. Farstad (eds), *The Greek New Testament According to the Majority Text* (Nashville: Thomas Nelson Publishers, 1982; 2nd edn 1985)

Hody, Humfrey, *De Bibliorum textibus originalibus, versionibus graecis, & latina vulgata: Libri IV* (Oxford: Sheldonian Theatre, 1705)

Holmes, M. W., 'Codex Bezae as a Recension of the Gospels', in Parker and Amphoux, *Codex Bezae*, pp. 123-60

Holte, Ragnar, *Die Vermittlungstheologie: Ihre theologischen Grundbegriffe kritisch untersucht* (Uppsala: University of Uppsala, 1965)

Holtz, L., 'L'écriture latine du Codex de Bèze', in Parker and Amphoux, *Codex Bezae*, pp. 14-55

Holzinger, Heinrich, *Über das Verhältnis des von den Septuaginta benutzten Textes des Ezechiel zu der heute rezipierten masoretischen Redaktion* (Unpublished)

Horsley, G. R. H., 'Papyrology and the Greek Language: A Fragmentary Abecedarius of Desiderata for Future Study', in *Acta of the 20th International Congress of Papyrology held in Copenhagen in August 1992*, ed. by A. Bülow-Jacobsen (Copenhagen: Museum Tusculanum, 1994), 48-70

Horsley, G. H. R., 'Reconstructing a Biblical Codex: The Prehistory of MPER n.s. XVII. 10 (*P.Vindob.* G 29 831)', in *Akten des 21. Internationalen Papyrologenkongresses Berlin, 13.-19.8.1995*, ed. by B. Kramer, W. Luppe, H. Maehler and G. Poethke, 2 vols (Stuttgart: Teubner, 1997), 1.473-81

Hoskier, H. C., *A Full Account and Collation of the Greek Cursive Codex Evangelium 604* (London: David Nutt, 1890)

Hoskier, H. C., *Concerning the Text of the Apocalypse*, 2 vols (London: Quaritch, 1929)

Howarth, David, *Lord Arundel and His Circle* (New Haven: Yale University Press, 1985)

Hunger, H., '7Q5: Markus 6,52-53-oder? Die Meinung des Papyrologen', in *Christen und Christliches in Qumran?*, ed. by B. Mayer, Eichstätter Studien, 32 (Regensburg: Pustet, 1992), 33-56

Hurtado, Larry W., *Text-Critical Methodology and the Pre-Caesarean Text: Codex W in the Gospel of Mark*, SD, 43 (Grand Rapids: Eerdmans, 1981)

Hutter, Irmgard, *Corpus der byzantinischen Miniaturenhandschriften*, 1-3: *Oxford, Bodleian Library* (Stuttgart: Hiersemann, 1977-82)

Jackson, Samuel Macauley (ed.), *The New Schaff-Herzog Encyclopedia of Religious Knowledge*, 12 vols (New York: Funk & Wagnalls Company, 1908)

Janin, Raymond, *Les églises et les monastères des grands centres byzantins (Bithynie, Hellespont, Latros, Galèsios, Trébizonde, Thessalonique)* (Paris: Institut français d'études byzantines, 1975)

Janko, Richard, 'Dissolution and Diaspora', in *Classics: A Discipline and Profession in Crisis?*, ed. by Phyllis Culham and Lowell Edwards (Lanham, MD: University Press of America, 1989), pp. 325-9

Bibliography

Jellicoe, Sidney, *The Septuagint and Modern Study* (Oxford: Clarendon Press, 1968)

Jobes, Karen H., 'A Comparative Syntactic Analysis of the Greek Versions of Daniel: A Test Case for New Methodology', *BIOSCS*, 28 (1995), 19-41

Jobes, Karen H., *The Alpha-Text of Esther: Its Character and Relationship to the Masoretic Text*, SBLDS, 153 (Atlanta: Scholars Press, 1996)

Jobes, Karen H., 'Karen Jobes Responds to Tim McLay', *BIOSCS*, 30 (1997), 32-5

Kahle, P., *The Cairo Geniza* (2nd edn; Oxford, 1959)

Kahle, P., 'The Greek Bible and the Gospels: Fragments from the Judaean Desert', *SE*, 1 (TU 73; Berlin 1959), 613-21

Keil, Günther, *Philosophie Geschichte: Von der Aufklärung bis zur Gegenwart*, 2 vols (Stuttgart: Verlag W. Kohlhammer, 1987)

Kemke, Johannes, *Patricius Junius (Patrick Young): Bibliothekar der Könige Jacob I. und Carl I. von England* (Leipzig: M. Spirgalis, 1898)

Kenyon, F. G., *The Palaeography of Greek Papyri* (Oxford: Clarendon Press, 1899)

Kenyon, F. G., *Handbook to the Textual Criticism of the New Testament* (London: Macmillan, 1926)

Kenyon, Sir Frederic, *The Story of the Bible: A Popular Account of how it came to us*, 2nd edn (London: John Murray, 1964)

Kenyon, F. G., *The Text of the Greek Bible*, ed. by A. W. Adams, 3rd edn (London: Duckworth, 1975; first published London: Duckworth, 1937)

Kidd, B. J., *Documents Illustrative of the History of the Church: Volume 2, 313-461 A.D.* (London/New York: SPCK/Macmillan, 1932)

Kilpatrick, G. D., 'Dura-Europas: The Parchments and the Papyri', *GRBS*, 5 (1964), 215-25

Kilpatrick, G. D., 'Luke 24:42-43', *Novum Testamentum*, 28 (1986), 306-8

Kim, K. W., 'Codices 1582, 1739, and Origen', *JBL*, 69 (1950), 167-75

Kirk, G. S. (ed.), *The Iliad: A Commentary* (Cambridge: University Press, 1985-1993)

Kraft, Robert A. and Emanuel Tov, 'Computer Assisted Tools for Septuagint Studies', *BIOSCS*, 14 (1981), 22-40

Kramer, B., W. Luppe, H. Maehler and G. Poethke (eds), *Akten des 21. Internationalen Papyrologenkongresses Berlin, 13.-19.8.1995*, 2 vols (Stuttgart: Teubner, 1997)

Laan, Nancy, 'Stylometry and Method: The Case for Euripides', *JLLC*, 10,4 (1995), 271-8

LaFleur, Richard A., '*Latina Resurgens*: Classical Languages Enrollments in American Schools and Colleges', *Classical Outlook*, 74 (1997), 125-30

Lagarde, Paul de, *Librorum Veteris Testamenti Canonicorum Pars Prior Graece* (Göttingen: 1883)

Lagrange, M.-J., *Introduction à l'étude du Nouveau Testament. Deuxième partie: Critique textuelle II: La critique rationnelle* (Paris: Gabalda 1935)

Lake, K., 'Some New Members of the "Ferrar Group" of MSS of the Gospels', *JTS*, 1 (1899), 117-20

Lake, Kirsopp, *Codex 1 of the Gospels and its Allies*, Texts and Studies, 7/3 (Cambridge: University Press, 1902)

Lake, Kirsopp, *The Text of the New Testament*, 6th edn (London: Rivingtons, 1928)

Lake, Kirsopp, J. de Zwaan, and Morton S. Enslin, 'Athos, Laura 184 [B'64] (Greg. 1739; von Soden α78), Acts Catholic Epistles, Paul', in *Six Collations of New Testament Manuscripts*, ed. by Kirsopp Lake and Silva New, Harvard Theological Studies, 17 (Cambridge, Mass.: Harvard University Press; London: Oxford University Press, 1932), pp. 141-219

Lake, Kirsopp and Silva, *Family 13* (London: Christophers, 1941)

Laks, A. and G. W. Most (eds), *Studies on the Derveni Papyrus* (Oxford: Clarendon Press, 1996)

Landon, C., *A Text Critical Study of the Epistle of Jude*, JSNT Sup. 135 (Sheffield: Academic Press, 1996)

Bibliography

Lane, W. L., *The Gospel According to Mark*, NICNT (Grand Rapids: Eerdmans, 1974), 18-21

Leaney, A. R. C., 'Greek Manuscripts from the Judaean Desert', in *Studies in New Testament Language and Text: Essays in Honour of George D. Kilpatrick on the Occasion of His Sixty-Fifth Birthday*, ed. by J. K. Elliott, NTSup 44 (Leiden: Brill, 1976), pp. 283-300

Leroy, Jules, *Les manuscrits coptes et coptes-arabes illustrés*, Bibliothèque archéologique et historique de l'Institut français d'archéologie de Beyrouth, vol. 96 (Paris: Paul Geuther, 1974)

Lewis, N., *The Documents from the Bar Kochba Period in the Cave of Letters: Greek Papyri* (Jerusalem: Israel Exploration Society, the Hebrew University, and the Shrine of the Book, 1989)

Lowe, E. A., 'The Codex Bezae and Lyons', *JTS*, 25 (1924), pp. 270-74, reprinted in *Palaeographical Papers 1907-1966*, ed. by L. Bieler (Oxford: 1972), vol. 1, 182-6

Lowe, E. A., 'A Note on the Codex Bezae', *Bulletin of the Bezan Club*, 4 (1927), 9-14, reprinted in *Palaeographical Papers 1907-1966*, ed. by L. Bieler (Oxford: 1972), vol. 1, 224-8

Manfredi, M., 'Opistografo', *Parola del Passato*, 38 (1983), 44-54

Martin, Annick, 'Alexandrie à l'époque romaine tardive: l'impact du christianisme sur la topographie et les institutions', in *Alexandrie médiévale I*, ed. by Christian Décobert and Jean-Yves Empereur (Cairo: Institut français d'archéologie orientale, 1998), pp. 12-15

Martin, J. P. P., *Quatre manuscrits de N.T. auxquels on peut ajouter un cinquième* (Paris: Maisonneure et Cie, 1886)

Martin, Maurice, 'Alexandrie chrétienne à la fin du XIIe siècle d'après Abû l-Makârim', in *Alexandrie médiévale I*, ed. by Christian Décobert and Jean-Yves Empereur (Cairo: Institut français d'archéologie orientale, 1998), pp. 45-49

Martin, Raymond A., *Syntactical Evidence of Semitic Sources in Greek Documents*, SCS 3 (Cambridge, Mass.: Scholars Press, 1974)

Martini, C. M., 'Il problema della recensionalità del codice B alla luce del papiro Bodmer XIV', *Analecta Biblica*, 26 (1966)

Martini, C. M. (ed.), *Novum Testamentum e codice Vaticano graeco 1209 (Codex B) tertia vice phototypice expressum in civitate Vaticana* (Vatican: in Bybliotheca Vaticana, 1968)

Martini, C. M., 'Note sui papiri della grotta 7 di Qumran', *Biblica*, 53 (1972), 101-4

Martini, C. M., 'Eclecticism and Atticism in the Textual Criticism of the Greek New Testament', in *On Language, Culture, and Religion: In Honor of Eugene A. Nida*, ed. by M. Black and W. A. Smalley (The Hague: Mouton, 1974), 149-56

Martini, C. M., 'Is there a Late Alexandrian Text of the Gospels?', *NTS*, 24 (1977-8), 285-96

Mayer, S. (ed.), *Christen und Christliches in Qumran?*, Eichstätter Studien, 32 (Regensburg 1992)

Mazarakes, Gerasimos G., *Symbolê eis tên historian tês en Aigyptoi orthodoxou ekklêsias* (Alexandria: Patriarchal Press, 1932)

Mazon, Paul, *Introduction a l'Iliade* (Paris: Les Belles Lettres, 1943)

McDonald, L. M., *The Formation of the Christian Biblical Canon*, 2nd edn (Peabody: Hendrickson, 1995)

McDonald, L. M. and S. E. Porter, *Early Christianity and its Sacred Literature* (Peabody: Hendrickson, 2000)

McLay, Tim, 'Syntactic Profiles and the Characteristics of Revision: A Response to Karen Jobes', *BIOSCS*, 29 (1996), 15-21

Mealand, D. L., 'On Finding Fresh Evidence in Old Texts: Reflections on Results in Computer-Assisted Biblical Research', *BJRL*, 74, 3 (1992), 67-87

Mealand, D. L., 'Correspondence Analysis of Luke', *JLLC*, 10, 3 (1995), 171-82

Mercati, G., 'Frammenti di Aquila o di Simmaco', *RB*, n.s., 8 (1911), 266-72

Mercati, Giovanni, 'I codici greci di Abramo Massad Maronita', *Studia Anselmiana*, 27-8 (1951), 15-37

Bibliography

Mercati, G., *Psalterii Hexapli reliquiae* (Vatican: in Bybliotheca Vaticana, 1958)

Messages: Millénaire de la Bibliothèque du patriarcat grec orthodoxe d'Alexandrie (952-1952) (Alexandria: Patriarchal Press, 1952)

Metzger, Bruce M., *Chapters in the History of the New Testament Textual Criticism* (Leiden: Brill, 1963)

Metzger, Bruce M., 'The Caesarean Text of the Gospels', in *Chapters in the History of New Testament Textual Criticism*, by Bruce M. Metzger, NTTS, 4 (Grand Rapids: Eerdmans; Leiden: Brill, 1963), pp. 42-72

Metzger, Bruce M., 'Explicit References in the Works of Origen to Variant Readings in New Testament Manuscripts', in *Historical and Literary Studies* (Grand Rapids: Eerdmans, 1968), pp. 88-103

Metzger, B. M., *The Early Versions of the New Testament: Their Origin, Transmission, and Limitations* (Oxford: Clarendon Press, 1977)

Metzger, Bruce M., 'St. Jerome's Explicit References to Variant Readings in Manuscripts of the New Testament', in *NTS* (Leiden: Brill, 1980), pp. 199-210

Metzger, Bruce M., *Manuscripts of the Greek Bible: An Introduction to Greek Palaeography* (New York/Oxford: University Press, 1981)

Metzger, Bruce M., 'Greek manuscripts of John's Gospel with "Hermeneiai"', *Text and Testimony: Essays on New Testament and Apocryphal Literature in Honour of A. F. J. Klijn*, ed. by T. Baarda, A. Hilhorst, G. P. Luttikhuizen and A. S. van der Woude (Kampen: Kok, 1988), pp. 162-9

Metzger, B. M., *The Text of the New Testament: Its Transmission, Corruption, and Restoration* (New York: Oxford University Press, 1968; 3rd edn, New York and Oxford: University Press, 1992)

Metzger, Bruce M., *A Textual Commentary on the Greek New Testament* (London and New York: United Bible Societies, 1971; 2nd edn, Stuttgart: Deutsche Bibelgesellschaft and the United Bible Societies, 1994)

Miller, R. J. (ed.), *The Complete Gospels* (San Francisco: HarperCollins, 1994)

Milne, H. J. M. and T. C. Skeat, *Scribes and Correctors of the Codex Sinaiticus* (London: British Museum, 1938)

Milne, H. J. M. and T. C. Skeat, *The Codex Sinaiticus and the Codex Alexandrinus*, 2nd edn, rev. by T. C. Skeat (London: British Museum, 1955)

Minnen, P. van, 'The Century of Papyrology (1892-1992)', *BASP*, 30 (1993), 5-18

Monks, George R., 'The Church of Alexandria and the City's Economic Life in the Sixth Century', *Speculum*, 28 (1953), 349-62

Morris, Ian and Barry Powell, *A New Companion to Homer* (Leiden: Brill, 1997)

Moschonas, Theodore D., *Hê Patriarchikê Vivliothêkê dia mesou tôn aiônôn* (Alexandria: Anatole Press, 1943)

Moschonas, Theodore D., 'L'église de Saint-Saba à travers les siècles', *Revue des conférences françaises en Orient*, (1947), 3-14

Moschonas, Theodore D., 'Codex Alexandrinus', in *Vyzantinon Diptychon: Alexandrinos Kôdix, Vyzantinê Alexandreia* (Alexandria, 1950), pp. 26-35

Moschonas, Theodore D., 'Byzantine Alexandria and its Relations with the Bible', *Analecta, Publications de l'Institut d'études orientales de la Bibliothèque patriarcale d'Alexandrie*, 20 (1971), 114-24

Moschonas, Theodore D. and Colin Davey, 'Codex Alexandrinus', *Analecta: Publications de l'Institut d'études orientales de la Bibliothèque patriarcale d'Alexandrie*, 22 (1973), 206-10

Most, Glenn W., '"With Fearful Steps Pursuing Hopes of High Talk with the Departed Dead"', *Transactions of the American Philological Association*, 128 (Atlanta: Scholars Press, 1998), 311-24

Bibliography

Mosteller, F. and D. L. Wallace, *Inference and Disputed Authorship: The Federalist* (Reading, MA: Addison-Wesley, 1964)

Mullen, Roderic L., *The New Testament Text of Cyril of Jerusalem*, SBLNTGF, 7 (Atlanta: Scholars Press, 1997)

Müller-Wiener, Martina, *Eine Stadtgeschichte Alexandrias von 564/1169 in die Mitte des 9./15. Jahrhunderts*, Islamkundliche Untersuchungen, 159 (Berlin: Klaus Schwarz, 1992)

Muro, Jr, E. A., 'The Greek Fragments of Enoch from Qumran Cave 7 (7Q4, 7Q8, & 7Q12 = 7QEn gr = Enoch 103:3-4, 7-9)', *RevQ*, 18 (1997), 307-12

Nasrallah, Joseph and Rachid Haddad, *Histoire du mouvement littéraire dans l'église Melchite du Ve au XXe siècle: Contribution à l'étude de la littérature arabe chrétienne*, III, 1 (Louvain: Peeters, 1983)

Neale, John Mason, *A History of the Holy Eastern Church: The Patriarchate of Alexandria*, 2 vols (London: Joseph Masters, 1847)

Nebe, G. W., '7Q4: Möglichkeit und Grenze einer Identifikation', *RevQ*, 13 (1988), 629-33

Nestle, Eberhard, *Die israelitischen Eigennamen nach ihrer religionsgeschichtlichen Bedeutung. Ein Versuch* (Haarlem: n.p., 1876)

Nestle, Eberhard, *Brevis linguae syriacae grammatica* (Berlin: Reuther, 1881), German translation, *Syrische Grammatik mit Litteratur, Chrestomathie und Glossar: 2. vermehrte und verbesserte Auflage* (Berlin: Reuther, 1888); English translation of second edition by R. S. Kennedy, *Syriac Grammar with Literature, Chrestomathy and Glossary* (London: Williams & Norgate, 1889)

Nestle, Eberhard, *Septuagintastudien*, 6 vols (Ulm: Wagner, 1886-96; Stuttgart: Stuttgarter Vereins-Buchdruckerei, 1899-1911)

Nestle, Eberhard, *Marginalien und Materialien* (Tübingen: Heckenhauer, 1893)

Nestle, Eberhard, 'Maulbron', *Realencyklopädie für protestantische Theologie und Kirche*, ed. by Albert Hauck, vol. 12, (Leipzig: J. C. Hinrichs, 1896), pp. 441-5

Nestle, Eberhard, *Einführung in das griechische Neue Testament* (Göttingen: Vandenhoeck & Ruprecht, 1897); 2nd edn, 1899; 3rd edn, 1909. English trans. of 2nd edn: *Introduction to the Textual Criticism of the Greek New Testament*, trans. by William Edie, ed. by Allan Menzies (London: Williams and Norgate, 1901)

Nestle, Eberhard, '"The Greek Testament" of the Bible Society of Stuttgart', *Expository Times*, 9 (1897-98), 419-20

Nestle, Eberhard [published anonymously, 1st edn], *Novum Testamentum Graece* (Stuttgart: Württembergische Bibelanstalt, 1898)

Nestle, Eberhard, 'Paul Anton de Lagarde', *Realencyklopädie für protestantische Theologie und Kirche*, vol. 11 (1902), pp. 212-18

Nestle, Eberhard, Erwin and J. Dahse (eds), *Das Buch Jeremia, Griechisch und Hebräisch* (Stuttgart: Privilegierte Württembergische Bibelanstalt, 1924)

Nestle, Eberhard, *Novum Testamentum Graece cum apparatu critico curavit Eberhard Nestle novis curis elaboraverunt Erwin Nestle et Kurt Aland Editio vicesima quinta* (Stuttgart: Württembergische Bibelanstalt, 13th edn, 1927)

Nestle, Eberhard, *Septuagintastudien*, iii (Stuttgart, 1888; repr. Göttingen: Vandenhoeck & Ruprecht, 1965)

Nestle, Eberhard (ed.), 'Aus Briefen von Eberhard Nestle', *Blätter für württembergische Kirchengeschichte*, 51 (1951), pp. 143-50

Nestle, Erwin, 'Eberhard Nestle. Zu seiner 100. Geburtstag', *Für Arbeit und Besinnung*, 5 (1951), pp. 194-7

Niccum, C., 'The Voice of the Manuscripts on the Silence of Women: the External Evidence for I Corinthians 14: 34-5', *NTS*, 43 (1997), 242-55

Nordenfalk, Carl, *Die spätantiken Kanontafeln* (Gotheburg: Oscar Isacson, 1937)

Bibliography

Nordenfalk, Carl, *Die spätantiken Zierbuchstaben* (Stockholm, 1970)

O'Callaghan, J., 'Notas sobre 7Q tomadas en el Rockefeller Museum', *Biblica*, 53 (1972), 517-33

O'Callaghan, J., '¿Papiros neotestamentarios en le cueva 7 de Qumran?', *Biblica*, 53 (1972), 91-100, translated by W. L. Holladay, *Supplement to JBL*, 91 (1972), 2.1-14

O'Callaghan, J., '¿1 Tim 3.16; 4,1.3 en 7Q4?', *Biblica*, 53 (1972), 362-7

O'Callaghan, J., 'Tres probables papiros neotestamentarios en la cueva 7 de Qumrân', *StudPap*, 11 (1972), 83-9

O'Callaghan, J., *Los papiros griegos de la cueva 7 de Qumrân* (Biblioteca de autores christianos 353; Madrid 1974)

O'Callaghan, J., 'Sobre la identificación de 7Q4', *StudPap*, 13 (1974), 45-55

O'Callaghan, J., 'Sobre el papiro de Marcos en Qumran', *FN*, 5 (1992), 191-8

O'Callaghan, J., *Introducció a la Crítica Textual del Nou Testament* (Barcelona: Claret, 1997)

Oates, J. F. et al., *Checklist of Editions of Greek Papyri and Ostraca*, BASPSup, 4, 3rd edn (Atlanta: Scholars Press, 1985)

Osburn, C. D., 'The Greek Lectionaries of the New Testament', in *The Text of the New Testament in Contemporary Research: Essays on the Status Quaestionis*, ed. by B. D. Ehrman and M. W. Holmes, SD, 46 (Grand Rapids: Eerdmans, 1995), 61-74

Outtier, B., 'Les *Prosermeneiai* du Codex Bezae', in Parker and Amphoux, *Codex Bezae*, pp. 74-8

Papadopoulos, Chrysostomos A., *Kyrillos Loukaris* (Tergeste, 1907)

Papadopoulos, Chrysostomos, 'Ho Athanasios II (1276-1316)', *Epeteris Hetaireias Vyzantinôn Spoudôn*, 6 (1929), 3-13

Papadopoulos, Chrysostomos, *Historia tês Ekklêsias Alexandreias (62-1934)* (Alexandria: Patriarchal Press, 1935)

Parker, David C., *Codex Bezae: An Early Christian Manuscript and its Text* (Cambridge: University Press, 1992)

Parker, D. C., 'The Majuscule Manuscripts of the New Testament', in *The Text of the New Testament in Contemporary Research: Essays on the Status Quaestionis*, ed. by Bart D. Ehrman and Michael W. Holmes, SD, 46 (Grand Rapids: Eerdmans, 1995)

Parker, David C., 'Professor Amphoux's History of the New Testament Text: A Response', *New Testament Textual Research Update*, 4/3 (1996), 41-5

Parker, David C., *The Living Text of the Gospels* (Cambridge: University Press, 1997)

Parker, David C. and C.-B. Amphoux, *Codex Bezae: Studies from the Lund Colloquium: June 1994*, NTTS, 22 (Leiden: Brill, 1996)

Pattie, Thomas S., 'The Creation of the Great Codices', in *The Bible as Book: The Manuscript Tradition*, ed. by John L. Sharpe III and Kimberly Van Kampen (London: British Library, 1998), pp. 61-72

Petersen, William L., 'Review of "The New Testament in Greek: The Gospel according to St Luke"', in *JBL*, 107 (1988), 758-62

Petzer, J. H., 'The Oxford Greek New Testament: A Review Article', *Neotestamentica*, 23 (1989), 83-92

Petzer, Kobus, (= J. H. Petzer), *Die Tekst van die Nuwe Testament. 'n Inleiding in die basiese aspekte van die teorie en praktyk van die tekskritiek van die Nuwe Testament*, Hervormde Teologiese Studies, suppl. 2 (Pretoria: Universiteit van Pretoria, 1990)

Petzer, J. H., 'The History of the New Testament – Its Reconstruction, Significance and Use in New Testament Textual Criticism', in *New Testament Textual Criticism, Exegesis and Church History: A Discussion of Methods*, ed. by B. Aland and J. Delobel (Kampen: Kok Pharos, 1994)

Philip, Ian, *The Bodleian Library in the Seventeenth and Eighteenth Centuries* (Oxford:

Clarendon Press, 1983)

Philippidis, N. S. and T. D. Moschonas, *Katalogoi tês Patriarchikês Vivliothêkês*, 3 vols (Alexandria: Patriarchal Press, 1945-47)

Pickering, S. R. and R. R. E. Cook, *Has a Fragment of the Gospel of Mark Been Found at Qumran?* (Papyrological and Historical Perspectives 1; The Ancient History Documentary Research Centre, Macquarie University, Sydney 1989)

Pickering, Wilbur N., 'Conflation or Confusion', in *The Identity of the New Testament Text* (rev. edn, Nashville: Nelson, 1980)

Pietersma, A., 'Kyrios or Tetragram: A Renewed Quest for the Original LXX', in A. Pietersma and C. Cox (eds), *De Septuaginta, Studies in Honour of John William Wevers on His Sixty-Fifth Birthday* (Mississauga, Ont.: Benben, 1984), pp. 85-101

Politis, Linos, 'Nouveau manuscrits grecs découverts au Mont Sinaï', *Scriptorium*, 34 (1980), 5-17

Porten, B. and A. Yardeni, *Textbook of Aramaic Documents from Ancient Egypt*, vol. 3 (Jerusalem: Akademon, 1993)

Porter, S. E. and C. A. Evans (eds), *The Scrolls and the Scriptures: Qumran Fifty Years After*, JSPSup, 26, RILP, 3 (Sheffield: Academic Press, 1997)

Porter, S. E. and W. J. Porter (eds), *New Testament Greek Papyri and Parchments: New Editions*, MPER, NS 28 (Vienna: Austrian National Library, forthcoming)

Porter, S. E., 'Dialect and Register in the Greek of the New Testament: Theory' and 'Register in the Greek of the New Testament: Application with Reference to Mark's Gospel', in *Rethinking Context, Rereading Texts: Contributions from the Social Sciences to Biblical Interpretation*, ed. by M. Daniel Carroll R. (Sheffield: Academic Press, 2000), 190-208

Porter, S. E., *The Grammarian's Rebirth: Dead Languages and Live Issues in Current Biblical Study* (London: Roehampton Institute London [1996]), 209-29

Porter, S. E., 'The Greek Papyri of the Judaean Desert and the World of the Roman East', in *The Scrolls and the Scriptures: Qumran Fifty Years After*, ed. by S. E. Porter and C. A. Evans (1997), 293-316

Puech, E., 'Les fragments non identifiés de 8KhXIIgr et le manuscrit grec des Douze Petits Prophètes', *RB*, 98 (1991), 161-9

Puech, E., 'Notes en marge de 8KhXIIgr', *RevQ*, 98 (1991), 583-93

Puech, E., 'Sept fragments grecs de la *Lettre d'Hénoch* (1 Hén 100, 103 et 105) dans la grotte 7 de Qumrân (= 7QHéngr)', *RevQ*, 18 (1997), 313-23

Quecke, H., 'Zu den Joh-Fragmenten mit "Hermeneiai"', *Orientalia Christiana Periodica*, 40 (1974), 407-14; 43 (1977), 179-81

Rahlfs, Alfred (ed.), *Septuaginta*, 2 vols (Stuttgart: Württembergische Bibelanstalt, 1935)

Ralston, T. R., 'The "Majority Text" and Byzantine Origins', *NTS*, 38 (1992), 122-37

Richards, W. L., 'Textual Criticism on the Greek Text of the Catholic Epistles: A Bibliography', *Andrews University Seminary Studies*, 12 (1974), 103-11

Richards, W. L., 'The Present Status of Text Critical Studies in the Catholic Epistles', *Andrews University Seminary Studies*, 13 (1975), 261-72

Richards, W. L., 'The New Testament Greek Manuscripts of the Catholic Epistles', *Andrews University Seminary Studies*, 14 (1976), 301-11

Richards, W. L., *The Classification of the Greek Manuscripts of the Johannine Epistles*, Society of Biblical Literature Dissertation Series, 35 (Missoula, MT: Scholars Press, 1977)

Richards, W. L., 'Gregory 1174: Alexandrian or Byzantine in the Catholic Epistles?', *Andrews University Seminary Studies*, 21 (1983), 155-68

Richardson, Samuel (ed.), *The Negotiations of Sir Thomas Roe in his Embassy to the Ottoman Porte for the Year 1621 to 1628 inclusive* (London: Society for the Encouragement of Learning, 1740)

Bibliography

Riddle, D. W., 'The Use of Lectionaries in Critical Editions and Studies of the New Testament Text', in *Prolegomena to the Study of the Lectionary Text of the Gospels*, ed. by D. W. Riddle and E. C. Colwell, SLTGNT, 1 (Chicago: University of Chicago Press, 1933), 74-5

Ritschl, Albrecht, *Geschichte des Pietismus*, 3 vols (Bonn: A. Marcus, 1880-6)

Roberts, C. H., *An Unpublished Fragment of the Fourth Gospel in the John Rylands Library* (Manchester: University Press, 1935)

Roberts, R. J., 'The Greek Press at Constantinople in 1627 and its Antecedents', *The Library*, ser. 5, 22 (1967), 13-43

Roberts, C. H., 'On Some Presumed Papyrus Fragments of the New Testament from Qumran', *JTS*, 23 (1972), 446-7

Roberts, C. H., *Manuscript, Society and Belief in Early Christian Egypt* (London: British Academy, 1979)

Roberts, C. H. and T. C. Skeat, *The Birth of the Codex* (London: British Academy, 1983)

Robinson, Maurice A. and William G. Pierpont, *The New Testament in the Original Greek According to the Byzantine/Majority Textform* (Atlanta, GA: Original Word Publishers, 1991)

Rogers, David, *The Bodleian Library and its Treasures, 1320-1700* (Henley-on-Thames: Aidan Ellis, 1991)

Ropes, James H., *The Text of Acts*, vol. 3 of *The Beginnings of Christianity Part 1: The Acts of the Apostles*, ed. by F. J. Foakes Jackson and Kirsopp Lake (London: Macmillan, 1926)

Runciman, Sir Steven, *The Great Church in Captivity* (Cambridge: University Press, 1968)

Šagi, Janco, 'Problema historiae codicis B', *Divus Thomas: Commentarium de philosophia et theologia*, 85 (1972), pp. 3-29

Schaff, Philip, *Germany: Its Universities, Theology, and Religion* (Philadelphia: Lindsay and Blakiston, 1857)

Schaff, Philip, *Theological Propaedeutic: A General Introduction to the Study of Theology*, 7th edn (New York: Charles Scribner's Sons, 1907)

Schmid, Josef, *Studien zur Geschichte des griechischen Apocalypse-Textes*, 3 vols (Munich: Karl Zink, 1955-6)

Schmid, Ulrich, *Marcion und sein Apostolos. Rekonstruktion und Historische Einordnung der marcionitischen Paulusbriefausgabe*, ANTF, 25 (Berlin: De Gruyter, 1995)

Schubart, W., *Palaeographie. I. Griechische Palaeographie* (Munich: Beck, 1925)

Skeat, T. C., 'The Provenance of the Codex Alexandrinus', *JTS*, n.s. 6 (1955), 233-5

Skeat, T. C., 'Early Christian Book-Production: Papyri and Manuscripts', in *The Cambridge History of the Bible. II. The West from the Fathers to the Reformation*, ed. by G. W. H. Lampe (Cambridge: University Press, 1969), 54-79

Skeat, T. C., 'The Codex Vaticanus in the Fifteenth Century', *JTS*, n.s. 35 (1984), 454-65

Skeat, T. C., 'The Origin of the Christian Codex', *ZPE*, 102 (1994), 263-8

Skeat, T. C., 'The Codex Sinaiticus, the Codex Vaticanus and Constantine', *JTS*, n.s. 50 (1999), 583-625

Skehan, P. W., 'The Qumran Manuscripts and Textual Criticism', *VTSup*, 4 (1957), 148-60

Skehan, P. W., 'The Biblical Scrolls from Qumran and the Text of the Old Testament', *BA*, 28 (1965), 87-100

Skehan, P. W., '4QLXXNum: A Pre-Christian Reworking of the Septuagint', *HThR*, 70 (1977), 39-50

Skehan, P. W., 'The Divine Name at Qumran, in the Masada Scroll, and in the Septuagint', *BIOSCS*, 13 (1980), 14-44

Skehan, P. W., E. Ulrich and J. E. Sanderson, *Qumran Cave 4.IV: Palaeo-Hebrew and Greek Biblical Manuscripts*, DJD, 9 (Oxford: Clarendon Press, 1992)

Smend, Rudolf, 'Der geistige Vater des Septuaginta-Unternehmens', MSU, 20 (Festschrift R. Hanhart; Göttingen: 1990), pp. 332-44

Bibliography

Smith, Thomas, *Miscellanea* (London: Samuel Smith, 1686)

Soisalon-Soininen, Ilmari, 'Die Infinitive in der Septuaginta', *AASFB* 132 (1965), 68-75

Sollamo, Raija, *Repetition of the Possessive Pronouns in the Septuagint*, SCS, 40 (Atlanta: Scholars Press, 1995)

Souter, Alexander, *The Text and Canon of the New Testament* (London: Duckworth, 1913), revised by C. S. C. Williams (London, 1954)

Spinka, Matthew, 'Acquisition of the Codex Alexandrinus by England', *Journal of Religion*, 16 (1936), 10-29

Spottorno, M. V., 'Nota sobre los papiros de la cueva 7 de Qumrân', *Estudios Clásicos*, 15 (1971), 261-3

Spottorno, M. V., 'Una nueva posible identificación de 7Q5', *Sefarad*, 52 (1992), 541-3

Stanton, G. N., *Gospel Truth? New Light on Jesus and the Gospels* (London: HarperCollins, 1995)

Stegemann, H., ΚΥΡΙΟΣ Ο ΘΕΟΣ ΚΥΡΙΟΣ ΙΗΣΟΥΣ: *Aufkommen und Ausbreitung des religiösen Gebrauchs von KURIOS und seine Verwendung im Neuen Testament* (Habilitationsschrift, Bonn, 1969)

Stephen, Gwendolen M., 'The Coronis', *Scriptorium*, 13 (1959), 3-14

Streeter, Burnett Hillman, *The Four Gospels: A Study of Origins* (London: Macmillan, 1924)

Streeter, Burnett Hillman, 'Codices 157, 1071 and the Caesarean Text', in *Quantulacumque: Studies Presented to Kirsopp Lake*, ed. by Robert P. Casey, Silva Lake and Agnes K. Lake (London: Christophers, 1937)

Summary Catalogue of Greek Manuscripts in the British Library, 1 (London: British Library, 1999)

Summary Catalogue of Manuscripts in the Bodleian Library, 6 vols (Oxford: Clarendon Press, 1895-1953)

Thiede, C. P., *Die älteste Evangelien-Handschrift? Das Markus-Fragment von Qumran und die Anfänge der schriftlichen Überlieferung des Neuen Testaments* (Wuppertal, 1986)

Thiede, C. P., *The Earliest Gospel Manuscript? The Qumran Fragment 7Q5 and its Significance for New Testament Studies* (Exeter: Paternoster, 1992)

Thiede, C. P., *Rekindling the Word: In Search of Gospel Truth* (Leominster: Gracewing, 1995)

Thompson, Edward Maunde (ed.), *Facsimile of the Codex Alexandrinus*, 4 vols (London: British Museum, 1879-1883)

Tillich, Paul, *Perspectives on 19th and 20th Century Protestant Theology*, ed. by Carl E. Braaten, (New York: Harper & Row, 1967)

Tillyridès, Andreas, 'Cyril Lucaris and the Codex Alexandrinus', *Analecta: Publications de l'Institut d'études orientales de la Bibliothèque patriarcale d'Alexandrie*, 24 (1975), 103-33

Tischendorf, Constantine, *Reise in den Orient*, 2 vols (Leipzig: Bernhard Tauchnitz Jr, 1846)

Tischendorf, Constantine, *Die Sinaibibel: Ihre Entdeckung, Herausgabe und Erwerbung* (Leipzig: Giesecke & Devrient, 1871)

Tischendorf, Constantinus (ed.), *Novum Testamentum Graece, editio octava critica maior*, 3 vols (Leipzig: (vol. 1) Giesecke & Devrient, and Hinrichs, 1869; (vol. 2) Giesecke & Devrient, 1872; (vol. 3) J. C. Hinrichs, 1894, ed. by C. R. Gregory)

Tov, Emanuel, 'The Orthography and Language of the Hebrew Scrolls Found at Qumran and the Origin of These Scrolls', *Textus*, 13 (1986), 31-57

Tov, Emanuel, 'Hebrew Biblical Manuscripts from the Judaean Desert: Their Contribution to Textual Criticism', *JJS*, 39 (1988), 1-37

Tov, Emanuel, 'The Socio-Religious Background of the Paleo-Hebrew Biblical Texts Found at Qumran', in H. Cancik and others (eds), *Geschichte – Tradition: Reflexion, Festschrift für Martin Hengel zum 70. Geburtstag* (Tübingen: Mohr, 1996), vol. I, pp. 353-74

Tov, Emanuel, *The Text-Critical Use of the Septuagint in Biblical Research*, 2nd edn (Simor:

Jerusalem, 1996)

Tov, Emanuel, with the collaboration of R. A. Kraft, *The Greek Minor Prophets Scroll from Naḥal Ḥever, ḤevXIIgr) (The Seiyal Collection I)* (DJD 8; Oxford: Clarendon Press, 1990; reprinted with corrections, 1995)

Tov, Emanuel, with the collaboration of S. J. Pfann, *Companion Volume to The Dead Sea Scrolls Microfiche Edition* (Leiden: Brill, 1995)

Tov, Emanuel and Benjamin G. Wright, 'Computer-Assisted Study of the Criteria for Assessing the Literalness of Translation Units in the LXX', *Textus* 12 (1985), 149-87

Trapp, Erich, *Prosopographisches Lexikon der Palaiologenzeit*, 8 vols (Vienna: Verlag der Österreichischen Akademie der Wissenschaften, 1976-96)

Turner, C. H., 'Notes on Markan Usage', in *JTS*, recently reprinted in *The Language and Style of the Gospel of Mark*, ed. by J. Keith Elliott (Leiden: Brill, 1993) (= *Novum Testamentum Supplements* 71)

Turner, E. G., 'Scribes and Scholars of Oxyrhynchus', in *Akten des VIII. Internationalen Kongresses für Papyrologie Wien 1955*, ed. by H. Gerstinger, MPER, ns 5 (Vienna: Rohrer, 1956), 141-6

Turner, E. G., *Greek Papyri: An Introduction* (Oxford: Clarendon Press, 1968)

Turyn, Alexander, *Dated Greek Manuscripts of the Thirteenth and Fourteenth Centuries in the Libraries of Great Britain* (Dumbarton Oaks: Centre for Byzantine Studies, 1980)

Ulrich, E., 'The Greek Manuscripts of the Pentateuch from Qumrân, Including Newly-Identified Fragments of Deuteronomy (4QLXXDeut)', in *De Septuaginta, Studies in Honour of John William Wevers on His Sixty-Fifth Birthday*, ed. by A. Pietersma and C. Cox (Mississauga, Ont., 1984), pp. 71-82

Ulrich, E., 'The Septuagint Manuscripts from Qumran: A Reappraisal', in *Septuagint, Scrolls and Cognate Writings: Papers Presented to the International Symposium on the Septuagint and Its Relations to the Dead Sea Scrolls and Other Writings* (Manchester, 1990), ed. by G. J. Brooke and B. Lindars, SCS 33 (Atlanta, GA: Scholars Press, 1992), pp. 49-80

Urbán, A. C., 'Observaciones sobre ciertos papiros de la cueva 7 de Qumran', *RevQ*, 8 (1973), 233-51

Urbán, A. C., 'La identificacion de 7Q4 con Num 14, 23-24 y la restauración de textos antiquos', *Estudios bíblicos*, 33 (1974), 219-44

Vaganay, L., *An Introduction to the Textual Criticism of the New Testament*, trans. by B. V. Miller (London: Sands, 1937)

Vaganay, Léon, *An Introduction to New Testament Textual Criticism*, 2nd edn, rev. by C.-B. Amphoux, trans. by Jenny Heimerdinger (Cambridge: University Press, 1991)

Valentine Richards, A. V., *The Text of Acts in Codex 614 (Tisch. 137) and its Allies* (Cambridge: University Press, 1934)

van Bruggen, Jakob, *De tekst van het Nieuwe Testament* (Gröningen: De Vuurbaak, 1976), English translation, *The Ancient Text of the New Testament* (Winnipeg: Premier, 1976)

van Bruggen, Jakob, 'Abba Vader! Tekst en toonhoogte van het Onze Vader', in *De biddende kerk*, ed. by C. Trimp (Groningen: De Vuurbaak, 1979), 9-42

van Haelst, J., *Catalogue des Papyrus Littéraires Juifs et Chrétiens*, Université de Paris IV Paris-Sorbonne série 'Papyrologie', 1 (Paris: Publications de la Sorbonne, 1976)

van Minnen, P., 'The Century of Papyrology (1892-1992)', *BASP*, 30 (1993), 5-18

von Baudissin, W. W., *Kyrios als Gottesname im Judentum* (Giessen: Topelmann, 1926-1929)

von der Goltz, E., *Eine Textkritische Arbeit des zehnten bezw, sechsten Jahrhunderts*, Texte und Untersuchungen, 2.4 (Leipzig: J. C. Hinrichs, 1899)

von Gebhardt, Oscar, *Novum Testamentum Graece et Germanice: Das Neue Testament griechisch nach Tischendorfs letzter Recension und Deutsch nach dem revidierten Luthertext* (Leipzig: Tauschnitz, 1881)

Bibliography

von Soden, Hermann, *Die Schriften des Neuen Testaments*, Part I: *Untersuchungen*, 3 vols (Berlin: Verlag von Arthur Glaue, 1902-10; 2nd edn, Göttingen: Vandenhoeck & Ruprecht, 1911); Part II: *Text mit Apparat* (Göttingen: Vandenhoeck & Ruprecht, 1913)

Wace, Alan J. B. and Frank H. Stubbings, *A Companion to Homer* (London: Macmillan, 1962)

Wachtel, Klaus, *Der byzantinische Text der katholischen Briefe: Eine Untersuchung zur Entstehung der Koine des Neuen Testaments*, ANTF, 24 (Berlin: De Gruyter, 1995)

Wachtel, Klaus, 'Response to Four Reviews of the James Volume of the Editio Critica Maior', *TC: A Journal of Biblical Textual Criticism* [http://shemesh.scholar.emory.edu/scripts/TC], 3 (1998)

Wallace, Daniel B., 'The Majority Text and the Original Text: Are They Identical?', *Bibliotheca Sacra*, 148 (1991), 151-69

Wallace, Daniel B., 'The Majority-Text Theory: History, Methods and Critique', *Journal of the Evangelical Theological Society*, 37 (1994), 185-215

Wallace, Daniel B., 'Historical Revisionism and the Majority Text Theory: the Cases of F. H. A. Scrivener and Herman C. Hoskier', *NTS*, 41 (1995), 280-5

Wallace, Daniel B., 'The Majority Text Theory: History, Methods, and Critique', in *The Text of the New Testament in contemporary Research: Essays on the* Status Quaestionis, *A Volume in Honor of Bruce M. Metzger*, ed. by Bart D. Ehrman and M. W. Holmes, SD, 46 (Grand Rapids: Eerdmans, 1995), pp. 297-320

Walters, P., *The Text of the Septuagint: Its Corruptions and Their Emendation* (Cambridge: University Press, 1973)

Walton, Brian (ed.), *Biblia Sacra Polyglotta: complectentia Textus originales, Hebraicum, cum Pentateucho Samaritano, Chaldaicum, Graecum ... edidit Brianus Waltonus* (London: Thomas Roycroft, 1657)

Warner, Sir George F. and Julius P. Gilson, *Catalogue of Western Manuscripts in the Old Royal and King's Collections in the British Museum*, 4 vols (London: British Museum, 1921)

Weiss, Bernhard, *Das Neue Testament*, Handausgabe (Leipzig: Hinrichs, I-III, 1894-1900)

Wessely, C., 'Evangelien-Fragmente auf Papyrus', *Wiener Studien*, 4 (1882), 198-214

Wessely, C., *Prolegomena ad Papyrorum Graecorum Novam Collectionem Edendam* (Vienna: Gerold, 1883)

Wessely, C., 'Analekten. 1. Neue Evangelien-Fragmente auf Papyrus', *Wiener Studien*, 7 (1885), 69-70

Wessely, C., *Aus der Welt der Papyri* (Leipzig: Haessel, 1914)

Westcott, Brook Foss, and Fenton John Anthony Hort (eds), *The New Testament in the Original Greek*, 2 vols (Cambridge/London: Macmillan and Company, 1881; 2nd edn 1896)

Wevers, J. W., *Genesis, Septuaginta, etc.* (Göttingen: Vandenhoeck & Ruprecht, 1974)

Wevers, J. W., *Text History of the Greek Genesis*, MSU 11 (Göttingen: 1974)

Wevers, J. W., *Deuteronomium, Septuaginta, etc.* (Göttingen: Vandenhoeck & Ruprecht, 1977)

Wevers, J. W., *Text History of the Greek Deuteronomy*, MSU 13 (Göttingen: 1978)

Wevers, J. W., 'An Early Revision of the Septuagint of Numbers', *ErIsr*, 16 (1982), 235*-239*

Wevers, J. W., *Numeri, Septuaginta, etc.*, vol. III.1 (Göttingen: Vandenhoeck & Ruprecht, 1982)

Wevers, J. W., *Text History of the Greek Numbers*, MSU 16 (Göttingen: 1982)

Wevers, J. W., 'An Apology for Septuagint Studies', *BIOSCS*, 18 (1985), 19-21

Wevers, J. W., *Leviticus, Septuaginta, Vetus Testamentum graecum auctoritate academiae scientiarum gottingensis editum*, vol. II.2 (Göttingen: Vandenhoeck & Ruprecht, 1986)

Wevers, J. W., *Text History of the Greek Leviticus*, MSU 19 (Göttingen: 1986)

Wevers, J. W., *Notes on the Greek Text of Exodus*, SCS 30 (Atlanta, GA: Scholars Press, 1990)

Wevers, J. W., *Exodus, Septuaginta, etc.* (Göttingen: Vandenhoeck & Ruprecht, 1991)

Wevers, J. W., *Text History of the Greek Exodus*, MSU 21 (Göttingen: 1991)

Wevers, J. W., *Notes on the Greek Text of Genesis*, SCS 35 (Atlanta, GA: Scholars Press, 1993)

Bibliography

Wevers, J. W., *Notes on the Greek Text of Deuteronomy*, SCS 39 (Atlanta, GA: Scholars Press, 1995)

Wevers, J. W., *Notes on the Greek Text of Leviticus*, SCS 44 (Atlanta, GA: Scholars Press, 1997)

Wevers, J. W., *Notes on the Greek Text of Numbers*, SCS 46 (Atlanta, GA: Scholars Press, 1998)

Weymouth, R. F., *The Resultant Greek Testament* (London: Elliot Stock, 1886; 3rd edn 1905)

Whitby, Daniel, *Examen Variantium Lectionum J. Milii* (London, 1710)

Wifstrand, A., 'Die Stellung der enklitischen Personalpronomina bei den Septuaginta', *Bulletin de la Société royale des lettres de Lund 1949-1950* (Lund, 1950), 44-70

Wilken, R. L., 'Alexandria: A School for Training in Virtue', in *Schools of Thought in the Christian Tradition*, ed. by P. Henry (Philadelphia: Fortress, 1984), pp. 15-30

Wilson, J. M., *The Acts of the Apostles Translated from the Codex Bezae with an Introduction on its Lucan Origin and Importance* (London, New York and Toronto: SPCK, 1923)

Wilson, N. G., *Scholars of Byzantium* (London: Duckworth, 1983)

Wisse, Frederik, *The Profile Method for Classifying and Evaluating Manuscript Evidence*, Studies and Documents, 44 (Grand Rapids: Eerdmans, 1984)

Wisselink, W. Franciscus, *Assimilation as a Criterion for the Establishment of the Text: A comparative Study on the Basis of Passages from Matthew, Mark and Luke* (Kampen: Kok, 1989)

Woide, C. G., *Notitia Codicis Alexandrini cum variis eius lectionibus omnibus*, ed. by Spohn, Gottlieb L. (Leipzig: Breitkopf, 1788)

Wright, Benjamin G., 'A Note on the Statistical Analysis of Septuagintal Syntax', *JBL* 104 (1985), 111-14

Württembergische Nekrolog für 1913 (1916), pp. 50-79

Young, Patrick, *Clementis ad Corinthios epistola prior ex laceris reliquiis vetustissimi exemplaris Bibliothecae Regiae, eruit, lacunas explevit, Latinè vertit, & notis brevioribus illustravit Patricius Junius ...* (Oxford: John Lichfield, 1633)

Young, Patrick, *Catena graecorum patrum in beatum Iob, collectore Niceta Heraclae Metropolita* (London: Royal Press, 1637)

Zahn, Theodor, *Geschichte der Neutestamentlichen Kanons: Zweiter Band* (Erlangen/Leipzig: A. Deichert, 1892)

Ziegler, J., *Duodecim prophetae, Septuaginta, etc.*, vol. XIII (Göttingen: Vandenhoeck & Ruprecht, 1943; 2nd edn: 1967)

Zuntz, Günther, *The Text of the Epistles: A Disquisition upon the Corpus Paulinum*, Schweich Lectures 1946 (London: British Academy, 1953)

Zuntz, Günther, *Lukian von Antiochien und der Text der Evangelien* (Heidelberg: C. Winter, 1995)

INDEX OF BIBLICAL AND EARLY CHRISTIAN TEXTS

Index of Biblical and Early Christian Texts

INDEX OF MANUSCRIPTS

Index of Manuscripts

GENERAL INDEX

General Index